Criminal Justice Under Stress

Criminal Justice Under Stress

Edited by

Eric Stockdale

and

Silvia Casale

BLACKSTONE
PRESS LIMITED

First published in Great Britain 1992 by Blackstone Press Limited,
9-15 Aldine Street, London W12 8AW.   Telephone 081-740 1173

© Blackstone Press Limited, 1992
The contributors hold the copyright for their respective chapters.

ISBN: 1 85431 222 7

British Library Cataloguing in Publication Data
A CIP catalogue record for this book is available from the British Library.

Typeset by Style Photosetting Ltd, Mayfield, East Sussex
Printed by BPCC Wheatons Ltd, Exeter

Contents

Stopping and searching people and vehicles — Lay visitors to police stations — Detention at police stations: access to solicitors — Codes of practice governing the general welfare of detainees, and in particular rights of access to a solicitor — Police complaints procedure — Relationship with the Crown Prosecution Service — Conclusions — References

Guiding principles — Bail and custody trends — The amount of crime committed on bail — Government initiatives to facilitate the use of bail and reduce time spent in custody — Conditions for remand prisoners — The focus on the remand population — Strangeways — The recommendations — The government's plans — Separate rules for remand prisoners — Conclusion: problems on the horizon — References

Objectives — Adversarial or inquisitorial? — Disparity of resources — Crown Court or magistrates? — Juries — Judges — Confessions — Tit for tat — Victims — Cracked trials — Conclusion — References

Contributors

The editors

Eric Stockdale, MSc, LLM, PhD, has been a Circuit Judge since 1972 and is the consultant editor of *Blackstone's Criminal Practice*. Judge Stockdale served on the Parole Board from 1985–89. This is his seventh book on criminal justice matters.

Silvia Casale, MA (Oxon), PhD (Yale), is an independent consultant in criminology. Dr Casale has worked in Sweden, the United States and the United Kingdom. A member of the Parole Board from 1987–90, she currently works as guest inspector with HM Prison Inspectorate, consultant to NACRO on prison policy, policy adviser on the National AIDS and Prison Forum, consultant for London Prisons Community Links and as a member of the Home Office Steering Group on Standards and the Feltham Working Group.

Her books include *Minimum Standards for Prison Establishments, Women Inside* and *Regimes for Remand Prisoners* (with Plotnikoff).

The authors

John Alderson, CBE, QPM, LLD, D Litt (HC), Barrister, is Honorary Research Fellow, the Centre for Police and Criminal Justice Studies, at the University of Exeter. Previously, he was Chief Constable of Devon and Cornwall (1973–82), following a career which began as a constable in Yorkshire in 1946. He held the important post of Commandant of the Police Staff College, Bramshill (1970–73), and senior posts in the Metropolitan Police, including that of Assistant Commissioner at New Scotland

Yard. He has travelled widely and written extensively on police affairs. His books include *Policing Freedom* and *Law and Disorder*. As consultant to the Education Committee of the Council of Europe he has prepared the textbook *Human Rights and Police*.

Rod Morgan, BSc, is Professor of Criminal Justice, University of Bristol and Dean of the Law Faculty. He is the author of many books and articles on criminal justice policy including *A Taste of Prison, The Future of the Prison System, Accountability and Prisons* and *Coming to Terms with Policing*. He was an Assessor to Lord Justice Woolf's Inquiry into the disturbances at Strangeways and elsewhere in 1990 and an expert advisor on custodial conditions to Amnesty International and the Council of Europe Committee for the Prevention of Torture. He is currently working on treatment programmes for sex offenders; the diversion of mentally disordered offenders; and the international inspection of custodial conditions.

Stephen Jones, BA, Dip Crim, Barrister, is a Lecturer in Law at the University of Bristol where he has taught criminal law, criminology and English legal system since 1974. He has written material on prisoners' rights and is a member of the Board of Visitors at Pucklechurch Remand Centre.

John Sprack, BA, LLB, Barrister, has practised for a number of years as a barrister and is now Principal Lecturer at the Inns of Court School of Law where he teaches criminal litigation and advocacy, among other subjects. He is one of the authors of *Blackstone's Criminal Practice* and *Emmins on Criminal Procedure*.

Joshua Rozenberg, MA (Oxon), Solicitor, is Legal Correspondent to BBC Television News and the only full-time Legal Correspondent working in British television. In 1984 he became BBC Radio's first Legal Affairs Correspondent and presenter of the Radio 4 series *Law in Action*. He moved to television in 1988. After reading law at university, he trained as a solicitor, qualifying in 1976. By then however, he had joined the BBC as a trainee journalist, where he worked as a producer and reporter before specialising in law.

He won the Bar Council's Legal Reporting Award in 1991. He is Jacksons Visiting Fellow in Law at the University of Teesside. His books include *The Case for the Crown* and *Your Rights and the Law*.

Martin Wasik, LLB, MA, Barrister, is Professor of Law at Manchester University. He was appointed Professor in 1992 and has taught there since 1980. He is the author of much published work on criminal justice and sentencing, including *Crime and the Computer*; co-author (with Pease) of *Sentencing Reform*; (with Taylor) of *Blackstone's Guide to the Criminal Justice Act 1991* and (with Munro) of *Sentencing, Judicial Discretion and Training*. He is one of the authors of *Blackstone's Criminal Practice*.

David Mathieson, BA (Hons), is Chief Probation Officer at Merseyside. He graduated at Manchester University where he also obtained a social science diploma prior to his appointment as a probation officer in 1963. During his probation career, he has held a number of posts in the north west and has also held national office in NAPO (National Association of Probation Officers) and ACOP (Association of Chief Officers of Probation). He has been a regular contributor over the years to several professional journals. He is a former editor of *Probation Journal* and is currently chairing the advisory group of the *Jarvis Probation Service Manual* and another group exploring the need for a new management journal for the Probation Service. He has a particular interest in public relations and chairs ACOP'S Parliamentary and Public Relations Panel. He has been Chief Probation Officer in Merseyside since 1981.

Stephen Shaw, BA, MA, PhD, is Director of the Prison Reform Trust, a post which he has held since 1981. Prior to that he worked in the Home Office and for NACRO. Originally trained as an economist, he has written widely on both economic and home affairs.

Mike Maguire, MA, B Litt (Oxon), is a Lecturer in Criminology and Criminal Justice at the University of Wales, Cardiff. He has written widely in the field of criminology and criminal justice. He is author of *Burglary in a Dwelling*; co-author of *The Effects of Crime and the Work of Victim Support Schemes* and *A Study of the Police Complaints System*; and co-editor of *Accountability and Prisons* and *Victims of Crime: A New Deal?* He has recently completed a study of detective practice for the Royal Commission on Criminal Justice and is currently editing the *Oxford Handbook of Criminology*. He was a member of the Parole Board from 1988–91.

Phil Parry, JP, LLB, MA, ACIArb, is a Principal Lecturer in Law at the University of Hertfordshire, where he teaches and researches in the area of criminal law, employment law and legal skills. He teaches a wide variety of students including those studying for law degrees, personnel managers, trade unionists, magistrate's court clerks and the police. He has been a magistrate in Inner London since 1978 and sits on both the Juvenile Panel and Family Proceedings Court.

Una Padel, BSc, has a Postgraduate Diploma in Social Administration and a Diploma in Social Work, and is at present Assistant Director to the Standing Conference on Drug Abuse. After working as a probation officer in Newcastle upon Tyne, she became Deputy Director of the Prison Reform Trust in 1985. While there, she wrote and campaigned about many aspects of imprisonment. In 1989 she became Assistant Director at the Standing Conference on Drug Abuse, managing projects designed to train prison staff to become HIV educators, and to improve the way in which the criminal justice system deals with drug users. She is the co-author with P. Stevenson of *Insiders: Women's Experience in Prison* and of *HIV Education in Prisons: A Resource Book* with R. Twidale and J. Porter.

Susan Edwards, BA, MA, PhD, is Lecturer in Socio-Legal Studies at the University of Buckingham. She has been teaching, researching, writing and campaigning on criminal justice issues for 15 years. She is author of *Female Sexuality and the Law, Women on Trial, Policing 'Domestic' Violence*, and editor of *Gender, Sex and the Law* and is a regular contributor to *New Law Journal*. She is currently researching into pornography and the law and has held many research grants over the years in areas of policing, and the criminal justice system. She is a member of the National Association for the Treatment of Sex Offenders and is on the Management Committee of CAST, an organisation serving the needs of female ex-offenders. She is currently consultant to the Metropolitan Police working Group on Domestic Violence.

Lucia Zedner, BA, D Phil (Oxon), is Lecturer in Law at the London School of Economics and Political Science (since 1989) and Assistant Director, Mannheim Centre for Criminology and Criminal Justice at the LSE since 1991. She was Prize Research Fellow at Nuffield College Oxford 1987–89 and since 1988, Research Associate at the Centre for Criminological Research, University of Oxford. She is a Council Member of the Howard League for Penal Reform and has also worked with NACRO and the Prison Reform Trust. Her recent publications include: *Women, Crime, and Custody in Victorian England*; with Dr Jane Morgan *Child Victims: Crime, Impact, and Criminal Justice*; and with Professor L. H. Leigh, *The Royal Commission on Criminal Justice Research Study No. 1 — A Report on the*

Administration of Criminal Justice in Pre-Trial Phase in France and Germany.

Adrian Grounds, DM MRCPsych, is University Lecturer in Forensic Psychiatry, Institute of Criminology and Department of Psychiatry at the University of Cambridge. He qualified in medicine at the University of Nottingham in 1977 and trained in psychiatry and forensic psychiatry at the Maudsley Hospital, Broadmoor Hospital and the Institute of Psychiatry. Since 1987 he has lectured in forensic psychiatry at the Institute of Criminology, Cambridge and is an Honorary Consultant Forensic Psychiatrist for Cambridge Health Authority and East Anglian Regional Health Authority.

Introduction

Eric Stockdale and Silvia Casale

'Another young prisoner hangs himself while on remand.' This sort of headline or opening sentence appears regularly in the newspapers. Each such news item has been preceded by appalling despair on the part of a prisoner who will never reach adulthood. Each such story has a number of lamentable factors underlying it. On occasion a spokesman for the criminal justice system (if such were to exist) might try to exculpate that system by saying that the young man was the suicidal type before he ever came into contact with the law or its enforcers, and that his death was inevitable once he accepted that he was going to be rightly convicted for a serious crime, and once he appreciated that a long sentence could not be avoided. On most occasions, however, such a spokesman would have to concede that failures of the system had contributed in large measure to the despairing decision to end it all.

The decision to commit suicide may well have been brought about by the despair caused by a combination of a number of the following factors:

(a)   The young man may have known that he was completely innocent, but may have been told by the police officers in charge of his case that they had manufactured enough evidence against him to put him away for a long time.

(b)   He may have been refused bail when there was no justification for such a refusal.

(c)   He may well be in a remand institution with appalling conditions. The physical conditions of the institution, the lack of facilities and bullying may all be enough to test the toughest of adults, never mind an inadequate young man away from home for the first time.

(d)   Staff shortages may well lead to most of the 24 hours of every day being spent in the cell, and to the absence of any worthwhile out-of-cell time.

(e)   Delays in the trial process for that prisoner may well have led not only to increased anxiety, but also to officers from the institution spending time out on escort duty. Absences of staff inevitably means more lock-up time.

(f)   The young prisoner may well have required more medical and psychiatric attention than was available to him.

From these points it can be seen that what happens in one part of the criminal justice process affects what happens in another. The more defendants there are awaiting trial, the more the remand institutions will become inadequate, and particularly so if the courts are refusing bail in a large number of cases when it could have been granted. What the police do affects not only those they charge with offences, but also the courts and the penal institutions. The actions of the courts obviously have a direct bearing on the numbers in prison. In making the crucial decision on whether a community penalty or a custodial sentence is appropriate, the courts will be guided to some extent by the information supplied and advice tendered by the probation service. That service will be influenced — if only to a minor extent — by directions from the Home Office. Although the courts are independent of the executive, inevitably — and quite properly — they may receive information from the executive, whether directly or via the probation officer presenting a pre-sentence report.

It is not only the defendant who suffers when the system is defective. If police officers perjure themselves sufficiently to obtain the conviction of an innocent man, the public will suffer — not only because it is being served by corrupt servants, but because the real offender has been granted immunity from pursuit and prosecution — by courtesy of two or three crooked officers. Also, the innocent prisoner may cause trouble in prison (although there is no history of large-scale disobedience by men claiming to be wrongly convicted: many of them have made model prisoners).

Whenever there are long delays in the completion of trials the public may suffer. Some witnesses for the prosecution change addresses and disappear, whilst others have fading memories. Even if their memories have not faded, counsel for the defence will be able to ask the classic question: 'How can you be sure after 18 months?' Research in America has confirmed that which might have been guessed: delay by and large favours the defence rather than the prosecution which, as a jury will be told on at least half a dozen occasions, bears the burden of proof.

Our system of criminal justice has been shown time and time again in recent years to be under stress. Sheer weight of numbers has played its part. Even if only a small proportion of offenders are caught and charged, the starting figure has become so vast that the numbers appearing in court are greater than ever before. The government has in the past 20 years increased the number of judges, courts and prisons substantially, but the system is constantly revealing a dearth of resources at different points. The system, like all other public services, has to compete for money with hospitals and schools. Increased facilities will ease stress at different points, and various chapters of this book discuss the improvements that can be made.

Unfortunately, increased resources cannot provide a remedy for one of the major problems revealed by the large number of miscarriages of justice — some of which are discussed by Joshua Rozenberg, the BBC's legal correspondent. In some of the major cases considered by him there have been wrongful convictions because the jury accepted evidence of police officers which has subsequently been called into question. Once a jury has convicted on the strength of false evidence, then assuming the judge made no technical error during the trial or in his summing-up, it is extremely difficult for any appeal to succeed. The Royal Commission on Criminal Justice will doubtless be considering ways of altering the powers of the Court of Appeal, Criminal Division, but it will not be able to make suggestions that will lead to all prosecution evidence being either truthful, or unmasked by the jury for what it really is. 'No system of trials is proof against perjury', as Lord Justice Farquharson has pointed out in the judgment cited by Joshua Rozenberg. The police service regularly assures the public that steps are being taken to deal with violent, corrupt or dishonest officers — and John Alderson, a former chief constable, reminds us of the steps taken by Sir Robert Mark to clean up the Metropolitan Police when he was Commissioner. When one or more officers have been exposed, the police force in question will say that it is regrettable, but every barrel contains a rotten apple. This may be true, but the sensible thing to do with rotten apples is to uncover them as soon as possible and to evict them from their barrel. Unfortunately, what has happened too often in the past is that honest police officers have not been prepared to speak up about their 'rotten apple' colleagues. It is probably a failing of all uniformed services that they have a common tradition that it is not done to let a colleague down — or to 'drop him in it' — even if he is a disgrace to his service. It is perhaps partly due to the in-bred loyalty tradition: the notion of the unbroken red, or blue, line: we must all stand together.

Fortunately, occasionally, honest officers are appalled by their colleagues' criminal behaviour and give evidence against them. Sometimes it has taken a considerable time for the better instincts to take over — as in the notorious case of the officers from the patrol van in North London who beat up some innocent youths for the fun of it. At other times they have come forward at once, as in the case of the officer who repeatedly stamped on a prisoner's face in a police van, presumably because he was black. In that case, incidentally, the honest, decent lead came from special constables, that is, from civilians.

The police force must tackle the problem of perjured evidence by its members in a determined manner. It is imperative that from their first days in the service all officers should be taught and reminded:

(a)   That crime prevention is one of their major functions. That includes the fundamental requirement that police officers should not commit crimes themselves — not even perjury in what they deem to be a 'good cause', such as framing a man they 'know' to be guilty of something or other.

(b)   That for an officer to lie in court about a defendant means that he is committing the serious crime of perjury.

(c)   That for two or more officers to concoct evidence involves their committing the serious crime of conspiracy.

(d)   That the police service has no place for criminals.

(e)   That it is wrong, in every sense of the word, for a police officer to turn a blind eye to the crimes of a colleague.

(f)   That they do not owe such criminal colleagues a thing — and certainly not supporting lies, misguided sympathy, or a Nelsonian blind eye.

(g)   That they owe it to themselves and to their decent colleagues, as well as to the service and the public, to prevent and to stamp out crimes by police officers. The Police and Criminal Evidence Act 1984 has provided some restraints on police misconduct, but the main policing of the police — as it is often called — must come, not from the courts, but from the majority of serving honest officers. The announcement that senior officers are to draft a Code of Ethics for the police is an encouraging sign. Other professionals must engage in similar self-examination, even though such a course may entail some painful criticisms of oneself and of colleagues.

For our example of the young offender who commits suicide we might substitute other types of prisoners reaching the end of their tether as they reach the hard end of the criminal justice process — prison. We have chosen a young male offender because the younger age bands represent the predominant offending group and because males far outnumber females at every stage of the criminal justice process.

The recent spate of suicides of young prisoners is one indication of stress in the criminal justice process. It represents the tragic culmination of successive failures of society to deal with young delinquent behaviour in the community and in custody. The recent cases of miscarriages of justice are likewise conspicuous signs of deep-seated problems in the criminal justice process. As Lord Justice Woolf noted with respect to the prison riots of 1990, they 'cannot be dismissed as one-off events or as local disasters or a run of bad luck. They are symptomatic of a series of serious underlying difficulties.' (Woolf 1991, para. 1.142.)

The criminal justice process is a concatenation of devices by which society has attempted over the years to enforce its norms and to deal with behaviour which it deems to be unacceptable. The links in the chain have developed variously. Divergent forces have shaped their growth. What we see today is the result of a somewhat haphazard evolutionary process. It is hard to regard the product as a 'system' of criminal justice. It is not always just, nor is it systematic in its delivery of justice.

In this compilation the authors focus on some of the more conspicuous flaws in the criminal justice process. The book draws together the different perspectives of academic, practitioner or journalist in two distinct ways. The chapters in the first half of the book focus on problems at the successive stages in the criminal justice process — from stop and search, through arrest, remand, trial and sentence to implementation of sentence whether in the community or in prisons and on parole. The discussion focuses on the agents of the State involved in delivering justice at each stage in the process.

The subsequent chapters focus on different types of people who become involved in the criminal justice process — the young, those with drug dependence, ethnic minorities, women, sexual offenders and their victims, and the mentally disordered. Thus the book attempts to look critically at current problems revealed at each stage in the process and at generic problems across the process.

The first three chapters deal with current issues in the process prior to conviction. It is here that the seeds of miscarriages of justice are sown and that the signs of differential treatment of various types of individuals coming into contact with the law first appear.

The chapter concerning the police adumbrates the concerns of the Royal Commission in examining the issues of public confidence and credibility, the boundaries between investigation and prosecution and the shift in balance of power in policing following the establishment of the Crown Prosecution Service in 1985. John Alderson discusses the difference between an objective inquiry into the truth of criminal behaviour and the collection of evidence to establish guilt, the need to balance police powers to interfere with the individual's liberty with freely available remedies for abuse and adequate safeguards, among them the involvement of lay visitors to police stations, access to solicitors at police stations and effective complaints procedures.

'Bail or jail' explores the rise in the remand population held in police cells and in prison, explodes recent myths about offending on bail, and considers initiatives for reducing the custodial population, including bail information services. The chapter examines the conditions for remand prisoners, and the role of remand prisoners and their problems in the prison riots of 1990. From the perspective of one of the assessors for the Woolf inquiry, Rod Morgan and his colleague Stephen Jones discuss the Woolf recommendations, focusing on the idea of community prisons and the emphasis on separate rules for remand prisoners.

Chapter 3 begins by re-examining the basic principles concerning the trial process and by suggesting priorities among competing objectives. John Sprack considers the differences between the adversarial and inquisitorial approaches to arriving at the truth. The discussion about the disparity of resources between the defence and the State at the trial stage focuses on ways of redressing the balance, in particular, arrangements for legal aid, the rules governing disclosure of evidence and the incentives and disincentives in the system which influence the behaviour and decisions of participants. The chapter concludes with an examination of the problems of modes of trial, the jury system and reliance upon confessions.

In 'Miscarriages of justice' Joshua Rozenberg reviews the series of cases in which convictions have been overturned after years of imprisonment and presents the stories of the struggle to make the system redress these wrongs. He considers the problems of evidence from confessions and expert opinion and the shortcomings of the appeal system.

Martin Wasik begins his chapter on sentencing by rejecting the outmoded notion of sentencing as an art rather than a science. The chapter proceeds to unravel the science of sentencing through a consideration of sentencing aims and an examination of the reductivist and the just deserts approaches. The recent shift towards the latter is discussed in relation to the Criminal Justice Act 1991. The principle of proportionality and the problem of the multiple offender are examined in the context of this far-reaching legislative attempt to redefine sentencing aims and to reduce unacceptable variation in sentencing across courts.

Chapter 6 deals with the involvement of the probation service in many different aspects of the criminal justice process from diversion, through various initiatives in the remand process — bail information services, bail hostels, bail support and the provision of social inquiry reports — to work related to sentence implementation — probation orders and other community penalties as well as parole supervision. David Mathieson considers the central role envisaged for the probation service in the Criminal Justice Act 1991 and examines the issues of care and control, tackling offending behaviour, accountability and the training of probation officers and volunteers.

Stephen Shaw's chapter on prisons contrasts the climate of optimism generated by falling prisoner numbers in 1990/91 with the current return to a rising prisoner population and the implications for implementing the Woolf report and the White Paper. Poor industrial relations and the recent shifts towards agency status and privatisation are seen as complicating factors in that process. The chapter brings an awareness of the gulf between policy and practice to bear on the discussion about taking forward Lord Justice Woolf's recommendations, most of which were accepted and endorsed in the government's response, *Custody Care and Justice* (Home Office 1991).

In chapter 8, Mike Maguire analyses shifting policy and practice in relation to the parole process, beginning with its shaky theoretical basis and tracing its patchwork development up to the report of the Carlisle committee. The chapter reviews the changes incorporated in the Criminal Justice Act 1991, focusing on the problems of assessing risk or resentencing, the anomalous restricted categories of cases and the issues of natural justice which arise most conspiciously in relation to life sentence cases.

Phil Parry examines how juveniles coming into contact with the law are dealt with by means of various mechanisms for diversion and how some nonetheless reach the juvenile court. He discusses the ambivalence of the juvenile court process concerning the justice or the welfare model. The chapter considers restrictions on the use of custody for juveniles and their implications for the remand process and for community penalties.

In 'Drug users', Una Padel discusses the relationship between drug use and crime and the conflict between sentencing and treatment, highlighting the debate about voluntary or compulsory treatment and sentences with conditions of treatment. The chapter describes and comments on various strategies for harm reduction in respect of drug-related offending. The examination of provision in relation to drug users in prison focuses on advice and treatment, counselling and support in general and in relation to HIV and AIDS issues in particular, and emphasises the need for prisoners to have access to outside agencies and for those agencies to have access to prisons in order to provide a range of services related to drug use.

'Perspectives on race and gender' looks at differential treatment of people of ethnic minority backgrounds and women through various stages of the criminal justice process. Susan Edwards describes the varying involvement of these groups in the process and presents patterns of disproportionate representation of ethnic minorities as shown in official statistics. The chapter illustrates how discrimination occurs through examples of black women's experiences of the criminal justice process, as associates, victims, defendants and offenders.

Lucia Zedner analyses the response of the criminal justice process to two types of sexual offending: child sexual abuse and rape. The discussion focuses on the problems of identification, investigation, prosecution and trial, examining the pros and cons of legalistic and non-legalistic approaches. The chapter also considers a variety of approaches to the treatment of sexual offenders and the options for treatment within the prison setting.

In the final chapter Adrian Grounds considers the stresses revealed in the criminal justice process in relation to people with mental health problems. The chapter looks at the various options for diversion, whether from criminal justice proceedings altogether or more narrowly from prison custody, and the gaps in provision for the mentally disordered in the context of the current changes in the National Health Service and the policy of care in the community.

A theme which recurs throughout the different contributions to this book is the lack of co-ordination of aims and incentives in the process of criminal justice. The stresses occurring at different stages and their effect on other parts of the process are revealed in their most recent and relevant manifestations. The combination of different perspectives is intended to provoke a rethinking of what we expect of a system of criminal justice. The discussions of conspicious variations in the delivery of criminal justice — among different police forces, across different courts, in different probation areas and for different kinds of people — prompt questions about the need for parity and the avoidance of disparity. In the criminal justice process the agents of the public are engaged in decisions which have profound implications for the lives and liberties of individuals. This book suggests that such work requires clear, coherent and consistently applied principles and standards for all aspects of the process, including openness of the system to public accountability, and professional training of all those to whom the State delegates its authority and in whom the public must put its trust.

References

Home Office (1991), *Custody, Care and Justice: the Way ahead for the Prison Service in England and Wales* (Cm 1647) (London: HMSO).
Woolf, Lord Justice (1991), *Prison Disturbances April 1990: Report of an Inquiry* (Cm 1456) (London: HMSO).

1

The Police

John Alderson

In our system of criminal justice the police are the agents of the prosecution. They are the first actors in the line of those whose coercive and judicial function affects the suspect, the accused, and the convicted offender.

As recently as 1981, the role of the police was thoroughly reviewed by the Royal Commission on Criminal Procedure, and subsequently by Parliament. The Police and Criminal Evidence Act 1984 (PACE), which followed, was the most comprehensive and detailed of all legislation affecting the police function in its history. It was designed to bring police practice into line with modern standards of justice, and with modern resources, including technology. The leading commentator on this piece of legislation said:

> I read all the Parliamentary debates in both Houses of Parliament from start to finish (if both Bills are counted, there was a grand total of 120 sittings, including 105 in committee) and struggled throughout to follow the bewildering sequence of hundreds of amendments that poured like confetti from the Home Office.
>
> There can rarely have been a piece of legislation that was subject to so many government amendments. (Zander 1985, p. i.)

The then Home Secretary, Leon Brittan, believed that the Act's success would depend on 'the extent to which its provisions are generally understood by the public, and to which its underlying philosophy is reflected in the actions of the individual police officer' (Zander 1985, p. ix). For the police, the Act imposed a massive and costly burden in training, administration and operations. Functions are affected by conflict and the resultant stresses in all systems and organisations; our system of criminal justice is no exception. To some degree these stresses are due to the peculiar place and perspective of the actors within the system.

Police officers' view of 'justice' is conditioned by their experience, which differs profoundly from that of lawyers, judges and administrators. Uniquely, police officers are often witness to the anguish and suffering of victims; they know the reputation, including the previous criminal convictions, of the accused; they labour, sometimes risking their safety, and even their lives, in the cause of criminal justice. Being human they sometimes suffer disillusion when the guilty go free, though in theory they should remain detached. They develop strong corporate loyalties which sometimes exact a high price in rectitude. For example, concern to support their colleagues and their own view of what justice is, can lead and has led to practices of falsely enlarging the evidence to fit the criminal accusation. Much of their work in the investigation of crime is carried out unobserved either by the public, or by their supervisors, and particularly by their most senior officers, whose remote position requires a peculiar strength of influence in order to prevail. Endowed, as they are, with a unique battery of powers over the rights and freedoms of people, they are vulnerable to corruption unless properly constituted, and imbued with adequate protection which flows from an ethical predisposition. They sometimes view the system of criminal justice with a jaundiced eye, as the following examples show:

> . . . our besetting national sin of complacency is seen at its worst in our attitude towards criminal justice, largely because so few people know anything about it, and we all want to believe that it is as good as we are told by those who have a powerful vested interest in maintaining the status quo. . . . there is no point in catching criminals if the system of trial is so inefficient that it lets them go free. . . . respected Metropolitan detectives can identify lawyers in criminal practice who are more harmful to society than the clients they represent, [and] who are practised in highly paid forensic trickery. (Mark 1975, pp. 148 and 155.)

A detective superintendent who uncommonly acquired a PhD in social anthropology, whilst covertly studying the behaviour of his colleagues, had this to say about the police:

Police ideology is sustained by the concept of crime at every turn, for the criminal justice system is a theatre of make believe with more than a touch of farce to its systems of production and presentation, and it is difficult for those who are sustained within its structures to admit this to themselves, never mind the outside world. (Young 1991, p. 390.)

Such plain speaking, when accurate, creates a considerable challenge to the leaders of the police, to ensure that their officers do not acquire warped and cynical views of their function.

An example of dangers besetting the system of criminal justice in its police context, arises where the investigators do become cynical, and in pursuit of what may seem to be justice, or a just end to their labours, resort to unjust means. This can represent a considerable temptation where crimes are horrific, the public alarmed, and where sections of the news media generate phobia. In such cases the whole system from investigators to the judiciary is placed under considerable stress. It is well understood, that the road to where the end justifies the means, leads ultimately to the justification of torture, or inhuman and degrading treatment. This happened in recent times in Northern Ireland (*Ireland* v *United Kingdom* (1978) Eur Court HR, ser. A, No. 25) and is a problem in at least one other member country of the Council of Europe today. Its roots go a long way back, to trial by ordeal, and most notoriously to the Inquisition.

The task of the police is to collect the evidence, to support the accusation that a criminal offence has been committed and that it was the accused who committed it. This is not the same as conducting an inquiry into the whole circumstances of the affair, for to do this in every case would far outstrip the resources and the expertise of the police. Though a suspect may be interrogated, once he is accused, or charged, the interrogating must stop. It is at the stage of treating a person as a suspect that the investigator has to avoid allowing a suspicion to become a conviction that the perpetrator of the crime has been identified. Subsequent inquiries may point to another person altogether; meanwhile valuable time and evidence are lost. An interesting illustration of a premature fixation of suspicion leading to a mistaken narrowing of the investigators' field of inquiry, is provided by aspects of the notorious 'Yorkshire Ripper' series of murders. The anonymous practical joker, whose spurious letters and tapes admitting guilt, personally addressed to the officer in charge, succeeded in causing an unwise and erroneous focusing of belief that the killer and the joker were one and the same.

Our adversarial system of criminal justice which characterises our mode of trial as a conflict out of which emerges proof of guilt beyond reasonable doubt or not, unsurprisingly also characterises the investigation. There is a subtle, but important, distinction between an objective inquiry into the truth of criminal behaviour, and the collection of evidence to establish guilt within the system and its rules. The testing of evidence for the truth is the responsibility of the courts. The investigator feels that he has done his job when he has delivered what he believes to be a case for the prosecuting authorities to steer through the court to victory (to use the language of combat).

There are those who, like the late Lord Devlin, see the role of the prosecution, including the investigator, as encompassing 'to a large and undefined extent . . . a duty of making inquiries for the benefit of both sides' (Devlin 1960, p. 62). Practising detectives would be amused, and bemused, if they were told to take such comment literally. Of course such evidence to help the defence which they may stumble across should be produced for the prosecuting authorities to offer to the defence. They also have enlightened self-interest in checking any alibi, often to disprove it, should it be damaging to their accusations of 'guilt'. But to suggest that they embark on inquiries to assist the defence may be a theory, but it does not coincide with practice.

Whether or not the stress arising out of conflict between the police and other sections of our system of criminal justice is inevitable, and constructive, may be argued, but stress there undoubtedly is. Reformers should examine the situation carefully, not only for defects of organisation, but also for the stress which arises from these differing experiences and perspectives. The Royal Commission on Criminal Procedure in its report of January 1981 spoke of the intractability of many problems with which they had been faced, of how 'interests conflict'; and of the fact that 'even those safeguards provided may at times be inadequate' (Royal Commission on Criminal Procedure 1981, p. 196).

Stopping and searching people and vehicles

Policing of streets and public places is laden with potential conflict, particularly at the point where police officers assert their authority to stop persons whom they have reason to suspect of being implicated in crime. The Vagrancy Act 1824 had given parish constables powers to arrest vagabonds, trespassers, and loiterers. These were the riff-raff of Georgian England, many of whom were the poverty-stricken veterans of Wellington's Peninsular and Waterloo campaigns. This piece of legislation was inherited by Sir Robert Peel's Metropolitan Police in 1829, and was used by patrolling constables throughout England and Wales, some of it until quite recently. The notorious provision which classified as 'rogues and vagabonds', persons loitering, and deemed to be suspected of intent to commit felonies (generally petty pilfering, but which might also include more serious crime) was widely used, and abused, by the police, particularly in London. This form of policing was comfort to the bourgeoisie, but to the street loiterers of the underclass, it caused chagrin and dismay. Colloquially known as 'sus', this provision was repealed in 1981, largely due to the refusal of racial minorities and other pressure groups to tolerate it. The Home Affairs Committee in 1980, described the 'sus' law as, 'unsatisfactory in principle', and 'a piece of law which is contrary to the freedom and liberty of the individual' (House of Commons Home Affairs Committee 1980a). Its repeal removed a serious cause of friction between the police and ethnic minorities, and others.

The powers and use of 'stop and search' have had a no less controversial existence than the 'sus' law itself, with the important difference that their use does not automatically result in a criminal charge. They are exploratory powers. First enacted for the use of the Metropolitan Police in 1839, their provision has represented the stock-in-trade of patrolling police officers in London and certain provincial cities for generations. They were, and to some extent still are, used as a measurement of a constable's industry. Due to 'stops' being recorded at police stations, supervisory officers find them to be an accessible source of information upon which to judge an aspect of a constable's performance. A good record of 'stops' leading to criminal charges is one way into the CID. Having 'a good nose', and being 'a good thief-taker', are regarded 'in the job' as being among the hallmarks of 'a good copper'. But policing a pliant underclass in this way is one thing; policing among the more sophisticated and articulate is another. Officers are quick to learn that excessive and crude use of their powers here can spell more trouble than it is worth. Complaints are made, legal action is threatened, and the officer's judgment is called into question.

The most comprehensive research into the use by the police of their powers to stop and search people, where reasonably suspected of having stolen or unlawfully obtained property (Metropolitan Police Act 1839, s. 66), or possessing dangerous drugs, or committing various motoring offences, was carried out by the Policy Studies Institute in 1983 (Smith 1983, pp. 89–113). They found, surprisingly, that 16 per cent of the population of London had been stopped by the police one or more times in a year. This is a high kind of policing activity, amounting to $1\frac{1}{2}$ million stops in a year. They also found that 'police officers do not make stops irrationally . . . they are using their powers intelligently'. But nine out of 10 stops produced no result, though numerically the 'yield' of successful stops was that 5 per cent led to an offence being reported, and 3 per cent to the person being arrested and charged with an offence.

Roughly speaking, this implies that people are arrested and charged with an offence as a result of a stop on 45,000 occasions a year and reported for an offence (generally a traffic offence) following a stop on 75,000 occasions a year. This is a very significant number of offences detected by means of stops. (Smith 1983, p. 117.)

The report concludes that:

The number of people who are opposed to police policy on this matter is small, but the intensity of their feeling may be much greater than among the majority. The police can justifiably point to the views of the majority in support of what they are doing, but this will not help to convince the people who are repeatedly stopped; on the contrary, it will highlight the conflict of views, and stimulate greater opposition among those who are affected. (Ibid., p. 323.)

It was revealed, for example, that the likelihood of being stopped and questioned by the police was highest for West Indians, lowest for Asians, and middling for white people (ibid., p. 96). Younger people of all groups are, unsurprisingly, more likely to be stopped than older ones. The mean number of stops of young West Indians in motor vehicles was 5.06, remarkably high compared with 1.94 for whites. On foot the disparity was 0.99 for West Indians against 0.43 for whites: approximately double (ibid., p. 100; for further discussion, see chapter 11 below).

It was Lord Scarman in his inquiry into the Brixton disorders of 1981 who found that the major factor in igniting latent social tensions was indiscriminate stopping and searching of black youths. Since then his recommendations for improved police awareness training have been implemented (Scarman 1981).

Before 1984 the laws granting powers of stop and search in the wider sense ranged from the theft of eggs of protected birds, to possession of dangerous drugs, firearms and ammunition. The Royal Commission on Criminal Procedure recommended the rationalisation of such powers, and the police in those areas where the basic powers of stop and search were lacking, strongly supported this view. The result is that ss. 1, 2 and 3 of the Police and Criminal Evidence Act 1984 rationalise the law and, importantly, the procedure in the stopping and searching of people and their transport, and the seizure of articles reasonably suspected of being stolen, or prohibited, e.g., offensive weapons at football matches. A duty is imposed on constables by s. 3 of the Act to make comprehensive records of searches. This is causing some police officers to describe the present position as having wrought a 'dramatic change'. 'We are just not doing it', was the view of many practising police officers.

The new and comprehensive systems of recording are making intuitive stops and borderline suspicions not worth the bother which may accrue from their supervisors, or from members of the public. Chief constables are now required to report annually on how many, and what kind of stops and searches, have been carried out within their police areas. These records will provide interesting indicators of the changes in, and variety of, stops and searches throughout the country. However, it will not be an indicator of how many people are being stopped and questioned by the police, since the records only apply to searches after a person or vehicle has, in the words of the Act, been detained. Judicious and skilful stopping and questioning will still be advocated by police trainers and supervisors; the kind of activity advocated by a senior detective in the following passage of his manual:

A stop in the street, whether of a motorist or a pedestrian, is really an interview being conducted by a police officer, who has chosen his subject, and the time and place to stop him, on reasonable grounds. The counter to 'What right have you to stop me like this?' is: 'It would be strange if policemen were forbidden to speak to people. We couldn't protect them or their property at all.' The counter to the old familiar, 'Do I look like a criminal, officer?' is: 'These days, as you see from the newspapers and courts, mere appearance counts for little or nothing.' The original question should be put again in a pleasant manner. (Powis 1977, pp. 162–3.)

Stopping persons or vehicles and, where necessary, searching them and seizing any property which is the subject of a crime are fundamental to the police function. However, the stopping and searching of innocent people is likely to have some adverse impact on relations between the police and the public. There may be times when it is in the public interest that people generally should be expected to cooperate with the police. But if this aspect of police duty is carried out with indifference, or recklessly, free co-operation of the public may at times be withdrawn. This may force the police to be excessively coercive. Where this happens the responsibility will rest with the police officer, though it is not unlikely that members of the public goaded into truculent resistance may even be prosecuted. The well trained and motivated police officer will understand that his basic function of stopping and searching people and their vehicles has to be carried out without unnecessary humiliation and deprivation of dignity.

There are signs that fewer instances of stopping and searching suspects are taking place, thereby reducing prospects of catching criminals 'red-handed'. On the other hand, fewer innocent people are having their rights and liberties interfered with. The balance, desired by the Royal Commission, between 'the interests of the community in bringing offenders to justice and the rights and liberties of persons suspected or accused of crime' may now be nearer than it was.

Lay visitors to police stations

Next to deprivation of life, the deprivation of a person's liberty is the most serious interference with fundamental freedoms imaginable in a liberal democracy. Police officers have many powers which enable them to interfere with these freedoms. It follows, therefore, that the rule of law has to be as unambiguous as humanly possible in this regard, and that remedies for abuse should be freely available to the injured party, as well as punitive sanctions being available, and applied, to perpetrators of such abuse.

It is of particular public concern that not only should deprivation of the liberty of the citizen be jealously regulated, but what happens to people whilst in police custody, and detention, should be safeguarded by every means possible. People are at their most vulnerable in these circumstances.

The Royal Commission on Criminal Procedure (1981), and subsequently the Home Office and Parliament itself, were content to leave the welfare of persons in police detention to the police themselves. There was much debate about the length of detention before any charge is preferred, which in the event was given a legal limit of up to 96 hours, by far the longest ever sanctioned by law. Successive stages of review are laid down by the Police and Criminal Evidence Act 1984, ss. 41 to 44, including a review by magistrates after 36 hours, and any subsequent period of 36 hours. (The European Court of Human Rights found a violation when persons detained under the Prevention of Terrorism (Temporary Provisions) Act 1974, for periods between four days, 16 hours, and six days, were held without being brought before a judge (*Brogan* (1988) Eur Court HR, ser. A, No. 145–B).)

Sections 37 to 39 of the Police and Criminal Evidence Act 1984 also provide for elaborate police procedures and safeguards of the rights of persons detained, and for those procedures and safeguards to be the responsibility of a custody officer. The idea of having independent sources of inspection does not seem to have been given serious consideration.

Addressing this issue in his report concerning the Brixton disorders in 1981, Lord Scarman was of the view that to leave the inspection of the conditions and detention of persons in police custody to checks by senior police officers was no longer sufficient (at p. 114). It was noted that the question of deaths in police custody, which had raised public anxiety about proper police supervision, had been considered by the House of Commons Home Affairs Committee in the preceding year (House of Commons Home Affairs Committee 1980b, para. 13). This committee had stressed the need for chief officers of police to arrange 'sufficient random checks to be carried out to ensure that procedures are properly observed'. It was also noted that the same issue had been raised by the Committee of Inquiry into Police Interrogation Procedures in Northern Ireland (1979) which was of the view that a scheme similar to the Boards of Visitors to HM prisons would be unlikely to have significant effect. The European Court of Human Rights found that the interrogation practices used on terrorist suspects in Northern Ireland amounted to inhuman and degrading treatment contrary to Article 3 of the European Convention for the Protection of Human Rights and Fundamental Freedoms (*Ireland* v *United Kingdom* (1978) Eur Court HR, ser. A, No. 25).

Lord Scarman went on to recommend provision for random checks on the interrogation and detention of suspects in police stations by persons other than police officers. He was of the view that such accountability might be exercised by members of the local police authority, or of the community/police consultative committees, which he also recommended should be introduced.

Following upon the Scarman report, a number of pilot schemes were set up in police forces under Home Office guidance, which in 1986 led to the Home Office asking all police authorities and their chief constables to institute such schemes. The objectives are generally to enable members of the local communities in which police detention centres are located to visit, observe and comment upon the conditions under which persons are detained and on whether the police procedures laid down by statute and local regulations are being properly observed. This is precisely what Lord Scarman recommended.

The Lay Visitors Scheme envisages that visitors should be suitable persons over the age of 18 years. Magistrates are disqualified. Visits are made by two visitors at a time. They arrange the date and times of their visits to ensure that the objects of the scheme are achieved. Police authorities are required to arrange adequate training of visitors, who need to have a sound knowledge and understanding of the many provisions laid down by the Police and Criminal Evidence Act 1984 and the Codes of

Practice under s. 66 of that Act. One scheme examined seemed rather keen in its advice to visitors to encourage them to give advance warning of their intentions to the police station to be visited! This would reduce the element of surprise which is one of the positive characteristics of effective schemes of inspection.

Visitors are expected to examine custody records, to visit detainees without interfering with the proper investigation of crime, and to report their findings to the various authorities. They are required to examine the condition of cells and detention rooms, attention being paid to juvenile or mentally disabled detainees. They are required to satisfy themselves that detainees are not held incommunicado, and that the right to legal advice has been adequately explained.

This reform is in its infancy, but it seems to be making a useful contribution to dealing with the problems affecting detained persons. The Home Office is anxious that the visitors should meet to discuss experiences, and that HM Inspectors of Constabulary should have regard to their role during inspections of police forces.

Many of these volunteers believe that they should now be allowed to form their own national association, and that they should be independent of police authority sponsorship. Many feel that a degree of independence would increase the value and objectivity of their observations and subsequent reports.

Detention at police stations: access to solicitors

The problems surrounding the need for persons to be questioned whilst in police detention are, and always have been, contentious. It is at this stage of the criminal justice system that considerable stress is generated, for a number of interests are in conflict. The police investigators who have arrested a person suspected of serious crime will regard themselves as acting in the best of public interests in seeking sufficient evidence pointing to the suspect's guilt to warrant formal charging with the crime or crimes. On the other hand, the detainee, whether guilty or innocent, has an interest in the exercise of legal rights, for example, the right to remain silent when asked questions by the interrogator. Society as a whole has an interest in procedures being exercised properly, efficiently and justly.

Active criminals who have experienced earlier passages through the criminal justice system often become adept in the exercise of their rights, and need little reminding of them, but many detainees require guidance and advice. There was an active criminal in London who on arrest and detention would produce his solicitor's visiting card, which was endorsed, probably by himself, with the words, 'My client is not to be interrogated until my arrival'. On the other hand, for most detainees, arrest, detention and incarceration can be traumatic. It is whilst the suspect is new to his circumstances that experienced detectives seek to carry out their questioning; they are required to act expeditiously in cases where their evidence is not yet adequate to charge the suspect formally, but is sufficient to justify the arrest.

A report on police interrogation commissioned by the Royal Commission on Criminal Procedure (Irving and Hilgendorf 1980) comments (at p. 23):

> In cases where the police already have substantial evidence, most suspects are likely to realise the futility of attempts at deception or remaining silent. They may therefore choose to answer questions truthfully, or may even offer a spontaneous confession. At the other end of the scale, with complex or serious crimes in which many people are involved, and the penalties are high, the process of reaching a decision about making a statement may be protracted.

Another problem which may arise from interrogation in police detention concerns persons who are innocent of any alleged crime, but nevertheless decide to confess their guilt. This may be due to pressure of interrogation techniques, but it may also be due to covering up for some other guilty person, or sometimes sheer irrational bravado. Psychologists comment, 'There are in theory many ways in which a suspect can be led, or can lead himself, to the conclusion that a false confession is the most attractive option open to him', and 'Some children are brought up in such a way that confession always seems to produce forgiveness' in which case a false confession may be one way of bringing an unpleasant situation (interrogation) to an end (Royal Commission on Criminal Procedure 1979, p. 25). It is for these and other reasons that the question of access to solicitors by detainees becomes very important, and often contentious.

The introduction of a solicitor into the relationship between the interrogator and the detainee certainly complicates the matter. It makes the task of the police questioner more difficult and protracted. An adversary has been introduced, often marking the beginning of the contest as a battle of wits and tactics. The police officer knows that almost invariably the solicitor's advice to his client will be to say nothing. This declares to the police officer, 'You are making these allegations. It is for you to prove them, for it is no part of the duty of my client to help convict himself.' The right to see a solicitor does not mean that a suspect is obliged to see one. Nor is it feasible, from present resources, for a confession to be valid only if validated by the presence of a solicitor. On the other hand, the Royal Commission felt that access to a solicitor when sought should be withheld by the police only in cases of suspicion of 'grave offences'. Terrorism, major organised crime, and crimes which seriously disturb right-thinking members of the public were no doubt in their minds.

Codes of practice governing the general welfare of detainees, and in particular rights of access to a solicitor

The question of the power of the police to delay access is set out in s. 58 of the Police and Criminal Evidence Act 1984 but remains contentious; and it seems inevitable that it always will, for there is a genuine conflict of interest. The police may only delay (not deny) access, where it is believed, on reasonable grounds (by a senior officer), that exercise of the right to consult a solicitor:

(a)   will lead to interference with or harm to evidence connected with a serious arrestable offence or interference with or physical injury to other persons; or

(b)   will lead to the alerting of other persons suspected of having committed such an offence but not yet arrested for it; or

(c)   will hinder the recovery of any property obtained as a result of such an offence.

There is a number of qualifications to this power which mark out the uneasy accommodation arrived at between the need to prevent and detect serious crime, and the importance of human rights.

Code of Practice C lays down detailed rules for the control of the situation once legal advice is being given, including the requirement by the police for the solicitor to leave the interview, should he act in such a manner 'that the investigating officer is unable properly to put questions to the suspect' (para. 6.9). But if a person decides to take advantage of his right of access to a solicitor (and the police *must* inform him of this right and record it), there still remains the question of the adequacy of solicitors to deliver it.

The police often point out the many cases, particularly outside 'office hours', when solicitors do not come, or send a clerk. Some police note that the administration of the payment of legal aid fees is of concern. As many as 60 per cent of claims in one police area were queried when checked against police records. The relationships between the police and solicitors in pursuing their often conflicting functions in these cases can, and does, give rise to allegations and counter-allegations of malpractice.

The introduction of the universal right of detainees to have free legal advice before charge was regarded by many as an important counter-balance to the extra powers of arrest, detention, search and seizure, given to the police by the Police and Criminal Evidence Act 1984. But if the duty solicitor scheme, funded by the government, is not giving adequate service, then the balance of power is tilted more in favour of the police than Parliament intended.

Once the detainee has been informed of his right to see a solicitor he may have his own solicitor contacted, or select one from a list of local solicitors, or he can choose a duty solicitor where such schemes exist. In spite of all these provisions some three out of four detainees decline to use the system. Solicitors put some of the blame for this on the police. In a paper presented to the annual members' conference of JUSTICE on 31 March 1990 (JUSTICE 1990, pp. 12–20), it was reported by researchers: 'We counted the kind of ploys the police use in discouraging suspects from exercising their rights, and we found that in around 42 per cent of all cases the police used one or more ploys aimed at discouraging suspects' (JUSTICE 1990, p. 14). It was reported at the same conference that juveniles suffer in particular by not having their rights read out to them properly until a parent or other adult arrives, but meanwhile both juveniles and the mentally disabled are left to their psychological trauma. It was recounted that one police officer said to a researcher, 'Now under PACE nothing has changed — you just read them their rights as quickly as you can, and get them to sign here, here and here, and there you are, nothing has changed' (JUSTICE 1990, p. 15). Numerous other police illegalities were recorded, in over 12 per cent of all the cases observed.

If the hapless detainee suffers sometimes at the hands of the police, he also has a likelihood of suffering by default of the system of legal aid or advice. 'Out of every 100 suspects who request legal advice, we estimate that 33 will be advised in person at the station by a solicitor, 24 will be advised in person at a police station by a representative, 20 will be advised over the telephone only, and 23 will not receive any advice at all' (JUSTICE 1990, p. 17). There is also concern about the use of non-qualified representatives in the more complicated and difficult cases. There are problems concerning visits by solicitors outside normal office hours, as well as the adequacy of response to requests for advice which is restricted to the telephone.

Both police and solicitors behave towards the letter and the spirit of access to legal advice in ways which are often predictable. The police see it as impeding their detection of crimes — the purpose for which they exist. Solicitors believe it can cost them time which may be more lucratively employed elsewhere; and though when called by a regular client they may respond, they may not feel the same urge to respond when the request comes from an unknown or unimportant individual. Both police and solicitors often feel that they are overworked, and at times not greatly appreciated.

In both cases there is a failure to follow the rules when it does not suit them. The police fail to follow the Codes of Practice, and PACE itself in a large minority of cases, and bend the rules in even more cases. The solicitors fail to follow their own rules of guidance and the rules of their scheme, and there is very little that the committees who control the scheme wish to do about that, even though those committees usually suspect that a certain amount of abuse is going on. (JUSTICE 1990, p. 18.)

Wherever the truth may lie, the Home Office Research and Statistics Department *Research Bulletin* (1991) reports the result of a limited piece of research, covering three police stations in different parts of the country, that since the Police and Criminal Evidence Act 1984, burglary suspects seeking legal aid rose from 6 per cent to 36 per cent. Visits by solicitors to police stations rose sixfold in these cases. Seventy-five per cent of burglary suspects now seek solicitors' services compared with 20 per cent before the Act, and solicitors attended 15 per cent of police interviews compared with 1 per cent before the Act.

Police complaints procedure

Concern about the effectiveness of the system of handling and resolving complaints brought to notice by members of the public reached serious proportions in the late-1950s following a succession of highly publicised incidents. This was one of the reasons for the then Home Secretary, R.A. Butler, deciding to appoint the Royal Commission on the Police in 1960. Its terms of reference included the requirement to consider 'the relationship of the police with the public and the means of ensuring that complaints by the public are effectively dealt with' (Royal Commission on the Police 1962). Its inquiry led it to the conclusion that putting the internal police machinery on a sound systematic footing, requiring alleged police crimes to be notified to the Director of Public Prosecutions, and requiring local police authorities to satisfy themselves that complaints against the police were properly dealt with, would be an effective answer to criticisms. In spite of provisions in the Police Act 1964 to meet these recommendations, dissatisfaction continued to persist, and to increase. The idea that the system would provide some kind of local government participation to reassure the public never could work in London, where the Home Secretary is the police authority. Nor was the Commission unanimous in its recommendations. Three members preferred some form of external check in the form of a commissioner of rights, to check on the way chief constables were discharging their task. The police being arbiters of their own conduct was to some no longer acceptable. Meanwhile the rank-and-file police officers often manifested the view that their task was being undermined by excessive regard for trivial and malicious complaints. Their representatives lobbied to resist the idea of outsiders being brought in to the complaint system which could involve police discipline. The senior officer who had done most in the early-1970s to root out police corruption and malpractice, Sir Robert Mark, ironically was to resign over the issue in 1976 when the Home Secretary appointed a part-time lay body, the Police Complaints Board, to monitor the system.

If the now defunct Police Complaints Board was given a role which seemed to satisfy no one, at least it opened the door to external involvement in the business of dealing with complaints against the police. It lasted barely 10 years. In its place a more robust and purposeful body, the independent Police Complaints Authority, was set up under the Police and Criminal Evidence Act 1984. It was now a full-time task with fresh powers of supervision and intervention to help balance the new powers given to the police by the Police and Criminal Evidence Act 1984. The manner in which complaints against the police were to be conducted now, it was hoped, would increase accountability for the uses and abuses of police power and authority. Serious complaints were singled out as a special responsibility of the Police Complaints Authority, which now must supervise these investigations conducted by the police. It is felt by some that even the investigation of these serious matters should be carried out by the Police Complaints Authority, though there are some difficulties with this. For example, it would require the setting up of a whole new investigative bureaucracy with an end result which might be no better, or perhaps even worse, than at present. The present system of internal police investigations externally supervised has fewer logistic and resource problems than a totally external system but still fails to allay public suspicions.

In addition to the serious complaints which it must supervise, the Police Complaints Authority has the power to intervene in cases where it is of the view that it is in the public interest to do so. For example, allegations of police corruption on a wide scale may suggest intervention. In these, and the 'serious' cases mentioned, the Authority may require that the investigation be carried out by an officer from a police force different from that to which the complaint has been made.

The Police and Criminal Evidence Act 1984 also introduced 'informal resolution' for minor matters which had formerly involved far too bureaucratic a treatment, when all that the complainant sought was a simple explanation or an apology. Provided that both complainant and police officer agree, a growing number of complaints are satisfactorily resolved in this way without recourse to formal disciplinary proceedings. It is the link with police discipline regulations which makes the disposal of complaints against the police so different from other public services.

The function of police officers, involving as it does such wide powers, has to be strictly controlled by internal as well as external accountability, but it is this involvement of external bodies in internal police discipline which is viewed by many in the police as questionable. Although the final responsibility for police discipline rests with the chief officer of police, when consideration of complaints raises the question of discipline, the Police Complaints Authority has been given powers of intervention.

Where a chief police officer does not prefer charges against one of his officers in matters arising out of complaints, the Authority may recommend that he ought, and if he still disagrees it may require him to do so. Of course, where a chief officer of police is consistently in conflict over these issues it would render him liable to censure from the Home Secretary, or, in serious miscarriages of justice, his fitness for his post would be queried. As for the discipline of the chief officers of police themselves, this is the responsibility of the police authority, and not of the Police Complaints Authority.

In fulfilling its disciplinary function the Police Complaints Authority may require the setting up of a tribunal consisting of the chief constable and two members of the Authority, who are otherwise not connected with the investigation of the case to be heard.

Interesting developments in the role of the Police Complaints Authority are presaged. It is now provided that a chief police officer may ask the Authority to supervise the investigation of incidents other than those which are the subject of complaints, in cases where the public interest requires this. For example, this might happen where a member of a police authority, or a friend of the chief police officer, was involved. The influence of the Police Complaints Authority, stemming from its wide experience, may help to modify police policies or police tactics, for example, those actions which generate significant numbers of public complaints, or grievances which happen in one part of the country and may be anticipated in another part.

The present system of dealing with complaints against the police is far more thorough, ordered and comprehensive than ever before. That it has become politically desirable and possible to bring about these improvements is due almost entirely to the refusal of the public to accept police behaviour which they feel is improper, and which exceeds the limits which law and custom define. However, there is no room for complacency.

Police disciplinary procedures give rise to concern. It is now the position that unless the case against a police officer appears to be beyond 'reasonable doubt', it is not the policy to hold a disciplinary inquiry. The standard of proof, i.e., 'beyond reasonable doubt', which was developed for criminal cases has now been agreed by the Home Office (under pressure from the Police Federation) to be appropriate in police disciplinary cases. This places police disciplinary inquiries above the standard of proof in civil cases, i.e., 'on a balance of probabilities', and certainly much higher than required in any other public service. This situation can, and does, result in people who have complaints of a serious nature no longer seeking satisfaction through police complaints and discipline, but rather through the civil courts. Damages awarded against the police in these cases are rising, as more and more complainants seek this kind of justice. But there is an even more perverse outcome. The damages awarded in civil cases come from the public purse, and do not touch the guilty police officer, who also avoids being disciplined and, even in fairly serious breaches of discipline, remains untouched by it all. The first step which needs to be taken is to impose the civil standard of proof in police discipline tribunals, i.e., 'on a balance of probabilities'. After all, police disciplinary hearings are more akin to civil proceedings than to criminal cases.

Further doubts about the present system for dealing with complaints against the police are expressed in recent Home Office sponsored research (Maguire and Corbett 1991, p. 13). The researchers identified four main objectives which the system should aim to achieve:

(a) maintenance of police discipline,
(b) satisfaction of complainants,
(c) maintenance of public confidence in the police,
(d) the provision of feedback to police managers for use in making necessary changes.

It was found that generally the members of the Police Complaints Authority and police investigators were committed and able, and that the system of 'informal resolution' of less serious complaints was developing satisfactorily. On the negative side, the researchers were struck by the failure of the system to achieve its aims. They comment, 'First, every way we measured complainant satisfaction, in relation to every category except informally resolved cases, indicated an overwhelming majority of "dissatisfied customers"' (Maguire and Corbett 1991, p. 194). The main reasons given for this state of affairs, including the high proportion of complainants and police officers complained against, was that complainants felt excluded due to excessive secrecy and bureaucracy; it took too long; they were not informed of progress; there were inadequate explanations for decisions; families suffered from stress and anger. Only a minority of people think that their complaints would be investigated fairly, and ignorance and misunderstandings predominate. This unsatisfactory state of affairs could be improved through better management.

It is the issue of police disciplinary tribunals and the unsatisfactory burden of proof which call for a change in the system. However, there seems to be little enthusiasm for doing anything about this at present. Perhaps as damages against the police in civil courts mount even further, there will be a demand for a review of this unsatisfactory state of affairs. In the words of the Home Office researchers:

> The position of the complainant against the police remains rather like that of the victim of crime in relation to the criminal justice system: he or she provides the initial input into a large impersonal system, which then takes over the case and processes it largely to meet organisational goals rather than in the interest of the individual. (Maguire and Corbett 1991, p. 197.)

Relationship with the Crown Prosecution Service

The reforms introduced in 1985 altered the balance of power in policing, and thereby created a new area of stress in the criminal justice system. So long as the police controlled the prosecution system they were able to use the power it conferred on their actions in a tactical sense when confronting criminal behaviour. The power to put people before the court, without having to convince any other body to do so, was in itself a coercive device, particularly when combined with the notion of a prima facie case to answer. It is significant that one of the first things which the new Crown Prosecution Service (CPS) did, was to abandon the concept of a prima facie case in favour of the test of 'a realistic prospect of a conviction', thus immediately raising the level of proof, and abandoning the more coercive and questionable standard employed by the police. The Royal Commission on Criminal Procedure (1981, pp. 130, 131) had already drawn attention to the unsatisfactory acquittal rate of police-initiated prosecutions, due, it was alleged, to their being grounded on inadequate evidence in the first place.

Apart from the anecdotal, there is now some evidence from early empirical research published by the Home Office Research and Statistics Department in its *Research Bulletin* 31 (1991), p. 25, that the Police and Criminal Evidence Act 1984 may be having the kind of influence on police practice which the framers of the legislation sought. The research indicates that the effects of the Act on the investigation of household burglary has resulted in fewer arrests from interrogation, but more from protracted inquiries and stops in suspicious circumstances. Detectives acknowledged that arrests were 'based on firmer evidence because: there was not time to acquire this after arrest; detectives could rely less on interrogation; custody reviews would reveal flimsy evidence; and the CPS would not take on weak cases'. On the other hand the same research supported anecdotal evidence that the introduction of the CPS and its methods caused some friction between it and detectives. The latter found increased case preparation work, organisational deficiencies, and a demand for too high a standard of evidence. Detectives also find the CPS use of powers of discontinuance to be irksome and frustrating; preventing them getting the accused before the courts, which at one time would have given the arresting officers greater satisfaction, even where acquittal followed. Termination of proceedings before trial is regarded more as a win for the crook, who escapes being put in jeopardy of being found guilty. Oral evidence of professional witnesses, such as the police, when given in court, can often be more telling and persuasive than might appear on the face of a written report.

There is no doubt that the introduction of the CPS suffered from conflict with the police which was aggravated by adverse publicity (Hetherington 1989, pp. 97–108). Sir Thomas Hetherington, then Director of Public Prosecutions, described the inherent nature of the organisational difficulties as 'formidable': 'Perhaps it is too much to hope that the day will soon arrive when the police will regard it as their only function to investigate an offence, once it has been committed' were views he expressed with approval and which seemed to reflect his own understated frustration (Hetherington 1989, p. 96). The real problem lies not so much in the attitude of chief constables and other senior officers as in the perspective of the active detectives grappling with the wiles and power found in the underworld of crime, who are disconcerted to find that the prosecuting authorities are no longer on their side, sometimes adding to the burden of their lonely task. They also are given to expressing the view that some in the CPS are no match for the 'forensic trickery' of their counterparts for the defence. It is generally admitted that the CPS was badly under-resourced, and hastily imposed, creating difficulties in attracting career-minded lawyers in some parts of the country, and this in turn leads to allegations of aggravating incompetence. Time, good management and a new sense of identity for the CPS will undoubtedly remove some of these current difficulties, but there is an in-built stress in these relationships which should not be under-estimated, and which should be acknowledged and minimised.

In the conflict of views concerning whether the CPS should be created as a local or national body, the Royal Commission on Criminal Procedure favoured local affiliation. After examining other common-law police and prosecution systems, their views were quite unequivocal: 'Our conclusion is that . . . a centrally directed national prosecution system for England and Wales is neither desirable nor necessary, and we do not recommend its establishment'. The government took precisely the opposite view. We now have a national prosecution system juxtaposed with localised police and magistracy. The trend towards the drawing of power away from local involvement goes on remorselessly. Meanwhile this potentially discordant arrangement will have to be well-managed to limit its negative character-istics.

Comments emanating from the lower operational police ranks suggest that cases which would have gone forward under the police prosecution system are not going forward under the CPS; too much 'plea bargaining' takes place, often due, it is alleged, to economic and managerial conveni-ence, rather than in the public interest; it is said by some police officers that the CPS does not have sufficient regard for, or understand, local sensitivities and problems which the police claim to understand.

The first Director of Public Prosecutions in charge of the new CPS and other influential voices now suggest that the CPS should play a greater, if not dominant, role in determining the policies for the cautioning of offenders, which hitherto has been under police discretion. It is argued, and it seems rational, that if the CPS has the power to discontinue criminal process at any stage on evidential, public policy or other grounds, then the decision whether or not to caution offenders should also be determined by it. The police, on the other hand, discern just another proposal to diminish their role and status within the system of criminal justice. But the suggestion which generates most reaction is that the CPS should play a gradually increasing role in the investigation process itself.

The Royal Commission on Criminal Justice appointed by the then Home Secretary, Kenneth Baker, following outrageous practices and short-comings of the entire system of criminal justice, revealed in such cases as the Guildford, Birmingham and Tottenham miscarriages of justice, has for its first two specific terms of reference to consider:

(a)   The conduct of police investigations and their supervision by senior officers, and in particular the degree of control that is exercised by those officers over the conduct of the investigation and the gathering and preparation of evidence.

(b)   The role of the prosecutor in supervising the gathering of evidence and deciding whether to proceed with the case, and disclosure of material, including unused material, to the defence.

There is clearly room for change in the business of gathering evidence in criminal cases.

Conclusions

There have been signs over recent years that the police institution has lost a great deal of its reputation for fairness and objectivity. Opinion polls, whilst still showing some respect for the police, indicate a steady and continuous decline in public satisfaction (Mayhew et al. 1989, app. A, tables 8 and 9). The police appear less sure of their place in the social order, and now the Police Federation, representing all the less senior operational ranks, has joined the call for the appointment of a Royal Commission on the police to set the service on a modern footing. There is much to commend this approach for political, as well as for operational reasons. Meanwhile the police, collectively, have articulated and promulgated their perceived professional common purpose and values. The police statement, among other things, declares its commitment to 'uphold the law fairly and firmly' and 'to pursue and bring to justice those who break the law' (which in one form or another means almost everybody who is active, including the police themselves). If this statement is meant to be taken literally, that they are to pursue and bring to justice everybody who breaks the law, including themselves, it may well bring the whole system of criminal justice to a halt. If it is one of those statements of rhetorical purpose, with a touch of crusading zeal, and an avenging spirit, it may be well-meaning, but it sets an unrealistic social agenda. Apart from laws which remain on the statute book but are obsolete or obsolescent (for example, some of the law on bigamy and drug-related offences, such as smoking cannabis), there remains a whole catalogue of regulatory laws which are honoured in the breach — for example, Sunday trading, obstruction of the highway by parked vehicles, and so on. Perhaps the statement does not mean each and every breach of the law, but only those laws which create serious offences. But again this presents a minefield of decision-making, choice and discretion.

Modern liberal democracies require much more of their police than a crusading zeal to fill the courts with offenders, however important that may be at times. There is now a growing moral awareness which impinges on the subject of criminal justice, namely the value of freedom and related human rights which require protection and enhancement, but which the police statement does not adequately address. This may be because in Britain we do not have a Bill of Rights for the police to address, or by way of which to become 'rights conscious'. Reference to a set of human rights values would reflect the spirit of the times and bring the best of modern policing principles into a new dimension. The basic principles of police in a modern liberal democracy might be couched in the following terms:

(a)   The protection of human rights and fundamental freedoms.

(b)   The protection of the institutions of a liberal democratic (in the ordinary philosophical, not the political meaning) government, and of public order.

Under (a) above, the inviolability of the person and peaceful enjoyment of property would be guaranteed. Under (b), all those measures, including security services, required to safeguard the State and public order would be justified. At every step of the police function, including the system of criminal justice, the principles of justice as informed by the laws of human rights and fundamental freedoms, as enacted and enforced under the European Convention, would influence ethical behaviour. Police action to the contrary would be *ultra vires*. The police would thus be enabled to see themselves in a positive role as protectors of human values, rather than merely seeing themselves in the negative avenging role which they otherwise may do. This spirit might make its mark on the system of criminal justice whichever form an amended police participation might take.

So far as police participation in the investigative and prosecution functions is concerned, serious consideration might well be given to a system of recruitment of law graduates directly into the Criminal Investigation Department. In a note of reservation to the report of the Royal Commission on the Police (1962), three members of the Commission expressed a similar view, and subsequent events have strengthened the purport of their comments. As the role of the criminal investigator evolves, and becomes more demanding, the need for more highly qualified entrants will be necessary.

Such officers would comprise a corps of detectives capable of working alongside other professions in joint investigating teams such as the Serious

Fraud Office and those joint European teams investigating international crimes which are envisaged after 1992. They would be expected to include a second European language amongst their skills in the latter cases.

However one views the future for criminal justice and the system, it seems unlikely that it will reach its full potential in the absence of wider constitutional reform. The steady recourse to the European Commission on Human Rights has already shifted the 'fountain of justice' in human rights and fundamental freedoms to Strasbourg and the European Court. The police are, and will be, judged not only for what they do and why they say they do it, but by what they represent; what is behind them; what is the source of their legitimacy. Anything which weakens their moral and constitutional stance will diminish their role in criminal justice itself. A Bill of Rights would set an agenda, and a framework, within which the police could judge and be judged, but that is another story.

References

Committee of Inquiry into Police Interrogation Procedures in Northern Ireland (1979), *Report* (Cmnd 7497) (London: HMSO).

Devlin, P. (1960), *The Criminal Prosecution in England* (London: Oxford University Press).

Hetherington, Sir Thomas (1989), *Prosecution and the Public Interest* (London: Waterlow Publishers).

House of Commons Home Affairs Committee (1980a), *Race Relations and the 'Sus' Law* (House of Commons Sessional Papers HC 559 1979/80) (London: HMSO).

House of Commons Home Affairs Committee (1980b), *Deaths in Police Custody* (House of Commons Sessional Papers HC 631 1979/80) (London: HMSO).

Irving, B., and Hilgendorf, L. (1980) 'Police Interrogation: the Psychological Approach', in *Police Interrogation* (Royal Commission on Criminal Procedure Research Studies Nos. 1 and 2) (London: HMSO).

JUSTICE (1990), Annual Members' Conference, Access to Legal Services. London, 31 March.

Maguire, M., and Corbett, C. (1991), *A Study of the Police Complaints System* (London: HMSO).

Mark, Sir Robert (1975), *In the Office of Constable* (London: Constable).

Powis, D. (1977), *The Signs of Crime* (London: McGraw-Hill).

Mayhew, P., et al. (1989), *The 1988 British Crime Survey* (Home Office Research Study No. 111) (London: HMSO).

Royal Commission on Criminal Procedure (1981), *Report* (London: HMSO).

Royal Commission on the Police (1962), *Final Report* (Cmnd 1728) (London: HMSO).

Scarman, Lord (1981), *The Brixton Disorders 10–12 April 1981: Report of an Inquiry* (Cmnd 8427) (London: HMSO).

Smith, D.J. (1983), *Police and People in London*, vol. 1 (London: Policy Studies Institute).

Young, M. (1991), *An Inside Job* (Oxford: Clarendon Press).

Zander, M. (1985), *The Police and Criminal Evidence Act 1984* (London: Sweet & Maxwell).

2

Bail or Jail?

Rod Morgan and Stephen Jones

Untried prisoners occupy the centre of a web of problems confronting our prison system. Between 1979 and 1989 the average daily prison population in England and Wales increased from 42,220 to 48,610. Seventy-eight per cent of that increase was attributable to the rise in the number of unconvicted prisoners awaiting trial. In April 1990 there occurred at Strangeways Prison, Manchester, the most serious disturbance and prolonged siege in English penal history. Untried prisoners were prominent among the rioters and the small group of prisoners who held officers at bay the longest. While the siege continued, disturbances occurred at over 20 other prisons. Some of the most serious of these disturbances also occurred at local prisons or remand centres (Bristol, Cardiff, Glen Parva and Pucklechurch) and, as at Manchester, untried prisoners either played a leading part or were wholly responsible for what happened. At Pucklechurch Remand Centre the damage to one part of the prison was so extensive that the Prison Department subsequently decided not to repair it, and the establishment is to close in 1993–94.

During the summer of 1990 the Council of Europe Committee for the Prevention of Torture and Inhuman and Degrading Treatment or Punishment (CPT) visited the United Kingdom for the first time. They concentrated their attentions on England and among the custodial institutions inspected were Brixton and Leeds Prisons, both of which are local prisons housing large numbers of unconvicted prisoners. The Committee, in a judgment unprecedented in any of their published reports to date, pronounced that the conditions in which many of the prisoners were being held were 'inhuman and degrading' (Council of Europe 1991, para. 57), a phrase not lightly used. It meant, by implication, that in the Committee's view the conditions breached Article 3 of the European Convention for the Protection of Human Rights and Fundamental Freedoms, which forbids the inhuman and degrading treatment of prisoners. Had the CPT visited any police stations in which Home Office prisoners (as opposed to police prisoners) are regularly held (over 1,400 of them at the time of writing) they might have been even more censorious. They assumed, wrongly, that detainees usually spend only a very short time in a police station, and yet, even on that assumption, found the washing facilities for police prisoners to be inadequate. Had the CPT appreciated that prisoners 'locked out' of prisons for various reasons are held in police stations often for weeks and sometimes for months, they would undoubtedly have condemned the arrangement unequivocally.

Crisis is an overused word. Yet, in relation to the custodial remand population, crisis is a reasonable description of the situation which has regularly prevailed in recent years. The population has often spilled over, as has the temper of that population.

These have been the pressures providing the backcloth to a package of initiatives pursued by the government to reduce the untried prison population, empty the police cells of them and radically to improve the conditions in which remand prisoners are held within the prison system. At the time of writing, pressures are being brought to bear which may undermine the success of these initiatives. Recorded crime in 1990 was 17 per cent more than in 1989. In the summer of 1991, in what appears to have been a campaign orchestrated by the Association of Chief Police Officers (ACPO), the press repeatedly carried stories, prompted by leaks from the police of research data not then published, maintaining that the number of offences committed by defendants on bail had dramatically increased. Thus the *Sun*, under an editorial headline of 'Jail Not Bail', asserted:

40 per cent of crimes are committed by suspects on bail. One dodger carried out another 274 crimes. The answer is not to give bail to people accused of serious, violent offences. If that means new jails, build them. Nothing is more important than society's protection. (*Sun*, 6 September 1991.)

Moreover, in 1991 — following a period of decline and stability during 1989–90 — the prison population, including the custodial remand population, began to rise again. Having fallen to below 45,000 in 1990, the prison population rose during autumn 1991 to about 48,000, including well over 9,000 remand prisoners, 21 per cent of the population.

This is the context within which the following account of the remand population must be set.

Guiding principles

There are three principles which should guide decision-makers in their treatment of defendants awaiting trial. First, unconvicted persons must be presumed to be innocent and treated accordingly. Second, and countervailing the first, the public have a right to be protected against individuals who are with good reason feared to pose a threat to person or property. Third, justice delayed is justice denied.

The first and second principles are incorporated in the Bail Act 1976. There is a presumptive right to bail and it can only be refused on conditions set out in the Act. Although the terms of the Act are capable of wide interpretation (which has led some commentators to call for their tightening — see, for example, Northumbria Police 1991, p. 58), the underlying doctrine is clear: unnecessary resort to custody is as legally wrong as it is morally offensive.

Unfortunately this principle has yet to be extended to the statutory framework governing the administration of imprisonment. Custody is not all or nothing. There are degrees of custody as there are levels of restrictions to liberty. Thus in the same way that the granting of bail may be accompanied by conditions (ranging from the requirement that defendants live at a given address through to the proviso that they abide by a curfew, or be electronically tagged and monitored), so also may custody be arranged with higher or lower levels of security. Indeed, the boundary between custody and bail might be blurred by the creation of 'secure' or 'more structured' bail hostels (Home Office 1988c). It should follow, therefore, that no defendant should suffer greater loss of liberty, both in duration or degree, than is necessary to secure the course of justice. However, as we shall see, this extension of the doctrine embodied in the Bail Act 1976 is officially admitted to be breached in prisons almost as a matter of routine. Indeed, all the evidence suggests that untried prisoners endure without justification the most oppressive conditions found in the prison system.

Bail and custody trends

The most appropriate starting-point for any assessment of the use of bail is 1975. Although the Bail Act 1976 was not implemented until 1978, it was preceded by a Home Office circular issued in 1975.

The period 1975 to 1980 saw a significant fall in the number of untried prisoner receptions. Not until 1985 did the number climb above the 1975 level. From 1985 to 1987 there was a further significant rise. What is striking about the receptions data is that the overall increase has been attributable to both the unconvicted and the sentenced, while the number of convicted but unsentenced and civil receptions has fallen substantially.

Although the total prison population has risen by 22 per cent since 1975 the number of sentenced prisoners has risen by only 12 per cent and the number of convicted and unsentenced and civil prisoners has fallen. By contrast, the number of untried prisoners has increased by a massive 142 per cent, an increase concentrated in the years 1976 to 1987, since which time there has been a modest decline. During 1991 the trend once again was upwards. These trends have dramatically altered the composition of the prison population. Whereas unsentenced prisoners comprised 12 per cent of the population in 1976, they made up 21 per cent of the prison population in 1989.

The principal explanation for this phenomenon is the changing duration of custody for the untried. Whereas untried prisoners spent an average 25 days in custody in 1975, this had increased to 56 days in 1987. The figures for untried female prisoners exhibit an even greater increase, albeit from a lower base. By the same token the stabilisation in the average population of untried prisoners since 1987 has been achieved largely as a result of a modest decline in the average duration of custody.

The prison data indicate, therefore, that the growth in the remand population is to only a limited extent explained by the courts refusing bail to an increased number of accused persons. The data suggest that court waiting periods have become longer. In fact the explanation is more complicated.

The proportion of defendants dealt with summarily who have their cases remanded and are refused bail declined from 16 per cent in 1978 to 11 per cent in 1989, though because of the substantial increase in the number of defendants involved this nevertheless represents an increase of approximately a quarter in real terms. However, custodial remands in summary proceedings are usually brief. The significant change in the size of the prison population has been the rise in the number of defendants committed by magistrates for trial in the Crown Court, and the proportion of those committals in custody. In 1975, before the Home Office bail circular and the Bail Act 1976, 20 per cent of committals were refused bail. That proportion fell to 17 per cent, but by 1985 had climbed back to 22 per cent, at which level it stabilised before falling to its present level of 19 per cent (Home Office 1992, table 8.7). This increased rate of committals in custody was until 1987 superimposed on a rise in the rate of all committals. In 1978–9 the number of committals declined, largely as a result of a major reclassification of offences as summary under the Criminal Law Act 1977. Between 1979 and 1987 the number of either-way cases committed (these constitute over 80 per cent of all committals) increased from 55,000 to 93,500, a rise of 70 per cent. This represented an increase from 15 to 23 per cent of all defendants proceeded against for either-way offences.

This upward trend — which largely accounts for the rise in the prison remand population — was halted and then reversed in 1988–9. In 1989 the total number of either-way cases committed to the Crown Court declined to 80,400 (a fall of 14 per cent from the 1987 high point) and the committal rate also declined from 23 to 21 per cent. The decline in the overall number of either-way cases largely resulted from a reclassification of offences under the Criminal Justice Act 1988. The decline in the committal rate and the committal-in-custody rate is more difficult to fathom, but is crucial. The higher the proportion of defendants who are committed in custody for trial at the Crown Court, the longer the waiting period and the higher the custodial remand population. This is the phenomenon at which recent government initiatives have been largely directed and, if the 1988–9 data are a guide, with a modest success.

We have argued that there are two competing principles governing the bail–jail decision and that, once that dilemma has been resolved in any particular case, the course of justice should be as expeditious as possible. How are we to determine whether there are too many remands in custody? This is not an easy question to resolve. Although some cases are complex and could not with justice be brought to trial speedily, there is little reason to believe that the number of such cases has dramatically increased. Yet, whereas the average number of untried prisoners in custody increased by 112 per cent between 1979 and 1989, the number who had been in custody for more than three months increased by 175 per cent and the number held for over six months by 216 per cent. In the period 1985–9 there were on average at least 100 untried prisoners who had been awaiting trial for more than one year (Home Office 1990b, table 2.3). Those data suggest that an increasing proportion of untried prisoners are held in custody for unacceptably long periods.

Are prisoners being avoidably refused bail? Many commentators have dealt with this question by considering the relationship between refusal of bail and subsequent conviction rates and sentencing decisions.

The proportion of untried prisoners subsequently acquitted or not proceeded against is probably around 14–15 per cent. (The available statistics do not enable us to be precise — the *Criminal Statistics* provide more of a guide than the *Prison Statistics* because the latter include high proportions of unknown outcomes.) This finding suggests that there is no room for complacency. Given that a remand in custody invariably carries severe social and financial costs, and that it is virtually impossible for a defendant found not guilty subsequently to obtain compensation, the fact that approximately one-eighth of all defendants denied bail find themselves in this position should be a cause for considerable concern. Ironically, the obverse can also be held to be true. The fact that persons are denied bail and are subsequently not convicted may be testimony to the fairness and impartiality of adjudicators.

The same paradox connects the denial of bail and the subsequent imposition of non-custodial sentences. A considerable proportion of the majority of untried prisoners who are subsequently convicted nevertheless do not receive custodial sentences — at least a third of males and a little over a half of females (the precise proportions are not clear from *Prison Statistics* for the reasons cited above). The proportions have marginally decreased in recent years. Does this constitute progress?

The answer is not straightforward. Bail and sentencing decisions are different. The high proportionate use of non-custodial sentences for offenders refused bail certainly raises a question about the necessity of their custodial remands, but it does not demonstrate that these custodial remands are unwarranted. Indeed, were all persons refused bail subsequently to be given custodial sentences that might be a greater cause for concern. Commentators in other jurisdictions report that sentencers feel obliged to pass custodial sentences at least as long as periods already spent in custody awaiting trial and sentence (Heinz 1989; Faugeron 1989). We know of no evidence that such an obligation operates in Britain. Indeed, the reverse is often said to be the case. It is precisely because an offender has been in custody on remand that sentencers feel that enough is enough and that a measure which could not legitimately have been imposed as a punishment has nevertheless served as one. A non-custodial penalty is therefore imposed. Had the offender not been held in custody then the outcome might have been different. It follows that the bail–sentence relationship is an equivocal one. We need to know what considerations impinge on sentencers' decisions in order to judge whether the current pattern is evidence of unnecessary custodial remands.

Further evidence can be brought to bear on this question. There are enormous disparities in the rates at which different benches refuse bail — as much as tenfold. These disparities cannot be explained by differences in the types of cases coming before different courts (Winfield 1984), and the government has repeatedly called for greater consistency (Home Office 1988a; see also the Home Secretary's speech to the West Midlands branch of the Magistrates' Association, November 1987). There is as yet no evidence that the practices of courts which are parsimonious in their use of custody could not be adopted by other courts without prejudice to public safety or the course of justice.

Of course, one essential difference between sentencing and bail decisions is that the latter have often to be made on the basis of little information. Making up that informational deficit was the object of the pioneering Vera Institute bail information project (Stone 1988) which served as the progenitor of the bail information projects which now make up the centrepiece of the government's effort to reduce the custodial remand population. The Vera project involved an initiative by eight probation services to provide information to the Crown Prosecution Service (CPS) in cases where the police indicated an objection to bail (probation services often possess information about defendants which could be relevant to the CPS assessment of whether to oppose bail). The eight schemes differed, as did the quality and extent of the information they provided. The schemes typically involved the verification of defendants' addresses, medical condition, employment record and probation supervision history. In some cases extra efforts were made to secure hostel accommodation or make referrals to drink or drug abuse centres or to employment schemes. The Vera Institute was cautious about the results. The number of cases in each project was small. Nevertheless, in all three areas where data on police and CPS recommendations were systematically collected before and after the project began, there was a significant decline in the proportion of cases for which the police recommended, and the CPS sought, a custodial remand. Further, in two of the three areas the correspondence between CPS and police recommendations for remands in custody was even lower in those cases for which the probation service supplied information. The declining correspondence did not mean that the police were necessarily overruled as a result of getting extra information. The police as well as the CPS were often persuaded that a remand in custody was unnecessary.

The Vera project demonstrated that large numbers of defendants were being avoidably remanded in custody. Further, there was no evidence that an increase in granting bail led to an increase in the failure rate. For the three pilot-project courts where full information was available, Vera found that the proportion of defendants who breached their bail was almost identical in those cases bailed following additional information as those bailed without it. This was true whether the test was arrest for a new offence, or for breach of bail conditions, or failure to answer bail.

Whatever the original Vera data showed, bail information schemes are now pervasive. But the police now appear less willing to accept that increased resort to bail has been achieved without increasing problems with bailees. A distinction has to be made between committing offences whilst on bail and breaching bail conditions — about which no data are routinely recorded — and failing subsequently to appear. In 1989 approximately 5 per cent of all suspects failed to answer police bail and about 6 per cent of all defendants granted bail by magistrates failed to appear. It is estimated that approximately 8 per cent of defendants on bail to appear in the Crown Court failed to do so. These proportions are marginally higher than the levels recorded in the late-1970s, but the changes are not significant. Moreover, some failures to appear may be legitimate and excusable. Failure to appear, however, is only one part of the story. The current focus of controversy concerns offences committed on bail.

The amount of crime committed on bail

ACPO, in response to increasing levels of recorded crime, is urging that the criteria for granting police and court bail should be tightened. During 1991 three police forces — the Metropolitan, Avon and Somerset, and Northumbria — produced reports for their areas on the apparent level of offending by people on bail.

The Avon and Somerset report claims that between 24 and 34 per cent of people who were arrested and 28 per cent of people who were charged were on police or court bail at the time. This finding was based on three different methods of data collection: surveys of detectives, a survey of all custody suites in police stations and an examination of court records (Brookes 1991). The Northumbria Police survey was based on all the cases dealt with in C Division, which is said to be broadly representative of the whole force area. It found that 23 per cent of all arrests were of people who were on police or court bail, and 17 per cent of people on court bail were found guilty of offences committed while they were on bail. However, this latter figure includes offences taken into consideration (TICs) by the courts and those dealt with by a formal caution (Northumbria Police 1991). The Metropolitan Police report was based on a sample of cases from 10 divisions, which are representative of both inner and outer London. It showed that 12 per cent of people on court bail were convicted of offences committed on bail (Nichols and Ennis 1991). Unlike the Northumbria study, this figure did not include TICs or cautions. The report comments that the situation does not seem to have changed greatly since the estimates for offending on bail reported in a Home Office study carried out a decade earlier (Home Office 1981). The Metropolitan Police report is the only one of the three which refers to that study, which was based on a sample drawn from all magistrates' courts throughout England and Wales in 1978 and showed an offending rate on court bail of 9 per cent, which rose to 12 per cent for the London area. These figures include a small number of TICs, but no cautions.

The government, facing the prospect of a general election, expressed concern at these police reports and said that the whole question would be considered by Home Office researchers. The Home Office Research and Planning Unit (RPU) produced its own survey in February 1992 (Morgan 1992). This comprised an evaluation of the three 1991 police reports, the earlier Home Office study, two reports from the Greater Manchester Police (Greater Manchester Police 1987 and 1988) and an RPU study based on 1986 and 1988 data on people convicted of one or more of four categories of offence in three magistrates' courts (Henderson and Nichols forthcoming).

In the 1992 RPU survey Morgan states that answers are needed to two 'key questions': the proportion of defendants on bail who commit further offences on bail, and the proportion of recorded crime that is committed by persons on bail. The findings outlined above are considered, together with the RPU analysis of the 1986 and 1988 data, which shows an offending rate on court bail of 10 per cent, and the Greater Manchester research. These studies, based on standard forms completed by arresting officers, found that 26 to 29 per cent of offenders charged were on police or court bail when charged. Morgan points out the difficulties of comparing the studies on account of the different methodologies adopted, and suggests that future research should concentrate on the proportion of defendants who are convicted of further offences while on bail, together with counts of the numbers of offences they commit. The second question is difficult to answer because two-thirds of reported crime is undetected. Moreover, as no earlier studies have considered the proportion of detected crime committed by people on bail, it is impossible to say whether this has increased in recent years. The use of arrest or charge as a test of 'offending' is convenient for police forces because collecting the data involves relatively little time and expense. However, such an approach is likely to produce higher levels than studies based on convictions.

Even after Morgan's analysis and the additional evidence from the Greater Manchester and RPU studies, the situation is far from clear. The research based on convictions for offences committed on bail seems preferable to that which uses numbers of arrests and charges as criteria for 'offending', and this gives lower offending rates than some of those that were receiving much publicity in 1991. This is not to deny the existence of a problem; as the number of defendants granted bail increases, there is a possibility that the number of crimes committed on bail will do so as well. Yet there is still much that we do not know. For example, although there is some evidence about the types of offences committed on bail, there is no information about their seriousness. Is it acceptable that between 10 and 17 per cent of people on bail are committing criminal offences? This depends on the nature and seriousness of the offences involved and balancing the cost to society of such crimes with the danger of wrongfully keeping people in custody. As the Metropolitan Police report pointed out, there are two types of 'wrong' decision concerning bail: the one that allows freedom to an individual who goes on to reoffend or abscond, and the one which results in withholding bail from an individual who would not have abused it. Even if 17 per cent of people on bail are offending, 83 per cent have not been shown to be.

The role of the police in this controversy is interesting. The Metropolitan Police report, originally given a restricted circulation, is a low-key document which states that no recommendations for action are being put forward. There is a balanced discussion of the problem of offending on bail which states that the greatest problem is the lack of available information about the accused. However, the tone of the Avon and Somerset and Northumbria reports is somewhat different, and it was the leaking of their findings to the press that caused the reports to be highly publicised in 1991. The Avon and Somerset report is concerned that officers are unable to refuse bail in some cases because s. 38(1) of the Police and Criminal Evidence Act 1984, which governs the granting of police bail, does not specifically provide that a fear of further offending can amount to grounds for such a refusal (Brookes 1991, p. 1). However, the provision does state that an arrested person may be detained, *inter alia*, 'to prevent him from causing physical injury to any other person or from causing loss or damage to property'. There can surely be very few cases where the police want a remand in custody which could not be justified on either of those grounds.

The Northumbria report goes even further. It claims that its findings 'call into question the increased use of alternatives to custodial sentencing, particularly where juveniles and young adults are concerned' (Northumbria Police 1991, p. 59). The meaning of this statement is not made clear in the report. It may be simply an expression of the police' belief in the deterrent efficacy of custodial sentences, but it does not seem to follow from, or be relevant to, the research findings relating to the level of offending on bail. There is also a claim in the foreword to the report by assistant chief constable, Gordon McMurchie, that bail information schemes have led to an increase in offending on bail: indeed, it was because of this belief that he initiated the project. McMurchie refers to 'anecdotal evidence' from his officers, but the Northumbria report does not deal at all with bail information schemes, and there is no published research evidence to support his view.

Following the publication of Morgan's report in February 1992, the Home Secretary made a statement in Parliament. He estimated that, of the nearly 500,000 people granted bail by courts in 1991, around 50,000 were convicted of an offence committed while on bail. Five years previously this figure was about 35,000. However, what this misleading use of figures did not show was that the number of people granted bail at that time was only around 350,000, so the percentage of estimated offending on bail remains the same. The Home Secretary felt that 'we must crack down on those bail bandits', and six new measures are to be introduced. Legislation will be brought in requiring courts to consider offending on bail as an aggravating factor when passing sentence, and to give the police statutory powers to arrest people immediately who breach police bail. Improved notices will be provided making the penalties for breach of bail conditions clear. New bail information projects involving different agencies in the criminal justice system will be set up in selected areas to ensure that those likely to offend will not be given bail. The training of magistrates in the criteria set out in the Bail Act 1976 to assist with risk assessment will be reviewed. The sum of £8 million will be provided over the next three years for bail accommodation and support, with 800 extra places by April 1995.

Clearly the 'offences whilst on bail' controversy cannot on the basis of existing evidence be said to have been resolved; more research is needed. What *cannot* be said on the basis of existing evidence is that offending by bailees has significantly increased in recent years. On the contrary, the data suggest that the proportion of defendants granted bail who commit further offences is much the same as it was 10 years ago. The same is true for breaches of bail conditions. Most commentators believe that bail is now more commonly accompanied by one or more conditions than was formerly the case, but it is far from clear that many bail conditions (such as reporting to police stations) are necessary or effective and that their breach should therefore be regarded in a serious light.

One way of increasing the credibility of bail is to attach restrictions to it. This is done extensively already, usually in the form of a requirement that the bailee report regularly to a police station, live at a particular address or refrain from visiting locations or persons associated with an alleged offence. In 1989 a pilot project was undertaken in three magistrates' courts involving the electronic tagging of defendants granted bail. This initiative encountered a good deal of opposition on the grounds both of principle and practicality. In the event it was not a success. Tagging was little used by the courts concerned and in those few cases where tags were applied compliance with the bail requirements imposed was poor (Mair and Nee 1990). The idea now seems to be less enthusiastically supported by Ministers, though provision for the electronic tagging of offenders sentenced to curfew orders is provided for in the Criminal Justice Act 1991, s. 13.

Another approach to bail credibility is represented in the growing interest in bail support schemes, which have for some time been provided to certain juvenile courts by social service departments and one or two voluntary societies. These schemes verify defendants' community ties and provide elements of supervision to bailees. Given that ss. 60 to 62 of the Criminal Justice Act 1991 provide for the phasing out of the use of Prison Service accommodation for juveniles pending trial or sentence and the laying of that responsibility on local authorities, bail support schemes are likely to increase in number and become more robust in quality. Despite a certain amount of opposition within the probation service to bail information schemes and bail support schemes, there is no reason why the principle of bail support — both advice and elements of surveillance — should not be extended to young adults or adults. This would be a controversial development not only because the boundary line between custody and liberty would become more blurred, but also because, as with all attempts to divert from custody by restricting liberty within the community, net widening of control may be the consequence.

In conclusion, the case against extending the use of bail is as yet not proven, although there is a good deal of evidence that many defendants currently refused bail could, following proper evaluation by the relevant agencies, be safely granted it. Moreover, and equally importantly, time spent in custody could almost certainly be reduced in many cases without damage to either prosecution or defence.

Government initiatives to facilitate the use of bail and reduce time spent in custody

From time to time Ministers exhort magistrates to make as sparing a use of remands in custody as possible. Moreover, during the late-1980s, the government has pursued several initiatives in an attempt to persuade the courts that they can release more prisoners on bail without significantly diminishing the protection of the public. Finally, several measures have been introduced in an effort to ensure that, where custody is resorted to, it is as brief as possible.

The first issue the government has tackled has been the question of consistency in the application of criteria and procedures under the Bail Act

1976. Courts have had their attention drawn to evidence of inconsistency (Home Office 1988a) and provision has been made to ensure that defendants are not inhibited from seeking bail, whilst safeguarding courts against frivolous or improper applications. In the 1980s, as a result of a Divisional Court decision ironically designed to clarify practice (*R* v *Nottingham Justices, ex parte Davies* [1981] QB 38), confusion arose as to whether more than one application for bail could be made on the basis of the same circumstances. Many remands in custody were uncontested for fear that if unsuccessful a subsequent bail application would not be entertained. Solicitors preferred to wait in order to make a thoroughly well-founded bail application (Brink and Stone 1988). The government has clarified the situation by statute. The Criminal Justice Act 1988, s. 154, which amends sch. 1 to the Bail Act 1976, provides that, once a defendant has been refused bail, any argument as to fact or law may be used to support a second application whether or not it has been used previously. Thereafter 'the court need not hear arguments as to fact or law which it has heard previously'. Thus, the court now has a discretion to hear these arguments on a third or subsequent application.

Second, on the grounds that remands in custody are often sought, or bail applications often fail, for want of information which might reassure the court that defendants will respond positively to bail, the Vera demonstration project has been commended as good practice and widely copied. More than 100 courts are covered by probation-run bail information schemes and 14 local prisons or remand centres operate bail schemes designed to assist prisoners refused bail to prepare successful applications (Home Office 1991a, para. 9.6). The evidence suggests that the proportion of defendants granted bail as a result of these projects has increased (Lloyd 1992).

Third, the government has funded expansion of the number of bail hostel places. At the beginning of 1992 there were 27 approved bail hostels offering 502 places and 82 combined probation and bail hostels offering 1,776 which together can accommodate approximately 1,000 bailees at any one time. An expansion programme is underway to double this number of places by the end of 1994 (Prison Service 1990, paras 3.21–3) and moves are being made to establish one or more hostels specifically for mentally disordered offenders.

Precisely what the net combined impact of these custody-avoidance initiatives has been, or might be if taken further, is difficult to assess. Whereas early studies of bail hostels showed that occupants were generally persons at high risk of custody (White and Brody 1980), more recent evidence indicates that some hostel residents would not otherwise be remanded in custody (Lewis and Mair 1989). Bail information schemes, on the other hand, show clear promise of reducing remands in custody, and there is as yet no clear evidence that offending by bailees is a significantly increased problem. If, on the basis of further evidence, that is shown to be the case, there may be a significant role to be played by bail support schemes for the continued credibility of bail for many defendants.

Probably as fruitful an approach — indeed, possibly more so, given the principal reason why the custodial remand population rose during the 1980s — are the initiatives being pursued to reduce delays in criminal proceedings. First, there has been a gradual application and now tightening of custody time-limits under provisions introduced by the Prosecution of Offences Act 1985 and the Prosecution of Offences (Custody Time-limits) Regulations 1987 (SI 1987 No. 299). At present, the limits are as follows: in triable-either-way cases, 70 days from first appearance to summary trial or committal, and 56 days from first appearance to summary trial if a decision about mode of trial has been made within 56 days; and in indictable cases, 70 days from first appearance to committal and 112 days from committal to arraignment. Any time-limit may be extended by the court, on more than one occasion if necessary, if the court is satisfied that there is 'good and sufficient cause' to do so and that 'the prosecution has acted with all due expedition'. However, there are two key difficulties associated with the fixing and operation of time-limits. First, any limit which did not lead to a significant number of breaches could be said to be relatively pointless in the sense that it exerted little downward pressure on current practice. Indeed, it could be counter-productive in that practitioners might be tempted more fully to use the time set below the limit. It follows that limits need to be set with some care and adjusted in the light of what proves to be achievable. Second, to the extent that there is a 'local legal culture' tolerant of delay, it is precisely those courts in which limits most need to be enforced that may be most ready to grant extensions. On both counts the operation of limits needs constantly to be monitored.

The evaluation of time-limits so far carried out is restricted to only a few areas and covers only 1987 and 1988 (Henderson 1991). Not surprisingly, no trend could be discerned and it was not possible to assess what effect the operation of time-limits was likely to have on the population remanded in custody. Extensions 'were treated as an almost automatic part of the process': indeed in the courts monitored not a single application for an extension was refused in 1987 (Henderson 1991, p. 24). This limited evidence suggests that the scepticism expressed by some commentators about the likely impact of time-limits may have been justified (Corbett and Korn 1987).

It is clear from available Home Office statistics that during the period 1986 to 1991 the average time taken to complete both summary and indictable cases increased significantly (for example, the average number of days from first listing to committal for indictable offences increased from 44 to 63 days) and that this increase was associated with a significant increase in the average number of adjournments. It was precisely for this reason that in 1989 a working group on pre-trial issues was established by the Lord Chancellor's Department. The group, which produced a report in 1990, includes representatives of the key agencies making decisions within the criminal justice system. The group has recommended, *inter alia*, that there should be national guidelines for the time to be taken between first appearance and critical decision points in criminal proceedings (such as pleas, trials and committals) and that compliance with these guidelines should be monitored by, among others, the 'court user committees' that many courts have now established (Lord Chancellor's Department 1990b). Among practising lawyers, however, there is a good deal of scepticism as to whether sufficient political will and resources have been devoted to the implementation of the working group recommendations. This issue, and how to reduce delays, is likely to be the first priority of the Criminal Justice Consultative Committee being established both nationally and locally following Lord Justice Woolf's inquiry into the Strangeways riot (Woolf 1991, para. 10.170; Home Office 1991a, para. 1.10).

The second initiative has been designed to stem the rising tide of committals in triable-either-way cases to the Crown Court. Cases may be committed either because the defendant elects to be tried there, or because the magistrates decline jurisdiction on the grounds that the case appears to them to be more serious than their limited sentencing powers allow for. Somewhat surprisingly, the official statistics do not record, and little research has been conducted on, the proportions of committals explained by these very different factors. Nevertheless, we know that committal rates vary considerably from one court to another and that the variation is not explained by differences in the types of cases dealt with. Further, a limited Home Office study has shown that a large proportion, possibly a majority, of committals involve magistrates declining jurisdiction in cases where defendants would have consented to have their cases being dealt with summarily if they had been given the option (Riley and Vennard 1988, p. 22). In most of those cases the magistrates' decision was in line with the recommendation of the CPS. This suggested that local legal cultures differed with regard to cases considered suitable for summary trial, a factor critical for the size of the custodial remand population.

It was with a view to ironing out inconsistencies in committal policy in triable-either-way cases that in 1989 a working group under the chairmanship of Lord Justice Farquharson was established to formulate national committal guidelines. Within the Home Office the hope was that the guidelines would encourage magistrates to accept jurisdiction in a higher proportion of cases. In 1990 guidelines were produced, published and disseminated to all those concerned with decision-making in magistrates' courts (Lord Chancellor's Department 1990a), although it is not at all clear that the content of the guidelines was informed by a clear statistical and substantive appreciation of the basis of existing committals policy. It follows that the use made and likely impact of the guidelines is unclear. However, as we have seen, the number of committals has declined from the high point in 1987.

Conditions for remand prisoners

It is clear that in the past remand prisoners received far less attention than the sentenced population, and this was largely because of the doctrine of 'treatment and training'. The philosophy underlying the present Prison Rule 1 — 'The purpose of the training and treatment of convicted prisoners shall be to encourage and assist them to lead a good and useful life' — began to dominate prison administrative thinking half a century ago. In effect, prisoners came to be classified as trainable or untrainable. Those deemed trainable (sentenced prisoners, except those serving very short sentences, for whom there was held to be insufficient time) and the recalcitrant (for whom the time had apparently passed) were to be allocated to a 'training' prison. 'Untrainable' short-term sentenced prisoners were to remain in the 'local' prisons, together with the untried and the unsentenced.

The 'treatment and training' model was never fully put into effect. The management expertise on which it depended did not exist, and for prisoners and prison officers alike it ran contrary to the coercive realities of prison life. However, 'treatment and training' dictated the manner in which resources were allocated and the prisoner population was distributed.

The overcrowding which, from the early-1950s, was a permanent and, until the 1980s, an ever-increasing problem, was borne by the old local prisons. The Prison Service argued that they had to assume this burden because their larger Victorian cells were capable of multiple occupancy to a degree that did not exist in the newer training prisons and modern remand centres. However, the small cells in the modern remand centres were also overcrowded, while the Victorian training prisons, many of which had large cells and had formerly been local prisons, were for the most part spared.

Only somewhat late in the building programme started by the Conservative government in 1979 was a new local prison built. Belmarsh, which opened in 1991, was the first new local for over a century. Previously, all the new building, with the exception of Holloway, which was to serve a multi-functional purpose for women, had been of training prisons or young offender establishments (although the latter included several remand centres built in the early-1960s). Every one of the local prisons before Belmarsh was Victorian.

The overcrowding in local prisons and remand centres might have been more bearable if those institutions had not been denied new facilities. During the 1960s and 1970s developments such as workshops, education blocks and sports halls usually went to training prisons. At the same time the daily regimes of local prisons and remand centres became less and less active, particularly for their remand population. This was eventually graphically illustrated in the regime monitoring data published by the Prison Service. In 1989–90 the inmates of remand centres and local prisons were on average spending only one-half or as little as one-third as much time (which meant less than two hours per day) engaged in such activities as work, education or PE as their sentenced counterparts in training prisons and young offender institutions. Unfortunately, the data did not distinguish untried and convicted prisoners. Had it done so, it would have shown that the untried were even worse off.

There were no provisions in either the Prison Act 1952 or the Prison Rules 1964 which could effectively have prevented the untried being made to bear the brunt of these pressures. The Prison Act 1952 required the Secretary of State to make special rules for the treatment of unconvicted prisoners (s. 47(4)(d)). Although successive Home Secretaries failed to formulate separate rules for remand centres, the Prison Rules 1964 contained nine separate provisions to protect the rights of the untried. They had to be kept out of contact with convicted prisoners 'as far as this can reasonably be done' (r. 3(2)); provided with the services of their own doctor or dentist 'providing there are reasonable grounds, and at his own expense' (r. 17(4)); allowed to wear their own clothing 'insofar as it is suitable, tidy and clean' (r. 20(1)); allowed to have their own food sent in 'at his own expense, or that of his friends' (r. 21(1)); and 'on payment of a sum' to occupy their own privately furnished and cleaned rooms (r. 25). They were also not subject to prison haircut regulations (r. 26(2)); did not have to work (r. 28(5)); could send as many letters and receive as many visits as they chose (r. 34(1)); and could have items such as books, newspapers and writing materials sent in (r. 41(1)).

However, as King and Morgan's study demonstrated (1976, ch. 3), these safeguards were either pointless (there were no rooms privately to furnish), or were ignored (young remand centre prisoners' own clothes were never judged to be 'suitable, tidy and clean'), or were nugatory (the vast majority of untried prisoners did not have the resources to have food and books sent in). In some cases they hid an almost cynical reversal of fortune: untried prisoners were not allowed to alter their hirsute appearance; or were not allowed access to the newspapers received by convicted prisoners because they could have their own sent in; or had to stay locked up all day if they chose not to work. As time went on, the Prison Rules increasingly failed to safeguard the status of the untried. With the growth in overcrowding, it became less practicable to separate the untried and convicted (Morgan and Barclay 1989). There was little work available for those untried who wanted it: because convicted prisoners were supposed to be employed, the few remaining jobs usually went to them. Meanwhile, the training prisons increased the amount of contact their prisoners could have with the outside world such that the untried in the remand institutions became relatively worse off. Restrictions on the number of letters convicted prisoners could send or receive were gradually abandoned. Many training prisons were able to allow their prisoners weekly visits which might last for over two hours. Open and low-security prisons began to introduce cardphones. Finally, in 1989, r. 21 was amended to remove the right of untried prisoners to have food and drink sent in. The Prison Department had regarded this as an awkward anomaly, a right rarely exercised, administratively inconvenient and allegedly a security hazard.

The consequence of all this was that the untried, without access to telephones, and restricted to 15-minute visits (which in most local prisons had to be accumulated) received in crowded and degrading visiting rooms, could no longer be said to be privileged — if they ever were.

Prison managers, in the absence of any legal hindrance, had no incentive to alter this unequal distribution of resources even when the philosophy of training began to be called into question. From the late-1960s the prison system was regularly disrupted by serious disturbances, almost all of which were in the maximum-security 'dispersal' training prisons. Individual remand prisoners might constitute a control problem, but collectively they seemed to be relatively quiescent despite their intolerable conditions. Therefore, from a control perspective, it appeared sensible to protect the jewels in the crown of the training sector; to provide more staff and resources, while at the same time increasing security at the long-term dispersal prisons.

Finally, it must be remembered that in the immediate post-war period, when the treatment and training model was at the height of its popularity, there were relatively few untried prisoners. Although remands constituted a relatively high proportion of receptions, they formed a small proportion

— always less than 10 per cent prior to 1960 — of the average daily prison population. Numerically, as well as ideally, the system was geared to the custody and treatment of sentenced prisoners.

The focus on the remand population

All this started to change dramatically in the 1970s. The philosophy of treatment and training came increasingly to be questioned. There was little evidence that different forms of training or treatment made imprisonment any more effective in terms of reconviction rates (Brody 1976). The Prison Service, however, failed to react to the growing disillusion, and this inertia was scarcely compensated for by the efforts of the official inquiry into the prison services in 1979 under Mr Justice May. The May Committee's proposal was that Rule 1 be replaced by a statement of 'positive custody' (Committee of Inquiry into the United Kingdom Prison Services 1979, para. 4.26). However, this concerned convicted prisoners; the Committee's formulation made no reference to the untried.

The policies of the Prison Service drifted during the late-1970s and early-1980s. Both overcrowding and staff industrial action led to considerable pressures. In 1975 the average daily prison population broke through the 40,000 barrier and rose steadily to exceed 50,000 in 1988. As we have seen, this increase was largely attributable to the dramatic rise in the population of untried prisoners. The average daily sentenced population changed little; it was only 13 per cent higher in 1988 (the high point) than it had been in 1975. This meant that remands now made up a substantial proportion of the daily population. In 1960 remand prisoners comprised 7.7 per cent of the average daily population. In 1970 the figure was 11.9 per cent, in 1980 13.7 per cent and in 1989 21.4 per cent.

Although some training prisons started to become overcrowded, most of the population increases continued to be in local prisons. On several occasions some of the local prisons were over 100 per cent overcrowded (Home Office 1988b, app. 4). Consequently, local prisons literally became insanitary, idle and inhumane warehouses. The Prison Rules had still not been amended to deal with this and the courts maintained their hands-off posture regarding prison conditions (Richardson 1985).

There were three ways in which this trend could be reversed. First, overcrowding could be alleviated by expanding the number of prisons. Second, the number of prisoners remanded in custody and the duration of their custody could be reduced. Third, existing resources within the prison system could be redistributed in favour of remand prisoners.

Following their election in 1979, the Conservatives initially adopted the first of these solutions. By the late-1980s some of the new prisons began to come into use and overcrowding was significantly reduced. However, by the mid-1980s it had become apparent that, if the building programme were not accompanied by a vigorous reductionist policy, there was a distinct possibility that the additional places would do little more than keep pace with the rising prison population. The prospect of an 'end to overcrowding', the government's proclaimed objective (Home Office 1986, p. 29), was receding. A series of reductionist measures, which have been discussed above, were then taken. Many of the initiatives appeared to be having some success. During the period 1989 to 1991 the remand population (as well as the sentenced population) was marginally reduced. Ironically, it was in the middle of this period of optimism that the prison disturbances of April 1990 occurred.

Strangeways

Evidence presented to Lord Justice Woolf's inquiry into the Strangeways riot showed that a demonstration — although not the riot and siege that developed — was planned, mostly by sentenced prisoners. However, once the disturbance had started, it was clear that prisoners of all types, including remand prisoners, took an active part. Although the vast majority of prisoners escaped from the mayhem as soon as possible, among the minority of prisoners who held out were remand prisoners. In fact, of the many establishments which experienced disorder in April 1990, five of the six most serious disturbances on which the inquiry concentrated its attention were in remand establishments, and remand prisoners played a leading or contributory part in what happened. Woolf found that they had good reason to feel aggrieved.

The governor of Strangeways, an overcrowded prison in which conditions were generally very poor, described the provision for remand prisoners there as 'grossly inadequate' (Woolf 1991, p. 49). Only a few cleaning jobs were available. The PE and educational facilities were very limited. Most remand prisoners were locked up, two to a cell without integral sanitation, for very long periods. Consequently, 'a large proportion of the inmates in the prison were sympathetic to the instigators of the disturbance and antagonistic towards the Prison Service' (ibid., p. 105). At Glen Parva, Woolf found there was a 'contrast in the conditions of the remand and sentenced prisoners the former being significantly less well provided for' (ibid., p. 114). The overcrowding at Glen Parva was mainly among remand prisoners (72 per cent overcrowded) rather than sentenced prisoners (7 per cent overcrowded).

The remand prisoners at Cardiff were able to spend much of their day out of cells. Although this lessened the impact of the extreme overcrowding to which they were subject (77 per cent overcrowded), they had no opportunity to work, attend educational classes or go to the trade training course available to sentenced prisoners (ibid., p. 163). Bristol was not seriously overcrowded at the time, but conditions in the wing where the riot took place were found to be particularly 'unacceptable' (ibid., p. 193). For many of the prisoners there was little or no association, and they were confined for much of the day to cells which, as elsewhere, lacked integral sanitation. At Pucklechurch, a purpose-built remand centre which was 17 per cent overcrowded at the time, there was no workshop or vocational training courses and the limited number of employment places tended to go to convicted or sentenced prisoners. The education and PE staff were found to have made vigorous efforts to lay on a full programme of activities. However, many of these had to be cancelled for want of escorts. The result of this was that prisoners spent long periods — $18\frac{1}{2}$ hours per day according to the regime monitoring data — in small cells without integral sanitation (ibid., p. 199).

The recommendations

Woolf realised that, whatever the view of the prison authorities in the past, remand prisoners have the capacity to cause serious problems. However, that did not mean the Prison Service had failed to subject remand prisoners to sufficiently secure conditions. Woolf found no single cause for the riots and no simple solution that would prevent them. He suggested that the stability of prisons is based on management paying sufficient attention to the elements of *security*, *control* and *justice*, and there being a balance struck between those three elements (Woolf 1991, pp. 225–6). In the case of remand prisoners there was imbalance. They were the object of excessive security, and the control measures to which they were subject were inappropriate. Moreover, they suffered a grave deficiency of justice. Woolf also doubted if so many remand prisoners need be held in custody for so long (ibid., p. 223).

As his terms of reference were limited, Woolf had to be circumspect about the use made of remands in custody by the courts. His inclinations were clearly reductionist, but he approached the question by considering the decision-making process. He pointed out that, in procedural terms, the question of bail is dealt with by the courts more casually than sentencing. Decisions are sometimes made hurriedly, without adequate information, by one or two, rather than three, magistrates, and without the benefit of High Court guidelines (ibid., p. 251). Meanwhile, he commended current government initiatives designed to increase the use of bail, or shorten the period that remands spend in custody (ibid., 251–3). In addition, his proposed Criminal Justice Consultative Council, together with parallel local committees, would be a mechanism ideally suited to develop initiatives designed to reduce the remand population.

Woolf's use of the terms 'security' and 'control' was relatively straightforward. 'Security' referred to the Prison Service's primary obligation to keep people committed to prison until they are due to be released. For remand prisoners, that meant until the time of their trial or sentence, unless granted bail in the interim. Control referred to orderliness within prison, a lack of which may spell the loss of security for other prisoners. A failure of control may sometimes lead to a breach of perimeter security.

Woolf's ideas of accommodation units for no more than 50–70 prisoners and secure 'firebreaks' between such units apply as much to remand as sentenced prisoners. However, they have a particular significance for the remand population because of his re-emphasis on separating the convicted from the unconvicted and the great importance he attached to accommodating prisoners as close as possible to their community ties in what he refers to as 'community prisons'. Woolf found that remand prisoners are currently subject 'to a degree of security and control which is frequently unnecessary' (ibid., p. 327), and proposed that they be treated, unless there is good reason to do otherwise, as the equivalent of security category C rather than B, their present classification. He also suggested that in the same way that the police, the CPS, the probation service and the courts co-operate to decide on the appropriate level of control needed over defendants granted bail, so those same agencies might assist the prison service by identifying defendants refused bail who may need to be subject to a higher security category (ibid., p. 327).

However, Woolf's use of the term 'justice' is more complex. It refers to the 'obligation' to treat prisoners with humanity and fairness and to prepare them for their return to the community in a way which makes it less likely that they will reoffend (ibid., p. 226). This definition is geared to the convicted, but Woolf elsewhere balances this by proposing that there be a separate body of prison rules for the untried. It is clear from the body of his report that his notion of justice involves more than both fairness and due process (ibid., p. 412). His recommendations that there be more active regimes for prisoners, access to sanitation at all times, properly paid work, education programmes, improved contact between prisoners and their families, and better clothing indicate that for him justice covers what Dilulio has more accurately described as *amenity* and *service* (Dilulio 1987).

The amenities and services available to untried prisoners should be different from those for convicted and sentenced prisoners. For example, the untried, subject to the presumption of innocence, should not be compelled to work. On the other hand, there is no case for denying them access to programmes on the ground that they have not been convicted of an offence. The vast majority of persons denied bail are seriously disadvantaged socially and economically. Many have a long record of previous convictions; that is often why they are denied bail. However, that is also why they 'should suffer no greater loss of liberty, both in duration and degree, than is necessary to secure the course of justice' (Morgan and Barclay 1989, p. 23) and why, according to Woolf, it must 'be part of the task of the Prison Service to enable the remand prisoner to spend his time in custody in as constructive a manner as possible' (Woolf 1991, p. 247).

The government's plans

The government appears to envisage a continuation of the initiatives developed in the late-1980s to keep more of the untried out of custody and to improve the lot of the (hopefully) reduced number of remand prisoners for whom custody is considered necessary.

However, serious problems stand in the way of achieving minimum resort to custody for the untried and decent conditions for those refused bail. The presumption of innocence is a legal doctrine belied by a good deal of practice within the criminal justice system. As recent miscarriages of justice vividly illustrate, police tactics and decisions are often dictated by a firm belief in a suspect's guilt. Bail is most frequently denied because magistrates think there is a likelihood of further offences being committed: the evidence for this usually comprises the defendant's record. We have already seen how the unconvicted are treated in prison.

This difference between theory and practice is not a purely English phenomenon. Surveys of international compliance with the UN Standard Minimum Rules reveal that breaches are most often admitted in relation to those rules concerning the untried (United Nations 1985, p. 14). In many countries, including some noted for their liberal penal systems, either the prosecutor or the court can severely restrict the conditions for prisoners awaiting trial (for example, by limiting visits) on the ground that the prosecution case would otherwise be undermined.

In addition, measures designed to divert the untried from custody can have 'net-widening' consequences. It was this consideration which, following consultation (Home Office 1988c), led the Home Office (and subsequently Woolf) to abandon the idea of establishing secure bail hostels. A similar problem arises from any insistence that the untried be physically separated from the convicted. This could only be achieved by further expanding a system arguably too large already. Yet, as we have seen, the integration of the convicted and unconvicted invariably signals the disadvantage of the latter.

The dilemma is shown in the government's response to the Woolf report. Competing aims 'may be irreconcilable'; a 'doctrinaire approach' will not do (Home Office 1991a, p. 47). The more that prisons are specialised, or different categories of prisoners are separated from each other, the less likely it is that the estate will be used efficiently, that overcrowding will be prevented and that prisoners will be kept as close to their community ties as possible. There will therefore need to be flexibility.

A minimum degree of insulation of the untried from the convicted will have to be maintained. The evidence suggests that, without this, the untried will suffer disadvantage. This insulation must be normative, and it is encouraging that the government has accepted Woolf's proposal of a separate set of Prison Rules for the untried. It must also be physical: untried prisoners should be held in discrete accommodation within prisons if not in separate prisons.

The difficulty of combining this physical insulation requirement with the idea of the community prison is obvious. Unless more new prisons are built specifically for remand prisoners, a prospect endorsed in the White Paper (ibid., para. 5.19) but which may be misplaced in view of the current effort to reduce the use of custody, prisoners can only be held in institutions close to their community ties if many spcialised institutions become multi-functional establishments within which different categories of prisoner, including remands, are not fully separated.

This is the crux of the problem. The government has suggested, for example, that it is preferable that young offenders and prisoners on remand should be located in less crowded conditions with prisoners of a different status than that they should be held separately in overcrowded conditions (ibid., para. 5.14). This is subject only to the proviso that they should never share cells. The government also considers that women might be accommodated in prisons which also receive men but are close to home, 'providing the accommodation is separate, fully secure and of an adequate size', and that the women have 'satisfactory facilities and regime activities' (ibid., para. 5.14).

It is clear that the acceptability of these pragmatic judgments depends on various factors including the perception of whether political will is being exercised to realise them. The government is arguably not doing all that it might to further these objectives. The consequence is a loss of sympathy by the penal pressure groups with the dilemmas confronting the Prison Service and their attempts to resolve them.

Not all critics of the policies spelt out in the recent government White Paper base their opposition on these contextual grounds. For example, some feminist commentators are more fundamentally opposed to women being accommodated in prisons which also house men. They contend that it will encourage more use of imprisonment for women by the courts, place women prisoners in danger and lead to women being deprived of facilities and regime activities. They also doubt that the arrangement will be cheaper (Tchaikovsky 1991, p. 12). These fears need to be addressed seriously, although the objective of saving money was never advanced by Woolf as an argument for the creation of community prisons.

The idea of a community prison is based on the fact that most prisoners are in prison for a relatively short period of time — a few weeks or months. The prison population is mostly a transitory one whose community ties need to be maintained as far as possible and whose financial security and social welfare on release need to be assured. Any policy which undermines these objectives is counter-productive in terms of reducing the likelihood of further offences. Community prisons would hold prisoners in the institution closest to their homes. They would also have better visiting arrangements, qualitatively as well as quantitatively, for prisoners and their families; better telephone access; improved provision of legal advice; and greater involvement by the community groups and statutory agencies with whom the prisoners will deal on release.

In some areas, with few institutions and few committals, the community prison ideal will have to be a multi-functional prison. In metropolitan areas it will be possible to have clusters of relatively specialised institutions. But, whatever the arrangements, the ideal will take time to achieve. More training prisons and young offender establishments will have to be redesignated as local or community prisons in which remand prisoners can be housed. If subsequently sentenced to imprisonment, these prisoners can continue to be housed close to home without need for transfer.

Woolf has also proposed that remand prisoners should be presumed to be security category C unless there is evidence that they pose a greater risk. Were that the case, many more institutions might house remand prisoners than at present. Although the government accepts that remand prisoners should be security categorised (Home Office 1991a, para. 5.21), it considers there is no evidence that remand prisoners could be held securely in category C accommodation and that, in any case, there are insufficient category C establishments in convenient locations. However, this view ignores the future disposition of most remand prisoners. It implicitly and uncritically accepts the excessively high security rating of some training prisons (see, for example, the Chief Inspector of Prisons' recommendations that Coldingley and Blundeston Prisons be security downgraded (Her Majesty's Chief Inspector of Prisons 1991a, 1991b)). It also ignores the potential many low-security and young offender institutions have to house remand prisoners. Almost half of all unconvicted prisoners (and two-thirds of all female unconvicted prisoners) are subsequently found not guilty or receive a non-custodial sentence. Of those who receive a custodial sentence the majority are categorised C or D. If more information were available, these prisoners could be given a lower security classification while on remand. It is doubtful whether the courts, which have no responsibility for prisons administration, should determine the level of security to which a remand prisoner should be subject; that is a matter better left to the prison authorities. However, there would be merit in the courts' adopting Woolf's suggestion and indicating which prisoners seem to warrant greater security than normal by marking their files.

Separate rules for remand prisoners

The government has reluctantly accepted Woolf's recommendation that there should be a distinct body of rules for unconvicted remand prisoners. What should the rules comprise?

Casale and Plotnikoff (1990) have set out the minimum physical standards of accommodation, duty of care, regime (such as exercise, skills development programmes and employment), welfare arrangements, and use of time and visiting facilities which should be incorporated in the prison rules for unconvicted prisoners. They have also indicated the importance the Prison Department should attach to ensuring that prisoners receive legal advice, information and access to the courts, thereby increasing the likelihood of bail being granted and cases being quickly brought to trial.

Three additional principles need to be added to the Casale and Plotnikoff prospectus. First, the unconvicted should be provided with an amount of money no less than the current minimum allowance awarded by the Department of Social Security for dependent persons. Further, unconvicted prisoners should be entitled to claim whatever benefits (including unemployment benefit) they would normally be eligible to, whilst they are in custody. Second, untried prisoners should be held in the remand establishment closest to their community ties. If their immediate families are distant from the court of committal and receiving prison, the prisoners' wishes should be taken into account when deciding where they should be accommodated. This same principle should apply to the question of women being held in single-sex or mixed establishments. Third, any prisoners held at a specified distance from their immediate family should, unless that arrangement is the prisoners' choice, be the beneficiaries of financial assistance to enable partners and children to visit.

The government has undertaken to 'prepare a model regime for local prisons and remand centres, taking particular account of the needs of unconvicted prisoners' (Home Office 1991a, p. 75). It is not yet clear what this model regime will comprise, but it could scarcely be inferior to that required by the tender document issued to potential contractors for the Wolds, Britain's first prison to be contracted out for management by a commercial company (Home Office 1991b). The regime at the Wolds will be based on prisoners being out of their cells for a minimum of 12 hours on weekdays and 10½ hours per day over the weekend. Prisoners will have an entitlement to six hours per week for education, another six hours for PE, two and a half hours each for visits to the library and the prisoners' shop, and 21 hours a week for requirements such as meals and showers. Meals will be eaten at the times they are normally taken in the community rather than being compressed into a short day determined by the working convenience of staff. There will be the opportunity of a daily change of underwear and convicted remand prisoners will be entitled to an hour-long visit each week instead of each fortnight.

Many people will be offended by the provisions in the Criminal Justice Act 1991 granting the employees of commercial organisations coercive powers to search, restrain and forcefully remove prisoners (ss. 85 and 86). Others will entertain doubts about the accountability of contracted-out arrangements (Sampson 1991, p. 16). However, it is clear that the regime for remand prisoners which will be provided at the Wolds (the unconvicted and convicted will not be strictly segregated) will be vastly superior to that which has for so long been provided in Prison Service establishments. Although the comparison may be unfair, the Wolds will provide the flagship regime which the Prison Service will thereafter be obliged to emulate.

Conclusion: problems on the horizon

The prospects for a genuine long-term reduction in the number of defendants remanded in custody and a significant improvement in their conditions lie in the balance. The principles enunciated by Lord Justice Woolf have been accepted by the government, and the Wolds Prison, which opened in April 1992, should provide a clear illustration of what can be done. There are storm clouds building, however. The prison population, including the remand population, is rising rapidly once again. At the beginning of 1992, there were nearly 1,500 prisoners being held in police cells. The then Home Secretary announced that plans to refurbish cells in some remand prisons were to be deferred in order to cope with the overcrowding (*Guardian*, 2 October 1991). Support from the public for the improvement of prison conditions for the untried is not likely to have been increased by the two major disturbances at Moorland, a £56 million young offender remand centre, which opened in the summer of 1991.

The foundations for a system in which bail may be granted more generously and remand prisoners may be better treated have been laid. What is in doubt is whether the political climate will allow a structure to be built on that foundation.

References

Brink, B., and Stone, C. (1988), 'Defendants Who Do Not Ask for Bail' [1988] Crim LR 152.

Brody, S. (1976), *The Effectiveness of Sentencing: a Review of the Literature*, (Home Office Research Study No. 35) (London: HMSO).

Brookes, S. (1991), *The Effect of Reoffending on Bail on Crime in Avon and Somerset* (Bristol: Avon and Somerset Police).

Casale, S., and Plotnikoff J. (1990), *Regimes for Remand Prisoners* (London: Prison Reform Trust).

Corbett, C., and Korn, Y. (1987), 'Custody Time-limits in Serious and Complex Cases: Will they Work in Practice?' [1987] Crim LR 737.

Council of Europe (1991), *Report to the United Kingdom Government on the Visit to the United Kingdom carried out by the European Committee for the Prevention of Torture and Inhuman or Degrading Treatment or Punishment from 29 July 1990 to 10 August 1990* (Strasbourg: Council of Europe).

Dilulio, J. (1987), *Governing Prisons: a Comparative Study of Correctional Management* (New York: Free Press).

Faugeron, C. (1989), 'Commentary on the Problems of Imprisonment' in *Crime and Criminal Policy in Europe: Proceedings of a European Colloquium*, ed. R. Hood (Oxford: Centre for Criminological Research).

Fitzgerald, M., and Sim, J. (1979), *British Prisons* (Oxford: Basil Blackwell).

Greater Manchester Police (1987), *Offenders Committing Offences on Bail* (Research Paper) (Greater Manchester Police).

Greater Manchester Police (1988), *Offences Committed on Bail* (Research Paper) (Greater Manchester Police).

Heinz, W. (1989), 'The Problems of Imprisonment' in *Crime and Criminal Policy in Europe: Proceedings of a European Colloquium*, ed. R. Hood (Oxford: Centre for Criminological Research).

Henderson, P. F. (1991), *Monitoring Time Limits on Custodial Remands* (Research and Planning Unit Paper 69) (London: Home Office).

Henderson, P., and Nichols, T. (1992), 'Offending while on Bail', *Research Bulletin* (Home Office Research and Statistics Department, Research Bulletin No. 32).

Her Majesty's Chief Inspector of Prisons (1991a), *Report of an Inspection of HM Prison Coldingley* (London: Home Office).

Her Majesty's Chief Inspector of Prisons (1991b), *Report of an Inspection of HM Prison Blundeston* (London: Home Office).

Home Office (1981), *Estimates of Offending by those on Bail* Home Office Statistical Bulletin 22/81.

Home Office (1986), *Criminal Justice: A Working Paper* (London: Home Office).

Home Office (1988a), *Bail* (Home Office Circular 25/1988, 11 May).

Home Office (1988b), *Report on the Work of the Prison Service April 1987–March 1988* (Cm 516) (London: HMSO).

Home Office (1988c), *Bail Accommodation and Secure Bail Hostels* (Consultation Paper) (London: Home Office).

Home Office (1990b), *Prison Statistics England and Wales 1989* (Cm 1221) (London: HMSO).

Home Office (1991a), *Custody, Care and Justice: the Way ahead for the Prison Service in England and Wales*, (Cm 1647) (London: HMSO).

Home Office (1991b), *Tender Documents for the Operating Contract of Wolds Remand Prison*, Schedule 2 and 3 (London: Home Office).

Home Office (1992), *Criminal Statistics in England and Wales 1990* (Cm 1935) (London: HMSO).

House of Commons Home Affairs Committee (1981), *The Prison Service*, vol. 1 (House of Commons Sessional Papers HC 412 1980/81) (London: HMSO).

Jacobs, J.B. (1983), *New Perspectives on Prisons and Imprisonment* (Ithaca: Cornell University Press).

King, R.D., and Morgan, R. (1976), *A Taste of Prison: Custodial Conditions for Trial and Remand* (London: Routledge).

Lewis, H., and Mair, G. (1989), *Bail and Probation Work II: the Use of London Probation Bail Hostels for Bailees* (Home Office Research and Planning Unit Paper No. 50) (London: Home Office).

Lloyd, C. (1992), *Bail Information Schemes: Practice and Effect* (Home Office Research and Planning Unit Paper No. 69).

Lord Chancellor's Department (1990a), *National Mode of Trial Guidelines* (London: HMSO).

Lord Chancellor's Department (1990b), *Report of the Working Group on Pre-Trial Issues* (London: Lord Chancellor's Department).

Mair, G., and Nee, C. (1990), *Electronic Monitoring: the Trials and their Results* (Home Office Research Study No. 120) (London: HMSO).

May Committee (1979), *Committee of Inquiry into the United Kingdom Prison Services Report* (Cmd 7673) (London: HMSO).

Morgan, P. (1992), *Offending while on Bail: a Survey of Recent Studies* (Home Office Research and Planning Unit Paper No. 65) (London: HMSO).

Morgan, R. (1989) 'Remands in Custody: Problems and Prospects' [1989] Crim LR 481.

Morgan, R., and Barclay, A. (1989), 'Remands in Custody: Problems and Prospects for Change. The Perrie Lectures 1988', *Prison Service Journal*, new series, No. 74 (April 1989), pp. 13–36.

Nichols, T., and Ennis, J. (1991), *Offending on Bail* (Metropolitan Police Directorate of Management Services Report No. 16/90) (Metropolitan Police).

Northumbria Police (1991), *Bail and Multiple Offending* (Research Project 1990–91) (Northumbria Police).

Prison Department (1990), *Evidence to Lord Justice Woolf's Inquiry into Prison Disturbances: Evidence for Phase 2* (London: Prison Service).

Richardson, G. (1985), 'Judicial Intervention in Prison Life' in *Accountability and Prisons: Opening Up a Closed World*, eds. Maguire, Vagg and Morgan (London: Tavistock)

Riley, D., and Vennard, J. (1988), *Triable-either-way Cases: Crown Court or Magistrates' Court?* (Home Office Research Study No. 98) (London: HMSO).

Sampson, A. (1991), 'Private Prisons: Fight is Fixed' *Prison Report*, No. 16 (Autumn).

Stone, C. (1988), *Bail Information for the Crown Prosecution Service* (London: Vera Institute of Justice).

Tchaikovsky, C. (1991), 'Mixed Prisons: Misogynistic and Misguided' *Prison Report*, No. 16 (Autumn).

United Nations (1985), *Implementation of the UN Standard Minimum Rules for the Treatment of Prisoners: Report of the Secretary General* (Milan: UN Congress on the Prevention of Crime and the Treatment of Offenders).

White, K., and Brody, S. (1980), 'The Use of Bail Hostels' [1980] Crim LR 420.

Winfield, M. (1984), *Lacking Conviction: the Remand System in England and Wales* (London: Prison Reform Trust).

Woolf, Lord Justice (1991), *Prison Disturbances April 1990: Report of an Inquiry* by the Rt Hon Lord Justice Woolf (Parts I and II) and His Hon Judge Stephen Tumin (Part II) (Cm 1456) (London: HMSO).

3

The Trial Process

John Sprack

Anyone who feels complacent about the criminal trial process in this country should take another look at what some of our leading legal lights have said recently.

> The judiciary are anxious about cases that have gone wrong. We all have a job to do in restoring public confidence. (Lord Chief Justice Taylor on his appointment.)

> The courts are coming under increasing strain and face unprecedented criticism. . . . The most dramatic evidence of the need for reform is in the criminal sphere, as the recent miscarriage of justice cases show. (Lord Irvine of Lairg QC, Labour spokesman on legal affairs in the House of Lords, writing in the *Guardian* on 4 March 1992.)

> In allowing these appeals we wish to express our profound regret that they have suffered as a result of the shortcomings of the criminal process. (Lord Justice Farquharson, delivering the Court of Appeal's unprecedented apology to the 'Tottenham Three', when it decided they had been wrongly convicted of the murder of PC Blakelock.)

As has become clear, there is a consensus among those involved in the criminal trial process that radical change is necessary. What is much more controversial is the precise form which that change should take.

This chapter is an attempt to sketch out some of the areas of concern, and to indicate the reforms which seem most urgent. The topics dealt with are:

(a)   the objectives of the criminal trial, in the context of the appointment of the Royal Commission on Criminal Justice (the Runciman Commission),

(b)   the adversarial nature of the English trial, and proposals to move towards an inquisitorial model,

(c)   the decision-makers in the trial, particularly the jury and the judge,

(d)   the material upon which decisions are made, concentrating upon the extent to which confessions by the accused should be relied upon, and dealing also with evidence of any previous convictions which the accused may have,

(e)   consideration for the victim and witnesses,

(f)   the need for speed and efficiency.

Objectives

Any critic of the criminal trial is under an obligation to nail his colours to the mast. Some attempt must be made to spell out the aims of the criminal trial, however subjective and determined by prejudice that process is bound to be. For it is only by exposing his prejudices in this way that the critic can signal the basis upon which criticism is put forward and, even more crucially, the rationale behind any suggested reforms.

It is suggested that the objectives of the criminal trial can be summarised as follows:

(a)   The innocent should be acquitted. As the Bar pointed out in its evidence to the Runciman Commission (Bar Council 1992, p. 2), this is not an entirely accurate way of putting it. To expand somewhat, this first objective requires that a person who has not committed an offence should not be tried. If he is tried, then he should not be convicted, and if he is convicted then his conviction should be quashed on appeal.

(b)   The trial should be conducted in conformity with civilised standards. This rather high-sounding formulation is based on the notion that it is not merely the result of the trial which is important. We are also entitled to expect, for example, that a criminal trial will be open to the public, that judges will act impartially, that the prosecution will not, by delay or deceit, abuse the process of the court, and that no one shall be subjected to double jeopardy by being tried for the same crime twice.

(c)   Any malpractice which threatens to contaminate the system of justice (for example, on the part of the police) should be prevented.

(d)   The guilty should be convicted.

(e)   Victims and witnesses should be treated with consideration.

(f)   The system should be speedy and efficient.

Clearly, there will be times when these objectives are in conflict, and we need to decide which is to have priority. Such a conflict occurs most clearly in relation to objectives (a) and (d) above. Most rules which have the function of protecting the innocent are likely to result in the acquittal of some who are guilty. To take an obvious example, the burden of proof in the English criminal trial is upon the prosecution, who must prove the accused guilty beyond reasonable doubt. If a less exacting standard were to be imposed upon the prosecution (for instance, that they should prove that it was more likely that the accused committed the crime than that he did not), then the number of guilty people convicted would soar. In itself, that might be a matter for celebration, but the unfortunate side-effect would be that there would also be many more innocent people convicted. Our criminal justice system has always been quite explicit on the priority where these two particular objectives clash. The innocent must be acquitted, even if some villains escape justice at the same time. Objective (a), we say, takes precedence over objective (d).

It is beyond the scope of this chapter to attempt to place all the objectives in order of priority — even if such a task were possible. What is important is that where a particular reform does appear to trigger off conflicting priorities, the objectives in question should be weighed critically against each other.

In this context, it is impossible not to feel some apprehension about the way in which the terms of reference of the Runciman Commission are framed. It was set up in the train of the revelations about the wrongful convictions of the Guildford Four and the Birmingham Six, and as it was becoming clear that the case of the Tottenham Three would soon end in the same way. Its *raison d'être* was to ensure that objective (a) in the scheme above — the acquittal of the innocent — was met more effectively. This historical purpose has been obscured by the Commission's terms of reference, which are to examine the effectiveness of our criminal justice system in:

(a)   securing the conviction of the guilty,

(b)   ensuring the acquittal of the innocent,

(c)   having regard to the efficient use of resources.

The first problem is the primacy which it appears to give to convicting the guilty. Second, it ignores entirely those aspects of a 'fair trial' which are not concerned with the result (see objectives (b) and (c) in the list at the beginning of this chapter). Third, much of the questionnaire circulated by the Commission to bodies submitting evidence deals with ways of streamlining the system and reducing costs. Whilst these are clearly legitimate concerns, they should not distract attention from the reason why the Commission was set up — the prevention of miscarriages of justice.

Adversarial or inquisitorial?

The distinguishing feature of the English criminal trial is its adversarial (or accusatorial) nature. It follows that some of the most sweeping proposals for its reform envisage the replacement of that adversarial model with its rival, the inquisitorial system dominant in countries like France.

Prominent among the critics of the adversarial system are the police. The evidence submitted jointly to the Runciman Commission by the various professional bodies which speak on behalf of the police service (Police Service 1991) embodies a full frontal attack upon the adversarial system:

> The reality is that it is increasingly difficult to gain significant evidence to sustain a conviction for a whole range of criminals. That difficulty is not only related to problems of investigation but is more profound because of the opportunities to exploit the considerable advantage which the accusatorial system gives to a defendant. (Police Service 1991, p. 12.)

In criticising the adversarial system, the police submission opposes it to the need to search for the truth:

> ... there need to be corresponding changes in the system of trial to move it away from an adversarial style to one that seeks the truth. (Ibid., p. 28.)

The attitude expressed in the police service's evidence provides an interesting contrast with that submitted by the Crown Prosecution Service:

> The accusatorial system should be retained. . . . Grafting parts of the inquisitorial system on to the present structure will only create confusion, and ultimately, injustice. (Crown Prosecution Service 1992, p. 8.)

The essential difference between the two systems is this:

(a)   Under the adversarial method, the person (or body) with the duty of deciding guilt or the lack of it leaves the responsibility to the prosecution and defence to present their case. It is inherent in such a system that one side or the other must bear the burden of proof. It is central to our version of the adversarial system that in a criminal case that burden is upon the prosecution, who must discharge it beyond a reasonable doubt.

(b)   In the inquisitorial system, the person charged with deciding guilt or its absence has the duty to carry out any necessary investigation. Neither side bears the burden of proof, since that onus is upon the tribunal.

The proponents of the inquisitorial system argue from a variety of positions. The evidence of the police service, for example, is clearly motivated by the link between the adversarial system, the role of the independent defence lawyer and the right of the suspect to preserve silence in the face of police interrogation. With some justification, it sees these three features of the English criminal system as being intimately connected. Somewhat more controversially, it would shed no tears if all three of them were to disappear:

If we are to have a more inquisitorial system of investigation the suspect must be encouraged to cooperate with the investigation and not impede it, as happens at present. The balance within the whole system should be 'right to comment' and the inferences a court may draw from failure to disclose a defence at the earliest opportunity. (Police Service 1991, p. 26.)

The 'right to comment' would allow the prosecutor and the judge at a subsequent trial to comment adversely on the accused's failure to answer questions when under interrogation. Whilst the suspect would retain, in theory, a right to silence, it would in practice be likely to be gravely undermined by this proposal. When one has decoded the police message, it is clear that they see the abolition of the adversarial system, and its replacement by the inquisitorial model, as part of a package to increase their powers and secure more convictions.

But support for the inquisitorial model comes also from sections of the public, who are uneasy with the adversarial system because of its 'confrontational' nature. The participant with whom many identify in the criminal process is the witness (perhaps also the victim). They see, or hear about, or actually experience, the examination and cross-examination of witnesses in styles which range from the cool and clinical to the unpleasant and aggressive. They assume that this process is unnecessary, and could with profit be replaced by a smoother, more neutral system, with a paternal judicial figure taking charge of all the questioning.

Yet is it legitimate to suggest that the adversarial system is somehow not a suitable vehicle in the search for truth? And is it realistic to yearn for a neutral person to take on the responsibility for that search?

It is suggested that the adversarial system of trial is in fact more likely to achieve the complementary objectives of acquitting the innocent and convicting the guilty. The danger in the inquisitorial system is that the judge may become prematurely committed to one outcome or the other. In doing so, he will not have had the full benefit of hearing the advocates representing defence and prosecution. Whilst in the adversarial system, each advocate knows that it is his responsibility to present the case for the defence or the prosecution, in the inquisitorial model the responsibility is more diffuse. As the Bar put it in its evidence to the Runciman Commission:

> The advocate cannot leave it to anyone else to adduce the evidence, argue points of law and seek to persuade the arbiter. If there is a loophole he must find it: he cannot say to himself 'I am sure the judge will find any loophole, so I do not need to worry'. In the words of an American President: 'The buck stops here'. If, on the other hand, the arbiter has the tasks of both establishing guilt and 'non-guilt' and of deciding the issue, his verdict is less likely to be right. In seeking to establish guilt, there is a likelihood that he will become convinced that the right verdict is one of guilt and become less willing to see 'non-guilt' as a possibility. Indeed he may become so convinced that he prematurely ceases any further investigation. (Bar Council 1992, pp. 11–12.)

What about the dissatisfaction felt by many an ordinary citizen with the confrontational aspect of the adversarial system? At the root of this feeling is a very real problem about the cavalier way in which the criminal justice system treats witnesses, and victims in particular — an issue which is discussed further below. Leaving that legitimate concern to one side for the moment, the dissatisfaction perhaps underestimates the value of cross-examination as a weapon in exposing lies. And it is the unpleasant reality of criminal proceedings that one side or the other (a cynic might sometimes be tempted to say 'both') is very often lying. If cross-examination is an effective weapon for the exposure of deceit, how can that weapon be deployed in the inquisitorial system? If the judge descends into the gladiatorial arena and cross-examines with the necessary vigour, then he risks compromising his impartiality, at least in the eyes of the witness being cross-examined. If that witness were the alleged victim and the cross-examination were to be followed by an acquittal, then insult would be added to injury. On the other hand, if the judge were to opt for discretion and leave cross-examination to the representatives of defence and prosecution, then that argument for a move to an inquisitorial system disappears.

In any event, the recent notorious miscarriages of justice which are the outward and visible signs of the crisis faced by our criminal justice system do not stem from the adversarial nature of that system. In fact the adversarial system, the right to silence, independent defence lawyers and the presumption of innocence are associated phenomena all of which are based upon a healthy suspicion of the State's use of its coercive powers. Unfortunately, those miscarriages of justice have shown that such a suspicion is all too justified.

Disparity of resources

For all its advantages, the adversarial system is bedevilled by a fundamental problem. It pits the State (in the form of the prosecution) against the individual defendant. Clearly, there is an inherent disparity of resources between the contestants. Of course, if the institutions of the State were neutral in the contest then any lack of resources on the part of the defendant would be irrelevant. It is the strength of the adversarial system, however, that it proceeds on the realistic assumption that the State's resources will tend to be thrown behind the prosecution. This is virtually inevitable, in view of the fact that its investigative agencies have formed at least a preliminary view that the accused is guilty. So there is, in practice, a disparity of resources. How can this be remedied so as to provide the defendant with a fair trial?

Some of the basic rights which the criminal justice system extends to the defendant are attempts to compensate for this disparity of resources and to put the adversaries on a more even footing. It is in this light that the presumption of innocence, the right to silence and the duty of the prosecution to disclose its case should be viewed.

To a limited extent, also, the deficiency in the resources of the defence is met by the provision of legal aid. In this country, legal aid for defendants is available, broadly speaking, subject to means and the seriousness of the case. In practice this means that the great majority of defendants in the Crown Court, at any rate, are in receipt of legal aid. Whilst legal aid covers the basic cost of legal assistance and representation in court, it has proved totally incapable of providing the investigative and forensic science resources which form part of the prosecution's armoury.

So further measures need to be taken to provide a level playing field. There are two main questions to consider. First, how can the information at the disposal of the prosecution be placed in the hands of the defence (the problem of disclosure)? Second, how can the defence be provided with improved resources?

As far as disclosure is concerned, the present position is that:

(a)   The defence at trial on indictment (but not at trial in the magistrates' court) are entitled to know in advance the evidence the prosecution intend to call.

(b)   The prosecution should disclose to the defence evidence which will not be part of their case — even if it contradicts their case. This duty is set out, as far as trial in the Crown Court is concerned, in the guidelines issued by the Attorney-General on the disclosure of 'unused material' (*Blackstone's Criminal Practice 1992*, app. 4). The guidelines provide that certain categories of unused material are not to be disclosed — such as when there are grounds for fearing that the disclosure of a statement might lead to the intimidation of a witness or the revelation of an informer's identity.

Even accepting these limitations, there have been grave failures to meet the prosecution's duty of disclosure, and a number of the recent miscarriage of justice cases have focused attention upon its deficiencies. In the Maguire case, for example, prosecution scientists suppressed information which showed that the defence case could be true (May 1990). Other failures to disclose material feature in the cases of the Birmingham Six, the Guildford Four and Judith Ward (see chapter 4).

In the Kiszko case, an innocent man was convicted of the murder of an 11-year-old girl and spent 16 years in prison before the Court of Appeal released him. Semen stains found on the girl's clothing could not have come from Mr Kiszko, who was infertile. At his appeal, it was stated that scientific evidence to this effect had been available at the time of the trial, and the police were still investigating the circumstances of its non-disclosure to the defence (*Guardian*, 18 February 1992).

Clearly, the prosecution's duty to disclose needs to be tightened up. The following reforms are required as a matter of urgency:

(a)   The prosecution's duty to disclose the evidence which it *does* intend to call must be extended to trial in the magistrates' court. The current anomalous position is that the prosecution must disclose evidence in their possession which they do not intend to call (e.g., the statement of a witness helpful to the defence (*R v Leyland Justices, ex parte Hawthorn* [1979] QB 283), but are under no such obligation in relation to the evidence which actually forms part of their case. As a result, the defence can find themselves facing a trial in the magistrates' court without sufficient knowledge of the prosecution case to be able to prepare or respond properly.

(b)   As far as trial in the Crown Court is concerned, the difficulty with the present system is that the Crown Prosecution Service may not know about evidence in the possession of the police. The CPS may therefore be able to say to the defence that they have handed over all unused material, but they can hardly be blamed for failing to disclose what they do not know about. As far as the police are concerned, whilst deliberate concealment is sometimes a problem, a more frequent difficulty is the failure to recognise the relevance or importance of the material which is consigned to limbo. What is needed is a system which imposes a discipline of disclosure upon the prosecution machinery as a whole, and the police in particular. In its evidence to the Runciman Commission, the CPS recognised this crucial need:

> A certificate of disclosure signed by a police officer, confirming that complete disclosure of all unused material has been made, should be required in order to introduce personal responsibility into this area and in order to allow the prosecution to comply fully with its duty of disclosure. (Crown Prosecution Service 1992, p. 11.)

(c)   It is wrong that an important matter like this should be left to the Attorney-General's guidelines. What is needed is a statutory provision, which could properly form part of the Police and Criminal Evidence Act 1984, placing a duty upon the police to disclose all evidence to the CPS, and a duty upon the CPS to disclose to the defence (subject in the latter case to the sort of exceptions as to sensitive information which form part of the guidelines). Failure to comply with these duties should become a criminal offence.

So much for tightening up the prosecution's duty to disclose. Any reforms in this area, however, can only provide a partial solution. What is needed is that the defence should have adequate resources to carry out their own preparation for trial. As the Bar put it in its evidence to the Runciman Commission:

> An important cause of miscarriages of justice has been the imbalance of resources between the prosecution and defence in respect of the analysis of forensic evidence. This appears to have made a material difference to the trial of the Birmingham Six, where the slender forensic resources of the defence were easily out-matched by the Crown. It is essential to a fair trial that the defence have access to forensic exhibits at an early stage and be provided with sufficient resources to analyse the same and to examine

critically the workings and conclusions of prosecution experts. At the present time, the resources provided are totally inadequate to the task. The problem is compounded by the complexity of modern techniques such as DNA analysis. (Bar Council 1992, p. 43.)

The Tottenham Three case provides an instance of the way in which inadequate defence resources can result in injustice. An additional report from a psychologist in relation to the mental age and suggestibility of one of the defendants could have led to his confession being rejected as inadmissible. As the Court of Appeal put it in quashing the convictions of all three defendants (on various grounds):

This appeal illustrates the difficulties confronted by solicitors where they need to obtain evidence from an expert. If the defendant is on legal aid and he receives a hostile opinion from an expert or one which his solicitors believe to be wrong, are they then disqualified from seeking a second or third opinion? While any form of 'expert-shopping' is to be discouraged there will be exceptional cases when the need for a further opinion can be demonstrated. (*Guardian*, 6 December 1991.)

The delays in the granting of legal aid are notorious, and it is often difficult to obtain authority in time to commission an expert's report before trial. Nor can there be any certainty whether that authority will eventually be obtained. The difficulties of the legal-aid solicitor, desperately walking the knife-edge between profit and insolvency can be readily imagined. Should he commission the report of an additional expert and face the risk that the legal aid fund will not pay up? Or will he be tempted to think that he has done his best with the resources at his disposal?

In order to redress the balance, there needs to be an established forensic service, at a centre of scientific excellence, which is primarily at the disposal of the defence. Its use would be covered by legal aid, which should be readily available for this purpose, given the role which it could play in the prevention of miscarriages of justice. The establishment of such an institution has been suggested by a number of bodies (for example, the Bar Council (1992, p. 14), the British Academy of Forensic Scientists (Forensic Science Service 1988) and the Legal Action Group (1991, p. 27)).

There is one particular proposal in the field of expert evidence which, it is suggested, would be positively retrograde. This is the idea which has been put forward from some quarters that experts should be appointed by the court on the French model. This innovation would substantially undermine the adversarial principle, and call into question the impartiality of the court. There is no reason to suppose that the introduction of an officially impartial expert would improve the situation. After all, the evidence adduced by the Crown is, in theory, supposed to be objective. The safeguards in the present system (cross-examination and the defence's right to commission their own expert) are valuable aids to truth, and must be preserved. Of course, they need strengthening in the ways canvassed above, but the hunt for a 'neutral expert' is a search for fool's gold (Howard 1991 and Spencer 1991).

Crown Court or magistrates?

The English system of criminal justice relies upon two different types of tribunal to carry out virtually all its work. The great majority of offences are tried in the magistrates' court. A minority of cases, generally confined to the more serious offences, are determined in the Crown Court. Where the case is heard in the magistrates' court, the decision-makers are usually justices, who have no legal qualification, advised by a clerk, who does. In some of the busy city courts, however, a stipendiary magistrate will hear the case alone. In the Crown Court, on the other hand, the trial will be presided over by a judge, the issues of fact being determined by the jury.

How is the decision taken as to the court in which a case will eventually be heard? It depends primarily upon the nature of the offence. Criminal offences are classified by Parliament into:

(a)   those which are summary only, i.e., can only be tried in the magistrates' court;
(b)   those which are triable only on indictment (in the Crown Court); and
(c)   those which are triable either way — in the magistrates' court or the Crown Court.

As far as category (c) is concerned, the decision as to whether the case will end up in the magistrates' or the Crown Court depends upon the decision of the magistrates and the accused. Only if both the magistrates and the accused agree will the case be tried by the magistrates. The magistrates for their part can refuse to accept jurisdiction, sending the case up to the Crown Court. A person accused of an either-way offence is entitled to elect trial by judge and jury in the Crown Court.

What then are the advantages and disadvantages of these two alternative modes of trial? How do they measure up to the objectives outlined above?

Where the accused is entitled to elect mode of trial and intends to plead not guilty, defence lawyers will usually, although not invariably, advise that he elect trial by judge and jury. Among the reasons for this advice are:

(a) There is a tendency for magistrates, who must hear cases with reasonable regularity, to become 'case-hardened'. In particular, where there is a conflict of evidence between the accused and a police officer, many magistrates tend to prefer the police version. This tendency, it may be thought, is one to which a number of judges are also prone, but with lay magistrates there is the additional danger that they have no legal training to keep the tendency in check. The Bar Council's evidence to the Runciman Commission puts it like this:

> Whatever may be the limitations on the fact-finding abilities of jurors, there is a strongly held view that full-time professional or part-time fact-finders (judges, stipendiary and lay magistrates) are more likely to convict innocent persons. It is felt that judges and magistrates may too easily see themselves as, not mere finders of fact, but as 'champions for law and order' in the community. Thus they may be too willing to believe police officers. Subconsciously, they may be more concerned with police morale than police fallibility or dishonesty. Jurors know that police officers can be arrogant, bullying and that from time to time they can lie. . . . Judges and magistrates are careful not to buy items in public houses. Judges and magistrates would know that it is stupid to lie to the police and, applying their standards, will too easily equate lying to guilt. (Bar Council 1992, p. 50.)

(b) Where trial is by judge and jury, the judge decides questions of law and the jury decide issues of fact. When the admissibility of a particular piece of evidence, such as a confession, is disputed, then the judge will rule on that dispute in the absence of the jury. If the decision is that the confession is inadmissible, then no harm will have been done, since the jury will not have heard it. The magistrates, by contrast, are the arbiters of both law and fact (although their clerk advises them on questions of law, the ultimate decision is theirs). In order to be able to decide whether the disputed evidence is admissible or not, they will inevitably discover what it is. If they subsequently determine that it is inadmissible, there is still a danger that they will be influenced by it.

(c) There is a similar problem in relation to the cross-examination of the accused about his or her previous convictions. Normally evidence of them is inadmissible, since it is thought to be likely to prejudice the trier of fact against the accused. However, in certain circumstances (for example, where the accused has impugned the character of a prosecution witness), the prosecution may be allowed to cross-examine the accused about his or her character (the rule is further discussed below in the section headed 'Tit for tat'). Before such cross-examination is allowed, it is always necessary for the prosecution to obtain the leave of the court. In the magistrates' court, as soon as such an application is made the bench is aware that the accused has a 'past' of some sort. Even if they decide to refuse the application, that knowledge will be difficult to ignore. The problem does not arise in the Crown Court, where the application is made to the judge in the absence of the jury.

(d)   At a trial in the Crown Court, the defence know exactly what evidence the prosecution propose to adduce since that must be disclosed in advance, in detail. Where the accused is charged with an offence which is triable either way, and has elected to be tried by the magistrates, then he is entitled only to a summary of the evidence (Magistrates' Courts (Advance Information) Rules 1985 (SI 1985 No. 601)). In cases triable only by magistrates, there is no obligation on the prosecution to disclose their case in advance of the trial at all. The overall effect is that the defence in the magistrates' court may have to deal with allegations without having had any chance to prepare a case. The prosecution, on the other hand, have the considerable advantage of surprise to add to their superior resources.

(e)   For Crown Court trial, legal aid is almost invariably granted, subject to the defendant's means, so that some 98 per cent of defendants in the Crown Court are in receipt of legal aid. By contrast, there are considerable variations in the willingness of magistrates' courts to grant legal aid for offences such as shoplifting and assault occasioning actual bodily harm.

If the acquittal of the innocent is to take the priority as an objective, it seems clear that jury trial should be the norm for any serious offence. It is, of course, a lot cheaper for a case to be tried by magistrates, particularly given the relative scarcity of legal aid. That consideration has tended to dominate recent thinking about which offences should attract the right to jury trial. It is worth bearing in mind, however, that an offence of theft, however small the sum involved, carries a stigma which may affect the offender's future quite drastically.

It may well be that too many cases end up in the Crown Court. There are alternative ways of reducing the number, without further erosion of the right to jury trial. As was said earlier in this section, for an offence which is triable either way to be dealt with by the magistrates, both they and the accused must agree. There are a number of cases where the accused is content to forgo his right to jury trial, very often with the intention of pleading guilty. Magistrates should be encouraged to accept jurisdiction in as many of these cases as possible. (In 1991, of the cases which went to the Crown Court for trial, 52 per cent went on the direction of the magistrates (Crown Prosecution Service 1991). An earlier study by Riley and Vennard (1988) concluded that, in more than half the cases committed by the magistrates to the Crown Court for trial, the sentence eventually imposed would have been within the magistrates' powers.)

For reasons of economy, it seems inevitable that a number of offences will continue to be triable only in the magistrates' court. It seems wrong that for that reason defendants should be kept in ignorance of the details of the case against them until the witnesses testify at their trial. Minimum standards of fairness surely require that the defence's rights to advance information should be extended to cases tried in the magistrates' court, at least where the offence in question is imprisonable.

Juries

How effective is the team of judge and jury which is entrusted with trial in the Crown Court?

Dealing first with the jury as an institution, there is a remarkable degree of unanimity among those submitting evidence to the Runciman Commission about its preservation. The only dispute seems to be about the *ambit* of jury trial (a subject addressed in the preceding section).

For the reasons already outlined, the jury scores high on the objective (to which our system rightly accords precedence) of acquitting the innocent. Some commentators have tried to lay the blame for the recent miscarriages of justice upon the jury. Certainly the verdicts in question were those of juries.

But two points need to be borne in mind. First, all serious cases are tried by juries. The miscarriages of justice which are the daily experience of those appearing in the magistrates' court do not often come to light. The sentences passed by the magistrates are inevitably short (a maximum of six months' imprisonment for any single offence). In a great number of cases, defendants do not think it worth appealing if they will have left prison by the time the appeal is heard. Second, in all the recent notorious miscarriage of justice cases, as the Bar puts it in its evidence to the Runciman Commission:

. . . it can, we believe, be said with a large degree of certainty that a judge trying the case alone would have reached the same conclusions as the juries had reached. (Bar Council 1992, p. 50.)

One cause for concern is that voiced by the Commission for Racial Equality (1991, pp. 15–20) about the composition of juries. The question which the CRE raises is whether the current practice in the selection of jurors produces a jury which is appropriate in a multiracial society. A black defendant is very often confronted with an all-white jury, and may feel, with some justice, that he is not receiving a trial by his peers. The problem is compounded, as the CRE points out, because the 'criminal justice system is administered by people who are overwhelmingly white which may reinforce the sense of isolation felt by ethnic minority defendants'.

The relatively small size of the ethnic minority population in Britain and its concentration in particular areas does mean that, with random selection, a black person is likely to face an all-white jury. In addition, there appears to be a practice of trying some defendants away from the area of the offence. For example, defendants from south London, which has a relatively high ethnic minority population, are sent to the Crown Court in Kingston-upon-Thames, which certainly does not. (This practice now has disturbing echoes of the Los Angeles trial of four police officers for the beating of Rodney King, which sparked off the riots in May 1992. That trial was moved, at the request of the defence, to the Los Angeles suburb of Simi Valley, a mainly white community where many serving and retired police officers live.)

Until a few years ago, there was built into the system a way of increasing the chances of securing a multiracial jury, and thus reducing the danger of racial prejudice against a black defendant. This was embodied in the right of each defendant to challenge up to seven, later three jurors, without the necessity of showing cause (i.e., there was no need to show that the person challenged was unfit to be a juror). This right of peremptory challenge was abolished (Criminal Justice Act 1988, s. 118) amid government allegations that it was being abused by defence counsel, particularly in multi-defendant cases, and was leading to unmerited acquittals.

In fact, the exhaustive research carried out at that time by the CPS on the use of peremptory challenge disclosed no link between the use of the challenge and acquittal rates (Vennard and Riley 1988). In the majority of trials, including those involving more than one defendant, defence counsel made no use at all of the right to peremptory challenge. It appears, then, that the fears which led to the abolition of peremptory challenge were groundless. On the other hand, the legitimate function which it fulfilled in a multiracial society such as ours was ignored. The problem posed for black defendants might be met by its restoration. But it would run the risk that white defendants charged with racial attack, for example, could use peremptory challenge to exclude black jurors from the jury. It is suggested that the problem might be addressed by allowing the trial judge to stand jurors by, in order to achieve a racially mixed jury in appropriate cases. The Court of Appeal has said that the trial judge has no right to do this (*R* v *Ford* [1989] QB 868, disapproving *R* v *Binns* [1982] Crim LR 52 insofar as it appeared to endorse such a practice), but it could of course be granted by statute.

As stated earlier, there is a consensus among those involved in the criminal justice system about the preservation of the jury, although there is a controversy over its ambit. At one end of the spectrum, there have been proposals that it be removed in respect of allegedly trivial offences. At the 'serious' end of the offence spectrum, there is also a set of proposals for reform, put forward by the Roskill Committee in relation to complex fraud cases (Fraud Trials Committee 1986).

The nub of the Roskill recommendations, as far as our present discussion is concerned, was that 'for complex fraud trials falling within certain guidelines, trial by a judge and two lay members (assessors) should replace trial by a judge and jury'. This proposal has not been implemented, although a number of its other recommendations (e.g., in relation to pre-trial procedure in serious fraud cases) have found their way on to the statute book.

The main reasons which the Roskill Committee put forward for the removal of the right to jury trial were:

(a)   that the length of complex fraud trials was such as to cause unacceptable disruption to the lives of the jurors;
(b)   that the evidence was so complex as to be beyond the 'limits of comprehension' of some jurors.

It should be stressed that this particular recommendation of the Roskill Committee ran counter to the views of the great majority of those who submitted evidence to it. Whilst the number of cases involved would not be great — a few dozen perhaps — there are important issues of principle at stake. Many other cases contain complex evidence, notably scientific evidence. Should they also be removed from the ambit of jury trial? The Committee's report seems to envisage this (Fraud Trials Committe 1986, para. 8.15).

One danger is that, where lawyers and experts constitute the tribunal, they tend naturally to carry on the arguments about procedure and technicalities for their own benefit. No one else would have to follow those arguments, and justice would not be seen to be done. Further, any acquittal might appear to be the result of an establishment carve-up — there is enough popular suspicion of what the City gets up to without reducing public involvement in the decision-making process.

The debate has been given fresh life recently by comments from High Court judges critical of the length and expense involved in major fraud trials over which they had presided. See, for example, the comments of McKinnon J, passing sentence in the Blue Arrow case: 'All involved in this case have been called upon to endure what no one in our courts should be asked to endure. That applies to the defendants, to the jury and to me.' (*Guardian*, 18 February 1992.)

What reforms could be carried out in order to ease this particular pressure point? Certainly those prosecuting will want to bear in mind the words of Gareth Williams QC, the chairman of the Bar: 'We must keep it simple, keep the number of defendants down'. As the Law Society put it in its evidence to the Runciman Commission:

> In fraud trials the indictment should be simplified by not including superfluous counts and confining the prosecution's evidence to disputed issues only. People on the fringes of an alleged fraudulent conspiracy should not be joined in the indictment. (Law Society 1992, p. 43.)

There remains the problem of ensuring that proceedings are not beyond the jury's 'limits of comprehension'. Detailed research needs to be done on the presentation of numerical information, improving jurors' understanding of the concepts involved, and overcoming difficulties in concentration. Such research is urgently needed, not only in relation to serious fraud cases, but to improve the functioning of the jury system across the whole spectrum of cases in which it is involved.

It is astonishing to find that any serious research into the way in which juries function is, in effect, prohibited by s. 8 of the Contempt of Court Act 1981, which makes it an offence to disclose, obtain or publish information about what took place in the jury room. Clearly safeguards are needed to protect the anonymity of all concerned and to prevent intimidation. Subject to that caveat, properly authorised academic researchers should be permitted to interview volunteer jurors after the verdict has been delivered.

Judges

As already stated, 'jury trial' is a label for a package which includes both judge and jury. What about the role of the judge? Is that working in accordance with the proper objectives of the criminal justice system?

The first issue which causes some concern is whether judges are sufficiently empowered to throw out cases which are inherently weak. In such a case, the position is that at the end of the prosecution evidence, the defence are entitled to make a submission of 'no case to answer', to which the prosecution reply. The judge then considers the evidence so far and has the power to decide that there is no case to answer. If the decision is that there is no case to answer then the judge directs the jury to acquit, without any necessity for the defence to call evidence.

The basis upon which the judge makes this decision is laid down in *R v Galbraith* [1981] 1 WLR 1039 in which Lord Lane CJ said (at p. 1042B–D):

> There are two schools of thought: (1) that the judge should stop the case if, in his view, it would be unsafe . . . for the jury to convict; (2) that he should do so only if there is no evidence upon which a jury properly directed could properly convict. . . . A balance has to be struck between, on the one hand, a usurpation by the judge of the jury's functions and on the other, the danger of an unjust conviction.

Somewhat strangely, the Court of Appeal in *Galbraith* indicated, in effect, that trial judges should be prepared to run the risk of an unjust conviction, in order to preserve the sanctity of the jury's role: 'We think the second of the two schools of thought is to be preferred.'

In the light of the analysis of the objectives of the criminal justice system outlined above, it is respectfully suggested that the Court of Appeal got its priorities wrong. The need to ensure the acquittal of the innocent ought surely to enable the judge to shelve any reluctance to usurp the jury's role. After all, even the staunchest of defenders of the jury should regard it as a means to an end, rather than an objective in itself.

In fact, partly no doubt as a result of *Galbraith*, the number of cases in which the judge directs the jury to acquit after a submission of no case to answer is very small: just over 2 per cent of all cases dealt with by the Crown Court (Lord Chancellor's Department 1992, tables 6.8 and 6.9). The dismissal of any such cases at a relatively early stage is beneficial not only in avoiding possible miscarriages of justice. It also spares the defendant from any prolongation of the ordeal of trial, and saves the public money which would be wasted if the trial went to its term.

Although there are some reported cases, both at first instance and in the Court of Appeal (see, for example, *R v Shippey* [1988] Crim LR 767 and *Blackstone's Criminal Practice 1992*, D12.31), which show attempts to relax the bonds upon the trial judge, the central authority of *Galbraith* holds sway in this area, and legislation would be needed to change the position to any appreciable extent. Such a change would have the merit of consistency. When the Court of Appeal considers an appeal against conviction, it must by statute allow the appeal if the conviction is 'under all the circumstances of the case . . . unsafe or unsatisfactory' (Criminal Appeal Act 1968, s. 2(1)(a)). The trial judge ought also to be able to direct an acquittal where a conviction would be 'unsafe or unsatisfactory'.

Confessions

No matter how diligent the decision-makers, errors will proliferate if their deliberations are based upon unreliable material. Nowhere is this more clearly true than in dealing with confessions. A number of the most notorious miscarriages have had at their centre a confession upon which the court wrongly relied.

False confessions were responsible for the hanging in 1950 of Timothy Evans (posthumously pardoned) and for the wrongful conviction of three juveniles who made detailed admissions to the police in the Confait case in 1972. More recently, there has been a spate of successful appeals relying upon allegations that the police had fabricated a confession relied upon at the trial. Some of these appeals were based upon the evidence proferred by the West Midlands Serious Crimes Squad during the period 1987 to 1989. Unreliable confessions were also, of course, a crucial part of the prosecution case against all of the Tottenham Three, and they contributed greatly to the miscarriages of justice against the Guildford Four, the Birmingham Six and Judith Ward.

A frequent, though not invariable, feature of the false confession cases has been lying evidence by the police. *The Times* remarked in an editorial on the tasks of the Runciman Commission:

> . . . members of the Commission must assume that as long as it is in the interests of the police to cheat, some of them will. Until the procedures of the law acknowledge that, miscarriages of justice will recur and damage will continue to the impartiality of the law of Britain. (*The Times*, 26 November 1991.)

How, then, can the procedures of the law acknowledge the fallibility of police evidence, particularly in relation to the production of confessions?

One step along this path is the introduction of tape recording, which is now required for any interview conducted after a suspect has been cautioned in respect of an indictable offence in all police areas other than Thames Valley. Tape recording is not required, however, in respect of less serious offences which are not indictable and hence must be tried in the magistrates' court. Nor is it required for terrorist offences (Code of Practice E issued under the Police and Criminal Evidence Act 1984).

Leaving aside these limitations to the ambit of tape recording, its introduction does not provide a sufficient safeguard in dealing with confessions. An officer can still put improper pressure on a suspect prior to interview. Further, even without impropriety, some suspects are particularly susceptible to the inherently coercive nature of detention and interrogation.

This reasoning has led to calls for a rule that confessions should be corroborated (i.e., that they should be supported by evidence from a source, independent of the confession, which tends to show that the accused committed the offence charged). Some such proposals have restricted the call for corroboration to interviews where no solicitor is present. Others have suggested that there should be a corroboration requirement whenever confession evidence is relied upon (Legal Action Group 1991, pp. 19–20; Liberty 1991, p. 4).

The experience of the courts in relation to those types of evidence where corroboration is already required (e.g., the evidence of a complainant in a sexual case) has not been a particularly happy one. The area is beset with technicalities, and the tendency of the higher courts has been to try to reduce the scope of the operation of any corroboration requirement.

Perhaps a safer precedent to follow is the obligatory warning of the need for special caution in identification cases, introduced with some success in the case of *R* v *Turnbull* [1977] QB 224 (for a detailed survey, culminating in a similar proposal, see Pattenden 1991). If such a rule were to be extended to confession cases, the judge would be obliged to warn the jury of false confessions which had been relied on in the past, and caution them about convicting upon the basis of a confession alone. He would go on to make reference to any evidence which either supported or undermined the confession, and he would have to draw the jury's attention to the circumstances of the confession, e.g., any breach of the various codes of practice issued under the Police and Criminal Evidence Act 1984. Whilst the adoption of *Turnbull* has not eliminated wrongful convictions based upon mistaken identity, it certainly seems to have reduced that particular problem. A similar approach to confession evidence might be an effective part of a package to reduce miscarriages in that area, too.

Tit for tat

One difficulty in rooting out false confessions is that there is a powerful disincentive to prevent the accused from alleging that the officers have fabricated the confession, or behaved in any seriously improper way. This disincentive is known as the 'tit-for-tat' rule. The usual position is that if the accused has any previous convictions, they will not go in front of the jury. But if the 'nature or conduct of the defence is such as to involve imputations on the character of . . . the witnesses for the prosecution', the accused loses the shield of protection from cross-examination about character (Criminal Evidence Act 1898, s. 1(f)(iii)). Hence, where they have a suspect with previous convictions, the police can attribute a false confession knowing that they are in a strong position. The defendant is left with a difficult choice. Either testify, deny the confession and risk exposing a criminal record to the jury, which is likely to make them think the testimony is not worthy of belief, or refuse to testify, and rely upon an advocate to discredit the police evidence in cross-examination, but without the benefit of any evidence to put in the scales against it.

The question which must be posed in the interests of the health of the criminal justice system is: do we really want to expose police malpractice? Or do we want to encourage the notion that an effective strategy for dealing with crime is to round up the usual suspects? If we are to promote objective (c) in the list at the beginning of this chapter (preventing malpractice which contaminates the system) then surely the 'tit-for-tat' rule should go.

Victims

No discussion of the shortcomings of the criminal justice system would be complete without some mention of the often cavalier way in which it treats the victims of crime. Any failures in this respect are obviously a matter of concern to the victims themselves — the system should aid their recovery from a potentially harmful experience, rather than hinder it. Proper and sensitive treatment of the victims is also in the interests of the justice system itself, since it depends upon them to report crimes and give evidence about them.

The difficulties faced by victims are dealt with in the evidence of Victim Support (1991) to the Runciman Commission. A continual problem is the lack of information. The need is for a two-way flow. On the one hand, the CPS should be in touch with victims so that the prosecution case can be soundly based when dealing with all aspects from charge, through bail, to trial and seeking the right amount of compensation. Conversely, the victim is often concerned and anxious about various aspects of the justice process, and deserves to be informed about developments. Victim Support quotes from research conducted by the University of Birmingham on their Victim/ Witness in Court Project (Victim Support 1991, p. 8), and points out that fewer than two in five of the respondents felt they knew sufficiently well the procedures within the court-room and what to expect there. A campaign to ensure better information at the various points of the criminal justice process would be well worth the effort and expenditure for its long-term effects.

A rather more thorny question is the way in which the time of witnesses is wasted. Victim Support's research shows (1991, p. 7) that in 37 per cent of cases where witnesses were required to attend, the hearing did not take place on the appointed day. Of the witnesses affected, 70 per cent were unaware of the change until they arrived at court. Nearly half had to wait for over four hours before being called into court.

Of interest in this context is the practice in some magistrates' courts of adopting a 'block listing' scheme. This gives the witness a definite time to attend (e.g., at 10.00 a.m. or 11.30 a.m.). Although no research has been conducted on these schemes, early fears that they would lead to much wasted court time appear not to have been justified.

The equivalent in the Crown Court, where the average trial is much longer, is a policy of giving as many trials as possible a fixed date, well in advance. But court administrators have been reluctant to travel down this path, because of the number of trials which are aborted (or, as the jargon puts it 'cracked'), frequently due to a last-minute plea of guilty by the defendant. The issues raised by this phenomenon are addressed in the next section.

One final point is most important in considering the impact of the justice process upon the victim. A wrongful conviction is an injury not just to the defendant, but to the victim of the crime (or the family). When Stefan Kiszko was cleared of the murder of Lesley Molseed after 16 years, her father said 'For us, it is just like Lesley had been murdered last week'. Her brother expressed his sympathy for Mr Kiszko and the hope that the new investigation would be successful, and then said: 'Somewhere is the man who killed my sister.' As Mr Kiszko's counsel, Stephen Sedley QC, put it:

> We acknowledge their pain in having to listen to some of the details surrounding their daughter's death and the new pain of learning that her killer has not, after all, been caught. (*Guardian*, 18 February 1992.)

Formal arrangements for offering support to the victims in such circumstances do not exist at present. Their provision must surely be a priority. And there is here further incentive, if it were needed, for the system to ensure the right decision in the first place.

Cracked trials

As indicated in the preceding section, the fact is that a great number of Crown Court trials, where a contest is expected, turn into guilty pleas at the last minute. This makes it very difficult to allocate court resources (court-rooms, judges, juries, lawyers) sensibly. It also plays havoc with the lives of civilian witnesses, and means that police officers are attending court unnecessarily, instead of preventing and investigating crime. Because of the uncertainty surrounding whether any particular trial will proceed, court staff are reluctant to allocate fixed dates, and this exacerbates the problems for witnesses in particular.

The reason why many defendants plead guilty is because of the discount which they expect to receive for their plea. In the Crown Court, a guilty plea traditionally results in a discount in the length of a custodial sentence — typically between a fifth and a third. It may even result in a lesser type of sentence. For example, in *R* v *Hollyman* (1979) 1 Cr App R (S) 289 two of the defendants pleaded guilty and received sentences of two months suspended. The third defendant pleaded not guilty, and received an immediate sentence of three months' imprisonment, although his case was in other material respects similar. (But see *R* v *Tonks* [1980] Crim LR 59, where it was thought that such disparity would leave the imprisoned offender with a sense of grievance.)

As far as the merits of the discount are concerned, it has been subject to some criticism. For example, Liberty suggests in its evidence to the Runciman Commission (Liberty 1991, p. 46) that 'it is wholly improper for defendants to be penalised for exercising their right to put the prosecution to proof'. It is submitted that this line of argument is basically flawed. As Stockdale and Devlin put it (1987, p. 50):

> You are not being punished for pleading not guilty, you are being rewarded for pleading guilty. The reward is based in part on the gratitude of the courts for the saving of time and money, partly on sparing the victim from the witness-box and partly because of the theory that a man who shows some contrition does not need to be punished so much as one who does not.

There is, then, a sound rationale for the discount. But is it applied in the right way? Surely each one of the factors justifying it operates even more powerfully if the plea is entered at an early stage. First, as has just been pointed out, the gratitude of the courts is greatly diminished by the fact that the matter had to be set down for trial. Second, although the victim may not have to enter the witness-box, it is too late to prevent what may have been an agony of anticipation. Third, surely contrition looks far less calculated when it follows close on the offence.

If this is the case, then the maximum discount ought to be available at the earliest stage of the criminal justice process, with the least discount being granted for the last-minute plea. There is authority from the Court of Appeal for this approach. Where an offender has delayed his plea to secure a tactical advantage, the discount may be reduced or even lost (*R* v *Hollington* (1985) 82 Cr App R 281). There is always a temptation, however, for the court to react more generously than might be properly merited to a late plea. A more formal policy of graduated discounts would assist in concentrating minds earlier.

The operation of the discount for a guilty plea is not the only factor behind a late change of plea. In a perceptive article, Bredar (1992) points out that defendants frequently refuse to make a final decision on their plea until they know whether the prosecution witnesses will turn up, which judge will preside, and that the final moment for a decision has arrived. Once these pieces of the jigsaw have been fitted into place, meaningful discussions can take place between prosecution and defence counsel about an informal plea bargain acceptable to the defendant and the CPS. The crucial question which he poses is: how can these discussions be forced to occur earlier? If that could be accomplished, then cracked trials, with all the adverse consequences which they imply, could be greatly reduced. Bredar puts forward a package, based upon a plea review conference 10 days before trial. There would be a rule of procedure that the charges could not be altered thereafter. Further, the defendant would have to plead guilty at the review in order to obtain a discount — any later plea would attract no sentencing benefit. The trial would be listed before a particular judge, irrevocably. The CPS would have to demonstrate the probability of key witnesses appearing to testify at trial. If they failed to do so, the count concerned would be dismissed.

Such a package would certainly have attractive features. Even if it proves too radical a departure, then some careful adjustment to the system of discounts for a guilty plea would have substantial merit on its own. It must be stressed that we are not dealing here with a question of finance. Certainly, cracked trials do cost a lot of money which could be more fruitfully spent in improving the quality of criminal justice. But more than that, they greatly disrupt the lives of those needlessly asked to attend court, as the evidence of Victim Support to the Runciman Commission makes plain.

Conclusion

Recent events have created a climate of willingness to discuss how the trial process can be improved. It is right to recognise that there is a lot wrong with the way in which justice is dispensed in our courts, but it is at least equally important to preserve those fundamental features which have attracted admiration, and a good deal of emulation, through much of the English-speaking world. In particular, it would be wrong to embark on a series of reforms motivated above all else by the desire to save costs.

The proposals set out in this chapter may be summarised as follows:

(a)   Any reforms should be carefully examined against the proper objectives of a criminal justice system.

(b)   The essential adversarial nature of our system should be preserved.

(c)   A statutory duty should be placed upon the police and the CPS to disclose to the defence material which is relevant to the case but which the prosecution do not intend to use.

(d)   The present duty of the prosecution to disclose their case to the defence prior to Crown Court trial should be extended to the magistrates' court.

(e)   A forensic science service should be established at a centre of scientific excellence, primarily at the disposal of the defence.

(f)   Magistrates should be encouraged to accept jurisdiction in more cases which are triable either way.

(g)   Careful consideration should be given to ensuring the right to a multiracial jury in appropriate cases, by ensuring that defendants are tried locally, and by giving the judge a right to stand jurors by in order to achieve this end.

(h)   Steps should be taken, by the prosecution in particular, to simplify proceedings in complex fraud trials as far as possible.

(i)   The veil which conceals the deliberations of the jury should be lifted, to allow serious research, subject to necessary safeguards.

(j)   The legal test of whether there is a case for the defence to answer should be altered, so that the trial judge can direct an acquittal where a conviction would be unsafe.

(k)   The jury should be warned about the danger of convicting upon a confession alone.

(l)   The 'tit-for-tat' rule should be abolished, so that the accused can challenge a confession without fear of losing the shield against cross-examination about character.

(m)   There must be better communication between the CPS and victims at the various stages of the criminal justice process; and special support must be provided for victims (and their families where appropriate) at appeals against wrongful conviction.

(n)   Dates should be fixed in advance for as many Crown Court trials as possible, so that disruption to the lives of witnesses is minimised.

(o)   Measures should be adopted to reduce the number of abortive trials, including a graduated discount depending on when a guilty plea is entered.

Appalling though the recent series of miscarriages of justice has been, the tragedy would be compounded if nothing was done to stop them happening again. All the participants in the criminal justice process deserve a quick, effective package of reforms which will help to achieve the proper objectives of the system.

References

Bar Council (1992), *The Bar Council's Response to the Royal Commission on Criminal Justice* (London).

Bredar, J.K. (1992), 'Moving up the Day of Reckoning: Strategies for Attacking the "Cracked Trials" Problem' [1992] Crim LR 153.

Commission for Racial Equality (1991), *Evidence of the Commission for Racial Equality to the Royal Commission on Criminal Justice* (London).

Crown Prosecution Service (1991), *Annual Report* (London: HMSO).

Crown Prosecution Service (1992), *The Evidence of the Crown Prosecution Service to the Royal Commission on Criminal Justice* (London).

Forensic Science Service (1988), *Minutes of Evidence* (House of Commons Home Affairs Committee) (House of Commons Sessional Papers 686–i 1987/88 and 686–ii 1987/88) (London: HMSO).

Fraud Trials Committee (1986) *Report* (London: HMSO).

Howard, M.N. (1991), 'The Neutral Expert: A Plausible Threat to Justice' [1991] Crim LR 98.

Law Society (1992), *Evidence of the Law Society to the Royal Commission on Criminal Justice* (London).

Legal Action Group (1991), *Royal Commission on Criminal Justice. Submission of the Legal Action Group* (London).

Liberty (1991), *Let Justice Be Done* (London).

Lord Chancellor's Department (1992), *Judicial Statistics England and Wales for the Year 1991* (Cm 1990) (London: HMSO).

May, Sir John (1990), *Interim Report on the Maguire Case* (House of Commons Sessional papers 556 1989/90) (London: HMSO).

Pattenden, R. (1991) 'Should Confessions be Corroborated?' (1991) 107 LQR 317.

Police Service (1991), *Evidence from the Police Service of England and Wales to the Royal Commission on Criminal Justice* (London).

Riley, D., and Vennard, J. (1988), *Triable-either-way Cases: Crown Court or Magistrates' Court* (Home Office Research Study 98) (London: HMSO).

Spencer, J.R. (1991), 'The Neutral Expert: An Implausible Bogey' [1991] Crim LR 106.

Stockdale, E., and Devlin, K. (1987), *Sentencing* (London: Waterlow).

Vennard, J., and Riley, D. (1988), 'The Use of Peremptory Challenge and Stand by of Jurors and their Relationship to Trial Outcome' [1988] Crim LR 731.

Victim Support (1991), *Royal Commission on Criminal Justice. Response by Victim Support* (London).

4

Miscarriages of Justice

Joshua Rozenberg

Anyone who still has any illusions about the ability of the criminal justice system to rectify miscarriages of justice should look up a statement made by the then Home Secretary Douglas Hurd in the House of Commons on 20 January 1987. In it he announced his conclusions on three cases which had recently been reviewed by his department.

Mr Hurd began with the case of the Maguire family. There was no new evidence, he said, which cast doubt on the safety of their convictions for handling explosives. He could see no grounds for referring the Maguires' case to the Court of Appeal.

On 26 June 1991 the Court of Appeal quashed their convictions.

Mr Hurd then dealt with the Guildford pub bombings. Again, there were no new points of substance. Again Mr Hurd could find no grounds to justify referring the case of the Guildford Four to the Court of Appeal.

On 19 October 1989 the Court of Appeal quashed their convictions.

Mr Hurd turned finally to the case of the Birmingham Six. He was satisfied that there *was* new evidence to justify referring their murder convictions to the Court of Appeal. But on 28 January 1988 the Court of Appeal decided not to allow their appeals.

On 14 March 1991 the Court of Appeal changed its mind and quashed their convictions.

To justify his refusal to reopen the cases of the Maguire family and the Guildford Four, Mr Hurd circulated two detailed memoranda in January 1987. Written by C3, the Home Office department responsible for investigating miscarriages of justice, they put forward eminently plausible arguments for not referring these two cases to the Court of Appeal — on the evidence then available. But as events were to prove, there *was* sufficient new evidence to clear all these defendants, if only somebody in authority was prepared to look for it.

The accounts that follow show how innocent people have suffered through official incompetence, narrow-mindedness and — occasionally — malice. It is only by looking in detail at what went wrong that we will have any chance of putting it right.

The Guildford Four

In October 1975, Patrick Armstrong, Gerard Conlon, Paul Hill and Carole Richardson were convicted of the five murders arising from the bombing in October 1974 of the Horse and Groom pub in Guildford. In addition, Mr Armstrong and Mr Hill were convicted of two murders arising from an explosion in November 1974 at the King's Arms pub in Woolwich. The prosecution case had been based almost entirely on confessions they had allegedly made to the police. All were sentenced to life imprisonment.

The Home Office memorandum of January 1987 paints a vivid picture of the Guildford Four. Summarising some of the representations made on their behalf, the Home Office noted the suggestion that 'the character and behaviour of the Four was such as to make them unlikely people to be terrorists, and that they were not the kind of people that the Provisional IRA would have used. In addition, it is pointed out that there is no evidence at all to show that all were involved with the IRA.'

The memorandum goes on to say that Patrick Armstrong and Carole Richardson in particular were suggested as most unlikely candidates for IRA bombers because they took drugs, lived in a squat, and were involved in petty crime. More remarkable still, the two had given their correct names and addresses to the police shortly after the bombings when they asked for help because Miss Richardson had been assaulted by a drunk.

The Home Office comment reveals the dangers of relying too closely on an adversarial system. 'The fact that some people may think it unlikely . . . that a particular person could ever have been involved in a crime of which he or she has been convicted is not an evidential point . . . . The points now being made cannot therefore be regarded as constituting new evidence or new considerations of substance which would justify the Home Secretary referring the cases to the Court of Appeal.'

But just two years later that was exactly what he did. In January 1989 Mr Hurd gave three reasons for his decision to refer the case back to the

Court of Appeal. First, Carole Richardson had been taking barbiturates and was suffering from withdrawal symptoms at the time she was arrested. The medical treatment she received in custody was open to question. Secondly, there was another account of Carole Richardson's movements on the afternoon of the Guildford bombings. And thirdly, there was another witness to support Paul Hill's alibi.

Whether this by itself would have been enough to clear the Guildford Four is something we shall never know. Their supporters were by no means confident: only a year earlier the Court of Appeal had dismissed appeals by the Birmingham Six, even though there had been enough new evidence to satisfy the Home Secretary that the Birmingham case should go to appeal.

But suddenly it all became quite academic. Quite unexpectedly, the dam burst: flood waters were to flow far beyond the Guildford case, washing away many more long-suspected miscarriages of justice and, through a Royal Commission, engulfing and perhaps cleansing the criminal justice system itself.

One of the most dramatic and tantalising letters ever to emerge from a fax machine reached solicitors for the Guildford Four on the morning of 17 October 1989. Chris Newell, the young and highly regarded director of headquarters casework at the Crown Prosecution Service, told defence lawyers that 'circumstances have recently come to the notice of the Director of Public Prosecutions which have caused him to conclude that it would be wrong for the Crown to seek to sustain the convictions'. An expedited hearing had been arranged for two days later. And it was only then that the Director would announce the reasons for his decision.

It was a courageous and unprecedented move by the DPP, Allan Green. At first sight it looked as if he was trying to bounce the Court of Appeal into accepting his view of the evidence. In a later case Lord Justice Russell was to criticise an approach of this kind: he firmly believed it was for the court to decide whether someone was to be cleared, not the prosecutor. But in practice the Crown's advice is invariably sought and normally followed: Lord Justice Russell's complaint was more a matter of form than substance. And in the Guildford Four case the Lord Chief Justice had been told in advance exactly what the Crown was planning to do.

Why then had the Crown thrown in the towel? Ultimately the Guildford Four owe their freedom to one woman. The name of Doreen Bryant is perhaps little known to the student of criminal justice, but she above all deserves the credit for breaching the dam which was holding back a whole raft of wrongful convictions. Not a relative, not a campaigner, not a journalist, in 1989 Doreen Bryant was a detective inspector in the Avon and Somerset Police.

Her force had been called in by the Home Office as long ago as 1987 'to investigate material which had recently come to light'. Once the case had been referred to the Court of Appeal in 1989, the superintendent in charge ordered a check of all interview notes obtained from Surrey police archives. Early in May 1989, Detective Inspector Bryant checked handwritten notes of interviews with Patrick Armstrong against typed notes of the same interviews. Her suspicions were aroused. The typed notes contained deletions and additions, both typed and handwritten, as well as some rearrangement of material. And yet the handwritten notes corresponded with the typed notes *in their corrected form*. It therefore looked to the Avon and Somerset Police as if the typed notes had been made before the handwritten notes. But at the original trial, Surrey police officers had claimed they had made handwritten notes during the interviews.

How could this be? The Surrey officers were interviewed. They could offer no satisfactory explanation. But Patrick Armstrong's confession was central to the prosecution case. Anything which cast doubt on it would undermine all four convictions. By early October, a full five months after Inspector Bryant's discovery, the DPP had decided that he should not oppose the appeal. In court, Mr Roy Amlot QC for the Crown said the typed notes must have been a draft of the evidence.

Giving judgment in October 1989, the Lord Chief Justice said there were two possible explanations. Either the typescripts were a complete fabrication, amended to make them more effective and then written out by hand to appear as if they were contemporaneous. Or the police had started with a contemporaneous note, typed it up to improve legibility, amended it to make it read better, and then converted it back to a manuscript note. Either way, Surrey police officers had not told the truth about a crucial document in the case against Patrick Armstrong. 'If they were prepared to tell this sort of lie,' he said, 'then the whole of their evidence became suspect'.

In the same matter-of-fact way as he delivered the rest of his judgment, Lord Lane ended by saying that the appeals were allowed and the convictions were quashed. The public gallery erupted into spontaneous cheers — perhaps the only sign that this was a case with immense implications, not just for other terrorist cases but for all prosecutions based on uncorroborated confessions.

The freeing of the Guildford Four made a significant dent in public confidence in the criminal justice system. Many of those in authority could only come to terms with it by telling themselves that just because a person is found not guilty it does not mean he did not commit the crime of which he was accused. Others were disturbed at the thought that the English legal system — which they had been brought up to believe was the best in the world — was capable of locking up the wrong people for so many years. Clearly, something had to be done. But what was to follow displayed all the muddle and delay which reformers have come to expect in this country.

At first, the authorities gave the impression of speedy action. Within an hour of the Guildford Four being freed, the Home Secretary announced the appointment of Sir John May, a retired Lord Justice of Appeal, to inquire into the circumstances surrounding the trials of the Guildford Four and the Maguire family. Equally quickly, the DPP ordered a police inquiry into allegations that Surrey police officers had lied in court.

In November 1989 Sir John May agreed to answer reporters' questions about his plans. As far as the Guildford Four were concerned, Sir John explained that he could not start taking factual evidence on their case while there was a possibility that Surrey police officers who had investigated the pub bombings might face criminal charges. But, said Sir John, there was no reason why these should not be completed within two or three months.

Reporters were incredulous. Sir John later earned much praise for his tenacious investigation of the Maguire case — which was to lead directly to their acquittal. But his estimate of the time it would take to prosecute the Surrey officers betrayed a staggering naïvety about the criminal justice system in which for some years he had been so intimately involved.

Sir John May was offered a chance to back down. Did he really mean two months?

'I hope so', Sir John told his questioner. 'Two months is an underestimate. I think three months. But you may be able to come and tell me in nine months' time that I was very wrong indeed and I have not yet started taking public evidence. But I cannot do it whilst the criminal investigations are proceeding, because that would be to the detriment of those persons involved.'

Sadly, Sir John was 'very wrong indeed'. It took the Avon and Somerset Police nine months just to investigate the case. It was a full year after Sir John's comment, in November 1990, before the DPP announced proceedings: retired Detective Chief Inspector (later Superintendent) Thomas Style, Detective Sergeant John Sutherland Donaldson, and Detective Constable Vernon Attwell would be prosecuted for conspiracy to pervert the course of justice. (Mr Donaldson and Mr Attwell had been suspended from police duties since October 1989 and later retired.)

Committal proceedings began in February 1991. They were to end, suddenly and dramatically, four months later. The Bow Street magistrate, Ronald Bartle, discharged the three men after ruling that the process of the court had been abused. It was a development so unexpected that not even Sir John May could be blamed for not foreseeing it.

The magistrate gave four reasons for his decision. They were immediately condemned as 'spurious' by the *Guardian* columnist Melanie Phillips. Mr
Bartle's first reason was that the 17 years' delay in bringing the case would
prejudice a fair trial. But as Phillips pointed out, a much older case, *R v
Pottle and Randle*, was even then being tried at the Old Bailey. Mr Bartle's
second reason was that the lapse of time would impose specific disadvantages on the men. Phillips's comment was to point out that the case
depended on documentary evidence rather than memory. The magistrate
then spoke of adverse media comment since the appeal. But on that basis
the Yorkshire Ripper should never have been charged.

However, it was Ronald Bartle's fourth reason that Phillips considered
'the most startling and misleading' of all. Mr Bartle said the Avon and
Somerset Police had failed to caution the three Surrey detectives before
interviewing them, an omission designed to conceal from them that they
were under suspicion of grave crimes and which deprived them of the
chance to seek evidence from others to assist their case. But these interviews
took place one month before the Guildford Four were released by the
Court of Appeal. They were not part of an investigtion into police
misconduct; the brief at that time was to see whether the Guildford Four
should be set free. At the same time, said Phillips, it was ludicrous to
suggest that the Surrey officers needed to be cautioned since, as detectives,
they would have known all too well that questions would be raised about
their own conduct if the Four were cleared.

There was consternation in the DPP's office. To have had the case
dismissed by a jury would have been disappointing, but for a single
magistrate to throw it out when the Lord Chief Justice himself had accused
police officers of lying was a bitter blow.

Where did all this leave Sir John May's inquiry? There could be no
appeal as such against the magistrate's order, so on the face of it Sir John
should have been able to begin investigating the Guildford Four case
without having to wait many months more for a trial to be completed. But
in July 1991 the Crown lodged an application for leave to seek judicial
review of the magistrate's decision, and at a hearing in October, two years
after the Four were cleared, the DPP was granted permission to apply for
judicial review at a full hearing before the Divisional Court in the new year.

The Attorney-General's decision to appear at the hearing in person
shows how high the stakes were: it was clear that former officers facing
charges arising from the Birmingham Six case would put forward similar
arguments. But to the Attorney's relief, the High Court came down in
favour of the prosecution. Lord Justice Neill, Lord Justice Taylor and Mr
Justice Rose decided that the magistrate's decision was unreasonable in the

sense that no reasonable magistrate could have reached it in the circumstances. The judges said that even though some of the publicity in 1989 had been hostile to the police, a jury would have been perfectly capable of deciding the case on the evidence — particularly because it was unlikely that a trial could be held before the autumn of 1992. And the judges said Mr Bartle had been 'wholly wrong' to conclude that the delay would prejudice a fair trial in a case which depended mainly on documentary evidence. The High Court said it had also been unreasonable of the magistrate to rule that the prosecution was unfair to the defendants. 'The principal concern of the investigating officers in the summer of 1989 was to obtain all relevant information to put before the Court of Appeal.' The case would proceed.

The estimate of two or three months Sir John May gave in November 1989 was now wildly inaccurate. The three were sent for trial in March 1992 but — partly because of the unavailability of their chosen counsel — the hearing could not start until more than a year later, in April 1993.

It followed that Sir John May would not have been able to begin public hearings into the Guildford Four case until some *four years* after his appointment. But even that was not to be. At the end of July 1992, Sir John threw in the towel. He announced there would be no public hearings after all. It would all be done in writing or in private.

The reason for this was said to be Sir John's wish to draw his conclusions from the Guildford case in time for the Royal Commission to consider them before it published its report in June 1993. But the Labour MP Chris Mullin said in Parliament that abandoning the inquiry became inevitable 'once it became clear that Sir John was unwilling to participate in a whitewash'; he said the decision would avoid 'embarrassment' for senior legal figures and police officers.

If anyone, Sir John May included, had known in November 1989 that the Guildford inquiry would be held in private, with its conclusions kept confidential for at least four years, the public would hardly have been reassured.

Even more disturbing, it became clear at an early stage that the police officers who interviewed the Guildford Four had no intention of giving evidence to Sir John May. Most disturbing of all, there was no way in which they could be compelled to testify. The Home Secretary had given Sir John May no powers whatsoever. Though few people realised it, his inquiry was purely informal; he could insist on nothing. How then was Sir John to find out what really happened?

Perhaps he was not meant to. Certainly when the Birmingham Six were released in 1991, no pretence was made of setting up an inquiry into the factual circumstances leading up to *their* conviction. Lord Runciman made it perfectly clear that this was not on the agenda for his Royal Commission on Criminal Justice.

So what should have been done? In his column in the *Financial Times*, the distinguished lawyer Sir Louis Blom-Cooper QC wondered whether the authorities should have gone ahead with a criminal prosecution in the first place. 'Criminal justice is a cumbersome and costly process, designed to punish the perpetrators of crime. It satisfies a proper public desire to control crime by way of focusing on defined criminal events, but its function involves only a limited exercise in determining individual criminal responsibility.' Sir Louis Blom-Cooper, who has chaired a number of public inquiries, suggested that an inquiry would have been more use than a prosecution. By the time a trial had taken place, the public would have heard all it wanted to know. 'And if the officers are acquitted,' he said, 'who would favour a rerun of the events which have been scrutinised by the jury?'

Writing in the summer of 1992, one cannot say what will become of the three Surrey detectives currently facing trial. But if they had been offered immunity from prosecution immediately and Sir John had started his inquiry straight away, we would probably have a much better idea by now of why the Guildford Four spent 15 years in prison for a crime they did not commit.

The Maguire family

In March 1976 Anne Maguire, her husband Patrick (known as 'Paddy'), her sons Patrick and Vincent, her brother Shaun Smyth, her husband's brother-in-law Patrick Conlon (known as 'Giuseppe') and a family friend called Patrick O'Neill were convicted of unlawfully possessing the explosive nitroglycerine in December 1974 (though not 'running a bomb factory' as the press often claimed). Mrs Maguire and her husband were each sentenced to 14 years in prison. The other adults were sentenced to 12 years (Patrick O'Neill's sentence was reduced to eight years on appeal). Vincent, then aged 17, was sentenced to five years, and Patrick, who was 14, to four years' detention. In 1980, Giuseppe Conlon died in custody. All the others served their sentences and were released. Mrs Maguire, who had been on bail awaiting her trial, was the last to be freed in February 1985.

Giuseppe Conlon had a son called Gerard who was one of the Guildford Four. Under questioning, he allegedly told the police that Anne Maguire, his aunt, was the person who had shown him how to make bombs at her home in London. That was why the police went to her house in the first place, two months after the Guildford bombings. Though no explosives were ever found, and there was no evidence of what the family were supposed to have done with them, the Crown alleged that the people arrested in the house had been moving or disposing of nitroglycerine. Tests were said to have detected minute traces of explosives on their hands (or, in Mrs Maguire's case, on her gloves). The Maguire family always maintained their innocence.

The freeing of the Guildford Four led directly to the clearing of the Maguire family. Though in fact there was no overlap between the two cases, it was taken for granted in the public mind that the bombs which exploded at Guildford were somehow linked to Mrs Maguire and her family. At the same time as he was asked to investigate the Guildford case, Sir John May was also asked to inquire into what had happened to the Maguires. When it became clear in 1990 that there would be little progress in his investigations into the Guildford Four, Sir John decided to concentrate on the Maguires; there was no possibility of prejudicing any prosecution as their convictions depended on scientific evidence rather than disputed confessions.

The Home Office memorandum of January 1987 had dealt with the grounds on which the Maguires' convictions had been challenged. One of these was the possibility that the defendants could have been innocently contaminated with nitroglycerine — in effect, that they could have had traces of explosives on their hands without deliberately or knowingly handling a prohibited substance.

Home Office officials dismissed suggestions of innocent contamination in a paragraph which must have returned to haunt them. 'These points were all raised at the trial', they said. 'No one has been able to suggest how the suspects could have become innocently contaminated.'

This was not strictly true. In 1982, Home Office scientists had published a paper in the *Journal of Forensic Sciences* called 'Transfer of Nitroglycerine to Hands during Contact with Commercial Explosives'. At the Maguires' trial, scientists had said that traces of nitroglycerine under their nails showed that each male defendant must have been handling or kneading the explosives. But the paper published in 1982 (reporting experiments carried out as long ago as 1977) proved that the explosive could 'migrate' under the fingernails from traces on the hands without the explosive being kneaded.

Explaining his decision not to refer the Maguires' case to the Court of Appeal in January 1987, the Home Secretary, Douglas Hurd, said that none of the arguments had succeeded in challenging the scientific evidence. The scientific validity of the TLC test — used to detect explosives — 'had not been undermined'. The main argument used by campaigners — that the samples must have been accidentally or deliberately contaminated — was 'not supported by the evidence'.

A blanket of secrecy normally covers the process of decision-making within the government. But a small corner of that blanket was lifted when the Home Office outlined the steps leading up to Mr Hurd's statement. It was summarised by Mr David Clarke QC, counsel to the May inquiry, at a public hearing in September 1991.

Mr Clarke said that in December 1986, the Home Office Criminal Policy Department had advised the Home Secretary to take no further action on the Maguires' case. In particular, he was advised against setting up the sort of inquiry which was to lead to the Maguires' eventual acquittal. Doubts which had been expressed about the case were — in counsel's words — 'not sufficiently cogent to justify a step of this magnitude'. The Home Office argued that an inquiry would be 'a massive and complex undertaking and raise numerous difficulties'. It would also 'set an undesirable precedent'.

The Home Office Minister David Mellor remained satisfied that the scientific evidence against the Maguires was 'unshaken by any subsequent developments'. Two days later Mr Mellor and the Home Secretary Mr Hurd met officials from the Criminal Policy Department and the Home Office Forensic Science Service. To his credit Mr Hurd seemed to be looking for a respectable way out of the problem. Was there a body of reputable scientific opinion, he wondered, which would now argue that there were doubts about the accuracy of the tests used to detect explosives on the Maguires? No, said the Home Office forensic scientists. Would it be worth setting up a group of scientists to look at the question? No, said the Home Office scientists. Mr Hurd decided to sleep on it.

The next day the Home Office prepared a further memorandum arguing against setting up a committee of scientists. This advice was apparently accepted: no more was heard of the idea after the Home Secretary reached decisions on the Maguire case — along with the Guildford Four and Birmingham Six cases — at a meeting of Ministers and officials shortly before his statement in January 1987.

It is worth looking a little more closely at the reasons of the Home Office for rejecting a committee of scientists. In summary: nobody had called for it; it would look as if the Home Office had doubts about the convictions; there was nothing wrong with the test used; but a committee was nevertheless bound to express surprise that no confirmatory test had been carried out. Most remarkable of all was the argument that a scientists' committee would amount to an attempt by the Home Office to unearth new evidence — that was not the government's function. But that was precisely what the Home Office did when it appointed Sir John May to investigate the Maguires' case; new scientific tests commissioned by the May inquiry were to lead directly to their acquittal.

Those tests were carried out in April 1990 by Professor Duncan Thorburn Burns, an analytical chemist. He decided to use a towel as a possible source of contamination because (not surprisingly) members of the Maguire family had said in evidence that they had washed and dried their hands on a towel in their bathroom. Professor Thorburn Burns handled a stick of explosives containing nitroglycerine. He then washed his hands and dried them on a clean towel which was subsequently used by others in the laboratory. The tests proved that significant amounts of nitroglycerine could be picked up from a contaminated towel, and smaller traces could be obtained by handling other contaminated household objects. This contradicted the evidence of scientists at the Maguires' trial, although it did imply that someone who had visited their home recently had been in contact with explosives.

Faced with this evidence, the Director of Public Prosecutions conceded in June 1990 that the convictions were unsafe and unsatisfactory on the ground of innocent contamination (but no other ground). Without waiting to hear what the courts might make of this, the Home Secretary David Waddington took the first opportunity to tell MPs what he thought the judges ought to do: 'I should say straight away that I don't believe the convictions can be allowed to stand', he said.

Quite apart from the question of innocent contamination, there were other aspects of the case which in Sir John May's view made the Maguires' convictions unsound. In his interim report published in July 1990, he concluded that a different explosive (called PETN) would have produced the same positive TLC test results. This in itself would not have helped the Maguires a great deal, but it was something that government scientists had failed to disclose; had the jury known this, Sir John said they would have viewed the scientists' evidence very differently. Prosecution lawyers were also criticised for their failure to let the defence team see the scientists' notebooks. Sir John believed that if the prosecution had 'been more open-minded to disclosure of the scientists' notebooks' it was 'very possible that events would have taken a different turn'.

Sir John had no hesitation in criticising men who until recently had been his close judicial colleagues. He said that in 1976 the trial judge Mr Justice Donaldson (later Lord Donaldson of Lymington, Master of the Rolls) had been wrong in directing the jury that they might ignore the evidence on the other explosive, PETN. Moreover he believed the Court of Appeal in 1977 (Lord Justice Roskill, Lord Justice Waller and Mr Justice Ackner) had 'erred in upholding the judge's directions'. Sir John May concluded that 'the whole scientific basis on which the prosecution was founded was in truth so vitiated that on this basis alone the Court of Appeal should be invited to set aside their convictions'.

After receiving this impressive and fearless report, it was not surprising that the Home Secretary David Waddington immediately referred the case to the Court of Appeal. The hearing began in May 1991 before Lords Justices Stuart-Smith, Mann and McCowan; a lengthy reserved judgment was delivered the following month.

All the Maguires were cleared. That included the late Giuseppe Conlon: the court decided, for the first time, that in a reference by the Home Secretary it had the power to acquit someone who was no longer alive. The acquittals were expected: the court could hardly have decided otherwise when Sir John May, the DPP and the Home Secretary had all said the convictions were no longer safe. But the court's reasons came as a bitter disappointment to the Maguires.

The first ground of appeal was that government scientists had misled or lied to the court at the original trial: the Court of Appeal said this claim had not been made out. The second ground was that the scientists had not disclosed important test results to the defence: the Court of Appeal found there had been a material irregularity in respect of some of the tests but no miscarriage of justice had occurred as a result. The third ground involved the admissibility of certain evidence: the Court of Appeal said this point had already been decided against the Maguires. The fourth ground was the possibility of innocent contamination from a towel — the only ground accepted by the Crown. The judges said it would be 'convenient to consider this ground at a later stage in the judgment'. The fifth ground was that the TLC test could not distinguish between nitroglycerine and the explosive PETN: this was rejected on the basis that the explosive must have been nitroglycerine. The sixth ground was that the Crown could not prove (as alleged) that the Maguires had been handling nitroglycerine: this too was rejected on the basis that neither side was suggesting it could have been PETN.

Finally the court returned to the issue of innocent contamination. Government scientists had said the Maguires must have been kneading or handling the explosives. But Professor Thornburn Burns had shown that substantial quantities can be transferred to the hands from a towel. The court accepted that evidence. 'It is possible,' said the court, 'that those whose hands were contaminated by nitroglycerine were innocently contaminated by contact with the towel. This itself must have been contaminated by one or more persons drying their hands on it. . . . The evidence does not enable us to conclude who the person or persons were who so contaminated the towel.'

The judges concluded: '. . . on the ground that the possibility of innocent contamination cannot be excluded and on this ground alone, we think that the convictions of all of the appellants are unsafe and unsatisfactory and the appeals are allowed and the convictions quashed.'

It was hardly the vindication and apology the Maguires had hoped for: indeed Gerard Conlon said it was 'the most evil judgment that had ever been handed down'. The family were innocent in the eyes of the law but apparently guilty in the eyes of the judges: at least one of them still stood accused at worst of handling nitroglycerine and at best of letting somebody into their house who had been in contact with explosives.

'There never were any explosives in my house', said Mrs Maguire after the judgment. And the Birmingham Six campaigner Chris Mullen MP scorned the 'magic towel' theory: 'No one can say where it came from, no one can produce it — a towel that somehow contaminated six or seven people in the house, and even contaminated a pair of rubber gloves and got under the finernails of somebody.'

It was a hollow victory for the Maguires. In newspapers the next day the Court of Appeal was accused of a grudging inability to admit mistakes, of damage limitation. The Maguire family pinned their hopes on Sir John May, who was planning to examine the possibility that the scientific tests which had convicted them had been contaminated in the laboratory. His findings would be passed on to the Royal Commission, of which he was a member. In addition, the House of Lords announced in January 1992 that it was to hold an inquiry into forensic science. A committee, to be chaired by the distinguished chemist, Lord Dainton, would look in particular at the question of innocent contamination.

The Birmingham Six

In August 1985, Hugh Callaghan, Patrick Hill, Gerry Hunter, Richard McIlkenny, Billy Power and Johnny Walker were convicted of the 21 murders arising from the bombing of two Birmingham pubs in 1974. All were sentenced to life imprisonment. The prosecution case rested mainly on confessions they had allegedly made to the police, together with scientific evidence which was said to prove that two of the men had handled nitroglycerine.

In January 1987 the Home Secretary referred the case back to the Court of Appeal. He gave two reasons: there was fresh scientific evidence casting doubt on the tests for nitroglycerine, and there had been allegations from a former policeman, Tom Clarke, that some of the men had been ill-treated while in police custody. But a year later all their appeals were dismissed.

Giving judgment in 1988 the Lord Chief Justice Lord Lane, sitting with Sir Stephen Brown and Lord Justice O'Connor, said that Mr Clarke was 'a most unconvincing witness'. The judges had no doubt that evidence 'suggesting his erstwhile colleagues in the West Midlands police force treated these applicants with brutality was false'. Other witnesses were also dismissed as lying or mistaken.

The court then dismissed claims that there had been a police conspiracy to fabricate evidence. Investigating officers from the Devon and Cornwall Police had found a document in the handwriting of former Detective Superintendent George Reade, who had been in charge of the West Midlands Police inquiry. The court said this document — which became known as the 'Reade schedule' — could not have amounted to a 'blueprint for perjury' as counsel for the men had claimed. It followed that their confessions, which the court had said were the true foundation of the prosecution's case, had not been undermined.

It was noted that in 1985 the Home Office scientist Dr Frank Skuse, who had given evidence at the trial, had 'accepted early retirement' (the court did not add that this had been as a result of 'limited efficiency'). However, the judges said in 1988 that nothing had emerged which caused them to doubt that the scientific evidence proved that one or more of the six had been in recent contact with explosives. Indeed, fresh evidence from another scientist, Dr Janet Drayton, had made the Court of Appeal 'sure that Hill's left hand is proven to have had nitroglycerine on it for which there is and can be no innocent explanation'.

The judges added that quite apart from the alleged confessions and the scientific evidence there was 'a wealth of evidence as to the surrounding circumstances . . . which by undesigned coincidence greatly strengthened the case' against the six men.

The Lord Chief Justice ended the court's judgment with remarks which were to become notorious. 'As has happened before in references by the Home Secretary to this court under section 17 of the Criminal Appeal Act 1968,' said Lord Lane, 'the longer this hearing has gone on the more convinced this court has become that the verdict of the jury was correct. We have no doubt that these convictions were both safe and satisfactory.'

Not only was Lord Lane saying Douglas Hurd had been wrong to send this case to the Court of Appeal, he was suggesting that the Home Office was too ready to refer other hopeless cases.

However, in 1990 a different Home Secretary, David Waddington, referred the case back to the Court of Appeal. He announced he was acting in the light of new information discovered by the Devon and Cornwall Police. Electrostatic document analysis had suggested that notes of a police

interview with Richard McIlkenny had not been recorded contemporaneously, as West Midlands detectives had claimed in court.

A month before the appeal hearing started the Crown announced that it
would no longer be relying on the scientific tests which were said to have
detected traces of explosives. Three weeks later the Crown went further and
conceded that the police evidence was no longer reliable either. Since the
remaining circumstantial evidence was not by itself enough to keep the men
in prison, counsel for the Director of Public Prosecutions Sir Allan Green
took the bold step of telling the Court of Appeal that he was no longer
seeking to sustain the men's convictions.

Although the outcome was by then in little doubt, the Court of Appeal
decided it should hear the evidence in public and decide the appeals in the
normal way. At the end of March 1991 Lords Justices Lloyd, Mustill and
Farquharson gave their reasons for allowing the appeals.

First, as the Crown had conceded, Dr Skuse's evidence could no longer be
relied on. Prompted by what Sir John May's team had discovered about the
Maguires' case, Home Office scientists had reviewed the explosives tests and
discovered that soap or detergent used to wash laboratory dishes could
produce the same results as nitroglycerine. They had also looked again at Dr
Drayton's more sophisticated experiments and found evidence, which she
now accepted, that other substances might have produced the same readings:
it appeared that she might have got a positive test result from anyone who
smoked cigarettes! That effectively disposed of the scientific evidence.

Turning to the alleged confessions, the court noted that the six were no
longer relying on the accusations of police brutality which had formed the
basis of their appeal in 1987. Instead, attention turned to alleged police
interviews with Richard McIlkenny.

Detective Sergeant Colin Morris and Detective Constable Terence
Woodwiss of the West Midlands police testified at the original trial that
they interviewed Mr McIlkenny on Friday, 22 November 1974, the day
after the bombings. Superintendent Reade said he was there. All three
swore that a contemporaneous note was taken. Mr McIlkenny always
denied that the interview had ever taken place.

In 1988, the Court of Appeal had considered Richard McIlkenny's
assertion that the contemporaneous note was a 'fraudulent concoction'. If
it was a concoction, said the judges, it was a very stupid one, because he
was quoted as claiming he had not known the other men until he met them
on the train. Moreover the alleged interview contained no admissions. The
court was quite convinced in 1988 it knew who was telling the truth:
'McIlkenny's assertion that he was not interviewed by the West Midlands
officers on the Friday is plainly unacceptable.'

But by the time of the second appeal the court had the benefit of electrostatic document analysis — the ESDA test. That, said the court in 1991, appeared to show that the note of the interview with Mr McIlkenny 'could not have been contemporaneous'. When questioned by the Devon and Cornwall police, Superintendent Reade could offer no acceptable explanation of the ESDA findings. Sergeant Morris and Constable Woodwiss declined to answer questions on the advice of their solicitors.

Sergeant Morris and Constable Woodwiss had also signed notes of an interview which they said Mr McIlkenny gave the following day, 23 November, in Birmingham. Detective Constable Rex Langford added his name as a witness. The Court of Appeal said that 'on any view the second interview could not have been noted contemporaneously, as the officers insisted'.

The court then turned to a discrepancy in the so-called Reade schedule. 'In the absence of any explanation from Superintendent Reade,' said the judges, 'it must cast additional doubt on the honesty and reliability of his evidence.'

In 1988 the judges said: 'We are certain that Mr Reade did not seek to deceive the court'. In 1991 they said: 'On the evidence now before us, Superintendent Reade deceived the court'.

The Court of Appeal concluded its 1991 judgment by saying that 'in the light of the fresh scientific evidence, which at least throws grave doubt on Dr Skuse's evidence, if it does not destroy it altogether, these convictions are both unsafe and unsatisfactory. If we put the scientific evidence on one side, the fresh investigation carried out by the Devon and Cornwall Constabulary renders the police evidence at the trial so unreliable that again we would say the convictions are both unsafe and unsatisfactory. Adding the two together, our conclusion was inevitable. It was for these reasons that we allowed the appeals.'

In November 1991 four retired detectives appeared in the dock at Bow Street magistrates' court charged with conspiracy to pervert the course of justice and perjury. They were George Reade, Colin Morris, Terence Woodwiss and Rex Langford. At the end of May 1992, Mr Reade, Mr Morris and Mr Woodwiss were committed for trial at the Old Bailey. Mr Langford was cleared by the magistrate of all charges. Reporting restrictions were not lifted. It was thought that the trial would not take place before the summer of 1993.

Throughout the drama of the Birmingham Six, there was a part to be played by almost every actor in the criminal justice system. The police of course were first on the scene, with officers from the West Midlands force interviewing suspects in the way they no doubt thought fit. The second act unfolded when the forensic science service carried out tests on the men in custody. That convinced the police that they had caught the bombers. But most disturbing of all, the third vehicle of the criminal justice system to fail the Birmingham Six was the appeal system itself — the three judges who dismissed their appeal in 1988.

Why did the Court of Appeal remain convinced in 1988 that the jury's verdict was correct? The judges genuinely believed in the confession evidence, the scientific evidence and important circumstantial evidence. But that apparently made them reluctant to accept the alleged police conspiracy put forward by the six men. In 1988 the judges did not have the latest evidence from explosives experts, or new scientific tests suggesting that police notes had been altered. But their devotion to the jury system made them rely too heavily on the original verdict. And a jury is only as good as the evidence it is given.

This view (first broadcast in 1991) received support from the Bar Council's evidence to the Royal Commission on Criminal Justice (published in January 1992). Speaking with remarkable frankness, the submission said that for the past 25 years, it had been the general belief of the criminal Bar that the Court of Appeal (Criminal Division) had been 'insufficiently disposed' to allow appeals against conviction on their legal merits. 'The accusation of "intellectual dishonesty" is frequently and seriously made by members of the Bar', it said. 'There is a tendency, to which many judges who have been advocates seem to become prone, to believe that juries do not convict those who are innocent.'

Ironically, the three parts of the system that failed the Birmingham Six in 1988 were to come to their rescue in 1991. The men owed their freedom to new police inquiries, new scientific tests and above all a more open-minded approach by the Court of Appeal. But none of that would have happened without a sustained campaign by journalists, lawyers and the men's supporters. Victory, though sweet, had come more than 16 years too late.

1991 will be remembered as the year the Birmingham Six were freed. But three more miscarriages of justice (one alleged, two confirmed) were to trouble the Home Secretary before the year was out.

Judith Ward

In September 1991 the then Home Secretary, Kenneth Baker, referred the case of Judith Ward to the Court of Appeal. She was given a life sentence in 1974 for offences including the murder of 12 people who died when a bomb exploded in a coach on the M62 motorway. She never appealed against her conviction. During her trial she made admissions and confessions, some of which could be shown to be clearly not true. Part of the scientific evidence against Judith Ward was given by Dr Frank Skuse, the Home Office forensic scientist who also gave evidence against the Birmingham Six. After his evidence in that case was declared unreliable, the Home Office started reviewing other cases in which he had been involved. Judith Ward's newly appointed solicitor, the tenacious Mrs Gareth Peirce, had been making representations to the Home Office in the meantime, but the Home Secretary announced that this was the first time the Home Office had reviewed a case on its own initiative. Officials pointed out that this showed a new approach to alleged miscarriages of justice, and indeed taking the initiative was an approach which the Home Office had effectively ruled out less than five years earlier.

Miss Ward's appeal opened in May 1992. On the fifth day of the hearing, when it became inevitable that she would be cleared, Judith Ward was freed on bail. She had spent 18 years in prison for crimes she did not commit.

Giving judgment in June 1992, Lords Justices Glidewell, Nolan and Steyn said they greatly regretted that a 'grave miscarriage of justice' had occurred. This was because:

> in failing to disclose evidence [to the defence] . . . one or more members of the West Yorkshire police, the scientists who gave evidence at the trial, and some of those members of the staff of the DPP and counsel who advised them . . . failed to carry out . . . their basic duty to seek to ensure a trial which is fair to both the prosecution . . . and the accused.

The judges said three senior scientists from the Royal Armament Research and Development Establishment, Douglas Higgs, George Berryman, and the late Walter Elliott, 'took the law into their own hands and concealed from the prosecution, the defence and the court, matters which might have changed the course of the trial'. Three weeks later the DPP, Barbara Mills QC, asked the police to investigate the role of Mr Higgs and Mr Berryman. She added that there were no grounds for action against anyone else involved in the case — including one of her own senior lawyers. It was announced that the two scientists would be questioned by the West Yorkshire police. That was the force which was criticised by the Court of Appeal for not disclosing evidence which would have helped clear Judith Ward.

The Tottenham Three

Also in September 1991 Mr Baker referred to the Court of Appeal the cases of Winston Silcott and Mark Braithwaite, convicted of murdering PC

Keith Blakelock in 1985 during rioting at the Broadwater Farm estate in North London. The case of their co-defendant, Engin Raghip, was referred to the Court of Appeal nearly a year earlier, in December 1990.

Winston Silcott had been refused leave to appeal when he first applied in 1988. The Lord Chief Justice, Lord Lane, was reported to have said his conviction was based on 'a solid foundation of evidence', and there was no need for the Crown to reply to his lawyers' submissions.

The new evidence in Winston Silcott's case was obtained by the Essex Police at Mr Baker's request. They arranged for scientific tests on police notes. Electrostatic document analysis — the 'ESDA' test — was to satisfy the Court of Appeal that vital parts of the notes were inserted after other parts of the interview were completed. Detective Chief Superintendent Graham Melvin, who interrogated Winston Silcott, was suspended from duty on the day the case was referred to the Court of Appeal.

In its judgment delivered in December 1991, the Court of Appeal found that notes of the police interview with Winston Silcott were not contemporaneous, as the officers had claimed. Since the foundation of the Crown's case had been destroyed and there was no other evidence against him, Mr Silcott was acquitted.

The court went on to say that if the trial judge had known of Chief Superintendent Melvin's alleged conduct, the other cases would have been withdrawn from the jury. As a result, Engin Raghip and Mark Braithwaite were also cleared.

Quite apart from any question of police misconduct, the Court of Appeal held that Mr Raghip was entitled to an acquittal on another ground. Before the trial had started, a consultant psychiatrist had found Engin Raghip 'of probably average intelligence'. A defence psychologist agreed, adding that his degree of suggestibility was average for a normal individual. But further tests carried out before the appeal hearing in 1988 showed that in fact Mr Raghip was of low intelligence and abnormally suggestible under the pressure of, say, a police interview. When Mr Raghip sought leave to appeal in 1988, his counsel tried to get the court to hear that new evidence, arguing that the jury would have been told about it if it had been available at the trial. However, the Lord Chief Justice said there had been no need to give the jury expert psychiatric evidence of Mr Raghip's mental condition at the time he was interviewed by the police. The court said it would not have made any difference to the verdict: 'The jury were in as good a position as the psychologist, if not better, to judge how amenable this young man was to suggestions'.

But in 1991 Lord Justice Farquharson, Mr Justice Alliott and Mr Justice Cresswell disagreed. The Court of Appeal said Lord Lane had been 'endorsing the "judge for yourself" approach in respect of the jury which [the Court of Appeal had held in an unreported case six months earlier] was the wrong approach for the judge'.

The earlier case was not cited to Lord Lane's court. But even if the Lord Chief Justice did not know what a court headed by his own deputy had decided on a similar point earlier in 1988, he must surely have appreciated that (in the words of the Court of Appeal) it had by then become 'the regular practice of judges to admit psychiatric or psychosocial evidence when considering submissions under the Police and Criminal Evidence Act'.

When it became clear that the Tottenham Three were to be cleared, the Home Secretary, Kenneth Baker, took some comfort from the fact that the case predated the Police and Criminal Evidence Act 1984, which came into effect at the start of 1986. Indeed, in September 1991 the Home Office told reporters that 'a repetition of the circumstances of recent miscarriage of justice cases where written interview evidence has been subsequently questioned therefore seems unlikely in the future'.

But when Winston Silcott was questioned in October 1985, three months before the Act came into effect, the Metropolitan Police had begun a 'dry run' — they were already observing the Act's codes of practice as if they were law. That policy was not suspended for the Broadwater Farm inquiry, although senior officers had been told they would not face disciplinary proceedings if they failed to observe the Act. Moreover, Mark Braithwaite was not arrested until February 1986, when the new law had been in force for more than a month. Yet he was denied the access to legal advice guaranteed by the Act. At the appeal in 1991 this was put forward as a new ground of appeal. In the light of what the judges had learned about Mr Melvin, they had no hesitation in granting Mr Braithwaite's appeal on that ground too. However, if the Act had worked as intended, he would never have been convicted.

The three judges ended their judgment with the first apology the court has made in overturning a recent miscarriage of justice. 'In allowing these appeals,' said Lord Justice Farquharson, 'we wish to express our profound regret that [the men] have suffered as a result of the shortcomings of the criminal process. No system of trials is proof against perjury, but this will be of little consolation to its victims.'

A week later the Crown Prosecution Service took out summonses against Detective Chief Superintendent Melvin alleging perjury and conspiracy to pervert the course of justice. Former Detective Inspector Maxwell Dingle, Mr Melvin's assistant on the Broadwater Farm case, was also accused of conspiring to pervert the course of justice. Mr Melvin made it clear that he would 'vigorously contest' the charges. The two men made their first appearance in the dock at Bow Street magistrates' court in January 1992. They were sent for trial in July 1992.

The Carl Bridgewater case

In October 1991, the Home Secretary asked for a new police investigation into the murder of Carl Bridgewater, the 13-year-old newspaper boy who was shot dead in 1978 when he disturbed burglars at a farm in Staffordshire. The following year, Michael Hickey, his cousin Vincent Hickey, and James Robinson were convicted of Carl's murder. A fourth man, Patrick Molloy, was convicted of manslaughter: he died in 1981. The case had been referred back to the Court of Appeal in 1987, but the convictions were upheld by the court in 1989.

The main evidence against the three men was Patrick Molloy's confession, which he subsequently retracted after claiming it had been beaten out of him. It was recorded by officers from the West Midlands Serious Crime Squad, which was later to be disbanded. The officer who took his confession was disciplined after allegations that statements in another case had been fabricated; he resigned on health grounds in 1990. A psychologist who examined Patrick Molloy's statement said there was less than one chance in a million that it was given in the circumstances described by the police.

The Staffordshire police asked officers from Merseyside to mount an inquiry, the fifth there had been into the original investigation. The Home Secretary made it clear that he would decide whether to refer this case back to the Court of Appeal after he had received the police report.

The Royal Commission

The government's response to the freeing of the Guildford Four was to set up the inquiry chaired by Sir John May. Cynics thought this was a way of buying time; if so, the price was rather higher by the time the Birmingham Six were cleared. But it would be wrong to be too cynical: by 1991 there was a clear feeling in government circles that fundamental reforms could no longer be avoided.

The appointment of Lord Runciman of Doxford to chair the Royal Commission on Criminal Justice was announced within minutes of the Birmingham Six walking free. From then on it was something of a public relations disaster. Lord Runciman, though otherwise the ideal person to chair a major inquiry of this type, appeared painfully shy in public and did nothing to reassure people that matters were now under control. Surrounding himself with officials who were equally frightened of the media, he delegated press inquiries to a junior Home Office press officer who was 'too busy' to return calls. On a personal level many of the Commission's members were approachable. But it went without saying that all the Commission's work was done in private. And the few 'photo opportunities' which did occur were thrown away by a Commission which clearly did not think it was under any obligation to restore public confidence during the two years or so it was intended to sit.

The Commission's terms of reference required it to examine the effectiveness of the criminal justice system of England and Wales in securing the conviction of the guilty and the acquittal of the innocent. In particular, it was to consider whether changes were needed in the conduct of police investigations and the extent to which they were controlled by senior officers; the role of the prosecutor and the extent to which he or she disclosed evidence to the defence; the role of expert witnesses and their relationship with the police; legal advice for defendants; the defendant's 'right to silence'; the possibility of giving courts an investigative role, particularly when faced with an uncorroborated confession; the role of the Court of Appeal in considering new evidence and the extent to which it should investigate allegations itself; and the arrangements for investigating alleged miscarriages of justice. The Commission drew up a list of 88 questions to which answers were invited.

Most of the submissions were in by the end of 1991 and members of the Commission spent much of their Christmas reading through them. Summaries were available, but the individual members of the Commission felt it right to read every word put in front of them. Although the Commission's recommendations will not be published before the summer of 1993, the submissions received may give some indication of what may end up in its final report.

Among the bodies which submitted evidence to the Royal Commission were the two government departments which appointed it. The Lord Chancellor's paper was purely factual, while the Home Secretary's submission looked more at the issues involved. It seemed a little odd that the Home Office should be calling on the Royal Commission to make recommendations back to the Home Office, but officials said they did not claim to have all the answers and it would be wrong to make changes piecemeal. On the whole, the Home Office confined itself to setting out the arguments for and against. But occasionally a view could be discerned. Also, officials clearly hoped that the Commission would give its backing to Home Office proposals which might otherwise be seen as an attack on civil liberties.

The Home Office evidence pointed out that somebody who is being questioned abut a serious fraud no longer has the right to silence, although anyone accused of murder or terrorism can refuse to answer questions. The Home Office suggested that in future all suspects could be questioned before trial by an examining magistrate: if they refuse to answer it would count against them.

Another suggestion which officials were keen to promote involved DNA profiling — genetic fingerprinting. This is seen as a valuable way of identifying suspects in rape or murder cases, but it is feared that guilty people may go free because the police have no power to force anyone to give a blood sample for testing. The Home Office thought it odd that blood could be taken from a drunken driver but not a suspected rapist. The police agreed.

In their own submission, the police also called for a more inquisitorial pre-trial procedure, although this would be followed by the familiar accusatorial trial. The three police representative bodies said the defendant's right to silence was an impediment to the search for truth: they believed the courts should be permitted to draw inferences from the defendant's refusal to mention a fact he relied on at the trial. In that way a person's silence could amount to corroboration. In any event the police thought that corroboration, though desirable, was not essential.

The police were also worried about being 'ambushed' in court. With minor exceptions, the defence are under no obligation to provide the prosecution with any details of the evidence they will use to rebut the prosecution case. The police said that meant the prosecution were at a disadvantage: advance disclosure by the defence would 'represent a move towards a criminal justice system based on openness and fairness'.

Advance disclosure by the prosecution was the subject of evidence from the then Attorney-General, Sir Patrick Mayhew. The government's senior law officer argued that new rules were needed setting out precisely how much should be disclosed: the present rules were now too vague. His view would be to give the defence an automatic right to see unused material held by the prosecutor; the defence would then have an additional right to material relevant to specific issues they had defined.

The Crown Prosecution Service said that despite all the changes since the pub bombing cases of the 1970s, there were 'still cases in which the rules governing police procedures are deliberately ignored and in which evidence is fabricated', and there were still cases 'in which improper investigative practices have occurred in an attempt to secure a conviction'. The CPS wanted the police to submit a much wider range of cases to them for advice before making a decision to charge the defendant. That would avoid cases being discontinued at a later stage, leading to frustration and annoyance all round. Strangely enough, the CPS cannot insist that further police inquiries are made once a charge has been brought. It argued that the DPP should in future have the power to order chief constables to make further inquiries. Turning to confessions, the CPS was against making corroboration compulsory, though new safeguards for the defendant should ensure less reliance was placed on confession evidence.

For many people the crucial question facing the Royal Commission was how to ensure innocent people could overturn wrongful convictions. The cases outlined earlier in this chapter show how difficult it was to challenge the jury's verdict, especially when leave to appeal had been refused. The Crown Prosecution Service was against creating a court of last resort to deal with alleged miscarriages of justice, but suggested instead that there should be a new court, under the Court of Appeal, to advise on the credibility of any fresh evidence. It would have specialised assessors and it could order new investigations.

The Law Society gave its support to the idea of an independent review body, made up of lawyers and lay people, which could arrange for cases to be reinvestigated and decide whether there was enough new evidence for the Court of Appeal to order a new trial before a jury. The defendant could appeal to the review body as soon as he had been convicted in the Crown Court; he would no longer have to ask the Court of Appeal for leave to challenge his conviction. Among the much wider grounds of appeal proposed by the Law Society would be poor legal advice by defence lawyers; witnesses not called at the trial; and insufficient disclosure by the prosecution. The Home Secretary would no longer have any part to play in the criminal justice system.

The Law Society also suggested, perhaps rather optimistically, that a continuous sound and video recording should be made of the police officer responsible for prisoners' custody at the police station. The aim would be to ensure that suspects were not persuaded into waiving their right to free legal advice. The solicitors' professional body also called for more 'ethical' interviewing by the police, aimed at fact-finding rather than confrontation. And defendants would keep the right to silence. But confessions would *not* have to be corroborated by other evidence.

The Law Society gave no support to the Continental idea of an inquisitorial system of justice. It said the present adversarial system was fairer because of the central role played by the independent defence lawyer. The barristers also believed that the adversarial system was more likely to achieve the right verdict and was more acceptable to those watching or taking part in the trial. But in complicated cases, they saw some merit in having a *juge d'instruction* — an examining magistrate — though this proposal was not developed in any detail.

The barristers also called for reform of the system of criminal appeals. To restore public confidence, the barristers called for an independent body with new powers to investigate alleged miscarriages of justice. It would refer cases back to the Court of Appeal if fresh evidence suggested the defendant had been wrongly convicted.

The barristers strongly supported keeping the existing right to silence. They were worried about the risks of false confessions and believed special rules were required for dealing with police evidence because of 'the danger that police officers may tell lies'. Police evidence, they suggested, should no longer be admissible unless there was some independent confirmation of it. But the Bar saw merit in the Scottish system of questioning a suspect before a judicial officer. The suspect would not have to answer questions but he would no longer be able to 'ambush' the prosecution in court; it could count against the defendant to give an answer at trial which he or she had failed to give at the initial hearing.

The Criminal Bar Association said that the admissibility of a confession should not depend on corroboration being available. And the London Criminal Courts Solicitors' Association agreed that uncorroborated confessions should not be ruled out automatically. They suggested the police should carry pocket tape recorders to record what was said before and after an arrest. And video cameras could be used where police raid premises to search for drugs or stolen property. The solicitors favoured an ombudsman to investigate alleged miscarriages of justice and a court of last resort to hear appeals.

The National Council for Civil Liberties — now known as Liberty — was also against adopting an inquisitorial system in England and Wales. Not surprisingly, it favoured keeping the right to silence. And its submission goes further than others in saying that 'it should not be possible to convict on confession evidence alone': independent corroboration would be needed.

One rather unusual question, posed by an individual member of the Royal Commission, was whether the dock should be abolished — as it has been in the United States. The Law Society said this was worth considering, so long as there was no risk of the defendant escaping and injuring somebody. The Bar said firmly that the dock should be abolished. 'Obviously some special arrangements will have to be made for those defendants who are security risks,' said the Bar, 'but those arrangements should not involve a dock'. When asked what they should involve, the Bar's spokesman said he had not yet thought about it.

The police saw no advantage in doing away with the dock. They said that prisoners in the United States (except, presumably, those on bail) are handcuffed to the chair and sometimes fitted with leg irons. Removing the dock would cost money and damage security. The Crown Prosecution Service agreed that the dock should be kept for security reasons: removing it might also undermine the 'seriousness and dignity of the court-room'.

In addition to inviting evidence from interested parties, the Royal Commission spent £40,000 on its own research programme. As well as academic studies, this included a major market research project: everyone — from the defendant to the judge — who was involved in any Crown Court trial held during two weeks in February 1992 was asked to complete a questionnaire.

It was against this background that Douglas Hurd — by then Foreign Secretary — decided to appear before Sir John May's inquiry in October 1991. Mr Hurd said, in effect, that without new evidence there would have been little point in referring the Maguires' case to the Court of Appeal in 1987. But he admitted that if he had appointed his own scientists to investigate the case in 1987, the injustice might have been remedied more quickly.

Mr Hurd then went on to make a damning condemnation of the criminal justice system: 'In this case and in other cases,' he said, 'the system and the way in which it was handled turned out to be inadequate for the purposes of justice'.

Mr Hurd's solution was equally radical. The Home Secretary, he now thought, should no longer decide whether a case should be reopened. Instead, that power should be given to an independent body, 'outside the political function'. The new tribunal would have the power to investigate alleged miscarriages of justice and the right to refer cases direct to the Court of Appeal.

Mr Hurd's proposals drew immediate support from the Bar Council, whose Chairman, Anthony Scrivener QC, said it was something he had been urging for some time. The government's response was to refer the idea to the Royal Commission, of which Sir John May is in any case a member.

The Royal Commission is expected to report in the summer of 1993. There will then be a period of consultation, and in due course the government will no doubt publish a White Paper setting out its proposals — perhaps early in 1994. A government Bill might be announced in the Queen's speech in November 1994; it would become law in the summer or autumn of 1995. Up to a year or more would be required to make regulations and retrain those affected: the reforms would therefore take effect late in 1996 or at the beginning of 1997. Only then can the system attempt to rebuild the public's shattered confidence.

January 1997 will mark the tenth anniversary of Douglas Hurd's decision to refer the case of the Birmingham Six back to the Court of Appeal. That was the first official acknowledgement that perhaps things were not as they should be. What has gone wrong with the criminal justice system is almost too dreadful to contemplate. The fervent hope must be that at least we get it right this time.

5

Sentencing: A Fresh Look at Aims and Objectives

Martin Wasik

Introduction

Sentencing is, of course, one of the key decision points in the criminal justice system. At this stage, the defendant has either admitted responsibility by pleading guilty to the charges or, if the trial was contested, has been convicted of the charges before lay or stipendiary magistrates or by a Crown Court judge and jury. The court now moves on to consider, and to pass, sentence. The procedure at sentencing is less formal and less clearly based upon a contest between prosecution and defence than the trial. Rules about the admissibility of evidence are relaxed. The judge, who during the trial has remained apart and somewhat aloof from proceedings, now assumes the central role in fixing the sentence. What is the framework for that decision?

Apart from laying down maximum sentences for each offence and prescribing the court's sentencing powers, which is done by Parliament through statute, it has been a long-standing characteristic of sentencing that the sentencer is left with a great deal of discretion in selecting the appropriate disposal for the offender. A view has grown up that sentencing is an area of law where statutory intervention is unhelpful and is one where the sentencer is best placed to make a judgment on the facts of the case. In order to inform that choice, the court will hear submissions from the defendant, or the defendant's advocate, in the plea in mitigation. This is an attempt to persuade the court to see the offender in the best possible light and to urge leniency upon the court. In many cases, particularly in the Crown Court, the sentencer will also receive a pre-sentence report prepared by a probation officer, which will give much more detailed information about the offender and seek to place the offending in its context. The report will also tell the court, where appropriate, what arrangements for punishment in the community the probation service can offer. More detailed information about the offender's past, particularly his previous record of offending, if any, will emerge from the police antecedents statement.

The court is prepared to listen to a wide range of matters relating to the commission of the offence, and the circumstances of the offender, which were not strictly relevant to the question of guilt or innocence. Matters which can influence the sentence include the context within which the offence arose; particular problems, such as financial or domestic difficulties, which were afflicting the defendant at the time the offence was committed; his motivation and perception of the offence; his remorse or lack of it. There are limits to the breadth of such an inquiry. The court should not be seeking to assess the general moral worth of the offender. Sometimes, though, events in the defendant's life quite unrelated to the offence have been taken into account by a court in forming a view about the person to be sentenced. According to Walker (1985, p. 50), 'Men have had prison terms shortened because they have fought well in a war, given a kidney to a sister, saved a child from drowning or started a youth club'. An example is *R* v *Reid* (1982) 4 Cr App R (S) 280.

Restating aims and objectives

What aims or objectives will the sentencer have in mind when selecting sentence? Sentencers themselves rarely seem inclined to discuss sentencing on anything but a practical case-by-case level, and rarely tend towards what may be called philosophical explanations of what they do. An unusual example of explicit reference by the Court of Appeal to sentencing theory may be found in *R* v *Sargeant* (1974) 60 Cr App R 74, where the court advocated retribution, deterrence, prevention and rehabilitation as being the four aims of sentencing, but without providing any explanation of how these aims might be reconciled. There has been a view that sentencing is an 'art' rather than a 'science', that it has to be absorbed through experience of doing it, rather than addressed by way of a set of principles capable of being set out and explained. This approach is now becoming outmoded, fortunately, and there is a greater willingness to consider the justification for particular sentencing policies and practices. Towards the end of this chapter I will deal with three specific sentencing issues which have proved troublesome to the courts over the years, but the main purpose of this chapter is to show how the solution to these and many other practical problems requires a clear understanding of sentencing theory. It is right to start, then, at a fairly high level of generality.

The first point to make is that sentencing is concerned with the imposition of State-authorised punishment upon that relatively small proportion of offenders who have been caught, prosecuted and convicted for their crimes (see Lacey 1988). The imposition of punishment by the State, depending upon its precise nature, will involve to one extent or another, the imposition of suffering upon offenders. Another way of expressing this is to say that sentences handed down by the court impose varying degrees of restriction of liberty upon offenders. The White Paper, *Crime, Justice and Protecting the Public* (Home Office 1990) puts it this way:

> Restrictions on liberty . . . become the connecting thread in a range of community penalties as well as custody. By matching the severity of the restrictions on liberty to the seriousness of the offence, the courts should find it easier to achieve consistency of approach in sentencing. (Home Office 1990, para. 4.5.)

Starting at the top of the range of punishments currently available to the courts in this country, imprisonment (or detention in a young offender institution for an offender under the age of 21) obviously imposes the most severe restriction upon liberty. Lesser, though still significant, restrictions are involved in the various community sentences. Curfew orders, which may be enforced by electronic monitoring, are a clear example. The offender is required to wear an electronic 'tag', which triggers an alarm if the offender fails to remain at a particular place, such as his home address, within periods of time specified in the order. Curfew orders are provided for in the Criminal Justice Act 1991 but, at the time of writing, it seems that the government may choose not to bring into force powers to enforce those orders by electronic monitoring. (See further Mair and Nee (1990).)

Community service restricts liberty by requiring the offender to give up a proportion of his or her leisure time to perform demanding unpaid work, on a specified project, for the benefit of the community. A probation order requires the offender to report to a probation officer at specified times, and keep the officer informed of any change of circumstances. This may seem a minimal restriction on liberty but, for an immature and disorganised individual it may impose a significant burden. Various conditions, more or less stringent, may be inserted into a probation order by the sentencer, requiring the offender to live at a specified address, such as a probation hostel, or to undergo treatment for a mental condition, or to attend a probation centre for practical advice or counselling, which forces the offender to address his or her antisocial behaviour. These requirements can be very demanding. The Criminal Justice Act 1991 extends further the variety of conditions which the sentencing court may insert into a probation order, including a requirement that the probationer undergo treatment for alcohol or drug dependency. In all cases the offender must consent to the making of a probation order.

Even financial penalties are restrictions on liberty, in the sense that the offender is being deprived of cash which he or she would have preferred to have spent on something else. For those on low incomes a fine can be a severe penalty, and sentencers are required to ensure that the offender's means are properly taken into account whenever a fine is imposed. The offender's ability to pay (disposable weekly income) forms part of the calculation of the unit fine to be imposed upon him: this means that the rich pay more and the poor pay less for commission of an identical offence: see the Criminal Justice Act 1991, s. 18; also Gibson (1990) and Moxon et al. (1990)).

Once it is agreed that sentencing involves the deliberate infliction of pain, in the sense of restriction of liberty, upon offenders, the second step in the discussion of sentencing philosophy, and sentencing policy, is to agree that this practice requires justification. How can the infliction of punishment by the courts upon individual offenders be justified? This is a question with which philosophers have grappled for many years (see the classic work by Hart (1968), upon which much of the subsequent literature builds). Broadly, two sets of ideas have emerged. They may be described as (a) the *reductivist* and (b) the *desert* approaches. They are outlined next.

The reductivist view is that the imposition of pain through punishment is justified whenever certain benefits are achieved by that punishment, and where those benefits outweigh the pain and make its imposition, on balance, worthwhile. This is the principle of utility, expounded by Bentham (1789). (For discussion see Smart and Williams (1973).) In particular, the imposition of punishment on the offender is designed to reduce the overall incidence of offending within society. The offender is used as an instrument by the court in an effort to achieve this effect. A number of distinct approaches shelter under the reductivist umbrella, and so the sentencer might impose a reductivist sentence by following one (or a mixture) of a number of different lines of thought. The first line is that the punishment will *deter the person sentenced* (individual deterrence), so that the person will desist from offending through fear of repetition of the penalty in future. The second line is that the punishment will *deter other like-minded people* (general deterrence). They will change their minds about offending when they see what penalty has been imposed upon an offender convicted of doing something similar. The third line is that by imposing a sentence of a particular type, such as a lengthy prison term, or a driving disqualification, on the offender, he will be *prevented from committing further offences* (incapacitation), at least for a limited period of time. The fourth line is that the sentence handed down by the court will *bring about a change of attitude* (reform) on the part of the offender, so that he will desist from offending in the future, not through fear of further punishment, but through a deeper realisation of the antisocial nature of offending.

These are all 'reductivist' theories. While it is helpful to draw distinctions between them, it will be apparent that a sentencer might, perfectly coherently, pursue more than one of these ends in the passing of a single sentence. What they have in common is the attempt, by the passing of sentence, to achieve a reductive impact upon the general level of offending in society. The reductivist objective is, in principle, empirically testable. It might be possible to demonstrate that a particular sentence has 'worked', in that it has had a particular net benefit in terms of the number of offences which were thereby prevented. In practice, however, such empirical claims are very hard to prove or disprove. It is extremely difficult to measure the impact of a particular sentencing decision, or a group of sentencing decisions.

Take, for example, general deterrence, which is that ground of reductivist theory which has probably held most sway over the mind of the English sentencer (see Walker (1985, ch. 7) and Beyleveld (1979)). If a sentencer imposes a markedly severe prison sentence for a house burglary, how can the reductive effect of that sentence be measured? Suppose that the official statistics for burglary record a downturn for that offence in the months following the decision. It would be tempting to assume that this downturn was the impact of the sentence. Such temptation should be resisted, however. For one thing, any such impact could not be measured by examining the official statistics of crime. These statistics relate only to offences which are reported to the police and are recorded by them. Unreported offending (a much larger figure) is not recorded. So, a decrease in reported house burglaries might conceal a real increase in burglaries (or vice versa). Even if it were possible to be sure that there had been a downturn in the real level of offending, it would still be dubious to assume that the sentencing decision had brought it about. The downturn may have been occasioned by some other factor, quite independent of sentencing, such as a change in police recording practices, the growth of neighbourhood watch schemes, an advertising campaign for home security, or simply a change in the 'fashion' of offending patterns. (On the problems of interpreting the official statistics of crime, see Walker (1985, pp. 57 et seq.).) In 1984 a special study was conducted by Farrington and Dowd (1986) to investigate why Nottinghamshire had the highest reported incidence of offences of violence against the person in the country. They found that this was due to unusually conscientious offence-recording practices by the Nottinghamshire police.

Further reflection reveals the lack of plausibility of most claims that sentencing has an impact upon the real level of offending. The argument presupposes that prospective house burglars make choices about committing burglary based, at least in part, upon their knowledge of current sentencing practice for burglary. This may be true in some cases and, certainly, there is an important element of rational choice in the selection of targets for house burglary, particularly by so-called professional offenders (Maguire 1982). A far more plausible general picture, however, is that most burglaries are committed by young men, often after drink, without much forward planning and with little or no speculation upon penalty levels. The criminological literature tells us that most young offenders tend to 'live for the moment', and rarely plan ahead or weigh the consequences of being caught against the excitement of breaking the law. (There are many theoretical and empirical studies. A pivotal account is Matza (1964).) In any event, a burglar sufficiently well-informed to have read the sentencing reports will also have read the criminological literature which tells him that the police detection and clear-up rate for burglary is less than 15 per cent. Penalty levels must become even less significant to offenders when they believe they have little chance of being caught.

There is, however, another point to be made about imposing a severe sentence for the house burglary. In *R v Mussell* [1991] 1 WLR 187, Lord Lane CJ commented that 'like any other kind of offence, dwelling-house burglaries vary in their seriousness . . . it is not always so serious that a non-custodial sentence cannot be justified'. In *R v Parry* (1990) 12 Cr App R (S) 69, 18 months' custody was reduced to nine months on appeal in respect of a single offence of burglary committed by an 18-year-old with no previous similar convictions. The house was ransacked while the occupants were out and a video recorder, camera, television, radio and tape deck, jewellery, coins and stamps were taken. In *R v Littler* (1990) 12 Cr App R (S) 143 an 18-year-old offender with no previous convictions had 12 months' custody reduced to 60 hours' community service for his part in the burglary of a house while the owners were away during which a microwave oven, two television sets, two music centres and jewellery were taken.

Suppose a Crown Court judge passes a sentence of five years' imprisonment upon an offender who has committed a relatively less serious
burglary, by reaching in through an open window and stealing a purse. In
order to 'clamp down' on house burglary which, according to the judge,
has reached epidemic proportions, the sentencer imposes the 'exemplary
sentence' of five years. The issue in such a case is not confined to the claims
and counter-claims about effectiveness. There is also the question of the
injustice of imposing a sentence upon an offender which is clearly more
than he deserves (in comparison with other sentenced cases) in an attempt
to achieve a general effect. The moral point is a strong one. Some people
may feel that even if the sentence's effectiveness could be demonstrated
empirically, and even if it could be shown that news of the sentence had
travelled fast and had prevented 10 house burglaries which otherwise
would have taken place, the five-year sentence should still be struck down
on the ground that it is unjust to the sentenced offender. (For discussion of
the moral arguments on deterrence see Walker (1985, ch. 7).)

We can say of those who adhere to reductivist sentencing strategies, such
as general deterrence, that they do so in the absence of convincing empirical
evidence and largely as an article of faith. The sentencer may feel that some
good can come through the sentences which are handed down; the world
can be made a better, safer place in which to live. To abandon reductivist
strategies may seem to make sentencing a pointless exercise. These views
may be very strongly held by individuals, and common sense may be
prayed in aid of them. Even those who are sceptical about deterrence would
concede that there is at least a grain of truth in the concept. Taken to
extremes, of course, deterrent policy would undoubtedly have an impact
upon offending patterns. If, for example, capital punishment were
tomorrow introduced as the penalty for illegal parking, it is likely that this
offence would decline sharply in popularity. But this still leaves the moral
problems. Can such a severe penalty ever be justified for a minor offence?
Surely not, since to impose it, or even to threaten it, would so distort our
sense of proportion between offence and punishment that it would leave no
room for dealing appropriately with those many offences which are
properly regarded as much more serious than illegal parking. How is the
blackmailer, rapist or murderer to be dealt with if illegal parking attracts
capital punishment?

A second view can be set in contrast to the reductivist one. The desert
approach to sentencing (Von Hirsch 1976, 1986) emphasises the moral
requirement of maintaining a proper proportion between offence and
punishment. It states that punishment involves censuring the offender for
his wrongful behaviour. Thus the prime determinant of sentencing should

be to ensure that the punishment imposed is that which is deserved for the offence, having regard to the seriousness of the harm caused or risked by the offender and the degree of that offender's culpability. It should be understood that, in sharp contrast to the various reductivist approaches, desert principles do not require that sentencing practice should impinge upon overall crime levels. Although desert theorists would, of course, welcome any reduction in overall offending patterns, desert theory treats the sentencing of offenders as an issue quite distinct from tackling the roots of offending in the community. The view is that the crime problem 'out there' in society can and should be tackled by a combination of strategies, such as economic policy, social policy, housing policy, environmental design and education, but to only a very limited extent through sentencing practice.

Desert theory has, at its heart, proportionality between the seriousness of the offence and the severity of the penalty imposed (Von Hirsch 1986, part 3). This sounds a simple idea and, in some ways and in general terms, it is. But the working out of desert theory in the kind of rigorous and detailed way which is required in a complex criminal justice system, such as that in England and Wales, brings with it considerable difficulty. 'Seriousness' is an elusive idea. What makes one offence more serious than another? A good starting-point would be the kind of harm, and the amount of harm, occasioned to the victim. If the victim's life is taken that is clearly more serious than if the victim is injured but survives. That, in turn, is more serious than a case where the victim suffers only loss of property, or money, or is merely inconvenienced, or distressed, by the offence. Various empirical studies of the public's perception of the relative seriousness of various crimes display a fair degree of consensus. See, for example, Wolfgang (1976).

Intuitively, most of us would agree that robbery is a more serious offence than theft. Indeed, the legal definition of the two crimes tells us that robbery is an aggravated form of theft: theft with the use of force or fear. But further reflection reveals that not all robberies are more serious than all thefts. A bag snatch involving minimal force and the loss of little of value would be regarded by most of us as less serious than the theft of £1 million from a bank. Many existing criminal offences describe criminal conduct in very broad terms, and offences overlap with each other in terms of their seriousness. This makes it difficult to draw up a clear hierarchy of offences for desert purposes. What is needed, as a first step, is subdivision of existing offences (Thomas 1978; Tonry 1982). Theft could be divided into, say, four categories depending mainly on the amount stolen. Robbery could also perhaps be divided into four categories, depending on the amount stolen, and the degree of force used to obtain it. Then we could begin to address, in a systematic way, the relative seriousness of the offences. Desert theory forces us to think carefully about offence seriousness. (For the fullest attempt to devise such principles, see Von Hirsch and Jareborg 1991.)

Offence seriousness is on one side of the scale. On the other side is penalty severity. Again, intuitively, most of us would agree that five years' imprisonment is a more severe sentence than five months' imprisonment and, perhaps, that imprisonment is inherently more severe than a sentence of community service. But devising a scale of penalties in terms of severity is beset with difficulties just as acute as those of comparing the seriousness of offences. Penalties are very different. How can one compare imprisonment with a probation order or a fine? A useful starting-point is to gauge all the various sentences in terms of their relative impact upon the average offender, or perhaps the extent to which they impinge upon and restrict the average offender's liberty (Von Hirsch 1986, ch. 8). This kind of scaling has always been part of the sentencing system in England and Wales, and it formed the basis of the description of the various sentencing powers available to the courts, which was given above. It is referred to in the books as the sentencing 'tariff' reflecting, in a rather non-specific way, the desert-based view that more serious offences require more severe penalties (Thomas 1979).

The traditional picture of sentencing is more complex than this, however. First, there is ambiguity about the 'tariff'. Sometimes the term has been used to describe the idea that an offender should progress up the sentencing ladder in the event of offence repetition (Sparks 1971; Ashworth 1983, pp. 433–5). Thus a burglar who was dealt with by community service last time must expect to receive something more severe if he reoffends. This approach, however, has much more to do with reductivist ideas of deterring persistence than with desert principles. Secondly, many of the available sentences have not traditionally been regarded as punishments at all. They have been seen as instruments designed to achieve a reductivist effect. The probation order is a clear example. The probation order has traditionally not been regarded as occupying any particular place in the tariff. Indeed, until very recently it was not strictly in law a 'punishment' or a 'sentence' at all (Home Office 1986, ch. 6). It was an individualised measure, addressed to the offender's needs, rather than to the seriousness of the offence. Thus, a probation order might properly be imposed in a case of minor shoplifting, but where the social inquiry report revealed that the offender, a person reliant upon social security payments, was in need of guidance in budgeting his or her income. It might also properly be imposed (as so-called 'last chance' probation: CSP, D2.3(a); R v Bradley (1983) 5 Cr

App R (S) 363; *R* v *Adamson* (1988) 10 Cr App R (S) 305) in the case of an offender convicted of house burglary, who had 20 previous convictions for similar offences. On this occasion, the social inquiry report revealed a 'glimmer of hope' in the offender's life, a new relationship with a woman, probation being preferred to custody in the 'almost certainly forlorn hope' of breaking the cycle of reoffending. The strongly reductivist base for many of the community sentences, such as probation, has led probation officers to urge them upon sentencers in their social inquiry reports, as being 'alternatives' to custody, likely to produce a more beneficial individual effect (Willis 1986).

David Thomas, a leading authority on sentencing in England and Wales, has characterised sentencing decisions in the following way (Thomas 1979, chapter 2). The primary decision for the sentencer is whether to choose a tariff (desert) or an individualised (reductivist) sentence. The secondary decision is, if the first path is chosen, to select the correct sentence in the tariff and, if the second path is chosen, to select the individualised sentence which the sentencer expects will have the most beneficial effect. It will thus be seen that English sentencing practice has, at its root, the irreconcilable diversity of sentencing aims which has been described so far in this chapter.

The 1990 White Paper and the Criminal Justice Act 1991

As has been explained above, sentencing in England and Wales has been characterised by a lack of legislative guidance on fixing the form and length of sentence. Sentence choice has largely been left to sentencers, who have adopted an eclectic approach (Walker 1985, para. 8.40 et seq.), sentencing in accordance with no single guiding principle in mind. Pressure for reform of this position has come from several sources, but three influences may be singled out.

The first was the continuing escalation, through the 1970s and 1980s, of the custodial population, which rose to unprecedented levels. The apparent ineffectiveness of the Court of Appeal in persuading sentencers to send fewer offenders to custody, and for shorter periods of time, has at last persuaded the legislature that this objective has to be achieved by legislative reform to fetter the discretion of sentencers. (For a discussion of the escalating custodial population and various strategies for its reduction, see Rutherford (1986).) A source of much valuable material on the prison system in England and Wales is the Woolf Report (1991).

The main development in sentencing law in the 1980s was the introduction of statutory restrictions upon the imposition of custody on offenders aged under 21, introduced in the Criminal Justice Act 1982, s. 1 and revised by the Criminal Justice Act 1988, s. 123. Now that the Criminal Justice Act 1991 has come into force these provisions have been repealed and replaced with new criteria for justifying the imposition of custody both for young offenders and for adults. These developments are set out more fully in chapter 9 of this book. Suffice it to say here that, after an initial period of reluctance and uncertainty, sentencers have adapted themselves to the new legislative constraints (*Blackstone's Criminal Practice 1992*, E3). The striking reduction in the custodial population for this age group which has followed is explained, in part, by the success of this legislation. In future, we will look back on the 1982 legislation as a highly significant first step in meaningful legislative control over sentencing patterns.

The second influence has been the belated official recognition of the unacceptable degree of sentencing disparity which exists in England and Wales (Ashworth 1983, pp. 50–1 and 431–3). The existence of sentencing disparity, in the sense of unprincipled differences in sentencing outcome from court to court and from sentencer to sentencer, has been confirmed in numerous empirical studies. Most have been carried out in magistrates' courts (Tarling 1979; Moxon et al. 1985; Turner 1992). Much of this disparity is probably explained by differing bench norms, arrived at in isolation, without reference to neighbouring benches, and sustained by the views of court clerks and senior magistrates, who train and constrain newer magistrates in their sentencing practices (Henham 1990; Parker et al. 1989). There are fewer studies of Crown Court sentencing, but nobody doubts that disparity exists there, too. One reason for the lack of information about Crown Court sentencing has been the reluctance of the higher judiciary to submit its sentencing practices to outside scrutiny. (See Moxon (1988), though this study was not aimed at identifying disparity.) Studies of Crown Court disparity in specific areas of sentencing have been carried out by Walmsley and White (1979) and McConville and Baldwin (1982). A large-scale exploratory study of sentencing in the Crown Court was begun by Ashworth et al. (1984) but was halted at a preliminary stage by Lord Lane's opposition.

The magistracy is to be commended not only for its acceptance of the problem of disparity but its efforts to design sentencing 'starting-points' for the lower courts, in an attempt to counter it (see the Magistrates' Association's *List of Suggested Penalties for Road Traffic Offences* and their *Sentencing Guide for Criminal Offences (Other than Road Traffic)*).

Despite the efforts of some practitioners to claim that disparities merely reflect acceptable local variations, or that the alternative to disparity is 'slot-machine justice', it is quite clear that sentencing disparity is a fundamental problem of equity. At the root of sentencing disparity is the diversity of sentencing aims, discussed above. If sentencers pick and choose their approach from case to case, in accordance with their own predilections rather than agreed sentencing policy, that is a sure recipe for sentencing disparity and injustice.

Thirdly, there has been a widespread disillusionment with reductivist sentencing goals, particularly reform, which have manifestly failed to deliver on the promise they seemed to offer in the 1960s and 1970s. As we have seen, reductivist goals are somewhat amenable to empirical testing, and reform is perhaps the most accessible of those goals. A famous survey of a large number of rehabilitative programmes was carried out in 1976. Its conclusions have been widely, though somewhat inaccurately, summarised with the dictum that 'nothing works' (Martinson 1974, 1976). The evidence is carefully considered by Walker (1985, ch. 6). In fact, the survey found that rehabilitative programmes sometimes did 'work', by having a discernible impact upon the reconviction rates of those made subject to them, but often only for highly selected 'good-risk' offenders in rather specialised situations, and over rather short follow-up periods. Many previously reported studies were dismissed as being methodologically unsound. Certainly, no general reductivist effect could be demonstrated. As a result, and remarkably quickly, rehabilitation went out of fashion as a sentencing goal. Other reductivist goals have proved more resilient, perhaps because the empirical evidence has been more difficult to collate. (For a critique of the various reductivist goals see Von Hirsch (1986), ch. 1 and part 4.)

At around the same time, in the United States, there emerged other concerns about reductivist goals in sentencing, which prompted a resurgence of the principle of desert. The main concern was that, in the pursuit of reductivist goals, sentencers were imposing very long and often indeterminate custodial terms. Much of the decision-making over sentence length was being left to members of parole panels who had been thought to be better placed to judge the rehabilitative effect of the sentence (Von Hirsch 1976). The new desert movement was outraged at the injustice of incarcerating offenders for periods of time out of all proportion to the seriousness of the offence which they had committed. This injustice was compounded by the paucity of evidence that these sentencing programmes actually worked. Accordingly, in the United States from the mid-1970s onwards, there has been a significant shift towards legislative involvement in sentencing. Many States have introduced mandatory or presumptive sentencing guidelines, which reduce the sentencer's discretion very considerably (Tonry 1987). The best-known of these systems, such as that operating in the State of Minnesota, are desert-based. The discretionary powers of parole boards have been reduced and, in some States, parole has been abolished altogether.

In the wake of the American developments, and for similar reasons, many other countries have been rethinking their sentencing principles. There have been important developments in Canada (as part of a comprehensive review of the criminal code, see Government of Canada (1984), (1990)), Australia (Lovegrove 1992) and several European countries, notably Sweden (Von Hirsch and Jareborg 1989).

In the United Kingdom comparable changes were signalled by the government in the path-breaking White Paper, *Crime, Justice and Protecting the Public* (Home Office 1990), which was issued early in 1990 (Wasik and Von Hirsch 1990; Ashworth 1990). This document proposed a comprehensive set of reforms of sentencing and early release arrangements. The aim was to create 'a coherent framework for the use of financial, community and custodial punishments'. The White Paper urged that proportionality should be the guiding criterion for deciding the severity of sentence (paras 1.6, 2.2 and 2.3), and was sceptical about relying on deterrence as the basis for determining sentence.

The White Paper advocated the adoption of desert principles in the determination of the form and length of all these sentences. Within the new desert-based sentencing structure the courts would continue to decide upon the deserved severity of penalties for each particular type of offence, and would decide upon the weight to be attached to aggravating or mitigating circumstances in each case. The White Paper proposals thus differed from the more radical American sentencing guidelines models, where normally recommended sentence levels are set in advance by the legislature. Reductivist goals were given a much lesser role in the new scheme. The White Paper specifically played down the importance of deterrence reasoning in sentence selection and implicitly it relegated issues of reform to a subsidiary role within the community orders. Most of the proposals in the White Paper have found their way into the subsequent legislation, the Criminal Justice Act 1991, which came into force in October 1992.

The best way to understand the Act is as laying down a set of general guidelines for sentencing. There is no American-style sentencing grid, so that guidance is by general principles expressed in words rather than by numbers (Von Hirsch 1987). The Act deals with custodial sentences, community sentences, fines and discharges, which can be seen as occupying four distinct levels in a pyramid, with custodial sentencing at the top and discharges at the base (Ashworth 1992). Selection of the appropriate level for sentencing in this hierarchy is crucially dependent upon the seriousness of the offence of conviction. Offence seriousness determines into which sentencing 'box' the sentence will fit, and also at what level within that particular 'box'. Of course, offence seriousness has always been an important element in sentence decision-making but, as we have seen, other factors have sometimes been used by sentencers to override it. The importance of the Act lies in its conceptual framework, and its emphasis upon proportionality between offence seriousness and penalty severity. It can be taken from this that the reductivist approach to sentencing will henceforth be much less prominent in English sentencing practice, though it is so ingrained in traditional thinking that it is unlikely to disappear overnight. The statute makes the passing of a disproportionate sentence on reductivist grounds in most cases impermissible and unlawful. The background to this may be found in the White Paper, rather than in the Act itself. In a notable passage (para. 2.8), the government states its view that deterrence should no longer form a central plank of sentencing policy:

> Deterrence is a principle with much immediate appeal . . . . But much crime is committed on impulse, given the opportunity presented by an open window or unlocked door, and it is committed by offenders who live from moment to moment; their crimes are as impulsive as the rest of their feckless, sad or pathetic lives. It is unrealistic to construct sentencing arrangements on the assumption that most offenders will weigh up the possibilities in advance and base their conduct on rational calculation. Often they do not.

There is, however, an exceptional class of custodial sentencing in the Act, where desert principles are compromised. This applies where the offender has been convicted of a violent offence or a sexual offence (as defined in the Act). The White Paper advocated a different approach for such offenders, against whom the government believed there was a requirement of protection of the public which should override normal desert principles. In such cases the main effect will be that the sentencer may pass a sentence which is longer, perhaps substantially longer, than that which could be justified on desert grounds (Wasik and Taylor 1991, pp. 29–37). Objection may be made to the special sentencing arrangements for these offenders. Given the nature of their offences, they would properly be dealt with severely under the desert model. To impose additional punishment on the basis of their anticipated dangerousness is a reductivist strategy which is open to all the moral and empirical objections which were discussed above.

Some specific sentencing problems

I turn now to consider three problem areas in sentencing. These are issues which cause day-to-day problems in the courts. My contention is that these issues can only be properly addressed and dealt with in the context of a clear understanding of the competing principles addressed in this chapter. Sentencers take different approaches to these problems because they are wedded to different basic sentencing philosophies. It will be suggested that the decisive change made by the legislature in the Criminal Justice Act 1991, from reductivist to desert principles, means that sentencers must now adopt the solution to these problems which is most in conformity with desert.

The multiple offender

When the desert model was sketched out, above, it was assumed for those purposes that the relevant offender had been convicted of a single offence. Even then, it was suggested, there were various problems in gauging offence seriousness and fixing the appropriate penalty, but some ways forward were suggested. Matters are more complicated, however, in the common situation where the court is dealing with a multiple offender, someone convicted on this occasion of two, three or more offences. He may, in addition, admit the commission of other similar offences and ask for them to be taken into consideration on sentence. What does the multiple offender deserve? At first sight it seems that an offender convicted of four burglaries should receive a sentence four times as severe as that which he would have received for one burglary. Sentencing practice, however, has rarely embraced this view (Ashworth 1983, pp. 250–71). While the commission of four burglaries does receive a heavier sentence than the commission of one burglary, the sentence is by no means four times as severe. Insofar as it is possible to detect a pattern in what sentencers do in such cases, it seems that each further offence attracts a smaller incremental increase in sentence. The difference between one burglary and two is rather greater than that between four burglaries and five, which is greater than that between 14 burglaries and 15. Indeed, by the 15th burglary, the increment may be so small as to be incapable of discernment. This sentencing pattern is referred to in England as the 'totality principle', and it is applicable to fines as well as to custodial sentences (see *Blackstone's Criminal Practice 1992*, E1.19). Examples are *R v Bocskei* (1970) 54 Cr App R 519 (custody) and *R v Chelmsford Crown Court, ex parte Birchall* (1989) 11 Cr App R (S) 510 (fines). When fining in respect of a number of offences the sentencer must review the total sentence and ensure that it remains proportional to the totality of the offending, as well as being within the capacity of the offender to pay.

The totality principle is not peculiar to England; it may be seen in other jurisdictions. What rationale, if any, underlies it?

Certainly, it is difficult to defend on a reductivist view. Persistent offending suggests the need for much heavier 'additive' sanctions, so as to effect deterrence or to incapacitate the offender. On a utilitarian view the erosion of sentencing differentials for the commission of a large number of offences is misconceived, since the deterrent effect of the threatened sentence is weakened with each repetition. If there is no discernible difference between the sentence for 14 burglaries and for 15 burglaries, then there is no disincentive for committing the 15th. Indeed, since the sanction failed to deter the offender on the second occasion, it would be coherent to argue on this view that each repetition should bring a greater, rather than lesser, incremental increase with each new offence. Some justification for the existing practice of the courts may, however, be found within the desert approach. The argument is as follows. If the desert framework is designed to reflect a proportionality between offence and penalty, and if we assume that the normal sentence for a house burglary is x months in custody, to impose a sentence of $14x$ months on a person who stands convicted of 14 burglaries would greatly distort the sense of proportion between the offence scale and the penalty scale. A sentence of $14x$ months would be a sentence appropriate for the commission of a serious offence of violence against the person; to impose it for burglary, even repetitious burglary, is wrong (Von Hirsch 1986, part 2).

What does the Criminal Justice Act 1991 have to say about the multiple offender? There are two relevant provisions. The first applies to the decision which the sentencer must make about the appropriate sentencing 'box'. As we have seen, this is crucially determined, in the Act, by offence seriousness. Section 1(2)(a) of the Act states that the sentencer may impose custody where:

> the offence, or the combination of the offence and one other offence associated with it, was so serious that only such a sentence can be justified for the offence.

It will be seen from this that the sentencer, when making the choice between a custodial sentence and a community sentence, can have regard to *up to two* of the offences of which the offender now stands convicted, or has asked the court to take into consideration. Parliament's choice of *two* offences is a compromise. To have permitted the sentencer to impose custody only if any *one* of the offences was serious enough to require custody would have paid no regard at all to the fact that the court is sentencing a multiple offender. Before the 1991 Act, the Criminal Justice Act 1982, s. 1(4A)(c) (in relation to offenders under 21), required the sentencer to consider whether any single offence was so serious that a non-custodial penalty could not be justified. The law was so established by the Court of Appeal in *R* v *Roberts* (1987) 9 Cr App R (S) 152, a case followed, not without reluctance, in *R* v *Davison* (1989) 11 Cr App R (S) 570, *R* v *Scott* (1990) 12 Cr App R (S) 23 and *R* v *Keane* (1990) 12 Cr App R (S) 132.

On the other hand, to allow the sentencer simply to aggregate all the offences of a multiple offender might mean that a petty persistent offender would receive custody merely by virtue of repetition, a position which is not compatible with desert principles.

The second provision in the Act which deals with the multiple offender question relates to the length of the sentence. Suppose that the sentencer has applied the criterion in s. 1(2)(a) and has decided that custody is justified. How long shall the custody be? Section 2(2)(a) says that it shall be

for such term (not exceeding the permitted maximum) as in the opinion of the court is commensurate with the seriousness of the offence, or the combination of the offence and other offences associated with it.

It seems odd, on the face of it, that the sentencer may have regard only to two offences when making the first decision, but may have regard to the totality of the offences when making the second decision. Before the 1991 Act, the Criminal Justice Act 1982, s. 1(4)(c) (in relation to offenders under 21), permitted the sentencer to take account of the totality of the offending when fixing sentence length (*R* v *Mussell* (1990) 12 Cr App R (S) 607).

There is a danger that allowing the sentencer to aggregate the offences when fixing sentence length will result in a sentence disproportionate to the nature of the offending. In an attempt to avoid this, and to preserve proportionality, s. 28(2)(b) of the Act declares that nothing 'shall prevent a court . . . in the case of an offender who is convicted of one or more other offences, from mitigating his sentence by applying any rule of law as to the totality of sentences'. This seems to restate, in a rather cumbersome manner, the common law totality rule, referred to above.

The criminal record

Of what relevance to the sentencing decision is the defendant's previous criminal record? If two offenders stand convicted of similar house burglaries, what difference, if any, in their respective sentences is appropriate to take account of the fact that one is a first offender and the other has 10 previous convictions for house burglary? It is difficult to be clear about existing sentencing practice. In most cases the sentencer will allow a 'discount' from the tariff sentence in the light of the offender's clean, or nearly clean, record. There are some offences, however, particularly very serious ones, which are regarded as being inappropriate for mitigation on this ground. For the repeat offender, however, successive sentences tend to increase in severity, but it is hard to discern a coherent principle at work. The increase is intuitive and the rationale underlying it, though a frequently encountered issue, is hardly ever discussed in sentencing cases (Wasik 1987).

This problem is similar, but not identical, to that of the multiple offender. The reductivist argument for increasing sentence to take account of criminal record is easy to understand. While, as was explained above, our ability to predict the future criminal behaviour of people is very limited and is prone to serious error, it is well-known that the best available predictor of future criminal conduct is past criminal conduct (Philpotts and Lancucki 1979). The reductivist sentencer would, in the light of this, tend to increase the sentence each time the offender was brought back before the court. The problem with this approach is the same as that encountered with the multiple offender: additive sentencing soon means that the latest sentence becomes disproportionate to the nature of the offending in which the offender has indulged. The Court of Appeal has, therefore, developed the idea of a 'ceiling' for a particular kind of offending (Ashworth 1983, pp. 226–30). The ceiling must be distinguished from the maximum penalty for the offence. The ceiling represents that level of sentence beyond which it would be inappropriate to go when sentencing the average case of burglary, no matter how many previous convictions for burglary the offender has.

Can differential sentencing be defended on a desert model? On one view, no. Some desert theorists have argued that since the cornerstone of desert sentencing is proportionality between the seriousness of the offence and the severity of the penalty, the commission of previous offences must strictly be irrelevant to sentence (Singer 1979). The offender has already received punishment for those, and their existence cannot in logic make the new offence more serious. Most desert theorists, however, take the view that previous convictions are relevant to sentence, while insisting that they are of *less* importance in determining sentence than is offence seriousness (Von Hirsch 1986, ch. 7). The position which has been reached is described as the theory of 'progressive loss of mitigation', whereby the first offender is entitled to a sentencing discount, and on subsequent reconvictions that offender will receive successively smaller discounts, so that by the time four or five offences are on his record all discount is lost and the offender has reached the sentencing ceiling for that offence. This model may sound rather similar to the one adopted by the reductivist, but the difference lies in the desert model's reference to the sentencing ceiling for the kind of offence which is being repeated, a limitation which is absent from the reductivist model.

What does the Criminal Justice Act 1991 have to say about previous convictions? Section 29 is the relevant provision:

(1) An offence shall not be regarded as more serious for the purposes of any provision of this part by reason of any previous convictions of the offender or any failure of his to respond to previous sentences.

(2) Where any aggravating factors of an offence are disclosed by the circumstances of other offences committed by the offender, nothing in this part shall prevent the court from taking those factors into account for the purpose of forming an opinion as to the seriousness of the offence.

This section is not easy to grasp, and there is uncertainty amongst criminal lawyers over how it will be interpreted by the courts. Section 29(1), however, seems to make a statement in line with the desert view on previous convictions. A more severe sentence is never justified merely because the offender has done it before. The section does not actually spell out the other part of the theory of progressive loss of mitigation, that a person with a clean, or nearly clean, record is entitled to a discount. That proposition seems certain to survive the Act, however, since s. 28(1) permits a sentencer to take account of any matter which, in the court's opinion, is 'relevant in mitigation of sentence'. Section 29(2) creates a very limited exception to s. 29(1). It allows the sentencer to have regard to the full *circumstances* of the commission of previous offences, where those circumstances are in some way relevant to, and throw light upon, the seriousness of the offence which is now being sentenced. One example which was given in the Home Office's *General Guide* to the Act (and discussed in Gibson 1992) is that of an offender now being sentenced for assault, committed upon a person of different ethnic origin. The offender has two previous convictions, for criminal damage. The circumstances of those offences were that they involved the spraying of racist graffiti on walls. These circumstances indicate that the offender is racially motivated in his offending, and this makes the current assault more serious than it would otherwise be. Seen in this light, s. 29(2) is coherent, but its main drawback is a practical one. Very often sentencers will not have the kind of detailed information about the circumstances of previous convictions which would permit these inferences to be made. Section 29(2) refers to 'other offences', not 'previous convictions', so it has application to multiple offending as well as to repeat offending.

Desert principles in community sentences

One of the most innovative parts of the Criminal Justice Act 1991 is its application of desert principles to community sentences. Community sentences are: probation orders, community service orders, combination orders, curfew orders, supervision orders and attendance centre orders. Under s. 6(1), it is made clear that a court shall not pass a community sentence 'unless it is of the opinion that the offence, or the combination of the offence and one other offence associated with it, was serious enough to warrant such a sentence'. Unlike the criteria for imposing custody, where there is the exceptional rule for offenders convicted of violent offences or sexual offences, the *only* justification for imposing any (or any combination) of the community sentences under the Act is offence seriousness. Until quite recently it had been assumed that desert principles were not applicable to community sentences. This view was challenged in Wasik and Von Hirsch (1988) and Bottoms (1989), arguments which seem to have found favour in the White Paper and the 1991 Act. Inherent in the scheme of the Act is the scaling of community sentences in terms of their relative onerousness, or the relative extent to which they impose restrictions of liberty upon the offender. Community sentences are no longer to be regarded as 'alternatives to custody', but as distinctive penalties in their own right. This will be a largely novel approach for sentencers. It also provides a considerable challenge for probation officers, who now have to rethink their approach to community sentences when tendering pre-sentence reports to the court. By the 1991 Act, social inquiry reports are replaced by pre-sentence reports, which will be substantially different in content and style. (For consideration of this see Wasik (1992).)

Unfortunately the Act provides very little detail about how the various community sentences will fit together in desert terms. Is, for example, a community service order to be regarded as more severe than a probation order with certain requirements inserted by the court? The details of the new hierarchy for community sentences will have to be worked out by the courts and the probation service together, over the coming months and years. Little of the pre-Act law will be relevant, and there is unlikely to be much guidance on this area of the Act from the appellate courts, since the vast majority of cases taken on appeal to the Court of Appeal are concerned with custodial rather than community sentencing.

What framework does the Act provide? Section 6(2) of the Act requires that the court, when passing a community sentence, must *achieve* (not seek to achieve) two objectives. By s. 6(2)(a) the community order or orders 'shall be such as in the opinion of the court is, or taken together are, the most suitable for the offender' and, by s. 6(2)(b), 'The restrictions on liberty imposed by the order or orders shall be such as in the opinion of the court are commensurate with the seriousness of the offence, or the combination of the offence and other offences associated with it'. The main difficulty with s. 6(2) is that the two objectives, (a) 'suitability' and (b) 'seriousness', will sometimes conflict with each other, and the statute gives no indication of which, in that case, should prevail over the other. To adopt no principle here would be to leave community sentencing largely unfettered by the Act with sentencers free to vary their reasons for community sentence selection from case to case.

It seems that the most coherent solution here is to say that the most suitable community order or combination of orders should be selected for the offender, but only imposed if this does not create a more onerous burden upon the offender than is justified by the seriousness of the offence. This would be to treat 'seriousness' as a limiting factor, and it would be in accord with the principle of desert which underlies the 1991 Act. Indeed, the first steps in this direction have already been taken. National standards which have now been issued by the Home Office seek to resolve some of the matters of detail left open by the Act. The National Standard on Pre-Sentence Reports (CPO 6/1992) clarifies the changing role of the probation service under the Act, and contains a section in which the service is encouraged to locate all the various community sentences within a matrix derived from 'offence seriousness' on one axis and 'offender need' on the other. The matrix will have the effect of ensuring that a community sentence which is more intrusive or onerous than can be justified on the basis of offence seriousness cannot be imposed on the ground of offender suitability. Once again, however, the details of the new arrangements will have to be worked out in cooperation between the courts and the probation service, within the new desert framework of the Act.

References

Ashworth, A. (1983), *Sentencing and Penal Policy* (London: Weidenfeld & Nicolson).
Ashworth, A. (1990), 'The White Paper on Criminal Justice and Sentencing' [1990] Crim LR 217.
Ashworth, A. (1992), 'Non-custodial Sentences' [1992] Crim LR 242.
Ashworth, A., et al. (1984), *Sentencing in the Crown Court* (Occasional Paper No. 10) (Oxford: Centre for Criminological Research, University of Oxford).
Bentham, J. (1789), *An Introduction to the Principles of Morals and Legislation*. Modern edition by J.H. Burns and H.L.A. Hart (1982) (London: Methuen).

Beyleveld, D. (1979), 'Identifying, Explaining and Predicting Deterrence' (1979) *British Journal of Criminology*, vol. 19, p. 205.

Bottoms, A.E. (1989), 'The Concept of Intermediate Sanctions and its Relevance for the Probation Service', in *The Criminal Justice System: A Central Role for the Probation Service*, ed. R. Shaw and K. Haines (Cambridge: University of Cambridge Institute of Criminology).

Farrington, D.P., and Dowd, E.A. (1986), 'Disentangling Criminal Behaviour and Police Reaction', in *Psychopaths, Dangerousness and Reactions to Crime*, ed. D.P. Farrington and J. Gunn (Chichester: Wiley).

Gibson, B. (1990), *Unit Fines* (Winchester: Waterside Press).

Gibson, B. (1992), *Criminal Justice Act 1991: Legal Points* (Winchester: Waterside Press).

Government of Canada (1984), *Sentencing*.

Government of Canada (1990), *Sentencing: Directions for Reform*.

Hart, H.L.A. (1968), *Punishment and Responsibility* (Oxford: Clarendon Press).

Henham, R.J. (1990), *Sentencing Principles and Magistrates' Sentencing Behaviour* (Aldershot: Avebury).

Home Office (1986), *The Sentence of the Court* (London: HMSO).

Home Office (1990), *Crime, Justice and Protecting the Public: the Government's Proposals for Legislation* (Cm 965) (London: HMSO).

Lacey, N. (1988), *State Punishment* (London: Routledge).

Lovegrove, A. (1992), 'Sentencing Reform and Judicial Training in Australia', in *Sentencing, Judicial Discretion and Training*, ed. C. Munro and M. Wasik (London: Sweet & Maxwell).

McConville, M., and Baldwin, J. (1982), 'The Influence of Race on Sentencing in England' [1982] Crim LR 652.

Maguire, M. (1982), *Burglary in a Dwelling* (London: Heinemann).

Mair, G., and Nee, C. (1990), *Electronic Monitoring: the Trials and their Results* (Home Office Research Study No. 120) (London: HMSO).

Martinson, R. (1974), 'What Works? Questions and Answers about Prison Reform' *Public Interest*, No. 22.

Martinson, R. (1976), *Rehabilitation, Recidivism and Research* (New Jersey: National Council on Crime and Delinquency).

Matza, D. (1964), *Delinquency and Drift* (New York: Wiley).

Moxon, D. (1988), *Sentencing Practice in the Crown Court* (Home Office Research Study No. 103) (London: HMSO).

Moxon, D., et al. (1985), *Juvenile Sentencing: Is There a Tariff?* (Research and Planning Unit Paper No. 32) (London: Home Office).

Moxon, D., et al. (1990), *Unit Fines, Experiments in Four Courts* (Home Office Research and Planning Unit Paper 59) (London: Home Office).

Parker, H., et al. (1989), *Unmasking the Magistrates* (Milton Keynes: Open University Press).

Philpotts, G.J.O., and Lancucki, L.B. (1979), *Previous Convictions, Sentence and Reconviction: a Statistical Study of a Sample of 5,000 Offenders Convicted in January 1971* (Home Office Research Study No. 53) (London: HMSO).

Rutherford, A. (1986), *Prisons and the Process of Justice* (Oxford: Oxford University Press).

Singer, R.G. (1979), *Just Deserts: Sentencing Based on Equality and Desert* (Cambridge Mass: Ballinger).

Smart, J.J.C., and Williams, B. (1973), *Utilitarianism: For and Against* (London: Cambridge University Press).

Sparks, R. (1971), 'The Use of Suspended Sentences' [1971] Crim LR 384.

Tarling, R. (1979) *Sentencing Practice in Magistrates' Courts* (Home Office Research Study No. 56) (London: HMSO).

Thomas, D.A. (1978), 'Form and Function in Criminal Law', in *Reshaping the Criminal Law*, ed. P. Glazebrook (London: Stevens).

Thomas, D.A. (1979), *Principles of Sentencing*, 2nd ed. (London: Heinemann Educational).

Tonry, M. (1982), 'Criminal Law: the Missing Element in Sentencing Reform' (1982) 35 Vand L Rev 607.

Tonry, M. (1987), 'Sentencing Guidelines and Sentencing Commissions: the Second Generation', in *Sentencing Reform: Guidance or Guidelines?*, ed. M. Wasik and K. Pease (Manchester: Manchester University Press).

Turner, A. (1992), 'Sentencing in Magistrates' Courts', in *Sentencing, Judicial Discretion and Training*, ed. C. Munro and M. Wasik (London: Sweet & Maxwell).

Von Hirsch, A. (1976), *Doing Justice: the Choice of Punishments* (New York: Hill and Wang).

Von Hirsch, A. (1986) *Past or Future Crimes* (Manchester: Manchester University Press).

Von Hirsch, A. (1987), 'Guidance by Numbers or Words? Numerical versus Narrative Guidelines for Sentencing', in *Sentencing Reform: Guidance or Guidelines?*, ed. M. Wasik and K. Pease (Manchester: Manchester University Press).

Von Hirsch, A., and Jareborg, N. (1989) 'Sweden's Sentencing Statute Enacted' [1989] Crim LR 275.

Von Hirsch, A., and Jareborg, N. (1991), 'Gauging Criminal Harm: a Living-Standard Analysis' (1991) 11 Oxford J Legal Stud 1.

Walker, N. (1985), *Sentencing: Theory, Law and Practice* (London: Butterworth).

Walmsley, R., and White, K. (1979), *Sexual Offences, Consent and Sentencing* (Home Office Research Study No. 54) (London: HMSO).

Wasik, M. (1987), 'Guidance, Guidelines and Criminal Record', in *Sentencing Reform: Guidance or Guidelines?*, ed. M. Wasik and K. Pease (Manchester: Manchester University Press).

Wasik, M. (1992), 'Rethinking Information and Advice for Sentencers', in *Sentencing, Judicial Discretion and Training*, ed. C. Munro and M. Wasik (London: Sweet & Maxwell).

Wasik, M., and Taylor, R. (1991), *Blackstone's Guide to the Criminal Justice Act 1991* (London: Blackstone Press).

Wasik, M., and Von Hirsch, A. (1988), 'Non-custodial penalties and the principles of desert' [1988] Crim LR 555.

Wasik, M., and Von Hirsch, A. (1990), 'Statutory Sentencing Principles: the 1990 White Paper' (1990) 53 MLR 508.

Willis, A. (1986), 'Alternatives to Prison: an Elusive Paradise', in *Alternatives to Custody*, ed. J. Pointing (Oxford: Basil Blackwell).

Wolfgang, M. (1976), 'Seriousness of Crime and a Policy of Juvenile Justice', in *Delinquency, Crime and Society*, ed. J. Short (Chicago: University of Chicago Press).

Woolf, Lord Justice (1991), *Prison Disturbances April 1990: Report of an Inquiry* (Cm 1456) (London: HMSO).

6

The Probation Service

David Mathieson

The probation service is in a period of major transition. The experience of change and challenge is not by any means new to the probation service — and over many decades, it has demonstrated an apparently inexhaustible capacity to adapt, develop and grow.

The current process of transition is, however, by far the most profound adjustment which the probation service has ever been required to make. Some people have even spoken, perhaps over-dramatically, of the 'birth of the probation service mark 2', which implies the emergence of a totally new kind of service.

The Criminal Justice Act 1991 will probably turn out to be the most significant piece of criminal justice legislation since the Criminal Justice Act 1948 — and it represents the government's intentions for major changes of emphasis and practice in the administration of criminal justice. The probation service finds itself at the heart of government plans for the implementation of the 1991 Act. Home Office Ministers describe the probation service as moving to occupy a 'centre-stage' position in the criminal justice system.

Before examining the implications of all these developments for the future of the probation service, it is useful to trace the essential nature of the probation service through a brief analysis of its history. In this way, it will be seen that there are many parallels between the challenges faced by the probation service currently and at its inception — but there are also significant differences in organisation and method.

History of the service

The Church of England Temperance Society established its Police Court Mission in some of the London courts in 1876. The purpose was to 'reclaim' people appearing at court for drunkenness — and it was the first organised attempt in this country to deal with offenders in the community rather than in custody.

The first two police court missionaries (the precursors of today's probation officers) were George Nelson and William Batchelor. They were ex-Coldstream Guardsmen and their aim was quite unapologetically evangelical: to reclaim the lives and souls of drunks appearing before the courts. They would ask the magistrates to bind individuals over into their care and they would undertake to secure their 'restoration and reclamation'.

One of the early police court missionaries, Thomas Holmes, wrote an account of his 'work among the poor and outcasts of London' (Holmes 1900). At the conclusion of a description of the complex human and social problems of the people with whom he was working, he stated revealingly:

I had to give them myself, for I had nothing else to give them in those days. And no one can say that I spared myself; but it meant something, for it nearly proved too much for me.

The early Police Court Mission was clear about the type of person suitable to be appointed as a police court missionary: 'a man (sic) of God, a man with a vocation, a man of character, a man with experience and tact and full of the milk of human kindness'. Thomas Holmes's account of his work brings all of these human qualities vividly to life — and demonstrates that the principal resource of the early police court missionaries was the depth of their own personalities.

The advent and success of the Police Court Mission played a large part in the formulation of new legislation in the form of the Probation of Offenders Act 1907, which enabled courts to appoint what were now being called probation officers. The Home Officer Minister of that time, Herbert Samuel, told the House of Commons that the purpose of having probation officers was so that:

certain offenders whom the court did not think fit to imprison, on account of their age, character or antecedents, might be placed on probation under supervision of these officers, whose duty it would be to guide, admonish and befriend them.

So the pioneering work of a voluntary, charitable organisation was now being incorporated into statutory functions and the scope of the police court missionaries was being extended to include a much wider range of offenders other than just drunks. The 1907 Act described the task of probation officers as being to 'advise, assist and befriend' people under supervision — words which were to have a potent effect in subsequent decades.

The work of probation officers became even more firmly rooted in 1926, when new criminal justice legislation established a standard administrative framework for the probation service and it became mandatory for every court petty sessional division to have one or more probation officers. The ground was now well prepared for the development of the probation service throughout the country.

The distinctive 'style' of the police court missionaries extended to the work of the early probation officers. Thereafter the Christian evangelical thrust gradually gave way to the influence of psychodynamic social work from the USA. The extent to which this particular style pervaded the probation service was demonstrated in an official Home Office report in 1962. The Departmental Committee on the Probation Service was appointed in 1959 by the Home Secretary, and under the leadership of Mr R.P. Morison (a distinguished lawyer), it spent three years taking evidence and reviewing the work of the probation service. The Morison report is one of the major landmarks in the history of the service. It described the probation officer as essentially 'a professional caseworker, employing in a specialised field skill which he (sic) holds in common with other social workers'. The Morison report saw it as the task of the Welfare State to deal with the material needs of offenders, thus freeing probation officers to establish with the probationer a social work relationship 'which will itself be a positive influence, counteracting and modifying the ill-effects of past experiences and of irremovable factors in the present'.

This individualised, psychodynamic social work ethos not only became extensively practised but was also officially endorsed by the Home Office in its recruitment and training of probation officers. It remained largely unchallenged until the late-1970s and early-1980s. The challenges came from two extremes of the political spectrum. From the left came the challenge to see the offender as a victim of an oppressive society with consequent demands for changes in the political and social systems. From the right came the challenge to see the offender as a menace to society so that his or her offending behaviour must be confronted and changed.

This is in some respects an oversimplification of the different challenges steadily mounted to the traditional and deeply rooted ethos of the probation service, but it serves to illustrate the state of turmoil which began to trouble the service. An additional factor which struck at the heart of the confidence of the service was some powerfully expressed academic evidence that 'nothing works'. This three-pronged attack produced a wilderness decade from which the probation service is at long last now emerging. It is emerging strongly with a new and clear thrust, but this in itself brings issues and tensions which have to be addressed.

Implications of new legislation

The sentencing aspects of the Criminal Justice Act 1991 came into effect in October 1992. Although the effects of the new legislation are likely to be of an evolutionary rather than a dramatic nature, nevertheless the probation service has to be fully prepared to work with the requirements of the new legislation. The Act installs *proportionality* as the primary aim of sentencing: the court should try to arrive at a sentence which is 'deserved', i.e., commensurate with the seriousness of the offence. The government's intention in introducing the Act is to ensure that serious offenders are sent to prison (both as a punishment and to protect the public) and that others (excluding petty offenders) are dealt with by means of 'punishment in the community' under the supervision of the probation service.

The Criminal Justice Act 1991 was preceded by the Home Office Green Paper, *Punishment, Custody and the Community* (1988) which stated that 'punishment in the community' should involve three basic principles:

(a)   restriction on the offender's freedom of action, as a punishment;
(b)   action to reduce the risk of further offending;
(c)   reparation to the community and, where possible, compensation to the victim.

In stating that an important feature of the Criminal Justice Act 1991 is to increase the use of community measures supervised by the probation service, the Home Office also emphasises that community measures must be 'tough, realistic and demanding'. It is, therefore, clear that the new legislation presents the probation service with a great challenge: to integrate traditional methods with the 'just deserts' requirements of the Act into a new framework of practice for supervising offenders in the community.

There is here a duality of issues for the probation service to resolve, i.e., philosophy and practice. The term 'punishment in the community' has been particularly difficult for the service to come to terms with and it continues to be important that it is analysed and debated openly and constructively if the service is to grasp the opportunities currently inherent in the changes taking place in the criminal justice system.

The probation service has always been fiercely proud of its values and has fought to protect them in an often hostile 'law and order' climate. Curiously, there is no probation service statement of values, but it is often accepted that the following extract from the Code of Ethics of the British Association of Social Workers appropriately encapsulates the essence of probation work:

Basic to the profession of social work is the recognition of the value and dignity of every human being — irrespective of origin, race, status, sex, sexual orientation, age, disability, belief or contribution to society.

The profession accepts responsibility to encourage and facilitate the self-realisation of each individual person with due regard for the interest of others.

The essence of probation work is respect for the individual without discrimination, a commitment to providing choices and opportunities and a consequent belief that, with proper support, people are capable of growth, responsibility and change. The issue of control has always been accepted as an integral part of probation work; the controversy has been about the balance between care and control. The service has often been criticised for getting the emphasis wrong and it is still frequently asserted that 'everything is done for the offender and nothing for the victim'.

The current climate not only revives the 'care–control' debate but also extends it to require the probation service to interpret the term 'punishment' within the philosophy of its fundamental values. If punishment means the deliberate imposition of pain or harm, then it cannot of course be contained within probation values.

The use of the term 'punishment in the community' is probably a deliberate attempt on the part of government Ministers to win public support for the increased use of community measures rather than custody. Any crime policy (like any public policy) ultimately requires the understanding and support of the general public for its success.

For good or ill, the term 'probation' is associated with offenders being let off. This albeit inaccurate notion has to be dispelled, hence the use of the term 'punishment in the community'. There is no evidence that the government or the new legislation requires that community measures should deliberately inflict pain or harm on offenders; rather is there evidence that 'punishment in the community' is a form of public relations shorthand for controlling offenders, diverting them from further crime and enabling them to become responsible citizens.

If this is so, there is no need for the probation service to be over-defensive and over-protective about its traditional values. There is plenty of scope for a constructive debate about reviewing and reinterpreting values in the context of new legislation which has the potential for dealing with more offenders in the community; and there is ample opportunity for the probation service to occupy a centre-stage position of influence in the criminal justice system.

Methods

Just as there is tension about values, so there is tension about methods of work within the service. The well-established practice of the service is that of the individual probation officer using a combination of his or her own personality plus social work skills with a discrete caseload of individual offenders. The impact of the Criminal Justice Act 1991 is to require a fundamental review of traditional practice, accompanied by a search for a much wider and more extensive range of work methods than ever before.

There is an added and powerful impetus to the search. The pessimism of the 'nothing works' conclusion has recently been replaced by a significant and growing body of research results which indicate that some things do work for some offenders in some circumstances. There is, therefore, an increasing climate of optimism that it is indeed possible to influence positively the attitudes and behaviour of many offenders, even those with extensive records of recidivism. These research findings point probation practice in three specific directions: first, a clear focus on confronting offending behaviour; second, a multi-model approach involving a range of methods and techniques; and third, exposure of offenders to peer-group experience and learning.

The emphasis, therefore, needs to shift away from an almost exclusive concentration by the individual probation officer on the individual offender as a person requiring casework help to a broad spectrum of programmes involving a wide range of personnel from the probation service itself, other statutory and voluntary agencies and voluntary associates from the local community. This is a fundamental and far-reaching challenge which is attracting a great deal of critical thought and debate within the service, for it implies not so much a shift as a huge leap in practice and methods. It also has tremendous implications for staff recruitment and training.

The challenge, however, has to be grasped. If more offenders are to be dealt with in the community rather than in custody, there are some crucial implications. First, the probation service is moving significantly up-tariff in terms of the offenders with whom it is working, i.e., they are likely to be more difficult and demanding. Second, the service has an increased degree of accountability to the courts and the public. In these circumstances, the service must be able to demonstrate that it can provide comprehensive programmes which realistically deal with offending behaviour and which enable offenders to move away from crime into more constructive and responsible patterns of behaviour.

There is an understandable reluctance to abandon the traditional welfare focus of the probation service (which traces its origins to the obligation contained in the Probation of Offenders Act 1907 to 'advise, assist and befriend') and the traditional one-to-one style of work. However, it is not a case of abandoning the past altogether, in favour of totally new styles and methods; rather is it a case of recognising that a much wider span of approaches to work with offenders is necessary to coincide with the reforms inherent in the Criminal Justice Act 1991.

Questions and challenges for the future

The Criminal Justice Act 1991 potentially marks the end of what has been called our carceral society, i.e., an overreliance on and therefore an overuse of imprisonment as a means of dealing with offenders. If that is too ambitious a description of the Act, it is nevertheless true that it seeks to diminish the role of imprisonment within the criminal justice system and to increase the role of community measures for dealing with offenders. In so doing, the Act establishes a new continuum of punishment, from substantial prison sentences through to what the government calls punishment in the community.

If the probation service is to play its part fully in helping these reforms to take off, then it must both recognise this new continuum and also be prepared to operate within it.

If the probation service is willing to take part in this process of change and challenge, a number of questions must be posed and debated. The questions which follow are by no means exhaustive and in no order of priority.

Staffing

Traditionally, the work of the probation service has been undertaken principally by the probation officer, i.e., a trained social worker. That position is already being questioned due to the growing shortage of qualified probation officers in a service which has to increase its staffing levels to cope with the extra work coming from the Criminal Justice Act 1991 and the extension of bail information schemes. On the basis of a clear analysis of the functions and requirements of the service, attention must be given without delay to the question of which tasks need the distinctive skills and qualities of staff with a social work qualification and which tasks can appropriately and effectively be performed by other staff.

This may seem to be a fundamental question, confronting the essential traditions of the probation service. But something rather different is suggested by the staffing statistics of the service, which clearly indicate that about half the staff of the service currently are non-probation officer grades. The use of ancillary and administrative staff in recent years has enhanced rather than diminished the work of probation officers. Therefore there is good cause in the present climate seriously to consider extending their recruitment and use. What is needed is a carefully thought out and comprehensive staffing strategy for the service at both national and local levels.

Additionally, the probation service has to give attention to two important partnerships: with other agencies (both statutory and voluntary) in the local community and also with voluntary associates. It is now increasingly accepted that for the most part, only experience *within* the community can fully restore an offender to the community. If this is the key to successful rehabilitation, then the probation service cannot afford to deal with offenders exclusively within its own confines; it must make full use of all the facilities and opportunities available within the local community. This means that the staffing strategy must be complemented by a partnership with other statutory and voluntary agencies rooted in the local community and also by the recruitment and use of volunteers from the local community. The use of volunteers is not by any means new to the probation service. Unfortunately, as Judge Eric Stockdale (1985) has pointed out, they are used differentially from one locality to another. The more extensive use of volunteers from each local community, including the appropriate recruitment of ex-offenders to be volunteers, is a challenge which must be accepted with fresh vigour by the service.

There is a further factor to be considered in the process of re-examining the staffing needs of the service. It is still traditionally believed that the managers of the service should be qualified probation officers who have been promoted through the ranks. Yet, in many probation areas, a growing number of non-probation officer personnel occupy posts in research, information, computers and public relations. And in the larger metropolitan areas which have their own in-house servicing arrangements, other professionals are heading finance, property and legal sections.

In addition, therefore, to a critical staffing analysis at fieldwork level, there is a need for a parallel exercise at management level. The question needs to be asked whether all managers in the probation service have to be qualified and experienced probation officers, or whether it is appropriate for people with other professional qualifications and experience to be appointed to management posts within the service. Of course, the ultimate question is whether the post of chief probation officer could be occupied by a person from outside the probation officer ranks.

In the debate on these major issues, it is important to avoid the traps of being either overprecious about the management of the service, so that the potential contributions of other professionals are totally excluded, or of being unfairly critical of existing management, so that outsiders are seen as the simple panacea. The key factor in the debate should be the changing requirements of management in the service, and the key question is what sort of qualifications and experience are needed in the managers of the future. There is, as always, an appropriate balance required between ability to provide leadership, to develop organisational objectives and priorities, to secure and use resources efficiently and effectively, to carry a high level of responsibility and to represent the service publicly — and the personal capacity to use these abilities within the distinctive ethos of the probation service.

Organisation

A second set of fundamental questions confronting the probation service are organisational. The probation service is still predominantly organised in a way which ensures that each geographically convenient area is served by a district office team working on a generic basis. The advantage is, of course, that the service is firmly rooted in and readily accessible to the local community.

Changes in recent years, however, and especially changes in practice and methods (referred to earlier) which the new legislation will require, mean that disadvantages are being identified in the traditional organisation of the service. Generic district offices cannot provide the range and depth of specific programmes now required to deal with an increasing number of up-tariff offenders in the community.

At least two other models of organisation are beginning to be prevalent in the service: that of providing a number of specialist units serving a wide geographical area and that of establishing one large multi-purpose probation centre serving a wide geographical area. Both models involve abandoning the traditional concept of the district office serving the local community in favour of concentrating staffing and resource expertise in one unit or centre.

Other models may be developed and it is right that new ways of organisation should be tried as part of the response to current challenges. However, it is essential that where new models are being implemented, they should be monitored and evaluated. There is an urgent need for reliable research information upon which to base future organisational changes.

Accountability

A third set of fundamental questions facing the probation service concerns how best to cope with the increasing demands of accountability. There can be no shrinking on the part of a statutory agency from the need to be accountable, but the history and traditions of the service have developed a culture in which there are varying degrees of resistance to the new accountability. The commitment to social work methods and the use of the probation officer's own personality gave rise to the hallowed tradition of the 'autonomy' of the individual officer. This particular culture together with the new accountability have produced an increasing level of tension within the service in recent years.

There is no clearly identifiable time when the challenge to the traditional culture began, but there is no doubt that the new kind of government which was elected in 1979 had a great impact not only on the probation service but on the public sector in general. It soon began to demonstrate antipathy to the public sector and, notwithstanding its own persistent protestations to the contrary, began a centralising process unprecedented in recent history. This new thrust gained increasing momentum as the government was subsequently re-elected in 1983 and 1987.

As far as the probation service was concerned, the government's twin commitments to 'value for money' and 'law and order' were bound to have an impact. The effects began to be felt in the early-1980s when the Home Office published a draft document entitled *The Future Direction of the Probation Service*. It was highly significant that, when the final version of that document was published by the Home Office in 1984, its title had become the *Statement of National Objectives and Priorities for the Probation Service*. This document represented the most penetrating government intervention ever in the affairs of the probation service and required each probation area to respond with its own local statement, to be measured against the Home Office's national statement. The process of tighter central control had begun.

There was to follow a series of further government initiatives. The Green Paper, *Punishment, Custody and the Community*, was published by the

Home Office in July 1988, quickly followed the next month by a Home Office letter to all chief probation officers, headed 'Tackling offending — an Action Plan'. Again each area was required to respond with its own action plan.

1989 saw the publication of the first 'national standards' document (on the operation of community service orders) and this process is continuing to the point that there will be a national standards document on almost every aspect of the work of the service.

The White Paper, *Crime, Justice and Protecting the Public*, was published early in 1990 and eventually led to the Criminal Justice Act 1991. A further Green Paper was published in 1990, entitled *Supervision and Punishment in the Community* (containing the government's thinking on the future organisation of the probation service), and another consultative paper, *Partnership in Dealing with Offenders in the Community*, was published in the same year. Then in 1991, a Blue Paper, *Organising Supervision and Punishment in the Community*, contained indications of government decisions about the future structure of the service.

In 1989, the probation service was the subject of major reports by the National Audit Office and the Audit Commission examining structure, organisation and resources. The Home Office's own Probation Inspectorate now conducts efficiency and effectiveness inspections in each probation area, and perhaps the culmination of the process of increased central control has been reached with the imposition of centrally determined cash limits on the budget of each probation area with effect from April 1992.

In summary, the past decade has seen an increasing tension between central government and local probation areas. It is fair to say that the probation service has accepted the need for accountability in the use of public resources and the requirement to be clearly committed to the prevention of crime and the reduction of offending. The fundamental and continuing controversy has been about whether an organisation like the probation service should be centrally or locally administered. The argument of late seems to have swung in favour of local administration and there does seem to be a diminishing political (and consequently civil service) thrust away from more centralisation. There is currently an intense amount of consultation taking place about many aspects of the future of the service, involving the Home Office, the Central Council of Probation Committees and the Association of Chief Officers of Probation. It is true to say that the future organisation of the service is still in the melting-pot and there will be some changes. But after much concerted debate and heart-searching, it is likely that the 'new' structure will be one which is based on the principle of a service which is locally organised but highly accountable to national government (which provides most of the finance).

Alongside this national–local controversy has been a growing tension between management and fieldwork staff. The probation service developed as an essentially basic-grade organisation and it was only following the Criminal Justice Act 1948 that management grades (i.e., principal and senior probation officers) started to have clearly defined roles. Thus a hierarchical structure began to develop, though not in any overly intrusive fashion.

In recent years, however, the service has experienced the ascendancy of a new managerial culture with its emphasis on the language of policies, objectives, planning, targets and monitoring and on the increasing use of research and new technology. The task of reconciling the new managerial culture and the traditional fieldwork culture has not been easy for the probation service and the process continues to need careful attention if unhelpful polarisation is to be avoided.

There can be no denying the importance of accountability for any agency in the public sector, and there can be no denying the need for the probation service to sharpen its organisation and to enhance its attractiveness to its stakeholders. The debate to resolve the tension between the managerial and fieldwork cultures must continue. The key to establishing a new unified culture is the fact that the business of the probation service is people not commodities. The service must continue to provide a human and humane service to the courts, the community and people under supervision. The framework of policies, objectives, planning, targets and monitoring has a proper place in the future of the service, provided that it exists to complement and facilitate the developing work of the service.

There is also a major tension experienced at committee, management and fieldwork levels within the service: that of discretion versus prescription. There is a fundamental and traditional ethos of discretion within the service but there has recently been increasing prescription from the Home Office down through the ranks of the service. This is a delicate situation and the twin requirements of public accountability and the necessary scope for spontaneity and initiative need to be kept in careful balance.

Image of the service

In assessing the overall capacity of the probation service effectively to occupy a centre-stage position in the criminal justice system, there is a wide range of factors to be taken into account. On the positive side, by reason of its substantial history and tradition, the service has a clear people-centred focus: staff are recognised as its main resource and its values are firmly based on the dignity and worth of individuals. Key strengths of the service are its commitment to persevering with difficult people and problems and also its commitment to equal opportunities and anti-racism policies and practices. The service is community based and possesses a wealth of knowledge of community personalities and issues at both management and fieldwork levels. A proven strength of the service is its capacity for creativity and for adapting to changing needs, and in the context of the high cost of custody, there is a growing awareness of the cost-effectiveness of the service. For a more influential future, the service needs to build on its undoubted strengths, but it also has to be aware of and work on less positive features, which can be examined in two broad categories: internal and external.

For an agency aspiring to a higher public profile, there is still a tendency for the service to be inward-looking and sometimes backward-looking. The service must listen even more closely to its stakeholders: the courts, other criminal justice agencies, the Home Office, local authorities and the general public. And in keeping with the principles of the Citizens' Charter, attention must be constantly given to improving the quality of service given to people under supervision and others for whom the service has a responsibility.

There are potential difficulties ahead in relation to public opinion. The public image of the probation service has always been imprecise, a situation graphically illustrated by some recent journalistic comments:

> It's probably fair to say that most of us don't carry a clear picture of the probation service in our minds. Mention the police or the prisons and an image already sharply defined rises to the surface. But the probation officers — what do they do? More to the point — what do they achieve? (Jon Silverman, BBC Radio 4 'Special Assignment', 23 February 1990.)

Whilst public perceptions of the probation service may be imprecise, public perceptions of crime are quite clear and are usually hostile. And often this hostility is displaced on to the probation service. This problem is likely to become more acute as the effects are felt of the implementation of the Criminal Justice Act 1991. The probation service will be required to take responsibility for more up-tariff offenders, both before or after custody. Therefore there is bound to be potential for some persons under supervision causing varying degrees of disruption to society. This will have implications for the probation service.

In these circumstances, there is an enormous challenge to the probation service to develop a more proactive public relations strategy. Public relations has been aptly described as 'the deliberate, planned and sustained attempt on the part of an organisation to establish and maintain mutual contact and understanding between itself and its public'.

Reference has already been made to the stakeholders of the service, which is another way of describing its public. Until comparatively recently, there was a reluctance and even hostility on the part of the probation service to using public relations methods. It was thought that PR was for the business and commercial world and certainly not for a confidential agency like the probation service, dealing with people and their problems.

There is now, however, a more positive attitude to PR, and indeed a growing number of probation areas have a PR section and a PR budget. Public relations is beginning to be integrated into the overall fabric of the service, but there are still a couple of fundamental dilemmas to be resolved.

First, who should speak for the service: a skilled public relations officer or the chief probation officer? In the highly charged situation of a public arena or in the sophisticated world of the media, particular skills are undoubtedly needed if the message is to be effectively communicated and the service properly represented. So which is the more important, the 'message' (which is the province of the chief probation officer) or the PR 'skill' (which is the talent of the public relations officer)? The answer is that they are both equally important, which points to the need for a new kind of partnership in the service, i.e., between management and public relations professionals. The probation service has arrived late on the doorstep of PR and it needs urgently to enter and embrace what has hitherto been thought of as an alien profession. Failure to resolve this dilemma positively could result in failure to occupy the centre-stage position in the criminal justice system.

The second fundamental dilemma is about the use of 'human' stories in publicising proactively the work of the service. Public audiences of whatever kind warm to real-life stories and photographs to illustrate talks and presentations. And the media are generally more interested in depicting a real live person rather than a policy document or a management statement. The service is constantly being asked to provide individuals (either currently or recently under supervision) for interview by newspaper reporters or for appearances on radio or television. If the service does respond to these requests, is this a proper use of individuals to enhance the public reputation of the service, or is there a risk in exposing potentially vulnerable people to the harsh world of media scrutiny and public gaze?

There is no easy answer to this particular dilemma because the service has a responsibility both to protect vulnerable people and also to account for its work to its stakeholders. There needs to be a balance between the two, and in a comprehensive public relations strategy for the service, this balance must be properly reflected. Where 'human' stories are contemplated in whatever form, the individual concerned should be fully consulted and advised in respect of giving consent, and where the media are involved, every effort should be taken to ensure that individuals are respected and not just used as 'media fodder'.

It will sometimes be necessary to veto the use of a human interest story in order to be fair to and to protect the individual concerned. However, with proper safeguards, there is no doubt that human interest stories are a powerful means of communicating important messages.

The challenge of restorative justice

The probation service has responded positively in recent years to a great many challenges, both philosophical and practical. There is, however, one challenge with which the service has yet to engage fully: that of 'restorative justice' both in concept and in practice. Restorative justice is the opposite to retributive justice, therefore its relevance to the work of the criminal justice system is controversial. Restorative justice is a profound and ambitious concept, the aim of which is to heal the wounds of every person affected by crime.

The present system of justice in this country establishes blame for offences, then deals in a variety of ways with the offenders. Whilst it is true that much progress has been made albeit belatedly in recent years to help the victims of crime, nevertheless as yet little is done to resolve the breach between offenders and the community and little to enable offenders to make amends for their offending. The ideal of restorative justice would be threefold:

(a)   a comprehensive system of compensation and support for the victims of crime;

(b)   opportunities for the community to benefit from reparation by offenders making amends;

(c)   the restoration to offenders of the responsibilities and privileges of full citizenship.

In the ideal of restorative justice, the three facets are interdependent and cannot be viewed in isolation from each other. Judged alongside the concept of restorative justice, the concept of punishment in the community (the heart of the Criminal Justice Act 1991) seems decidedly narrow. Restorative justice is wider, more imaginative and much more challenging.

The probation service is particularly well placed to play a major part in promoting the development of restorative justice by reason of its unique knowledge and experience gained over the years, but the service still needs convincing of the potential of restorative justice as a concept and its own capacity for turning the concept into practice.

The community service order is the obvious starting point. Introduced in the Criminal Justice Act 1972, it benefits the courts by providing a clear alternative to custody; it benefits the community by providing a workforce for tasks that may otherwise not be undertaken; it benefits offenders by giving them a sense of worth.

Community service is a form of indirect reparation by offenders to the community and as such is widely practised and well known. Direct reparation is sparsely practised and little known, which is a pity because it means that the community in general and crime victims in particular are denied the benefits of reparation. It also means that offenders are denied the opportunity of translating guilt for their crimes into positive forms of advantage for the victims of their crimes.

Direct reparation can take several forms:

(a)   an oral, face-to-face apology from the offender to the victim;
(b)   a written apology;
(c)   compensation from the offender to the victim;
(d)   unpaid work either directly for the victim or for an organisation of the victim's choice.

The process of direct reparation is delicate and must always be supervised by skilled staff and always initiated with the full consent of the victim. The fact that there are so few reparation schemes in this country is proof that the potential of reparation as a highly constructive approach has still not been fully grasped by the probation service and the criminal justice system,

In wider terms, the implementation of the Criminal Justice Act 1991 should be seen by the probation service as a springboard for further progressive reforms in the criminal justice system; hence this is the time for close attention to be given to the concept of restorative justice. The route to the restoration to offenders of full citizenship is via a proper means of ensuring that victims and the community receive fair treatment. There is an immense challenge here for the probation service.

Summary and conclusion

The probation service is in a period of major transition, which places it under varying degrees of stress and which brings a number of crucial challenges. There is a striking similarity between today's situation and the situation which prevailed when the Police Court Mission was established in 1876, i.e., the urgent need to deal with more offenders in the community rather than in custody.

The difference between then and now is that the role of imprisonment is now diminished by statute; there is a very real prospect of seeing the end of the carceral society and there is growing acceptance of the fact that successful rehabilitation of the offender has to take place in the community. After many decades of proving its worth, this is truly a time when the probation service can move decisively centre-stage.

The reward of this challenge is the thrill and excitement of being even more highly valued in society. The cost is the need to analyse and change traditional philosophies and practices. The probation service has a demonstrable capacity to respond to challenges, but there is an unprecedented and concentrated period of challenge ahead.

No organisation has an inexhaustible capacity to change without experiencing difficulty, and the probation service will be no exception to this rule. Its strength in coping successfully with the stresses ahead is its continuing commitment to a fundamental value base and its depth of experience within what is now known as the criminal justice system. The real test will be the extent to which the service can not only play a positive part in the implementation of the Criminal Justice Act 1991 but can also offer something even more progressive and compelling to society in its quest to deal more successfully with the complex problem of crime.

References

The following texts will form additional useful reading alongside this chapter:

Bochel, D. (1976), *Probation and After-care* (*its development in England and Wales*) (Edinburgh: Scottish Academic Press).

Haxby, D. (1978), *Probation: A Changing Service* (London: Constable).

Holmes, T. (1900), *Pictures and Problems from London Police Courts* (London: Thomas Nelson and Sons).

Jarvis, F.V. (1972) *Advise, Assist and Befriend* (*a History of the Probation and After-care Service*) (London: National Association of Probation Officers).

Jarvis, F.V. (ed. Weston, W.R.) (1987), *Probation Officer's Manual* (London: Butterworths).

King, J.F.S. (1969), *The Probation and After-care Service*, 3rd ed. (London: Butterworths).

King, J.F.S. (ed.) (1979), *Pressures and Change in the Probation Service* (University of Cambridge Institute of Criminology).

Monger, M. (1967), *Casework in After-care* (London: Butterworths).

Monger, M. (1972), *Casework in Probation*, 2nd ed. (London: Butterworths).

Raynor, P. (1988), *Probation as an Alternative to Custody: A Case Study* (Aldershot: Gower).

Shaw, R. and Haines, K. (1989), *The Criminal Justice System: A Central Role for the Probation Service* (University of Cambridge Institute of Criminology).

Stockdale, E. (1985), *The Probation Volunteer* (The Volunteer Centre).

Vass, A.A. (1990), *Alternatives to Prison (Punishment, Custody and the Community)* (London: Sage Publications).

Walker, H. and Beaumont, B. (1981), *Probation Work (Critical Theory and Socialist Practice)* (Oxford: Basil Blackwell).

Walker, H. and Beaumont, B. (1985), *Working with Offenders* (London: Macmillan).

Wood, C. (1991), *The End of Punishment (Christian Perspectives on the Crisis in Criminal Justice)* (Edinburgh: Saint Andrew Press).

7

Prisons

Stephen Shaw

Just like the poor, it sometimes seems that the crisis in the prisons is always with us. That crisis may take different forms: yesterday prisoners on the roof, today industrial action by prison officers, tomorrow overcrowding flowing into police cells. But whatever its manifestation, there can be little doubt that for the last two decades the prison service has been characterised by a succession of scandals, disputes and misfortunes without parallel in the public sector.

The question at the beginning of 1992 was whether, at long last, an end to this state of endemic crisis was in sight. By common consent, the Woolf report, published in February 1991, was the most important and far-reaching report on the prison system for a century. The principles that lay behind that report were also prominent in the government's White Paper on the prisons, *Custody, Care and Justice* (Cm 1647), published in September 1991, although there was considerable doubt about the pace at which it would be implemented. By talking about a time-scale of up to 25 years, Home Secretary Kenneth Baker was in danger of exacerbating that prison service syndrome most decried by HM Chief Inspector of Prisons in his 1990–91 Annual Report — that of 'a lack of expectation that matters can ever change for the better'.

Furthermore, after falling substantially in 1989 and 1990, the prison population appeared to have restarted its climb. There was concern too about the effects of the Criminal Justice Act 1991. Industrial relations continued to be in a parlous condition, and the impact of agency status and privatisation was still to be tested.

In this chapter, I will discuss these and other issues principally through the eyes of the Woolf report and the subsequent White Paper. This is a top-down approach which obviously has some limitations. Not least it may seem a long way removed from the everyday experience of both prisoners and staff on prison wings and landings. Nevertheless, it will serve to demonstrate that whatever else the prison service lacks in the 1990s, it is not short of policies, new initiatives and recommendations for reform.

The people in prison

At the end of December 1991, the prison population stood at 45,319, including some 995 prisoners who had been farmed out to police cells. The figure was over 1,300 higher than that of 12 months earlier, but still significantly lower than the all-time high of 51,000 in August 1988. Even allowing for seasonal factors (the prison population always falls during the winter months), the benefits to the system made during 1989 and 1990 when the number of prisoners fell by over 10 per cent had not entirely been lost.

Unfortunately, the Home Office's own projections show a steady rise in the number of prisoners over the 1990s. According to the present director general, Mr Joe Pilling:

> Current predictions envisage that . . . the prison population will continue to grow over the next few years at the rate of about 2,000 prisoners per year.

Although these Home Office projections have a poor track record for accuracy, the number in custody has risen most years since 1945. The United Kingdom regularly tops the European league table for the proportion of its citizenry in custody — 96.5 per 100,000 of the population in 1989 — compared with our nearest rival the former West Germany at 83.8 per 100,000 of the population. However, the UK lags well behind the United States and most of the countries of the former Soviet bloc.

Just under one-quarter of the prison population are awaiting trial or sentence on remand, a proportion which doubled during the 1980s reflecting increased delays in the courts. Of the sentenced population, around one-third have been convicted of offences involving sex, drugs or violence (a proportion which is also increasing). Over 5 per cent are serving life sentences (the United Kingdom has more life-sentence prisoners than the rest of Western Europe *put together*). However, the majority of convicted prisoners are serving short or medium-term sentences for non-violent property offences — principally burglary and theft. When those held on remand are also taken into account, it can be seen that for most people who enter prison the experience is a transitory one. However, at the other extreme, a total of six persons have served over 30 years consecutively in custody and 84 have served over 20 years.

The people in prison also include the 30,000 staff (two-thirds of them uniformed prison officers). Although not quite so labour-intensive as policing, wage costs represent around two-thirds of the prison budget of £1.3 billion. The average annual cost of imprisonment per prisoner was £20,070 in 1990/91.

Following recent research undertaken for the Home Office by the Office of Population Censuses and Surveys, we have a pretty good idea of the socio-economic status of prisoners (Prison Reform Trust 1991). Levels of homelessness and unemployment are much higher amongst people who receive prison sentences than amongst the population as a whole. Some 43 per cent have no educational qualifications, including around 10 per cent who have a reading age of 10 years or less. Nearly one-quarter of adults, and almost 40 per cent of young prisoners have experience of local authority care. A study on behalf of the Association of Chief Officers of Probation also indicates that prisoners are significantly more likely to have been *victims* of crime than the public at large.

Around one-third of prisoners suffer from some form of psychiatric disorder. Research by a team from the Institute of Psychiatry has indicated that drug abuse or dependence is the single most common diagnosis, affecting over 10 per cent of adult male prisoners and about one-quarter of women (Gunn et al. 1991). The research found 1.9 per cent of prisoners with psychoses, 5.3 per cent with neurotic disorders and 8.2 per cent with personality disorders. In total, it was estimated that 1,140 prisoners urgently require hospital treatment.

Perhaps related to this psychiatric profile is the disproportionately high incidence of suicide and self-injury in prisons. The prevention of suicides is the subject of an important report by HM Chief Inspector of Prisons (1990) which in many respects complements the Woolf report itself. The prison suicide rate doubled in the 1970s, doubled again in the 1980s, and is currently running at one death every week. In July 1990, a 15-year-old boy held in a strip cell in Swansea Prison became the youngest prison suicide since child imprisonment was abolished.

The number of such very young prisoners has fallen markedly during the 1980s as a result of increased cautioning by the police and the growth of alternative-to-custody projects. One result is that many young offender institutions (YOIs) have been operating at little more than 75 per cent of capacity and young prisoners have been held many miles from their homes. Feltham YOI, on the edge of London, takes boys from as far away as Cornwall, for example.

The age structure of the prison population as a whole is heavily skewed towards the ages 17–40, with nearly 20 per cent under the age of 21 and nearly two-thirds under 30. The vast majority of prisoners are male, the proportion of women prisoners having consistently remained between 3 and 4 per cent for many years, slightly below the European average. However, in no member State of the Council of Europe is the proportion of women prisoners known to exceed 7 per cent, an indication of the degree to which crime is a male-dominated activity.

There is a significant race dimension to any discussion of the prison system. In total over 16 per cent of the prison population is made up of people from minority ethnic groups. For women prisoners, the proportion is over 26 per cent and in some prisons — particularly in the South-East — black people are even more strongly overrepresented. In all, about 11 per cent of the male prison population and 21 per cent of the females are known to be of African or Afro-Caribbean origin.

Compared to white prisoners, black people are more likely to be refused bail despite having fewer previous sentences. They are also serving much longer sentences than whites (44 per cent longer in the case of men and twice as long in the case of black women), although these figures are significantly influenced by the number of foreign nationals imprisoned on drug importation charges (Prison Reform Trust 1991).

The Home Office has developed some excellent policies on paper to try to ensure that the prison service operates in an anti-racist manner. In many ways, these policies are a model for any other employer or provider of services — whether in the public or private sector. However, as on the question of suicide prevention — where a series of important policy initiatives has been taken — there seems to be a gap between what the policy is designed to achieve and its implementation and performance in practice. This — rather than a lack of concern and imagination — is perhaps the most fundamental problem currently facing the administration of the prisons.

The Woolf report

As the discussion above indicates, the prison population includes a wide range of individuals: both those serving a few days for fine default and those who may never be released; mothers with babies and men who have committed vile crimes against children; boys of 15 and men of 70. The prison system itself is subdivided into different types of institution offering different types of security and regimes to reflect the different needs of its charges.

The most familiar image of a prison is as a dank Victorian pile situated in an inner-city area: prisons like Walton in Liverpool, Winson Green in Birmingham, or Brixton, Wandsworth and Pentonville in London. But in fact there are now as many new prisons as old ones, and perhaps the largest single category is made up of buildings converted during the last 50 years from some other civil or military use. Sudbury open prison, for example, was previously an American military hospital; Ashwell and Deerbolt are two of many which are on former army bases; Kirklevington Grange was the home of an industrialist; the main building at the women's prison at East Sutton Park is an Elizabethan mansion with added Jacobean features.

Each prison — whether urban or rural, old or new, for young people or adults, male or female, sentenced or convicted — has its own distinct culture and traditions. It is no more sensible to regard all prisons as the same as to think of all prisoners as identical. Equally, the assumption that modern prisons are somehow 'good' and Victorian prisons 'bad' would be endorsed by few prisoners or staff. Indeed, although they may not suffer the squalor and decrepitude of the 19th-century estate, many modern prisons are ill-designed, claustrophobic and staff-intensive.

Furthermore, what matters most to the prisoners is the quality of relationships with staff and (most important of all) proximity to their relatives. There would be few London prisoners who would not swap good conditions in Albany for the squalor of Wandsworth just to be closer to their families, for example. Most prisoners want to be in close and regular contact with their family, and to be treated as reasonably responsible adults. Physical conditions and a progressive regime tend to be accorded a much lower priority. Certainly a list of the major prisoner disturbances of the past two decades would show little correspondence between the level and frequency of unrest and the age of the buildings.

Indeed, that prisoner unrest has become one of the distinguishing features of the prison system. Virtually all of the top-security 'dispersal' prisons have experienced major breakdowns in control, and in the 1980s the disturbances became increasingly frequent in lower-security institutions. At the end of April 1986, there were disturbances in 40 establishments in what the then Chief Inspector of Prisons, Sir James Hennessy, termed 'the worst night of violence the English prison system has ever known'. Northeye prison in Sussex was virtually razed to the ground.

Strangely, the riots of 1986 seem to have been forgotten by most commentators, and Hennessy's subsequent report is little quoted and its recommendations ignored. But bad though it was, the 1986 unrest pales into insignificance compared with the events of April and May 1990 at Manchester's Strangeways Prison and elsewhere. These riots were the most severe and most widespread disruption ever suffered by British prisons. They led directly or indirectly to at least three deaths, to damage amounting to tens of millions of pounds, to the loss of over 1,500 prison places, and to political embarrassment for Her Majesty's Government as television pictures of the disorder were flashed across the world.

Within days of the outbreak of the disturbances, the then Home Secretary, David Waddington, invited Lord Justice Woolf to conduct an inquiry. The reliance upon lawyers and judges to conduct inquiries into matters of which they have no prior knowledge is one of the peculiarities of public administration the world over. In the case of Woolf, the tradition of judicial inquiries has proved a triumphant success.

The genius of the Woolf report lies in its ability to locate a grave breakdown in law and order in the context of the long-standing problems of the prison system — overcrowding, decrepitude, poor management, a lack of justice and humanity. The full history of the Woolf inquiry has yet to be written, but it was clear to observers that David Waddington and his senior civil servants were appalled by the breadth of approach which Woolf immediately brought to his task. It would have been easy, safe even, for Woolf to have concentrated on the locks-and-bars aspects of security and control. It is to his very considerable credit that, with one or two exceptions, he avoided such an approach.

The Woolf report — which some sources say was written by Woolf in longhand — is very much his personal statement. Co-signatory Judge Stephen Tumim, HM Chief Inspector of Prisons, seems to have played only a peripheral part. Equally unusual for an inquiry of this kind, the influence of the inquiry's secretary on the shape of the final report was very limited. The approach throughout was also an extremely open one, with public seminars used to debate and discuss areas of concern. Questionnaires were prepared for — if not always distributed to — all prisoners and staff. The medium of the Woolf inquiry was also its message: openness, involvement, consultation.

Both literally and figuratively, the Woolf report is a weighty document, 600 pages long and costing £38.00. It contains some 204 specific proposals and a host of other ideas and suggestions on virtually every page. But of no less significance than Woolf's conclusions and recommendations are the underlying principles in the report. These are perhaps summed up by the words: justice, care, respect, individual treatment, and support for staff. All too often the philosophy of what prisons are for (to punish, reform, deter, or whatever) has been muddled with the philosophy by which prisons should be run. Whatever size of prison population we have, and whatever transgressions of the law we choose to penalise by incarcerating the offender, Woolf believes that a wholly new ethos should govern the running of the institutions themselves.

Woolf distils his massive report into 12 main recommendations, each of which is worth considering in turn. The first of these recommendations promotes closer cooperation between the different parts of the criminal justice system. For this purpose, Woolf says, a national forum and local committees should be established.

Ever so discreetly, what Woolf is suggesting is that there is a need to plan the criminal justice system. Unfortunately, when the Criminal Justice Consultative Council was set up in January 1992 it appeared to be running into opposition from other senior figures in the judiciary. On the doubtful proposition that coordination with other services threatens judicial independence, no judge was to serve on the local committees. Nor was a judge to chair the national body, which instead was to be chaired by the permanent secretary in the Home Office. Fortunately, the ban on judicial involvement was dropped following the appointment of Lord Taylor as Lord Chief Justice. But the very fact that machinery to establish coordination could prove so controversial to the judges is itself evidence of the need for that coordination.

Establishment of a properly functioning Criminal Justice Consultative Council does not obviate the need for further administrative reform. In particular, it is questionable whether a sustained improvement to the prison system will ever be possible unless the prison population is brought under control. Woolf emphasised that his proposal was not for a sentencing council, the fear of which exercises a tremendous hold on the judicial mind. There is, however, a strong case for such a council to be established, charged with providing a framework for sentencing policy.

Woolf's second recommendation is for more visible leadership of the prison service by a director general who is, and is seen to be, the operational head and in day-to-day charge of the service. To achieve this, Woolf calls for a 'compact' or 'contract' between Ministers and the director general of the prison service, who should be responsible for the performance of that 'contract' and publicly answerable for the operations of the service. Woolf's proposal for a strong leader of the prison service is not a new one. But it derives special resonance from the widespread press and political criticism of the then director general, Christopher Train, whose one media appearance during the Strangeways riot was widely regarded as a shambles.

More conspicuous leadership has been promised — and is being delivered — by Christopher Train's successor, Joe Pilling. A greater focus upon the director general is also likely to be one of the results when the prison service assumes a form of 'agency status' in April 1993. The idea that the prison service should operate at arm's length from the Home Office was the key proposal in the report by Sir Raymond Lygo (1991) into prison service management which was established by the then Home Secretary, Kenneth Baker, following the escape of two alleged IRA prisoners from Brixton in August 1991. This proposal — but not Lygo's idea for a two-tier management board — is to be put into effect quickly not least because Joe Pilling himself is a strong enthusiast for agency status. However, some critics of the proposal believe it may result in a loss of public accountability.

Woolf's third and fourth recommendations are for increased delegation of responsibility to governors of establishments and an enhanced role for prison staff. Both proposals are welcome, although the first assumes that all governors are trained and motivated for their enhanced task, and will be provided with additional back-up staff to support them. As a corollary, it also calls into question the present size of prison service headquarters. In principle, the second proposal could come about both through establishing a more purposeful working environment or by offering increased opportunities for training. It is regrettable therefore that increased staff training appears already to have been rejected by the government because of resource constraints.

The idea of 'compacts' or 'contracts' — the words seem interchangeable — is a recurrent theme of the Woolf report. Recommendation 5 argues for a compact for each prisoner setting out the prisoner's expectations and responsibilities in the prison in which he or she is held. This proposal is currently being piloted at the progressive Latchmere House Prison in South-West London, although it is unclear what additional benefits prisoners would enjoy from a compact if they were all offered individual sentence plans and a code of standards were in place. There seems little value in paper commitments which prisoners cannot enforce.

It is also unclear how far the prisoner's compact would alter as he or she 'progresses' through the prison system. The idea of a graduated system of privileges as an incentive to good behaviour was at the heart of the 1984 report of the Home Office's Control Review Committee, made up of senior governors and officials. However, subsequent liberalisation of prison regulations on such matters as visits and letters has tended to offer equal rights to all prisoners and has done little to diminish the relatively greater privileges and better facilities enjoyed by prisoners in top-security establishments over those in lower-security and short-term institutions.

Perhaps the biggest surprise in the Woolf report is the recommendation for a national system of accredited standards with which, in time, each establishment would be required to comply. Proposals for a system of standards are presently under discussion in the Home Office. However, the idea for a system of accreditation — a proposal based on American experience with standards — appears to have been met with less enthusiasm. Standards (the phrase 'minimum standards' seems to have lost its currency) are essential if sensible resource allocation is to be ensured. However, it is clearly going to be some years before the more down-at-heel institutions are able to offer a reasonable level of accommodation and range of facilities. Nor does it seem likely that the government will accept the enforcement of standards through the courts. (It is interesting to note that on three separate occasions — most recently in its report *Prison Education* published in March 1991 — the House of Commons Select Committee on Education has recommended a new Prison Regimes Act. The Act would introduce *statutory* minimum standards to ban enforced cell sharing and guarantee access to work, education, exercise and decent sanitation. The standards would also cover such matters as access to baths and showers.)

The one recommendation in the Woolf report which has been rejected outright by government is the idea of a new Prison Rule that no establishment should hold more prisoners than is provided for in its certified normal level of accommodation, with provision for Parliament to be informed if exceptionally there were to be a material departure from that rule. Woolf's procedure for tackling the problem of overcrowding certainly looks cackhanded, but the proposition that no prison should hold more prisoners than those for which it is designed is surely right. Indeed, one only has to change the word 'prison' to 'hotel' or 'aeroplane' or 'hospital' to see how unexceptional it is.

Woolf's eighth recommendation is a timetable to provide access to sanitation for all prisoners not later than February 1996. This timetable for ending slopping out has been accelerated by the Home Secretary. The present plan is that no prisoner will be slopping out after the end of 1994.

Clearly this is a reform of historic significance. Although it is true that (in)sanitary arrangements have not featured at the top of prisoners' lists of complaints, the reliance on the plastic pot as a toilet has been one of the most disgusting aspects of the prison system. Incredible as it now seems, in the 1960s prisons like Risley were still being commissioned, designed and built without proper sanitation. It may therefore appear churlish to criticise the accelerated programme of integral sanitation — a reform for which prison reformers have been campaigning for years. Nevertheless, there is evidence that ill-suited sanitation is being installed because of the new 1994 deadline. Integral sanitation must allow for proper screening and should not result in cellular accommodation which is even more cramped than at present. Installing toilet facilities in cells without adequate screening in effect condemns the prisoner to living in a lavatory. Unfortunately, this is exactly what is happening in many places rather than the more acceptable method of installing integral sanitation by converting three cells into two. In the short-term, the accelerated programme has also meant a loss of accommodation, exacerbating — but not directly causing — the continued reliance on police cells as overflow accommodation.

In practice, therefore, Woolf's target date of the end of 1992 for 'outlawing' prison overcrowding may never have been feasible because of the accelerated programme to end slopping out. But bearing in mind Woolf's original plan under which both the new Prison Rule and the end of slopping out would have been achieved by the end of 1996, this date would seem to be a far from unmanageable target by which the principle — if not the letter — of Woolf's recommendation could be put into effect.

Woolf's recommendation 9 is for better prospects for prisoners to maintain their links with families and the community through more visits and home leaves and through being located in community prisons as near to their homes as possible. This use of the term 'community prison' is perhaps the most significant phrase in the whole report. Yet Woolf is remarkably vague about what he means. In part, the notion is one of a gaol playing a full part in the community — prisoners doing good works for the community, integration of community and prison facilities, plenty of sporting ties and so on. He also has in mind what might be termed 'comprehensive prisons', with both short and long-term prisoners, remand and sentenced, adult and young, even male and female, sharing one site but housed in discrete units. Where this is not possible, but to ensure that prisoners are in prisons close to their homes, Woolf argues for 'clusters' of prisons each serving a different specialist purpose. The idea of 'clusters' is related to work on the organisation of the prison estate already underway in the Home Office. However, it calls into serious question the present division of the prison service into 15 'areas', a division which seems to have been done with little or no regard for function.

The idea of community prisons has major implications for the prison building (and closure) programme. In principle, Woolf's recommendation 10 that prisons should be divided into small and more manageable units also has much to recommend it. However, there is no particular science in Woolf's view that units should only house between 50 and 70 prisoners. Indeed, not all prisoners want to live in small units and some staff do not like working in them. The refurbished remand centre at Strangeways struck this writer as extremely claustrophobic, and the succession of electronic gates dividing up the wings into units restrict movement and therefore may restrict access to education and other activities.

Woolf's eleventh recommendation is for a separate statement of purpose, separate conditions and generally a lower security categorisation for remand prisoners. This is also welcome, although of course statements of purpose — and the other modern management tools which have been adopted so enthusiastically by senior prison service officials in recent years — are only as good as the degree to which they inform practice. Although most prison staff can recite the prison service's mission statement by rote, it is questionable how far they can relate it to their day-to-day tasks. There is a case for interpreting the mission statement — perhaps through a separate statement of the values which should inform all the work of the service, and against which it could be judged.

The final core recommendation in the Woolf report is for improved standards of justice within prisons. These include the giving of reasons to prisoners for any decision which materially and adversely affects them, a grievance procedure and disciplinary proceedings which ensure that the governor deals with most matters under his present powers, relieving boards of visitors of their adjudicatory role, and providing for final access to an independent complaints adjudicator. Along with the notion of the 'community prison', his advocacy of 'justice' in prison may well come to be regarded as Woolf's most lasting and significant contribution to prisons policy.

Abolition of the role of boards of visitors in adjudications, the establishment of a complaints investigator, and the giving of reasons to prisoners, are all reforms which should significantly enhance prisoners' 'rights'. Like most features of the Woolf report, none of these changes requires legislation and therefore the Home Office has been able to move reasonably speedily to implement them. However, in the longer run, it would be better if all the new arrangements were to be placed on a statutory basis. There should be new and comprehensive legislation to replace the Prison Act 1952. Such new legislation would have many benefits. Not least, it would be the surest possible indication of the strength of the government's commitment to lasting reform of the prison system.

In any report — even one of this significance — there are of course omissions and confusions. One or two of Woolf's suggestions — for example, the idea that prisoners should earn a discount on their sentence if they work well in prison workshops — are an embarrassment. The notion that some prisoners should be released earlier because they are more productive workers seems utterly wrong in principle as well as being fraught with difficulties in practice. Similarly mistaken is Woolf's proposal that information should be provided to magistrates about where the defendant would be confined if bail was not granted and about the regime available. Although much more information could usefully be provided to magistrates and judges, specific information about specific prisons or remand centres should not be relevant to the remand decision (it is certainly not relevant to the statutory exceptions to the presumption of bail). Neither is there much to be said for Woolf's notion that 'consideration should be given to requiring the prison service to provide routinely for the sentencing court a report on the manner in which a remand prisoner had behaved while in custody'. Again, such information is not germane to the sentencing decision or to the new framework for sentencing policy introduced in the Criminal Justice Act 1991.

Sentencing policy is perhaps the most significant omission from the Woolf report (although Woolf stretched his terms of reference to the limit to enable him to discuss the range of offenders he wanted to see diverted from custody). He is also uncritical of the prison building programme, and expressly excluded consideration of the senior management reorganisation which took place in September 1990. There is no mention either of women prisoners (a reflection of the fact that women prisoners tend not to riot). The ideas of justice, care, respect, individual treatment and support for staff apply equally (but differently) to the approach which should be taken to women's prisons, and there is a strong case for a separate in-depth inquiry.

Most surprisingly, Woolf makes next to no mention of privatisation (contracting out), which may well be one of the most significant penal 'innovations' of the 1990s, and is certainly one of the most controversial. The first contracted-out prison (the Wolds on Humberside) opened its gate to prisoners in April 1992. In addition, plans were being made to contract out the new prison at Blakenhurst near Redditch (a prison taking both convicted and unconvicted prisoners) and some court escort duties. The government has also embarked on a programme of 'market testing' both services (like education) within prisons and entire institutions themselves. Strangeways itself will be the first prison to be market tested, with the government mounting its own bid in competition with the private sector. At a fringe meeting at the 1991 Conservative Party conference, the Prisons Minister, Mrs Angela Rumbold, talked about up to half the gaols eventually being in private hands. The contract terms for the Wolds should offer prisoners much enhanced conditions compared with those available to remand prisoners in the public sector. However, privatisation raises major practical and ethical questions, as well as risking the creation of a commercial lobby with a material interest in a growing prison population.

It is also perhaps worth saying that despite being free with their management advice, Woolf and his co-signatory Judge Tumim have little managerial experience themselves. Woolf's treatment of resources is somewhat cavalier and it is arguable that he should have added an economist and someone expert in industrial relations and public service management to his team of advisers. The Treasury was never likely to share the Woolf report's happy assumption that fewer prisoners here could release resources to pay for better regimes and conditions elsewhere in the system.

Finally, it should not pass without comment that the report makes little reference to the issue of alleged staff brutality — the allegation most frequently cited by the Strangeways rioters themselves. Even the outrageous treatment of young prisoners at Pucklechurch in the aftermath of the disturbance there is not the subject of as strong a condemnation as might have been expected.

The White Paper on the Woolf report

With publication of the Woolf report on 25 February 1991, the Home Secretary, Kenneth Baker, announced a series of immediate reforms to the prison system. In addition to the accelerated programme to end slopping out, these were:

(a)   home leave for prisoners in open prisons to be increased from three to six times a year;

(b)   routine censorship of letters to be abolished in all gaols except the dispersal prisons;

(c)   the introduction of cardphones in all establishments;

(d)   the consolidation of convicted prisoners' second monthly visit as a right not a privilege;

(e)   improvements to the assisted prison visits scheme so that prisoners' families will be eligible for assistance immediately a relative is received into prison.

This was a limited but not unpraiseworthy list of immediate changes, although Mr Baker rather spoiled things by using the term 'holiday camps' and referring approvingly to 'austere' conditions in his statement to the House of Commons. The Home Secretary went on to announce the preparation of a White Paper on the prisons. To some degree a White Paper was not necessary — if it chose to do so, the Home Office could simply have got on with the business of implementing the Woolf report, especially as no immediate legislation was planned. (When legislation eventually was forthcoming it took the form of a Prison Security Bill, the principal clause of which introduced a new offence of 'prison mutiny', a proposal not actually in the Woolf report and which had been rejected by the government itself in 1985.) It can be argued, therefore, that the White Paper exercise simply resulted in an unnecessary six-month period during which any further action was placed on hold. Nevertheless, the White Paper has provided an opportunity for the government to set down markers for the future, and to outline some of the fundamental principles by which it believes the service should be run.

More than that, the White Paper, *Custody, Care and Justice*, contains the bulk of the proposals made by Lord Justice Woolf in his report and gives substance to the Home Secretary's stated commitment to implementing those reforms. Implicitly, too, it models itself on the Woolf report: 12 key priorities echo Woolf's 12 major recommendations, and the structure closely follows that of part II of the Woolf report. Of those 12 recommendations, 11 are represented in the White Paper in some form. Proposals such as the establishment of a Criminal Justice Consultative Council, a system of prisoner 'compacts' and a code of prison standards are all present. Particularly welcome are the speedy abolition of board of visitors' adjudications (which took effect on 1 April 1992), and the commitment to the separate statement of purpose for remand prisoners.

Publication of the White Paper therefore marks an important step on the road towards the creation of a civilised and constructive prison system. Kenneth Baker perhaps deserves more credit than he has received for not overturning the Woolf principles when his own career was on the line after the Brixton escape. It is widely believed by staff who were in post at the time that the prison service was thrown off course in the 1960s by an excessive reaction to the escapes of the Great Train Robbers and the spy George Blake.

However, while the spirit of the White Paper is strong, its flesh is much weaker. In particular, the rejection of Woolf's recommendation that there should be a cap on prison overcrowding (discussed above), and the absence of any new proposals to reduce the size of the prison population, have caused considerable anxiety. The present Home Office forecast is that the prison population will reach between 56,000 and 57,000 by 1999, a rise over the decade of 25 per cent.

The Woolf report was unambiguous about the effect overcrowding has had on the prison system, and quoted with approval the (then) director general of the prison service:

The life and work of the prison service have, for the last 20 years, been distorted by the problems of overcrowding. That single factor has dominated prisoners' lives, it has produced often intolerable pressure on staff, and as a consequence it has soured industrial relations. It has skewed managerial effort and it has diverted managerial effort away from positive developments. The removal of overcrowding is . . . an indispensable precondition of sustained and universal improvement in prison conditions.

However, the White paper proposes only 'to avoid recourse to police cells because suitable accommodation cannot be found in prison cells; [and] to reduce overcrowding — and in particular avoid having to hold three prisoners in cells designed for one'.

Equally disappointing is the absence of any new proposals in the White Paper to tackle the root causes of overcrowding. In the absence of these, the White Paper appears to accept that despite the prison building programme and the effects of the Criminal Justice Act 1991, overcrowding will continue to beset the system. In a section entitled *Future Direction*, the White Paper admits that attempts to move prisoners out of police cells may require 'an element of overcrowding in prisons'.

Anxiety about the future size of the prison population is exacerbated by the government's lack of urgency in implementing the reforms, as implied by the cautious language in which the proposals are framed in the White Paper, and the lack of any firm time-scale for the majority of the measures. The indication that resources to implement almost all the reforms will have to be found out of existing budgets causes additional worry. Taken together, these factors may put the future success of the reforms in doubt.

Moreover, some of the proposals made by Woolf and Tumim have been watered down. For example, the increase in prisoners' pay to a figure of £10 per week proposed in the Woolf Report is met in the White Paper with a commitment to aim for a figure of £8 per week. (In practice, prisoners were initially offered a rise of only £1, a figure widely regarded as derisory.) Moreover, the language in which the White Paper is written gives the impression that the government's commitment to prison reform is less than whole-hearted. Phrases such as 'will consider' and 'is developing a strategy towards' recur. Even where the government has already timetabled reform, the White Paper seems reluctant to admit it. A case in point is the proposal for a Prison Complaints Adjudicator (Prison Ombudsman). The White Paper says only that the government is 'attracted to the notion' whereas in fact the Complaints Adjudicator will probably be in post by December 1992.

Although the fall–out from the Brixton escape has not been allowed to interfere too much with the Woolf reforms, security considerations are noticeably more prominent in the White Paper than they were in the Woolf report. Woolf was careful to argue in his report that observing the needs of security was but one part of the proper role of the service: he sought 'a proper balance within prisons between security and control on the one hand and humanity and justice on the other'. That proposition is accepted in principle in the White Paper. However, the prevention of escapes is called the 'first priority' of the prison service, and the White Paper proposes the doubling of the maximum penalty for aiding an escape. As noted earlier, the government has now legislated for a new offence of prison mutiny, a measure Home Office officials themselves admit privately is of little or no value and will probably never be used.

The paragraphs in the White Paper relating to prison staff are also weak. The availability of in-service training for prison officers is mainly addressed in the context of accreditation for existing prison officer tasks or training for newly promoted middle-grade governors. The Woolf proposal of 15 days per year in-post training is nowhere mentioned.

The final area of concern in the White Paper centres upon implementation of the measures it contains. Implementation requires resources and commitment to planned change. The Woolf report did not cost its proposals, and although it argued that many of the reforms it proposed would require little or no extra resources, it did not shirk the fact that 'some recommendations and proposals have financial consequences'. The Woolf report also called for 'a planned programme of change', with the package of measures in the report being 'moved forward together'.

However, the White Paper ducks both these issues. Ministers have made it clear that, with the exception of measures to install integral sanitation and improve security, money to implement the reforms will have to be found from within existing budgets. This is emphasised by constant references in the White Paper to reforms being implemented 'when resources allow'. Moreover, there is little in the White Paper which suggests a planned process of change: the timetable of reforms which was issued alongside the White Paper includes but a fraction of the proposed reforms, and the White Paper itself does not refer to planned time-scales. To give but one example, it is disappointing — as the House of Commons Employment Committee said in a report in late-1991 — that the government has set no target date for the general introduction of sentence plans. Nor has the government given any indication when the new primary legislation to replace the Prison Act 1952 is to be expected. This, allied to the Home Secretary's statement that the process of reform may take a quarter of a century, does not give the impression that the White Paper proposals will be implemented as a matter of urgency.

Nevertheless, despite these reservations, the prisons White Paper is a positive and constructive response to the Woolf report. If it were resourced in full, it would go a long way towards creating a prison system of which this country could be proud. Certainly Home Office civil servants have been feverishly writing position papers on such matters as standards and model regimes (although the word 'regime' is an unfortunate one suggesting a uniformity of approach when what is needed is diversity of activities available on the basis of prisoners' individual preferences and needs). Pilot projects have been set up on prisoners' pay and in-cell television, and governors have done what they can to take forward the Woolf agenda in their own establishments.

But it must equally be said that the majority of prisoners would not regard progress to date as adequate. Few people would pretend that the general quality of life for prisoners has shown much improvement. And we are still a very long way from the active and purposeful 'community' prisons which Woolf saw as constituting the prison system of the future.

Looking to the future

While international comparisons are fraught with difficulty, there is a strong case for saying that for many years the British prison system has been the worst in Western Europe. And although disturbances have occurred elsewhere in Europe too, it seems likely that the British prison system has also been the most prone to riots and acts of concerted indiscipline. It is difficult to believe that these facts are unrelated, and the whole thrust of the Woolf report — with its emphasis upon the balance between security, control and justice — confirms that view. The central themes, and the many specific proposals, in the Woolf report have provided the government a historic opportunity to transform our prison system into one which compares favourably with practice elsewhere in Europe and the rest of the industrialised world.

Although the Woolf report followed the worst riot in British prison history, in other respects its timing was fortunate. During 1989 and 1990 the prison population fell by around 5,000, a fall without precedent in the post-war era. Much of the optimism which the Woolf report engendered was related to this reduction in pressure on the system. Subsequently, some of that optimism has been lost as the number of prisoners began to rise again during 1991. It was particularly regrettable that the Home Secretary did not follow the example of all his recent predecessors by endeavouring to 'talk down' the prison population by advocating the sparing use of custody. On the contrary, on a range of 'issues' — 'joyriding' and 'squatting' among them — Mr Baker appeared to be encouraging a *greater* not a reduced reliance on imprisonment.

For this reason and others (notably his on-the-record criticisms of the quality of prison service management), relationships between the Home Secretary and senior prison service officials have been at rock-bottom. Furthermore, with financial restrictions beginning to bite, prison officers regularly at loggerheads with management, and a recent spate of prisoner disturbances, the state of the prisons remains balanced on a knife-edge.

The Woolf report and the *Custody, Care and Justice* White Paper have shifted prisons policy in a reformist direction to a degree which would have been unimaginable even five years ago. Yet day-to-day practice remains locked into a cycle of poor regimes, resource shortages and crisis management. A survey of prison governors carried out by the Prison Reform Trust at the beginning of 1992 indicates that, although there is great commitment to the Woolf report, reforms with significant resource implications — such as changing the times at which prisoners eat their meals — do not seem to have got very far.

I have before me a letter from a remand prisoner in a London prison, subject to 23 hours a day lock-up, denied a working radio, books and a pen, his requests for help allegedly ignored by staff. It is doubtful if that prisoner or his family feel they have yet gained a great deal from Lord Justice Woolf's endeavours.

References

Gunn, J., et al. (1991), *Mentally Disordered Prisoners* (London: Home Office).
Her Majesty's Chief Inspector of Prisons (1990), *Report of a Review by HM Chief Inspector of Prisons for England and Wales of Suicide and Self-harm in Prison Service Establishments in England and Wales* (Cm 1383) (London: HMSO).
Home Office (1991), *Custody, Care and Justice: the Way Ahead for the Prison Service in England and Wales* (Cm 1647) (London: HMSO).
Home Office Control Review Committee (1984) *Managing the Long-term Prison System* (London: HMSO).
House of Commons Education, Science and Arts Committee (1991), *Prison Education* (House of Commons Sessional Paper 311 1990/91) (London: HMSO).
House of Commons Employment Committee (1991), *Employment in Prisons and for Ex-offenders* (House of Commons Sessional Paper 30 1991/92) (London: HMSO).

Lygo, Sir Raymond (1991), *Management of the Prison Service: a Report* (London: Home Office).

Prison Reform Trust (1991), *The Identikit Prisoner* (London: Prison Reform Trust).

Woolf, Lord Justice (1991), *Prison Disturbances April 1990: Report of an Inquiry* (Cm 1456) (London: HMSO).

8

Parole

Mike Maguire*

The parole system in England and Wales was constructed upon shaky
theoretical foundations, its procedures have always reflected a tendency to
place administrative convenience above the requirements of 'justice', and
it has been subject several times to manipulation by Home Secretaries to
ease immediate political pressures. Not surprisingly, it has generated
cynicism and discontent among prisoners, unease among Parole Board
members, and continued criticism from academics about its lack of
principle and consistency. It has also been the subject of challenges in the
domestic and European courts, mainly on the grounds of breaches of the
principles of natural justice.

Yet despite its imperfect history, there have been relatively few influential
voices in the UK (unlike in the USA) calling for the total abolition of
parole. The possibility of early release, it is generally recognised, injects
some humanity and flexibility into an otherwise harsh penal system: it gives
prisoners a ray of hope, allows account to be taken of change over time,
and helps to ameliorate harsh sentencing practices. It is useful to prison
staff as a carrot to encourage compliance from prisoners, and it provides a
weapon to government for easing the chronic problems of prison
overcrowding without interfering directly in judicial decision-making or
appearing to condone softer sentencing policies.

*I am grateful to Dr Roger Hood and Mr Terry Russell for comments on a draft of this article.

The combination of hidden agendas and lack of clear thought about the fundamental purposes of parole will form a recurrent theme in this chapter. I shall comment briefly upon some of the main shifts in parole policy and practice which have occurred over the past two decades, putting them in the context of general shifts in criminal justice policy. I shall discuss the thinking behind the major legislative changes, arising from the Carlisle report (Home Office 1988) and incorporated in the Criminal Justice Act 1991, which will significantly alter the system in the 1990s. I shall refer to debates about specific procedural arrangements — most of them related to concerns about natural justice — which continue to reflect stresses in the system despite the reforms. Finally, I shall briefly consider issues relating to the release of life-sentence prisoners on licence, which, although not strictly 'parole', constitutes one of the Board's most important responsibilities. I shall draw throughout both upon published material and my own experience as a Parole Board member between 1988 and 1991.

The shifting sands of policy and practice

Parole was introduced in England and Wales under the Criminal Justice Act 1967. The rhetoric of its designers — expressed in the White Paper (Home Office 1965) which preceded the Act — drew heavily upon the concept of rehabilitation. Specifically, the White Paper made play of the notion of a 'recognisable peak in training', representing the ideal point at which to release a prisoner in order to reduce his or her chances of reoffending. This assumed that imprisonment entailed a programme of treatment or training, to which an inmate's response could be assessed by experts. At the right moment, the prisoner could be released under the supervision of a probation officer, who would continue the rehabilitative programme in the community. Prisoners could be released at any time between the one-third and two-thirds point of their sentence, the option being retained of recalling them to captivity if they failed to cooperate or if their behaviour gave cause for concern. Many of the people to whom such decisions were entrusted were recruited from professions with apparent expertise in the area of rehabilitation. The Parole Board had by statute to include probation officers, psychiatrists and academics, while local review committees (LRCs, see below) had to contain probation officers and prison governors — although there were also 'independent' or 'lay' members and representatives from sentencing or adjudicatory bodies (Crown Court judges on the Board, members of boards of visitors on the LRCs).

However, as many commentators (e.g., Morgan 1983; Bottomley 1984; Fitzmaurice and Pease 1986; Home Office 1988) have pointed out, there was also a powerful political motive underlying the introduction of parole: concern about prison overcrowding. The late-1960s had seen an unprecedented increase in recorded crime and a consequent rise in the prison population. Efforts to persuade sentencers to pass shorter terms of imprisonment were meeting with little success and a back-door way of easing the pressure on accommodation held great attractions: there would be no publicity about sentence length and no need for direct interference in judicial decision-making.

Early assessments

During the first few years of the system, the 'rehabilitative' model dominated decision-making practice. The first chairman of the Parole Board, Lord Hunt, repeatedly emphasised that release on licence was a privilege to be earned rather than a right to be expected, and a policy of caution was followed, both by the Board itself and, equally importantly, by the local review committees attached to each prison, which acted as a preliminary filter to reduce the pressure of cases on the Board. Until the mid-1970s, LRCs consistently made negative recommendations in over 60 per cent of cases, most of these decisions being accepted by the Home Office without reference to the Board. Moreover, many positive recommendations by the LRCs were subsequently reversed by the Board, the overall effect (even after legislation in 1972 which allowed releases of short-term prisoners on the recommendation of the LRC alone) being that during this early period over two-thirds of all eligible prisoners were refused parole. Almost by definition, too, the system favoured shorter-term prisoners with lesser offences and light records, who were naturally considered a lower risk than recidivists or long-termers (though in the latter case, the true risk was often grossly overestimated). The Board pointed to the low recall rate (little over 5 per cent) as a vindication of its practice and as a mark of the success of the system, but criticism was soon directed at what was seen as excessive caution (see, for example, West 1972). It was also pointed out that scarce probation resources were being expended upon the supervision, over periods too short to have an impact, of ex-prisoners who had relatively little need of it, while more serious offenders and people with greater problems continued to be released 'cold' into the community after many years in prison, with only voluntary after-care to fall back upon.

A further set of criticisms arose over a perceived lack of natural justice in the system. For example, Hawkins (1973) noted major inconsistencies in decision-making between local review committees, but no opportunity for prisoners to question — or even to know — the basis upon which such decisions were arrived at. Hawkins proposed regionalisation of the Parole Board to improve central monitoring and control of local practice, with the development of clear criteria for release. Such arguments, together with those for personal appearances by prisoners to put their case, the routine provision of reasons for refusal, and the possibility of judicial review of the Board's decisions, were subsequently aired — albeit sceptically — by Hall Williams (1975) in two well-known articles in the *Criminal Law Review* and have since featured regularly in debates about the system. (For summaries of these and other early concerns, see a special issue of the *British Journal of Criminology*, vol. 13 (1973); Thomas 1974; Bottomley 1990.)

But the most fundamental criticisms of the parole system were expressed, in particularly cogent fashion, by Hood (1974, 1975), who questioned the key premises underpinning its introduction and operation. He pointed out that there was simply no evidence of a 'peak in training', or that, even if such a thing existed, it could be identified by the Board: indeed, it was questionable if any meaningful training at all took place in many prisons. The system encouraged manipulation and dissimulation by prisoners and was profoundly unfair. Above all, it was wrong in principle for what were *de facto* sentencing decisions to be taken by a secret and unaccountable executive body, which gave no reasons for its decisions and which was not subject to appeal. He proposed the replacement of parole for all those serving under three years with a system of automatic release at the one-third point, followed by compulsory supervision up to the end of the sentence. This would come much closer to meeting the demands of justice and would leave decisions about the length of time that a prisoner should serve principally in the hands of a recognised sentencing body, the judiciary, whose decisions are taken in open court.

It is significant that Hood was to play a major role 14 years later in the Carlisle committee (Home Office 1988), whose conclusions, as we shall see, were based on similar arguments of principle. His ideas were taken up by an important pressure group, NACRO (Cavadino 1977) and came close to implementation in the early-1980s following their broad acceptance by a Home Office working party (Home Office 1981), only to be steamrollered off the government agenda by political and judicial opposition (see below).

The expansion of parole

Meanwhile, however, the problem of prison overcrowding had reasserted its influence, stimulating important changes in parole practice. In 1975, the then Home Secretary, Roy Jenkins, encouraged both the Board and LRCs to adopt a more generous policy of release, in particular towards prisoners with a history of relatively minor property offending who, despite presenting a greater risk of failure, would be unlikely to commit serious offences on parole. At the same time, he extended the range of cases in which release could be granted on the recommendation of LRCs without reference to the Parole Board (Home Office 1976). The effect of this initiative, which was largely motivated by a desire to thin out the population of lesser property offenders in prisons, was a considerable rise in the proportion of licences granted, from an average of 32 per cent over the period 1970–4 to 49 per cent over the period 1976–80. *De facto*, therefore, parole began to shift from being an occasionally granted privilege towards, if not a right, at least a reasonable expectation, particularly on the part of prisoners sentenced to between 18 months and three years.

Jenkins's action raised a number of interesting issues, which have continued to be pertinent and controversial in the parole process. First of all, it represented the first significant attempt by a Minister to influence or control the overall policy of the Board. While the Board was set up only to advise the Home Secretary, the latter retaining full powers to overturn its recommendations to release, in practice Ministers had left both the decision-making criteria and the determination of individual cases almost entirely to the Board, accepting all but a tiny handful of positive recommendations. Although, from the point of view of most penal reform groups, his actions were very welcome, the policy-setting precedent he established was a double-edged sword. As we shall see, it was used by a later Home Secretary, Leon Brittan, in a quite different way — virtually to halt the release of whole categories of offender — a development which caused dismay among the same reformers.

Secondly, Jenkins at the same time introduced — and made public — the first set of specific criteria to be employed by the Board in arriving at its decisions. These were, in short:

A   The nature of the offence.
B   The offender's previous history.
C   Behaviour in prison.
D   Medical considerations.
E   Home circumstances.
F   Likely response to supervision.

These criteria still remain in force at the time of writing, although they will change in October 1992, when the Criminal Justice Act 1991 is implemented. Every negative decision made by the Board is accompanied by a brief written reference (retained by the secretariat, though not revealed to prisoners) to one or more of the criteria: for example, 'No, on the grounds of A, B and F'.

Some of these grounds clearly relate to post-sentence changes in the prisoner or to future circumstances outside prison, but the first two (the nature of the offence and previous history) are unalterable matters of past record. Certainly, the nature of the offence may be highly relevant, in conjunction with information about post-sentence developments, to the assessment of risk. But when, as occurs on many occasions, 'A' is given as the sole criterion, serious questions have to be asked about the basis of the Board's interpretation of its own function. As was pointed out quite early on in the history of parole (Hawkins 1973; Hood 1974), to refuse early release purely on the grounds of the seriousness of the offence amounts to resentencing: this feature of the case, together with the convicted person's criminal history, has already been taken into account by the judge and the length of sentence has already been increased accordingly. To deny parole to one offender on these grounds, but to grant it to another no better qualified to receive it according to the remaining criteria, is to distort the differential between the original sentences passed, significantly narrowing (or even eliminating) the gap between them in terms of time actually served. Moreover, this is done on grounds unrelated to the original guiding principles of parole, i.e., that it should be granted to those whose response to training in prison offers a good chance of rehabilitation.

A third question raised by the intervention by Roy Jenkins in 1975, and still not resolved today, is whether there should be a presumption for or against parole. This issue has been sidestepped by successive chairmen, but it is of considerable importance to the numerous borderline cases which arise in Parole Board panels' day-to-day business. Failure to resolve it has also contributed to the inconsistency of decision-making which has frustrated prisoners and added fuel to critics' arguments for many years. For members who, consciously or unconsciously, adopt a presumption in favour of release, there is no reason to refuse a prisoner who arouses no serious doubts in relation to any of the six criteria — for example, one who possesses a fairly light criminal record, 'keeps his nose clean' in prison and has a reasonable release plan. Others, however, believe that the grant of parole demands positive signs of change in attitude or behaviour, and may find the above factors alone insufficient to earn release.

A final important issue raised by the Jenkins initiative is that of the interpretation of the concept of risk in parole decisions. Prior to 1975, both the Board and LRCs had shown a general reluctance to grant parole to prisoners who, though suitable on other grounds, had lengthy criminal records — this in itself indicating a high risk of reoffending. However, Jenkins made known his willingness to endorse the release of more people who, though higher risk in this sense, had records of relatively minor property offending and were therefore unlikely to present a threat to public safety. This approach has since been reflected in numerous government attempts to influence sentencing policy, particularly in the Criminal Justice Acts of 1982, 1988 and 1991, which have all included provisions to restrict the use of imprisonment for less serious offences, particularly those committed by young adults. It embodies a growing acceptance of the belief that imprisonment is primarily a punitive, rather than a rehabilitative, sanction and that the long-term goal of crime reduction is better served by non-custodial measures, including supervision by a probation officer, even when the objective risk of (relatively minor) reoffending is quite high (see, for example, Brody 1976; PAPPAG 1980; Home Office 1990).

The Brittan rules

Since the Jenkins initiative, the most important — and certainly the most contentious — intervention in parole policy by a Home Secretary occurred in 1983, when Leon Brittan announced that (a) the threshold of eligibility for parole (i.e., the minimum period to be served before it could be granted) would be reduced from 12 months to six months, (b) parole would not normally be granted at all to prisoners serving over five years for violent offences or drug trafficking, (c) Ministers would set a minimum tariff period to be served by life-sentence prisoners, dependent upon the circumstances of their offence and (d) specified categories of lifer would not be released until they had served a mimimum period of 20 years.

The first of these moves, the lowering of the parole threshold, was in the liberalising tradition of Roy Jenkins and was aimed, once again, at reducing the numbers of less serious offenders in prison. It was also a politically astute substitute for a proposed scheme of automatic release for short-termers after one-third of their sentence, similar to that originally put forward by Hood (1974), which had been floated by the Home Office Working Party on Parole (Home Office 1981), but which had been effectively buried by a combination of opposition from the senior judiciary and attacks upon the previous Home Secretary, William Whitelaw, at the 1981 Conservative Party conference for his soft law-and-order policies (Bottomley 1984). Brittan's alternative scheme, which retained discretion in release decisions, appeared on casual scrutiny to be merely a technicality and its implications — a significant increase in the numbers paroled — were not widely understood. Moreover, attention to it was diverted by the other elements of his initiative, the restrictions on parole for serious offenders and on release on licence for lifers. Although affecting much smaller numbers of prisoners, these measures were clearly attractive to the powerful law-and-order factions in his party and enabled the Home Secretary to ease the prison overcrowding problem while at the same time portraying himself as tough on crime.

To others, however, the new measures represented a usurpation of the responsibilities of the judiciary and of the Parole Board. Where the shorter-term prisoners were concerned, they had the effect of seriously distorting the differentials between sentences passed in court and time actually served (see below). Equally important, where prisoners serving long sentences for violent or drug offences were concerned, they virtually removed the decision-making powers of the Board (see, especially, Home Office 1988, also discussed below). Cases continued to be considered, reports to be written and prisoners' hopes to be raised, when in fact the prisoner had almost zero chance of being released. In most cases in which it considered release acceptable, the dilemma for the Board was whether to recommend parole in the knowledge that the decision would be overturned by the responsible junior Minister in the Home Office, or simply to take a realistic view and play the game, refusing release against members' better judgment. In time, Ministers let it be known that they would allow a period of up to eight months on parole for offenders in this category, so the Board then had to choose between recommending, say, 12 months, in which case the prisoner would quite likely be turned down by a Minister and receive no parole at all, or to forward date the release to leave precisely eight months.

In fact, the Board has generally adopted the realistic approach, rarely recommending release for a longer period than it knows to be acceptable to Ministers. While this may have benefited some prisoners, it has also distorted the statistical record of the Board's decisions, which has continued falsely to indicate broad agreement between members and the Home Secretary: in 1990, for example, Ministers overruled release recommendations in only 36 cases (Home Office 1991).

Where lifers are concerned, the Board has not had even this option. Fairly early in a lifer's sentence, the Home Secretary, having first consulted the Lord Chief Justice and the trial judge, now sets a minimum period to be served to 'meet the interests of deterrence and retribution'. The prisoner's case does not come before the Board until three years before this point is reached, so that (as the release process for lifers is a slow one, normally involving transfer to open conditions followed by a period on a pre-release hostel scheme) it is unlikely that he or she will leave prison prior to the tariff point set by the Minister. In certain categories of case — those involving the murder of police or prison officers, the sexual or sadistic murder of children, murder by firearms in the course of robbery, or murder in the furtherance of terrorism — this means that the papers are not considered until at least 17 years have elapsed.

In the short term, this policy led to a number of cases of heartless treatment of individual prisoners who had reached the penultimate stages of release, but were suddenly transferred back from open prisons into the closed system and told that they would have to serve several more years to satisfy their new tariff (*Re Findlay* [1985] AC 318). More generally, it raised serious questions about the respective roles of the executive and the judiciary. A study by the Oxford University Centre for Criminological Research in the late-1970s (Maguire et al. 1984) indicated that, in fact, many judicial recommendations on the minimum period to be served before the requirements of justice have been met (which are communicated to the Home Secretary in writing and attached to the parole dossier) were for considerably shorter periods than those subsequently laid down by Ministers — a phenomenon later confirmed in Home Office evidence to the House of Lords Select Committee on Murder and Imprisonment (1989). In other words, the appropriate punishment for different kinds of murder has since 1983 been determined more by the Home Secretary than by the courts. (As we shall see, the position for lifers convicted of offences other than murder is somewhat different.) At the same time, the role of the Parole Board has been restricted primarily to the assessment of risk once the tariff period has been served. Further comment on these issues will be made towards the end of this chapter.

The Carlisle committee

The anomalies which had always been present in the parole system, but which were greatly exacerbated by the Brittan rules, formed the subject of a thorough inquiry by a committee chaired by Lord Carlisle of Bucklow (Home Office 1988). The inquiry was set up partly in response to judicial misgivings about the distorting effect of remission and parole on sentence differentials (see below), but ranged well beyond this issue. In contrast to the tinkering approach of previous reviews, the committee showed itself willing to confront fundamental questions about the purposes of the parole system and the balance between political, judicial and independent inputs in determining real sentence lengths. Its recommendations, too, were based more upon principle than upon expediency.

The committee recognised, first and foremost, that as parole decisions are — in effect, if not in name — sentencing decisions, they should be subject to considerations of natural justice. It also recognised the broad ideological shift which had taken place, since the introduction of parole, in assumptions about the purposes and effectiveness of the criminal justice system as a whole: in essence the decline of faith in both the effectiveness and the ethical justifiability of the rehabilitative ideal and the growing acceptance of punishment-based ideologies such as 'just deserts' (see, for example, Von Hirsch 1976; Hudson 1987; Home Office 1990). From these foundations, the committee began to rethink the place of parole within the criminal justice system. The implications were that principles such as 'justice', 'consistency', 'fairness' and 'openness' should be central to the system, thus challenging the pre-eminence of unfettered individual discretion and the secrecy and unaccountability of the existing decision-making process.

This approach not only focused attention upon specific practical issues such as open reporting on prisoners, the right to a personal hearing and the possibility of appeal, it also strengthened the judicial argument that greater heed should be paid to 'proportionality' — i.e., that the lengths of time actually served by different prisoners should bear a closer relation to the relative lengths of the original sentences passed. As the Carlisle report pointed out, the changes made by Leon Brittan in 1983, and the subsequent introduction in 1987 of automatic remission at the half-time point for all those sentenced to 12 months or less, had greatly eroded differentials in real time served. For example, a broad presumption in favour of parole for relatively short-term offenders meant that most people sentenced to between 12 and 18 months were released after six months. Again, a person sentenced to 33 months was quite likely to be released after 11 months, actually serving less time than one sentenced to 18 months who was refused parole. As few decisions in these categories were taken by the Parole Board itself (most being left to LRCs under s. 33 of the Criminal Justice Act 1982), there were serious problems of inconsistency, leading many prisoners to refer to the system as a 'lottery'.

At the same time, the Brittan policy of restricting parole for serious offenders had heightened a general tendency towards 'bifurcation' (Bottoms 1977) in the penal system, with a much wider gap in real time served between those sentenced to up to five years and those sentenced to over five years. For example, a person sentenced to 60 months had a fair chance of release after 20 months, while a person sentenced to 63 months could well serve over 40.

The committee's main proposals can be summarised as follows:

(a) Discretionary parole should be abolished for all prisoners sentenced to four years or under. Instead, all should be granted automatic conditional release (later dubbed 'ACR') at the *half-time* point in their sentence. However, they would remain at risk of being sent back to prison to serve the remainder (or part of the remainder) of their sentence, should they be convicted by a court of a new offence committed during this period. In addition, all those sentenced to between one and four years would be subject to supervision by the probation service up to the three-quarters point in their original sentence. During this period, they would be subject to recall to prison for a serious breach of licence, although such decisions would be taken by a magistrates' court rather than, as now, the Parole Board.

(b)   All offenders sentenced to over four years would be subject to a system akin to the present parole arrangements, except that:

(i)   the Brittan rules limiting the release of those convicted of serious violent or drug offences would be abolished,

(ii)   release would not be possible until the halfway point in the sentence (rather than, as now, the one-third point),

(iii)   they would be supervised up to the three-quarters point (and, in contrast to those sentenced to under four years, subject to recall on the decision of the Parole Board) and would remain at risk of recall until the full expiry of the sentence.

(c)   The Parole Board should become independent of the Home Secretary, with full powers and responsibility for conditional release decisions, except in the case of life-sentence prisoners — in other words, Ministers would lose their powers to refuse parole for determinate-sentence prisoners.

(d)   The system should be reformed to meet the requirements of justice, particularly through the introduction of open reporting on prisoners (i.e., they should, except in special circumstances, see all reports about them considered by the Board), the giving of reasons for decisions, the opportunity for prisoners to ask for reconsideration of negative decisions, and the provision of advice and assistance to prisoners in the preparation of their cases.

(e)   The criteria for parole should be prescribed by statute, and decisions based primarily on the specific test of the risk to the public of the person committing further serious offences.

(f)   Local review committees should be abolished.

After a period of wavering, the government accepted the bulk of these proposals (Home Office 1990) legislating the changes in the Criminal

Justice Act 1991. Some of the proposals were modified — for example, automatic conditional release will apply to those sentenced to *under* four years, rather than four years or under — while one of the central tenets of the committee's argument, that the Parole Board should become fully independent of the Home Secretary, was rejected. Instead, the latter will retain the power to give the Board 'directions as to the matters to be taken into account by it in discharging any [of its] functions' (s. 32(6)). It was also stated in the White Paper (Home Office 1990, para. 6.16) that the Home Secretary's intention was 'that he should continue to consider the release of those serving very long determinate sentences of seven years or more': in other words, the only release decisions for which the Board would assume full responsibility were those concerning people sentenced to between four and seven years. The consequences of this are that, although (as in pre-Brittan days) the Board's release recommendations for longer-term prisoners may well be followed by Ministers in most instances, the maximum amount of time on licence that members will be able to grant to a prisoner against the Home Secretary's wishes will be little more than one year (i.e., the period between the half-time and two-thirds point of a $6\frac{1}{2}$-year sentence). Nevertheless, the reversal of the Brittan rules and the advent of automatic conditional release (which came into effect in June and October 1992, respectively) are significant reforms which will doubtless go some way towards meeting some of the major criticisms made over many years.

Apart from the failure to grant independence to the Board, key areas in which serious contention is likely to re-emerge include the setting of the parole eligibility threshold at half-time rather than one-third, the interpretation of 'risk', and the system of release for life-sentence prisoners. There are also important practical and procedural questions — several of them bound up with the arguments about natural justice — still to be settled regarding the composition of the Board, the role of the new community Parole Board members, the translation into practice of open reporting and the giving of reasons, and the nature of the appeal mechanism. I shall return to lifers in the final section. First, however, I shall comment in varying degrees of detail on the other issues listed above.

The parole eligibility threshold

The Carlisle committee's recommendation to set the minimum period to be served before release at half, rather than one-third, of the sentence passed, was prompted above all by the desire to produce a system palatable to the judiciary. It was on this very point that William Whitelaw's plans to introduce a system of automatic release had foundered in 1981: as a BBC television 'Panorama' programme at the time revealed, a cabal of senior judges had made it very clear to him that they considered automatic release at the one-third point unacceptable. However, as the committee recognised, unless there is a corresponding reduction in average sentence lengths, the inevitable consequence of keeping all shorter-term prisoners until the halfway point in their sentence will be a considerable increase in the prison population — a result desired by neither the Carlisle committee nor the government. For example, the majority of prisoners sentenced to terms of 18 months are currently released on licence before they have served nine months (in 1990, parole was granted in 76 per cent of all cases considered of sentences under two years: Home Office 1991, table 9); under the new scheme, *all* such prisoners will have to serve nine months. While the effect of this change will be offset to some extent by earlier release of the minority who do not currently receive parole, without a significant change in sentencing practice the overall effect will be an increase in total time served. The Carlisle committee's 'best guess' (Home Office 1988, para. 434) was that it would require an overall reduction in sentencing levels of about 5 per cent to 'balance the books'.

The committee's resolution of this problem was, in my view, an over-optimistic one. In short, it expressed the 'hope and expectation' that its proposed scheme would be met by a *quid pro quo*: a new willingness among the judiciary to pass shorter sentences. They stated:

> We believe that there is every prospect that the judiciary will not only welcome these new release arrangements but reduce sentence lengths in recognition of the greater meaning which will have been restored to the sentences which they pass. This would mean that the overall impact on the size of the prison population would be at worst neutral and at best beneficial. (Home Office 1988, para. 297.)

However, the committee then went on to qualify its 'belief':

> But much hinges on this and on the commitment of the government to work for lower overall sentences. There is the risk that the disappearance of release at a third and the increased liabilities which we propose for the latter part of the sentence could add, possibly substantially, to the prison population.

One does not have to be especially cynical to conclude that this risk is a very substantial one. Previous government exhortations to the judiciary to soften its sentencing practices have had notoriously little effect (see, for example, Ashworth 1983). Moreover, the committee's expressed desire to influence sentencers conflicts with many statements elsewhere in the report to the effect that sentence lengths are a matter for judges and magistrates alone, to be arrived at on the merits of the case, without consideration of the possible effect of post-sentence developments. For example, in para. 242 it is clearly stated that:

> We believe that it is right that judges and magistrates should continue to set the sentence in terms of the total sentence which the offender merits for what he has done, rather than taking as their starting-point the actual period of time which he should spend in custody.

Elsewhere (e.g., in ch. 2) there is much thinly veiled criticism of current sentence lengths, but at the same time an understandable reluctance to stray beyond the inquiry's brief into the question of whether and how sentencing reform should be attempted. All the committee can say is that, if its hopes for sentencing changes are not realised, 'we are satisfied that the case for a root and branch review of sentencing law and practice, and its early release mechanisms, would become irresistible' (para. 298). Considering the complex constitutional questions (particularly that of judicial independence) which such a review would raise, the massive opposition that it would meet from the judiciary, and the political risk to whatever government attempted it, this seems to be an unrealistic conclusion. In sum, the practical effect of the half-time release arrangements, however much fairer they are than the present system, will almost certainly be an increase in the prison population.

The risk factor

The Carlisle committee (Home Office, 1988, para. 244) made the important statement that:

> . . . our observations have led us to believe that, quite separately from the restricted policy, prisoners are commonly denied parole because they 'have not done long enough' for their crime, even though they clearly pose no possible risk for the future. Under the present system this is understandable; in our view it is not, however, satisfactory.

This describes the phenomenon, mentioned above in the context of the Jenkins criteria, which is often referred to by the somewhat imprecise term of 'resentencing' — i.e., the denial or postponement of parole on the grounds that the prisoner has not yet been sufficiently punished for what he or she did, even if there is every prospect of a crime-free return to society. From my own experience on the Board, I can confirm the Carlisle committee's belief that this is by no means uncommon. Both in panel meetings and in LRCs' written reasons for a negative recommendation (which are forwarded to the Board), the phrases 'Not enough time yet' and 'No, on the grounds of A' are familiar refrains. Moreover, some members tend to adopt a punitive approach in relation to particular types of crime which they consider especially abhorrent, or which, they believe, warrant a deterrent message to potential offenders through the frequent denial of parole (this approach is especially overt in the case of drug trafficking). I even recall one member who adopted the rule of thumb that anyone coming before the Board should serve at least one year in prison from the time of sentence before release should be contemplated (even if time had previously been served on remand), purely on grounds of retribution and general deterrence. (For a similar experience recorded by an observer, see Tata 1990.)

In order to bring to an end this approach to parole decisions, the Carlisle committee argued that the criteria for release should be statutorily laid down (in either primary or subsidiary legislation) and that the overriding consideration should be that of 'the risk to the public of the person committing further serious offences at a time when he would otherwise be in prison' (Home Office 1988, paras 318–24). By raising the eligibility threshold to that of half the sentence passed, the committee argued, the problem of insufficient punishment would be eliminated, it being a reasonable assumption that this proportion was sufficient to meet the requirements of justice. From then on, full attention could be turned to the question of risk to public safety (with due regard to factors such as willingness to cooperate with supervision). This principle was accepted by the government (Home Office 1990, paras 6.21–23), although it preferred a 'general policy direction' to specific legislation to implement it.

While the new approach sounds unexceptionable in principle, there are several doubts about how well it will work in practice. To what extent, for example, will members manage to overcome the temptation to resentence when the offence was particularly abhorrent to them, justifying retributive decisions by a process of post-rationalisation on the subject of risk? Even if they can avoid this, to what extent will they be able accurately and objectively to assess risk? And what relative weight will they give to the very different questions of (a) how likely is the prisoner to commit another offence and (b) if he or she does reoffend, how serious is the crime likely to be?

The first question (avoidance of resentencing) is impossible to answer. Parole Boards are generally very jealous of their independence and are quite willing to ignore guidelines if they disagree with them (a good example is provided by deportation cases, on which clear Home Office instructions were consciously ignored by many members during my period on the Board — see below). There will be no break in membership during the changeover period, and it is likely that members will find it difficult to break long-established approaches and habits.

The question of how good members will be at assessing risk depends to some extent upon training (which, until recently, has consisted essentially of one day's explanation of procedures and practices combined with reading and sitting in on a panel considering cases), but even with comprehensive training the problem remains a difficult one. Research has consistently indicated that even experts such as psychiatrists are not notably successful at predicting serious criminal behaviour, except in the very short term. In particular, there is a general tendency to over-predict 'dangerousness' — the well-known problem that false positives (those predicted to reoffend but who do not) invariably outnumber true positives (those correctly predicted to reoffend) — see, for example, Bottoms (1977), Brody and Tarling (1980) and Monahan (1984).

At present, members are provided in some cases with a 'reconviction prediction score' (RPS), calculated by the Parole Unit using a formula based upon the prisoner's age, sex, type of offence, previous convictions and other known factors, which represents the estimated percentage chance that he or she will reoffend within a given period. However, this is largely ignored by panels, who prefer to base their decision on the individual circumstances of a case, rather than the potential parolee's membership of a particular risk group ('Otherwise, what are they paying us for?' as one member put it to me). It has been argued forcefully by one of the criminologist members of the Board, Professor Pease, that, under the new system, an improved version of the RPS should be developed and should play a central part in both the making and monitoring of parole decisions (see Hann et al. 1991), but I have not been able to detect much enthusiasm for this idea among members. Moreover, the RPS tends to be less reliable in the more serious cases which will in future occupy the Board: while it provides a good indication where a recidivist burglar is concerned, it is of less use to the consideration of a case of rape or serious violence by a first offender. Certainly, it is important to know the basic fact that only a small proportion of such offenders repeat their crimes, but the grave consequences of making a mistake over *which* offenders will do so lead members, not unnaturally, to pay much more attention to qualitative assessments, such as psychiatric reports, than to statistics.

The above points, of course, also raise the issue of the membership of the Parole Board. If, as the new criteria for release imply, one is looking for experts in the prediction of risk, it seems to follow logically that the Board should be composed of psychiatrists, psychologists, criminologists and possibly probation officers and ex-police or prison officers, all of whom can claim either professional knowledge or close acquaintance with serious offenders. On the other hand, it now seems difficult to justify, except on pragmatic or political grounds, the inclusion of judges, and it may be asked whether independent members such as business people, however great their experience of life, are equipped to make good judgments about whether a given prisoner will commit another serious offence. They may bring some welcome common sense to bear, but, judging by my own past experience, independent members (along with judges) are generally more likely than the expert groups to give weight to retributive and deterrent consider-ations, and hence to be less concerned about charges of resentencing.

The final question raised above, concerning the relationship between the risk of reoffending and its potential seriousness, is perhaps the thorniest of all. How, for example, is one to weigh an 80 per cent chance of future non-violent (but perhaps substantial) property offending against a 50 per cent chance of supplying drugs or a 5 per cent chance of a sexual assault? The Board will almost certainly receive no clear guidance on such issues, and will thus be left to form its own definitions of 'seriousness'. At present, where the existence of criterion A (the nature of the offence) effectively allows members to vote against parole because they do not feel a prisoner has served sufficient time to atone for his or her crime, one can, as noted above, quite easily identify many individual members' beliefs about the relative seriousness of different kinds of offences: some will take consider-able persuasion to agree to release *any* drug trafficker, others are reluctant to release child molesters, others take a particularly harsh view of violence against women, and so on, while they may be quite liberal in relation to kinds of offence considered particularly heinous by other members. When the exercise of blatant resentencing of this kind is made more difficult, the assessment of seriousness will be unambiguously transposed from judg-ments about past offending to the area of possible future offending. However, while one member may feel that, for example, the fairly high risk of further burglary offences is acceptable but the much lower risk of a violent offence is not, another member may take a different view of the relative seriousness of the two types of crimes and hence come to opposite conclusions.

In sum, there is a danger that the concept of risk assessment will be used, consciously or unconsciously, to camouflage other grounds for decisions, in particular those of deterrence and retribution. Of course, if one took the philosophy of the new system literally, it might be argued that decisions should be taken entirely on the basis of the best statistical predictions available, thus obviating the need for personal judgment and discretion entirely. After all, there is little evidence that, over large runs of cases, parole boards can out-perform statistically derived risk scores in their ability to predict reoffending (Ward 1987; Hann et al. 1991). But if we accept that there is a place for parole at all, then there must be a place for discretion in individual cases. What is necessary, it seems to me, is to ensure that:

(a) As much information as possible is available to the Board about the statistical likelihood of reoffending among the broad risk group into which any prisoner falls (at the very minimum, information of the order that, for example, first-time violent offenders constitute a low-risk group while, say, repeat arsonists constitute a very high-risk group), so that, however the data are eventually interpreted, decisions are at least not made on the basis of incorrect assumptions in areas about which firm criminological knowledge exists.

(b) The problem of possible reversion to resentencing practices under another name is squarely addressed and continuously monitored.

Only then can it be at all convincingly asserted that cases are considered in accordance with the principles of 'justice', 'fairness' and 'consistency' which underpin the Carlisle committee recommendations.

Procedural issues and natural justice

The concept of natural justice, or due process, is also highly relevant to other arrangements surrounding the decision-making process. It is a fundamental principle of natural justice that when a decision is made about a person's liberty, that person should have the opportunity to put his or her case and to know what other evidence has been used to arrive at the decision. Similarly, he or she should be given reasons for the conclusion reached and should have the opportrnity of challenging it on procedural grounds (see, for example, Griffith and Street 1973; Garner 1989). As noted earlier, such questions were considered briefly in the context of parole some years ago by Hall Williams (1975), who concluded that, as parole was a privilege rather than a right and the proceedings were administrative rather than judicial in principle, there was no overwhelming argument for applying to them the strictest requirements of natural justice. While desirable, he argued, reforms such as the right of prisoners to be heard in person, to be legally represented or advised, to see reports about them, to be given reasons for decisions, or to appeal, could be reasonably resisted on the grounds of practical difficulties and administrative inconvenience. This view has been echoed several times in the British courts, initially in the case of *Payne* v *Lord Harris of Greenwich* [1981] 1 WLR 754, in which the applicant's claim that he was entitled to reasons for being refused parole was rejected on similar grounds. However, as will be discussed below, the European Court of Human Rights has taken a more robust line in the context of decisions about life-sentence prisoners, and the Carlisle committee (Home Office 1988, para. 346), although eventually recommending against personal hearings in determinate cases on the grounds of cost, noted that the 'inconvenience' objection may have a limited life:

> We suspect that the developing jurisprudence of the European Court of Human Rights may well require the introduction of Parole Board hearings in due course.

Although the issue of appearances in person — on which the Carlisle committee itself was split — has clearly been shelved until such a decision materialises, several of the other natural justice issues raised by the Carlisle committee have come under active consideration. They were not covered by the Criminal Justice Act 1991, which left procedural arrangements mainly for executive decision, and discussions on these matters seem likely to continue almost to the last minute before the Act is implemented. Here I shall look briefly at options in the areas of (a) the role of community Parole Board members; and (b) arrangements for open reporting, the giving of reasons and the questioning of decisions.

Community Parole Board members

The Carlisle committee recommended the abolition of local review committees, principally on the ground that, with the number of cases to be considered coming down from 24,000 to around 4,000 per year, the Parole Board would have no need for assistance from another decision-making body. However, in addition to their decision-making role when sitting as part of the committee, individual LRC members perform the important function of interviewing prisoners prior to hearings in order to allow them to put their case verbally (members' first duty in this role is to record what the prisoner says, rather than to make personal judgments — although the latter may well influence their vote subsequently as a member of the panel).

The Carlisle committee's final proposals entailed the removal of all personal contact between prisoners and those making decisions about them, although its commitment to more justice in the system had led it to consider seriously ideas such as allowing parole applicants to receive legal advice or to appear in person before the full Board, possibly with legal representation. In the end, it recommended the recruitment at a local level of trained parole counsellors, who would assist prisoners in the preparation of written representations to the Parole Board, but would play no part in decision-making.

This idea has since metamorphosed into the planned appointment of 'community Parole Board members' (CPBMs), whose role will be similar to that previously carried out by the LRC interviewer, although with additional administrative responsibilities such as ensuring that parole dossiers are complete before being sent to the Board. However, they will not perform the function of a 'friend' or 'counsellor'. Rather, the CPBMs will sit on panels themselves as full voting members — albeit not hearing cases in which they have met the prisoner. This separation of roles in individual cases seems to be an improvement upon the old LRC system, but the lack of advice is a serious omission. A possible solution might be to ask boards of visitors to perform the 'counsellor' function as part of their general watchdog role in prisons (Maguire and Vagg 1984). As boards have now lost their adjudicatory function, they are less likely to be regarded by prisoners as part of the establishment (Martin 1975; Committee on the Prison Disciplinary System 1985).

Open reporting, reasons and challenges to decisions

The government has broadly accepted the principles of open reporting and the provision of reasons as laid down by the Carlisle committee. From October 1992, prisoners will be able to see virtually everything in their parole dossier. However, questions still surround the circumstances in which exceptions will be allowed — obvious candidates being cases where disclosure might harm a third party (e.g., negative information supplied by a member of the prisoner's family), some police reports and, perhaps, psychiatric reports which a doctor feels might exacerbate a condition, were the prisoner to see them. There is also a danger that prison staff, or other report writers who have to live with a parole applicant after a refusal, will be less frank than they should be in recording their reservations, in order to avoid any unpleasant consequences of being blamed by the prisoner for the result. However, experience in other countries suggests that problems with open reporting generally turn out to be less serious than anticipated and it is to be hoped that the principle does not become diluted by excessive qualifications or attempts to convey sensitive information to the Board secretly.

Where the giving of reasons for parole decisions is concerned, earlier commentators, including Parole Board chairmen, argued that it was both time-consuming and difficult to carry out in practice, as it was difficult to summarise panels' wide-ranging conversations (cf. Hall Williams 1975). While such arguments are dubious in the broad context of administrative law (many other forms of tribunal face the same problems but regularly provide reasons), a more serious problem, in practice, will be to avoid the provision of bland or routinised reasons. A brief experiment in giving reasons some years ago foundered on these rocks, with panels doing little more than ticking boxes equivalent to the official criteria (A, B, C etc.). Such an exercise is of little use to a prisoner in comprehending what he or she can do to improve later chances of parole. On the other hand, panels may be reluctant to give more detailed reasons, on the ground that this may offer prisoners more ammunition to dispute the decision.

Although this argument, too, seems difficult to defend in principle, it illustrates the important point that the giving of reasons is closely tied up with a further element of natural justice, that of appeals against decisions. What if a prisoner disputes the factual basis of one of these reasons — for example, that his home circumstances are unsettled when, in fact, he has a family to return to? The current proposal is that he should be permitted to complain to the Parole Board Chairman, who would be able to order a rehearing if doubts arose about the initial decision on procedural grounds. However, it is likely that many prisoners will also seek judicial review, on the grounds either that the reasons provided are not consistent with the published criteria for parole, or that they are based on factual inaccuracies. As the criteria are not statutorily defined, it may be that the courts will not entertain actions on the first ground — although it could equally be argued that the central principle of risk has been clearly specified in many official pronouncements. But whatever view they take, there is a great deal of potential trouble in store, which could be avoided by the introduction of a formal right of appeal, on clearly defined grounds. The above issues are good illustrations of the half-hearted approach to natural justice which underlies many of the proposed reforms — a comment which, as we shall see, applies with even more force in the case of life sentence prisoners.

Deportees

Before leaving the subject of determinate sentences, a few comments should be made about a problem which goes to the heart of arguments about the purposes of parole: that of decisions concerning prisoners who are subject to deportation orders. By far the largest group in this category are those convicted of drug trafficking offences, principally people referred to in the drugs trade as 'mules' or 'donkeys' — i.e., overseas residents, often from Third World countries, who are paid to smuggle drugs through British customs. Many of these receive substantial sentences and hence were subject, until June 1992, to the Brittan restrictions on parole. But whereas a British citizen sentenced to over five years for an identical offence is quite likely to be granted eight months on licence, most foreigners in this position who are subject to deportation have been refused parole entirely, receiving only the one-third remission to which all prisoners are entitled. Indeed, for those on shorter sentences not subject to the Brittan rules, the tendency to refuse parole to deportees often results in even greater disparities. The principal arguments used by Parole Board members reluctant to grant release in such cases are (a) that refusal sends a strong deterrent message back to potential smugglers in drug-producing countries and (b) that the main purpose of parole is to prevent reoffending through supervision by probation officers and that such supervision is not available abroad (or, even if it is, failure to abide by the conditions will not result in recall to prison).

The first of these arguments is totally untenable if one accepts the principle that parole should not entail resentencing. The second has more substance, but comes up against the strong counter-argument that prisoners should not be penalised simply for the fact of being foreigners. In the great majority of cases, drug mules possess no previous convictions, have good family circumstances, show remorse and contrition, behave well in prison and are unlikely to become involved in drug trafficking again (at least in this country, if only because they are now known to HM Customs and Excise). In these circumstances, they are excellent bets for parole, the only possible reasons for refusal being the serious nature of their crime and the fact that they cannot be supervised by a British probation officer.

In fact, Home Office policy — conveyed in a memo to the Parole Board — is that people in this situation should be treated *as if they had a satisfactory release plan in the UK*. However, this has been consciously ignored by many Board members, for the reasons outlined above.

The Carlisle committee found this situation unacceptable and suggested that deportees should be removed from the parole process altogether. This recommendation was adapted in the Criminal Justice Act 1991, with the effect that those sentenced to under four years will be released, like all other prisoners, at the halfway point in their sentence, while the remainder will be considered by the Home Secretary without the benefit of the Board's advice. However, simply to transfer the responsibility in this way is not to solve the problem — indeed, it is likely that Ministers will follow a tough policy, but that the decisions will be even less publicly visible than they are now. An alternative approach might be to formulate an automatic release system for all deportees — though here, again, there is no obviously fair way of determining the point of release. For example, should they be released at the half-time point in their sentence (in which case, British drug traffickers serving over four years, who will remain subject to discretion on release, would be disadvantaged by comparison) or at the two-thirds point (in which case the deportees would be unfairly treated in comparison to British offenders)? A compromise suggestion is that they should be granted automatic remission at a point somewhere between the two — perhaps after serving 60 per cent of their sentence. A more radical proposal is that much greater use should be made of the facility to transfer deportees to prisons in their own countries at an early stage in their sentence — although the counter-argument here is that, depending on where they come from, they may receive either much more lenient or much harsher treatment (in terms of both prison conditions and release provisions) than they would in this country.

These questions are not subject to easy solution — indeed, I can envisage no arrangements which would be regarded as totally fair to all sides. However, there is no doubt that the present situation is indefensible, while the proposed solution gives little cause for confidence. Above all, there is no doubt that many of the people involved suffer greatly by being cut off from their families, unable to speak English and having little prospect of parole from what are often very long sentences (the average length of sentences for drug trafficking has increased markedly over the past few years). While there is little public sympathy for the perpetrators of what is clearly regarded by the judiciary as one of the most serious offences coming before the courts (although some argue that those caught smuggling drugs are often sentenced too harshly for the sins of others — many are 'expendable pawns', themselves victimised and exploited by professional criminal organisers), this should not divert attention from basic principles of fairness and consistency. While the idea of removing them from the parole system entirely seems a reasonable solution — so long as clear principles are established determining what proportion of their sentence they should serve — perhaps the best argument is that, if risk is to become the principal criterion for release, this can be assessed in the case of drug traffickers just as well as in any other type of crime, and that they should therefore remain subject to parole (but not to resentencing) like everybody else.

Life-sentence prisoners

The arrangements for the release on licence of life-sentence prisoners — not strictly 'parole', although the Parole Board plays a vital part in the process — has received considerable media attention recently, primarily as a result of some important decisions in the European Court of Human Rights (ECHR) in Strasbourg and of a government defeat in the House of Lords during debates on the Criminal Justice Bill in 1990. The court cases have mainly concerned so-called 'discretionary' lifers: that is, people sentenced to life imprisonment for offences other than murder (where the life sentence is mandatory). These at present account for only about 20 per cent of all lifers, although if current campaigns for abolition of the mandatory life sentence are successful, *all* such sentences will be discretionary and hence subject to the court rulings. (The strength of opinion in favour of abolition was reflected in a vote to this effect in the House of Lords in April 1991, during the committee stages of the debate on the Criminal Justice Bill. Although government opposition to the reform led subsequently to a reversal of the vote in the Commons, the fact that the amendment was strongly supported by the Lord Chief Justice and many other senior judges suggests that a change in this direction is likely before too long. For other authoritative discussions of this issue, see PAPPAG 1986; House of Lords Select Committee on Murder and Life Imprisonment 1989; Windlesham 1989.)

The main areas of contention surrounding release on life licence include arguments for procedural reforms already discussed in relation to parole — access to records, the right to put one's case in person, the provision of reasons for decisions and so on — as well as the issue of recall to prison (discussed below), which has generated several important court cases. However, perhaps the most critical attention has been directed at the timing of Parole Board reviews, under the system introduced by Leon Brittan in 1983. The key concept here is that of the tariff. Prior to 1983, life-sentence cases could be reviewed at intervals on the basis of a prisoner's progress, but thereafter cases have not been heard by the Parole Board until a minimum 'tariff period' has been served. As mentioned earlier, the length of this period, which is explicitly intended to reflect the requirements of deterrence and retribution, is set quite early in a prisoner's sentence by the Home Secretary, after obtaining the views of the Lord Chief Justice and the trial judge: moreover, for certain categories of murder the tariff period is virtually automatically set at a minimum of 20 years, no matter what the judicial view.

In its evidence to the House of Lords Select Committee on Murder and Imprisonment (1989), the Home Office reported that in 1988 Ministers had set a higher tariff than that recommended by the judiciary in almost two-thirds of cases considered. The committee noted that:

subsequent witnesses [expressed] surprise and shock at the extent to which a junior Minister could increase the tariff in this way. It was greatly felt that the question of the tariff, reflecting the requirements of deterrence and retribution, was properly a matter for the judiciary, and for them alone, to determine, and should not subsequently be revised (upwards or downwards) by the Home Secretary or any of his junior Ministers.

Similarly, there was widespread condemnation by witnesses of the Home Secretary's decision in 1983 to introduce, without Parliamentary approval, 20-year minimum sentences for those convicted of certain categories of murder. Witnesses saw this as usurping the rightful prerogative of the judiciary in determining the appropriate tariff.

Similar sentiments, including serious concern about the effect of the policy change upon a small number of prisoners whose expectations of imminent release were suddenly dashed after it was announced (see *Re Findlay* [1985] AC 318, referred to earlier), have been expressed by many other commentators. Ministerial practice has been modified in respect of discretionary lifers since 1987 as a result of a court ruling (*R v Secretary of State for the Home Department, ex parte Handscomb* (1991) *The Times*, 4 March 1991) that the tariff should be set in such cases strictly according to the recommendations of the judiciary, but this principle has not been extended to murder cases (*R v Secretary of State for the Home Department, ex parte Smart* (1991) *The Times*, 19 January 1991). It is quite likely, however, that the ECHR will eventually rule against any involvement in setting tariffs. If this occurs, of course, the focus will shift to the secrecy of *judicial* recommendations, strengthening the argument for tariffs to be set in open court, as well as for the right of judges to pass determinate sentences upon those convicted of murder.

Turning now to the natural justice issues discussed earlier in relation to parole, the ECHR — with belated support from the British courts — has adopted a particularly forthright approach to discretionary (non-murder) lifer cases. In 1990, the ECHR held that the Parole Board's review procedures were in breach of art. 5(4) of the European Convention for the Protection of Human Rights and Fundamental Freedoms (*Thynne, Wilson and Gunnell v United Kingdom* (1990) Eur Court HR, ser. A, No. 190). The court argued that, once the tariff point for the offence in such cases had been passed, the only matter to be decided was that of risk to the public:

this should be determined by proper legal proceedings, with prisoners having full access to reports about them, the right to put their case in person, the right to legal representation, and the right to know the reasons for the decision arrived at. The English Court of Appeal subsequently overturned domestic precedent to allow Wilson access to his file (*R* v *Parole Board, ex parte Wilson* [1992] 2 WLR 707), although it is clear from the decision in *Smart* referred to above that the domestic courts, like the British government, have continued to draw a sharp distinction between murder and non-murder cases with regard to such principles. Murder cases, of course, form the bulk of those dealt with.

The practical result of the ECHR judgment was the incorporation into the Criminal Justice Act 1991 of a new procedure for the determination of discretionary life sentence cases. A new kind of tribunal will be set up, along the lines of Mental Health Review Tribunals (for an account of these, see Peay 1989), in which cases will be heard in the presence of the prisoner by a judge and two other Parole Board members — probably a psychiatrist and either an independent member or a senior member of the probation service (the composition of the panels is yet to be finalised). Prisoners will have full rights to disclosure of documents and legal representation. However, satisfactory as this outcome may be, it is likely to be only the first stage in a long legal saga in which mandatory lifers struggle for the same treatment (or, alternatively, until all lifers become discretionary through the abolition of the mandatory penalty for murder).

A final issue concerning lifers which has both attracted criticism from penal reform groups and exercised the courts for some years is that of recall to prison. The life licence extends for the remainder of a released prisoner's life and he or she is subject to recall, on the recommendation or confirmation of the Parole Board, at any time his or her behaviour 'gives cause for concern'. In the case of those originally convicted of murder — as with prisoners on parole from determinate sentences, who have made similar complaints about the system — no specific reasons have to be given for the recall and there is no appeal mechanism beyond written representations to the Parole Board (following the ECHR judgment, recalls of discretionary lifers will be reviewed by the new tribunals).

The arguments here have largely focused upon the same issue which has dominated the debate about release procedures — i.e., the extent to which natural justice should be built into the decision-making process — and it is likely that any future reforms will apply to both areas. A point of particular importance in recall cases is that, if prisoners dispute the *facts* of the allegation which has led to their recall, it seems highly unsatisfactory for them to not to be allowed a hearing and representation to do so. Indeed, the latter are constitutionally required in the United States (R. Hood, personal communication). However, whatever procedural arrangements obtain, it is important also to ask the substantive question of what criteria should be applied to recall decisions. For example, should unsubstantiated accounts of aggressive behaviour be sufficient, or should firmer evidence be necessary? Again, what weight should be attached to new criminal convictions? Under the ordinary parole system, a further conviction of any kind tends to be regarded as sufficient reason for recall, even when the new offence is much less serious than, or of a different character to, the original crime. Because recall to a life sentence is so much more devastating to the individual, lifers are often treated more leniently if they reoffend in a minor, non-violent way. Nevertheless, there are examples of, say, 'domestic' murderers being recalled because they have slipped into a pattern of petty property offending, although this does not appear to increase their risk of killing again. Whether this is justifiable is a question which has rarely been openly debated — though it was argued by one witness to the select committee (House of Lords Select Committee on Murder and Life Imprisonment 1989) that European case law demands a close link between the original offence and any ground for subsequent recall.

Finally, one unsatisfactory aspect of recall which might beneficially be altered without any need for legal intervention is its 'all or nothing' character: once recalled, the prisoner has to go through the same protracted release procedures as before, so may spend an unjustifiably long time in custody after the initial cause for concern has receded. It might be possible, as some probation groups have suggested, to institute some form of temporary recall, in order to deal with cases where a specific but probably short-lived risk has arisen (say, in relation to a particular relationship), or where it is felt there is a need for assessment in safe conditions before the final decision is made.

Concluding remarks

For all the effort put in by the Carlisle committee, and the undoubted improvements which will flow from its recommendations, the stresses which have been evident in the parole system from its early days are unlikely to disappear. Indeed, developments born out of a desire for fairness and a broadly liberal philosophy could well backfire in the form of an unwanted rise in the prison population: judges may not reduce overall sentencing levels to counterbalance the raising of the parole threshold; once selection for release is removed at the lower sentencing bands, a higher proportion of prisoners on conditional release may be recalled for breaches of licence; the Parole Board may interpret 'risk' little differently from its present interpretation of the current criteria; and — a point not yet mentioned — the introduction of 'supervision for all' after release will remove the rationale for the current practice of giving many higher-risk prisoners a 'short launch' (usually about three months) purely in order to prevent them coming out cold after several years in custody, the likely result being a significant fall in the proportion of positive decisions. (A similar phenomenon was observed in Canada when universal supervision was introduced there.)

In addition, despite the welcome discontinuance of the Brittan rules, the new system will not reverse the trend to bifurcation in the treatment of short and long-term prisoners — on the contrary, the four-year cut-off point helps to legitimise it; developments such as open reporting and the giving of reasons for decisions will go only part-way towards the aim of meeting the requirements of natural justice (prisoners will no longer address in person anyone concerned in the decision in their case, and there is no entitlement to representation or appeal), a situation which, exacerbated by the lack of statutory criteria for release, may generate a flurry of attempts at judicial review; the lack of clarity and insufficient safeguards in the criteria and procedures for recall will attract continuing criticism; and the differential treatment of mandatory and discretionary lifer cases will almost certainly lead to fresh challenges in the European Court.

While some of these weaknesses may be resolved through further reforms, the fundamental problem which has dogged the parole system since its inception — the lack of clear agreement about its purposes — is likely to re-emerge into the open at regular intervals. Although the Carlisle committee was admirably clear in its own view of the purposes of parole, it has to be remembered that many of those involved at ground level have differing opinions in this regard, which are unlikely to be permanently changed by abstract penological arguments. As Tata (1990) rightly points out, the broad support which the idea of parole has enjoyed in Britain has been the result of what he calls a 'nebulous consensus': the very contradictions and lack of clarity which have characterised the system in the past have allowed people of quite different political and penological persuasions to support it for very different reasons. For example, it can be justified on the grounds that it assists rehabilitation, or that it limits the damaging effects of custody, or that it protects the public through post-custodial supervision, or that it saves money, or that it aids control in prisons. The fact that four-person panels consisting of, among others, judges, academics, probation officers, psychiatrists, ex-police officers and prison governors, or business people, can come to unanimous agreement (often, one suspects, for very different reasons, as well as through a certain amount of unspoken dealing — conceding some cases in order to get one's view accepted on others) in 93 per cent of the cases before them, reflects the remarkable durability and flexibility of this consensus. One of the Carlisle committee's main aims was to expose the contradictions and confusions which lay behind it and to attempt to replace them with stronger logic and coherence. But one wonders whether the new focus upon risk will do any more than simply introduce a new rhetorical framework for the same hidden conflict of penological philosophies, rather than, as is intended, genuinely changing the basis of decision-making.

References

Ashworth, A. (1983), *Sentencing and Penal Policy* (London: Weidenfeld & Nicolson).

Bottomley, A.K. (1984), 'Dilemmas of Parole in a Penal Crisis', *Howard Journal*, vol. 25, No. 1 (February 1984), pp. 24–40.

Bottomley, A.K. (1990), 'Parole in Transition: a Comparative Analysis of Origins, Developments and Prospects' in *Crime and Justice*, vol. 12, ed. M. Tonry and N. Morris (Chicago: University of Chicago Press), pp. 319–74.

Bottoms, A. (1977), 'Reflections on the Renaissance of Dangerousness', *Howard Journal*, vol. 16, pp. 70–96.

Brody, S. (1976), *The Effectiveness of Sentencing* (Home Office Research Study No. 35) (London: HMSO).

Brody, S., and Tarling, R. (1980), *Taking Offenders out of Circulation* (Home Office Research Study No. 64) (London: HMSO).

Cavadino, P. (1977), *Parole: The Case for Change* (London: NACRO).

Committee on the Prison Disciplinary System (1985), *Report of the Committee on the Prison Disciplinary System* (Cmnd. 9641) (London: HMSO).

Fitzmaurice, C. T., and Pease, K. (1986), *The Psychology of Judicial Sentencing* (Manchester: Manchester University Press).

Garner, J.F. (1989), *Garner's Administrative Law* (London: Butterworth).

Griffith, J.A.G., and Street, H. (1973), *Principles of Administrative Law* (London: Pitman).

Hann, G., Harman, W.G. and Pease, K. (1991) 'Does Parole Reduce the Risk of Reconviction?' *Howard Journal*, vol. 30, No. 1, pp. 66–75.

Hawkins, K. (1973), 'Parole Procedure: an Alternative Approach', *British Journal of Criminology*, vol. 13, No. 1, pp. 6–25.

Home Office (1965), *The Adult Offender* (Cmnd 2852) (London: HMSO).

Home Office (1976), *Report of the Parole Board, 1975* (London: HMSO).

Home Office (1981), *Review of Parole in England and Wales* (London: HMSO).

Home Office (1988), *The Parole System in England and Wales: Report of the Review Committee* (Cm 532) (London: HMSO).

Home Office (1990) *Crime, Justice and Protecting the Public: the Government's Proposals for Legislation* (Cm 965) (London: HMSO).

Home Office (1991), *Report of the Parole Board, 1990* (London: HMSO).

Hood, R. (1974), 'Some Fundamental Dilemmas of the English Parole System' in *Parole: Its Implications for the Penal and Criminal Justice System*, ed. D.A. Thomas (Cambridge: Institute of Criminology).

Hood, R. (1975), 'The case against executive control over time in custody' [1975] Crim LR 545.

House of Lords Select Committee on Murder and Life Imprisonment (1989), *Report of the Select Committee on Murder and Imprisonment* (House of Lords Paper 78 1988/89) (London: HMSO).

Hudson, B. (1987), *Justice through Punishment* (Basingstoke: Macmillan Education).

Maguire, M., Pinter, F. and Collis C. (1984), 'Dangerousness and the Tariff: the Decision-making Process in Release from Life Sentences', *British Journal of Criminology*, vol. 24, No. 3, pp. 250–68.

Maguire, M., and Vagg, J. (1984), *The Watchdog Role of Boards of Visitors* (London: Home Office).

Martin, J.P. (1975), *Boards of Visitors of Penal Institutions* (the Jellicoe Report) (London: Barry Rose).

Monahan, J. (1984), 'The Prediction of Violent Criminal Behaviour: a Methodological Critique and Prospectus' in *Crime and Justice*, vol. 3, ed. N. Morris and M. Tonry (Chicago: University of Chicago Press).

Morgan, N. (1983), 'The shaping of parole in England and Wales' [1983] Crim LR 137.

Nuttall, C. (1977), *Parole in England and Wales* (Home Office Research Study No. 38) (London: HMSO).

PAPPAG (1980), *Too Many Prisoners* (London: Parliamentary All-party Penal Affairs Group).

PAPPAG (1986), *Life Sentence Prisoners* (London: Parliamentary All-party Penal Affairs Group).

Peay, J. (1989), *Tribunals on Trial: A Study of Decision-making under the Mental Health Act 1983* (Oxford: Clarendon Press).

Tata, C. (1990), *Coherence and Consensus: Parole Policy in England and Wales*. Unpublished dissertation. Department of Politics, University of Hull.

Thomas, D.A. (1974), *Parole: Its Implications for the Penal and Criminal Justice System* (Cambridge: Institute of Criminology).

Von Hirsch, A. (1976), *Doing Justice: The Choice of Punishment* (New York: Hill and Wang).

Ward, D. (1987), *The Validity of the Reconviction Prediction Score* (Home Office Research Study No. 94) (London: HMSO).

West, D.J. (1972), 'Board on parole', *New Society*, 15 June 1972, pp. 567–8.

Williams, J.E. Hall (1975), 'Natural Justice and Parole' [1975] Crim LR 82, 215.

Windlesham, Lord (1989), 'Life Sentences: the Paradox of Indeterminacy' [1989] Crim LR 244.

9

Juveniles

Phil Parry*

Introduction

The sheer scale of involvement in crime of those aged 16 and under surprises many. In 1989 they comprised 21 per cent of the males and 23 per cent of the females found guilty or cautioned for indictable offences in England and Wales. In the case of burglary, theft and handling stolen goods their proportionate involvement was just under one-third of the total. The majority of offences they committed, however, were relatively minor and were committed against property. Just 11 per cent were involved in indictable offences of violence, 2 per cent sexual offences and 1.5 per cent robbery (Home Office 1990a). As Professor West has commented:

> For most youngsters law-breaking is not a steady occupation, but something that happens sporadically, usually when they are not too busy with their ordinary affairs, when the time and place and company are propitious and a tempting opportunity presents. . . . The totality of youthful crime includes occasional offences by vast numbers of different individuals and repeated offences by a small number of versatile and persistent delinquents. (West 1982, p. 142.)

---

* Phil Parry writes in a personal capacity and his views should not be taken as necessarily representative of the views of magistrates in general or the Inner London commission area in particular.

The number of juveniles proceeded against in the juvenile courts has steadily declined for several years and today, at 55,000, is only about half the 1983 figure. This can be accounted for by a drop in the general juvenile population of 23 per cent and by a large increase in the numbers diverted from the court system by means of police cautioning. But there has also occurred a significant fall in the numbers of juveniles found guilty or cautioned per 100,000 in the 10–16 age group. This is in contrast to the overall growth of crime for all ages which appears to have been rising at between 4 and 5 per cent per annum since 1980. The sentencing patterns of the courts are changing as well and are in general far less punitive and custody-orientated than previously. In 1989, 2,300 males aged between 14–16 were sentenced to immediate custody, less than one-third of the figure for 1979. During the same period the proportionate use of immediate custody for this group in relation to indictable offences fell from 12.8 per cent to 9.1 per cent (Home Office 1990a, para. 7.21). The courts' use of fines has also decreased whilst their use of supervision orders, absolute and conditional discharges and attendance centre orders has increased.

This picture of juvenile crime is therefore at considerable variance with the popular view, often encouraged by dramatic and selective media coverage of particular incidents, of a youth crime picture rapidly spiralling out of control (Pearson 1983). These 'moral panics' are for most of us based largely on the fear of crime rather than its reality, but they do nevertheless lead to a deterioration in the quality of life for a significant number of citizens, particularly the elderly. These fears can play a major role in policy development, for example, by influencing political parties so that they may be publicly perceived as tough on law and order, and supportive of the police.

The statistics therefore appear to illustrate a healthy picture of decreasing offending, with the police and the Crown Prosecution Service committed to diverting large and increasing numbers of offenders away from the stigmatising process which involvement with the court system often entails, and a magistracy increasingly imposing non-custodial sentences if this is at all practicable. There are, however, serious points of stress within the system.

Diversion

Diversion from the courts can occur at two points in the system of juvenile justice. Since the 1960s most police forces, encouraged by the Home Office (see Home Office circular on the cautioning of offenders (No. 59/1990), which followed Home Office circular No. 14/1985), have been diverting large numbers of juveniles away from the court process by using a system of cautioning. In 1989, 64 per cent of males aged 14–16 (82 per cent of females) were cautioned in respect of indictable offences compared with 35 per cent in 1979 (59 per cent for females) (Home Office 1990a, tables 5.2 and 5.3). The police can choose to administer an informal caution on the spot or, if specified conditions are met, a formal caution or severe telling-off by a uniformed senior officer at the station. The necessary conditions are:

(a)   there must be sufficient evidence to give a realistic prospect of conviction,
(b)   the offender admits the offence,
(c)   the offender, or his or her parents, give an informed consent to being cautioned.

If these conditions are met, Home Office circular 59/1990 recommends the police to take into account whether a caution would be in the public interest and thus directs attention to the nature of the offence, the likely penalty, the offender's age and health, attitude towards the offence and previous criminal history.

The decision to caution rather than to recommend a prosecution to the Crown Prosecution Service may be made as a result of the facts of the case having been referred to a multi-agency cautioning panel. These now exist in many, but by no means all, local authority areas. The panels vary greatly in their purpose, personnel and the types of cases they consider, but most often they are composed of representatives from various agencies such as social work, education welfare, police and the probation service. Their purpose is to consider the background and circumstances of the offender and the offence he or she has committed in order to establish whether a caution is the most appropriate way of dealing with the case. They can usually only make recommendations to the police and may or may not have a policy of suggesting to the offender and his or her parents that they take advantage of the help and assistance which other statutory and voluntary agencies may be able to provide.

The rationale underpinning cautioning is that courts should only be used as a last resort. This is because, first, it prevents juveniles becoming stigmatised by others and seeing themselves as criminals. Secondly, a rather frightening caution administered in a police station is likely to have more impact than a court appearance and hence help reduce the chances of reoffending. To quote Professor West again, 'The niceties of justice are totally lost on the average unsophisticated offender who finds himself caught up in a meaningless and frightening ritual of uncertain outcome' (West 1982, p. 143).

Lastly, and considered by many police officers to be particularly important, it is an inexpensive method of dealing with crime, particularly minor, opportunistic and transient crime, compared with the alternative of prosecution.

Even if the police do recommend prosecution, the Crown Prosecution Service retains the discretion to discontinue the proceedings or refer the case back to the police for further consideration. The activities of the CPS are governed by a Code for Crown Prosecutors which recognises that 'the stigma of a conviction can cause irreparable harm to the future prospects of a young adult' and urges prosecutors to consider carefully the possibility of dealing with the offender by means of a caution when considering whether it is in the public interest to prosecute. Prosecutors are urged to make themselves aware of the arrangements for inter-agency consultation in their area and to contribute their experience to the development of these procedures. The Code clearly establishes the important principle that before deciding upon prosecution, the prosecution must be satisfied that not only the letter but also the spirit of the cautioning guidelines have been complied with (Code for Crown Prosecutors, paras 8(iii), 21 and 22).

Little research has been conducted into the degree to which these recommendations are followed or the effect they have in practice of ensuring that the CPS is truly independent from the police in this respect. The evidence available suggests that in two particular sample areas 95.8 per cent of cases recommended by the police for prosecution were in fact prosecuted (Gelsthorpe and Giller 1990). If this is typical it raises concern because of the considerable evidence available which demonstrates diversity of practice between and within particular police forces and the differences in view about appropriate prosecution policies between different Crown Prosecutors. As has been pointed out by the leading researchers in this area, Gelsthorpe and Giller (1990, p. 164), it is right to question whether such general statements of intent, however well-meaning, achieve their purpose when they do not contain specific objectives which can be measured and monitored and lead to practice being altered in the light of the results.

Cautioning by the police has never been placed on a statutory basis and is covered only by the Home Office circulars to chief constables issued in 1985 and 1990, both of which have attempted to establish national standards. There are problems, however, and these relate to variations in cautioning practice and the scope that still remains to extend its use. The cautioning rates for 14–16-year-old males in respect of indictable offences in 1989 vary from 60 per cent (Hampshire, Greater Manchester) to 86 per cent (Dyfed-Powys) (Home Office 1990a, para. 5.8). There are also considerable variations between different areas in the same police force; for example, in the number of previous cautions which will be allowed before a recommendation to prosecute is made. Police forces employ widely different methods of organising the consultative process prior to the decision being made and may employ different criteria to define 'serious' or 'non-serious' offences. Research evaluating the 1985 Home Office circular concluded that, whilst it had led to an overall increase in cautioning rates, variations between forces had narrowed only slightly (Wilkinson and Evans 1990).

Considerable scope exists to extend cautioning even further. Of those juveniles who were not cautioned in 1989 and who were subsequently sentenced in the court, 50 per cent of the males (64 per cent of females) aged 10–13 years were given some form of discharge, as were 29 per cent of the males (51 per cent of females) in the 14–16 age group (Home Office 1990a, tables 7.2 and 7.3). Many of these youngsters might have benefited more from a caution than from being processed through the legal system and at little risk to the public. Indeed, if the number of 10–13-year-olds given a caution (88 per cent of males, 95 per cent of females) (Home Office 1990a, p. 102) is combined with the large numbers given a discharge by the courts, a strong case can be argued in favour of not only extending the practice of cautioning but also of increasing the age of criminal responsibility from 10 to 14 years of age. The argument would be even stronger if 'cautioning plus' schemes were extended so that young people who previously would have committed criminal acts, but for the raising of the age of criminal responsibility, were encouraged to avail themselves of the services offered by local caring agencies.

The 1990 Home Office circular aims to resolve many of these problems, its major proposal for promoting change being a recommendation that every area establish multi-agency consultative arrangements. There is little doubt that cautioning is most effective where these exist. The problem is that until cautioning is put on a statutory basis with a requirement for every local authority and police force to participate on a panel, it is doubtful if more than marginal change will occur. The task is particularly urgent since the jurisdiction of the juvenile court was extended to cover 17-year-olds in 1992. Many magistrates and police officers believe 17-year-olds to be qualitatively different from juveniles because they supposedly commit more serious offences, have more previous convictions and are often less suitable for community service sentences. They are therefore seen as less suitable for cautioning. It is hardly surprising to note that whilst the cautioning rate for 15-year-old males in 1989 was 61 per cent it was only 13 per cent for 17-year-olds. These suppositions are in fact open to serious doubt. Research conducted by Evans (1991) in Northamptonshire, an area with a high cautioning rate, shows that about one-third of the male young adult offenders were in fact making their first appearance in the adult court, half of them had no criminal convictions as juveniles and four-fifths of them had no citable cautions! Just 17 per cent were charged with offences involving violence against the person. It would seem, therefore, that there is indeed considerable scope for extending cautioning to this age group, particularly if the 'cautioning plus' schemes mentioned above were extended to provide assistance with accommodation, unemployment and training schemes. Evans estimated that if the 1990 guidelines had been applied to his sample the cautioning rate could be increased by between two and four times.

The juvenile court

Juvenile courts were established by the Children Act 1908. Their jurisdiction has been extended by the Criminal Justice Act 1991 to include 17-year-olds and the Act also renamed them youth courts. In 1988 nearly 90 per cent of the juveniles appearing before them were aged 14 to 16. The government estimates that about three-quarters of defendants in the new court will be aged 16 to 17 (Home Office 1990b, para. 8.30). Nationally, it is estimated that this measure will increase the work of the court by 50 per cent. The problem we face is similar to that before the 1991 Act, '. . . the weight of evidence points to the juvenile court meeting neither its objectives nor the new demands made of it' (Morris and Giller 1987, p. 241).

Take, for example, the determinants of the sentencing decisions reached by the courts. Many practitioners believe, supported by considerable evidence, that instead of one national system of juvenile justice, England and Wales in fact consists of a large number of discrete, localised systems. Each may display major variations in its sentencing practices and may not use the disposals available to it in any methodical way (Moxon et al. 1985; Children's Society 1988). Thus the experience of the offenders and the sentence they receive can depend upon the geographical area in which the court they attend is situated. The danger, of course, is that juveniles and their parents see justice itself as irrational and biased, with the process lessening their respect for the rule of law generally. Most juveniles do not like being punished, but they expect it; their disillusionment may come about from what they perceive as similar cases being treated in dissimilar ways. Several reasons account for this.

First, there is the confusion in the minds of many of those who work in the court, be they magistrates or lawyers, about what their role is supposed to be. Are they there to apply a 'justice' or a 'welfare' model? In the former, emphasis is placed on the adversarial approach with the full benefit of procedural safeguards afforded to the accused. Sentencing is by reference to the tariff operating in the locality and is directly related to the seriousness of the offence. If the welfare approach is adopted, however, less weight is placed upon these factors and emphasis is given to establishing the reasons why the juvenile offended and which sentence would best facilitate his or her individual needs both now and for the future. These differences in approach will obviously result in widely different sentencing practices. Secondly, educational provision, the presence and quality of social worker involvement and the availability of alternatives-to-custody schemes in the area can result in variations in disposals. Third, there is considerable variation in the quality of legal representation available to the juvenile. Most juveniles are now offered the opportunity of free legal representation but its quality, and indeed relevance, can vary widely. This is particularly important if the local bench adopts a 'justice' model, because legal and procedural requirements are accorded considerable importance. All too often, young and inexperienced lawyers are allocated the case at the last moment and appear ill-prepared. In the writer's experience barristers are sometimes even unaware of the courts' sentencing powers!

Fourth, the language used and procedures adopted frequently confuse both juveniles and their parents. Often they are told to sit down in what is to them a formal and intimidating court setting and are expected to remain silent for the great majority of the time. They usually take little active part in the proceedings and appear to have only a limited understanding of what is happening. For example, when asked if they have anything to say, the answer is almost invariably no. When asked if they have understood the sentence which has just been passed, it is often clear that they have failed to understand what it involves or why it was passed. Thus the entire proceedings can seem to them to be a theatrical production in which they feel they ought to be taking the principal role but which in fact relegates them to the wings, unnoticed and unvalued for the most part — a play run by and for the benefit of the professionals.

Sentencing and custody

Given the dramatic reductions in the numbers of juveniles sentenced to custody over the last 10 years it might reasonably be anticipated that those who are so sentenced are those who pose a grave and direct threat to the community. In fact this is often not the case. In 1989 just 25 per cent of those in custody had committed crimes involving violence or robbery

(Home Office 1990c, p. 56). Nor do the majority of those sentenced to custody have long criminal records. In 1986 53 per cent of those sent to detention centres had two or fewer previous convictions and 27 per cent sentenced to youth custody had two or fewer previous convictions (Children's Society 1988; the custodial sentence for young people is now detention in a young offender institution).

Serious questions must be asked about what objectives are being achieved by these sentencing practices. With reconviction rates of 70 to 80 per cent within two years of release, they do not generally deter the offender and there is increasing evidence that they do not deter others from committing crimes. (See Home Office 1990d, which makes the point that research studies suggest 'that a sentence should not normally be justified on merely deterrent . . . grounds' (para. 3.6). In fact it is the probability of arrest and conviction that is likely to deter offenders (para. 3.4).) What the period of custody may well do is to turn the offender into a more sophisticated, confirmed and effective criminal. Custodial sentences do not even protect the public, other than in the short term, as the average length of sentence served is just 4.4 months (Home Office 1990a, para. 7.26). Nor are they cost effective. It costs between £311 and £375 per week to hold a youth in custody (Home Office 1990d, p. 110) compared with the costs of alternative disposals such as intermediate treatment which costs about £700 for each juvenile's complete placement (NACRO 1991, p. 10).

Prior to 1992 custodial sentences for young offenders were governed by the terms of the Criminal Justice Act 1988. The Act provided that, subject to s. 53 of the Children and Young Persons Act 1933, which deals with the long-term detention of young offenders for very serious crimes, custodial sentences were to be served in young offender institutions (s. 1(3A)). The sentence could be imposed on males between 14 and 20 years and females between 15 and 20. Subject to a number of exceptions the minimum term of detention was 21 days and the maximum 12 months. Custodial sentences could only be imposed where:

(a)   the nature and gravity of the offence were such that if the offender was over 21 the court would pass such a sentence, and,

(b)   the offender had a history of failing to respond to non-custodial penalties and was unable or unwilling to respond to them, or,

(c)   only a custodial sentence would be adequate to protect the public from serious harm from him, or,

(d)   the offence was so serious that a non-custodial sentence could not be justified (Criminal Justice Act 1982, s. 1(4) as amended by the Criminal Justice Act 1988).

The criteria for custodial sentences are now to be found in the complex provisions of s. 1(2) of the Criminal Justice Act 1991 and these apply now to all offenders irrespective of their age.

A custodial sentence can now only be imposed where the offence, or the combination of the offence and one other associated with it, was so serious that only a custodial sentence can be justified, or, where the offence is a violent or sexual offence, that only such a sentence would be adequate to protect the public from serious harm from the offender. Section 1(4A)(a) of the Criminal Justice Act 1982 is therefore repealed. This permitted custody where the offender had a history of failing to respond to non-custodial penalties.

The court is required to state its reasons for imposing a custodial order and to explain why it formed that view. It must normally consider a pre-sentence social inquiry report prior to sentencing (Criminal Justice Act 1991, ss. 1(4) and (5) and 3).

The courts may no longer impose custodial sentences on 14-year-old boys and the minimum period of detention for persons aged 15 to 17 is now two months (Criminal Justice Act 1991, s. 63).

The 1991 Act modifies and restricts the criteria contained in the Criminal Justice Acts 1982 and 1988 and is a statutory recognition that courts should be reserving custodial sentences exclusively for serious offenders. But it is not entirely clear how effective statutory sentencing criteria are in changing the sentencing practices of the courts. David Thomas, for example, believes that reductions in the number of custodial sentences have got little to do with the statutory restrictions (*Guardian*, 28 November 1991). The weight of informed opinion, however, supports the other side of the argument which is that whilst the 1982 and 1988 criteria were ignored, at least initially, by some courts, subsequently they have come to play a more important role in decision-making, particularly in borderline cases (NACRO 1990). This can be accounted for by the large number of successful appeals against sentence to the Crown Court between 1983 and 1988 where lawyers used the statutory wording as the basis of the appeal. At the same time the Court of Appeal was delivering guideline judgments on the meaning of the criteria for the benefit of magistrates and lawyers alike. This, combined with the pressures placed upon magistrates during the 1980s to employ structured decision-making processes, has led to a position whereby the language of the statute has increasingly pervaded the proceedings in the court and the seriousness with which the statutes are treated by those who sentence.

There are, therefore, some grounds for hoping that the new criteria in the Criminal Justice Act 1991 might further restrict the number of custodial sentences passed. But there remains a number of associated problems. Within England and Wales there is widespread inconsistency between different magistrates' courts in their use of custodial sentences. Juvenile justice is highly localised and individual benches develop their own customs and practices, often without regard to, or indeed knowledge of, those prevailing in neighbouring areas. A relatively small number of areas are responsible for a high level of custodial sentencing. Thus, while the overall custodial rate for 14–17-year-old males in 1989 was 8 per cent, this masks variations in different areas of between 1 per cent (West Sussex) and 15 per cent (Cleveland) (NACRO 1991, p. 57). Indeed, within the same city substantial variations may exist between different benches. In 1988, for example, 4.8 per cent of those sentenced in the inner London borough of Camden received a care or custodial sentence, whilst in the inner London borough of Hackney the corresponding figure was 30 per cent (see *NACRO London Newsletter*, No. 5 (May 1990), p. 6; NACRO makes the point that variations may be due to differences in cautioning rates and the availability and credibility of community-based alternatives as well as differences in the sentencing climate). If there is to be a substantial reduction in the number of juveniles sentenced to custody, it is to the 'high-custody' courts that we must look to establish whether the new criteria are actually influencing sentencing practices and action taken in the event that they are not.

Even where a particular court tries its best to apply the criteria it is still faced with a multitude of problems. The Act is highly complex and even with the legal advice of a qualified court clerk, many lay magistrates are likely to experience difficulty in applying it. They will have to take into consideration the large number of Court of Appeal guideline judgments which attempt to define 'seriousness' and 'public protection' in a wide variety of circumstances (see *Blackstone's Criminal Practice 1992*, E3). They must also agree upon the weight they should attach to information concerning the circumstances of the offence which might take the case above or below the 'seriousness' threshold. Section 3(3)(a) of the Act requires the court to consider any aggravating or mitigating factors, and thus variables such as good or bad motive, intoxication, premeditation, age of victim and intellectual capacity, will need to be taken into account. At best the courts are likely to experience a lengthy learning period — with some help from the Judicial Studies Board — until appeals to the Court of Appeal establish clear guidelines which the magistrates understand and use in their deliberations. Until the new rules have been mastered it is probable that little progress will be made towards reducing inconsistencies of sentencing practice. Indeed the situation may deteriorate in the short term.

Alternatives to custody

Do we need to sentence to custody more than the small number of offenders who pose a direct and serious threat to the public — for example, those who have committed an offence involving serious violence? There is considerable evidence that effective and credible alternatives to custody exist which reduce offending in the long term. In addition they protect the public more effectively than custody and are considerably less expensive. 'Intermediate treatment' (IT) has been described as consisting of a

> wide variety of recreational, educational and socially valuable activities designed to secure the involvement of the juvenile within a community context. . . . The term indicates that the provision is 'intermediate' between the removal of the juvenile from home and relying solely on the support of social work with the juvenile or his family. (Home Office 1990d, para. 11.24.)

Various forms of IT schemes have been operated by a number of local authorities for some years, but their provision has been patchy and the monitoring of their effectiveness often poor or non-existent. The usual method of ensuring that an offender participates in such a scheme is for the social worker or probation officer to request the court to make a supervision order. Magistrates have the power to insert various conditions into such orders, for example, that the offender participate in an IT programme (either at the discretion of the offender's supervisor under the Children and Young Persons Act 1969, s. 12, or as stipulated by the court under s. 12A(3)) for a stipulated number of days up to a maximum of 90 (ss. 12(3) and 12A(5)). In certain circumstances the court can also require the young person to live in local authority accommodation for up to six months (s. 12AA). The procedure for making the order is now contained within the Criminal Justice Act 1991 and this requires, among other considerations, both that the court consider a pre-sentence report and that it considers whether the offence was serious enough to warrant such an order (ss. 6, 7 and 68).

In 1983 the Department of Health and Social Security made available £15 million over a three-year period to voluntary organisations which were willing to work together with local authorities to provide intensive programmes for juvenile offenders as a direct alternative to custody (Local Authority Circular LAC 83(3)). The IT initiative was also intended to promote an inter-agency approach to dealing with juvenile crime and to act as 'seed-corn' money to allow local authorities the time to transfer their resources from the declining residential care sector to the expanding community-based programmes. In the result 110 projects were established in 62 local authority areas (58 per cent of the local authorities in England).

Projects vary considerably in their activities and working methods but a useful illustration of what might typically be involved is the Children's Society Tracking Project in Kirklees (Curtis 1989, p. 96 et seq.). This is aimed at serious and persistent offenders who would almost certainly be sentenced to custody in the absence of IT. The project staff would normally request the court to make an initial 28-day conditional bail order so that they can assess the offender's attitude and suitability. If this is judged satisfactory they return to the court asking for a one-year supervision order containing a specified activities clause (under the Children and Young Persons Act 1969, ss. 7 and 12). The offender initially meets a 'tracker' each day and this continues for four months, gradually decreasing in frequency. The offender is helped to organise his or her time in a constructive way and is provided with considerable support and advice in dealing with common problems, such as those involving family, finances, unemployment and training. They meet as a group on two evenings each week and discuss together matters such as personal relationships, offending, employment problems, the law and criminal justice.

There is now considerable evidence that projects such as this are successful. The large majority of offenders manage to complete their orders successfully and levels of reoffending have decreased (and often when reoffending has occurred it is for less serious offences) (Curtis 1989; NACRO 1991, p. 52 et seq.). Projects such as these are increasingly persuading magistrates that a serious, hard alternative to custody exists which is both a strong and a demanding response to delinquency. It is also more likely to benefit both the community and the offender. Indeed, the IT initiative led Mrs Virginia Bottomley, Minister of State at the Department of Health, and a former Inner London Juvenile Court magistrate, to comment, '[The initiative] has proved that serious and persistent offenders can be managed and supervised without recourse to institutions and that courts can have confidence in community-based sentences' (NACRO 1991, p. 3).

One reason in particular accounts for this success. All the projects had a management committee composed of representatives from a broad range of statutory and voluntary agencies such as social work, education, police, probation and, significantly, the local magistracy, who were represented on 75 per cent of all committees, see NACRO 1991, p. 30. The process was facilitated in 1985 when the Lord Chancellor gave his approval to magistrates serving on these committees, see *The Magistrate*, vol. 42, No. 3 (1986), p. 34.

Research consistently demonstrates that the most effective method of promoting alternative-to-custody schemes is to involve juvenile court magistrates. If they have knowledge of local schemes and have confidence in them they will use them, otherwise not. Bringing together all the separate agencies involved in the system of juvenile justice and employing an inter-agency approach, not only results in a more effective use of resources by avoiding duplication, but also facilitates the accomplishment of specific policy objectives such as the reduced use of custody which any one agency working in isolation would be unable to achieve. For example, NACRO, who were charged by the DHSS with monitoring the initiative, stated: 'The key to success is an effective local strategy involving an inter-agency approach subject to scrutiny and review' (NACRO 1991, p. 49).

Despite this success, we still imprison young people who have not committed violent crimes and who pose no direct threat to society. The key to positive future developments might therefore involve obliging every local authority to establish at least one alternative-to-custody project and to establish a multi-agency juvenile crime authority for its area as advocated by the Children's Society (1988, p. 20). Recent legislative developments provide some grounds for optimism. The Children Act 1989, s. 7, for example, obliges local authorities to take reasonable steps to encourage children within their area not to commit crimes. Guidelines issued by the Department of Health advise local authorities to review their existing range of facilities and emphasise the importance of an inter-agency strategic approach (Department of Health 1991, p. 70). The Criminal Justice Act 1991 has abolished custody for 14-year-old boys. This Act has also raised the upper age limit for supervision orders to include 17-year-olds (s. 68 and sch. 8) and has given the court new powers to impose curfew orders on those over 16 (s. 12, which allows the curfew to be monitored by electronic tagging). Section 11 of the Act will allow the court to combine previously separate penalties so that a sentence of probation can be combined with a community service order. Hopefully these new powers will convince many magistrates that tough alternatives to custody are possible. Many will certainly need convincing if they are to use them on a large scale with 17-year-olds. In 1989, 2,788 17-year-olds were sentenced to custody. This is more than the total number of juveniles of all ages sentenced to custody (they were also given an average sentence of nine months which is more than double the average for under-17-year-olds).

If magistrates feel increasingly able to use community penalties and all local authorities actually provide alternative-to-custody schemes we would be well on the way towards abolishing imprisonment for all young people, except for the small number of those who pose a direct and violent threat to the public. But even for this category of offender it is questionable whether sending them to prison service establishments does anything but brutalise them still further. Both they and the community to which they will eventually have to return would benefit from their being placed in specialist secure local authority accommodation with staff trained both to contain and manage them in a more humane way (see NACRO 1989 for details of conditions in a number of young offender institutions).

Remands in custody

If the 1980s witnessed a sharp drop in the number of juveniles sentenced to custody this was not matched by similar reductions in the numbers remanded by the courts before conviction or between conviction and sentence (rising from 1,544 in 1982 to 1,704 in 1987). The problem is compounded because many of them are charged with non-violent offences and a large number are subsequently acquitted or given a non-custodial sentence (over 40 per cent in 1988). Juveniles are entitled to the safeguards provided by the Bail Act 1976 in the same way as adults. If bail is refused then the juvenile is remanded to the care of the local authority who have wide discretion as to where he or she should be placed. Prior to the Criminal Justice Act 1991, in certain circumstances the authority could apply for a certificate of unruliness (Certificate of Unruly Character (Conditions) Order 1977 (SI 1977 No. 1037)) in respect of 15 and 16-year-old boys (but not girls). If this were granted, the juvenile would be held in a Prison Service establishment. There is general agreement that this is unsatisfactory (see, for example, Home Office 1990b, para. 8.20). The Chief Inspector of Prisons, for example, commented in his Annual Report for 1989 that 'probably the most disturbing aspect to emerge from our inspections was the number of juveniles who continue to be held in prison establishments'. The Criminal Justice Act 1991 therefore provides in s. 60 that where bail has been refused the remand or committal *must* be to local authority accommodation. The certificate of unruliness procedure is abolished and instead the court may require the young person to comply with any conditions which could have been made under s. 3(6) of the Bail Act 1976, e.g., relating to residence, curfew, reporting to the police, or a ban on entering a particular geographical area. The local authority may be charged by the court with ensuring that the young person complies with the conditions. The court can also order that the young person be *not* placed with a specified person. Of equal importance, the court can also specify, subject to certain conditions, that the authority place people of at least 15 years of age in secure accommodation without this being dependent on an application by the local authority. The court must believe that only secure accommodation would be adequate to protect the public from serious harm from the offender (Criminal Justice Act 1991, s. 60(1)).

This development is to be welcomed but a number of problems still remain. First, at the present time there is insufficient local authority secure accommodation available and until this matter is resolved the courts have no alternative but to remand certain juveniles to a remand centre, if one is available, or to a prison if it is not and it believes that this is the only way to protect the public adequately from serious harm (Criminal Justice Act 1991, s. 62). No definite date exists for the abolition of juvenile remands to prison service establishments, only target dates. Secondly, the courts will still be remanding people to local authority accommodation who are not charged with serious offences involving violence. The Bail Act 1976 has not been altered in line with the 1991 Act and thus it is possible that courts will deny bail to people who will not subsequently receive a custodial sentence.

Every local authority should be developing a bail remand strategy in order that as many young people as possible are kept away from not only penal establishments but also secure accommodation. If this were made a statutory requirement, every court could be required to supply detailed reasons in the event that it declined to use it in a particular case.

A number of local authorities have developed bail support schemes which contain elements of containment, supervision and support, even for people charged with serious offences. They are tough in the sense that they convince the magistrates that the juvenile will appear before them when required, that the juvenile will not commit further offences whilst on bail and that the juvenile will be promptly returned to the court if he or she breaches the conditions. Typically the conditions of bail may prescribe such matters as residence, curfew, attendance at a five-day-per-week support unit, education, and provision for the juvenile to be escorted to and from the scheme by a parent or social worker. Because of the seriousness of the alleged offence it might also involve the defendant spending a short period in custody whilst scheme workers consider the suitability of the juvenile for inclusion on the scheme and prepare a bail package to present to the court. This can in itself encourage the juvenile to adopt a serious attitude to the conditions.

Few local authorities have remand strategies as yet. The establishment in every local authority area of at least one bail support scheme designed as an alternative to custody for young people charged with serious offences could be one of the key tasks for the proposed juvenile crime authority. But crucial decisions will have to be made concerning who will pay for them. Even in the short term, many local authorities will look towards central government for grants to develop this type of activity, particularly as prison service expenditure on juveniles remanded to their care is progressively reduced. Central government could usefully consider financing a 'remand strategy initiative' similar to the IT initiative, whch has worked so successfully in providing alternatives to custody.

Conclusion

The system of juvenile justice is changing rapidly. Indeed many of those who work within the system find it difficult to keep up to date with the pace and complexity of legislative reform. Many of the changes introduced by the Children Act 1989 and Criminal Justice Act 1991 are positive and progressive but there is still a number of serious shortcomings which could and should be corrected. Many of them relate to inconsistent practice within and between the various agencies involved with juvenile justice. The evidence suggests that justice is best achieved when they come together and become involved in establishing and monitoring strategies to deal with local offending. The most effective method of dealing with this lack of integration would be for the various agencies to come together and form a local juvenile crime authority. At the same time central government should take steps to restructure the financial framework within which each of the agencies operates. Present funding arrangements almost encourage reliance on centrally funded custodial penalties whilst discouraging alternatives which have to be paid for locally.

Until these initiatives are taken we will continue to tinker with the system in a piecemeal and sporadic fashion and continue to place ideology on a pedestal higher than the evidence warrants. More importantly we will continue to betray large numbers of our young people.

The legal system must ensure that every young person is left in no doubt that serious delinquent behaviour is antisocial, that it will not be tolerated and that it will be met with a firm response. But it should only bring within its formal machinery of adjudication those who pose a real and demonstrable threat to society. For these offenders the sentence passed should be the minimum consistent with the principle of proportionality and determinacy. Last, but by no means least, custodial sentences should only ever be imposed on juveniles as a last resort where no alternative method of protecting the public exists. As this chapter has sought to establish, this is far from being the case for many of those in custody at the beginning of the 1990s.

References

Children's Society (1988), *Penal Custody for Juveniles. Report of the Children's Society Advisory Committee on Penal Custody and its Alternatives for Juveniles* (London: Children's Society).

Curtis, S. (1989), *Juvenile Offending: Prevention through Intermediate Treatment* (London: Batsford).

Evans, R. (1991), 'Police Cautioning and the Young Adult Offender' [1991] Crim LR 598.

Gelsthorpe, L., and Giller, H. (1990), 'More Justice for Juveniles: Does More Mean Better?' [1990] Crim LR 153.

Home Office (1990a), *Criminal Statistics England and Wales 1989* (Cm 1322) (London: HMSO).

Home Office (1990b), *Crime, Justice and Protecting the Public: the Government's Proposals for Legislation* (Cm 965) (London: HMSO).

Home Office (1990c), *Prison Statistics England and Wales 1989* (Cm 1221) (London: HMSO).

Home Office (1990d), *The Sentence of the Court: a Handbook for Courts on the Treatment of Offenders* (London: HMSO).

Morris, A., and Giller, H. (1987), *Understanding Juvenile Justice* (London: Croom Helm).

Moxon, D., et al. (1985), *Juvenile Sentencing: Is There a Tariff?* (Home Office Research and Planning Unit Paper No. 32) (London: Home Office).

NACRO (1989), *NACRO Briefing: Detention in a Young Offender Institution — the First Year* (London: NACRO).

NACRO (1990), *NACRO Briefing: Criteria for Custody* (London: NACRO).

NACRO (1991), *Seizing the Initiative: NACRO's Final Report on the DHSS Intermediate Treatment Initiative to Divert Juvenile Offenders from Care and Custody 1983–1989* (London: NACRO).

Pearson, G. (1983), *Hooligan: A History of Respectable Fears* (London: Macmillan).

West, D.J. (1982), *Delinquency* (London: Heinemann).

Wilkinson, C., and Evans, R. (1990), 'Police Cautioning of Juveniles: the Impact of HO Circular 14/1985' [1990] Crim LR 165.

10

Drug Users

Una Padel

The sufferer is tremulous, and loses his self-command; he is subject to fits of agitation and depression; he loses colour and has a haggard appearance. The appetite falls off, and symptoms of gastric catarrh may be manifested. The heart also suffers; it palpitates or it intermits. As with other such agents, a renewed dose of the poison gives temporary relief, but at the cost of future misery.

Not the effects of heroin, 'crack' cocaine or ecstasy, but a description of coffee excess from *A System of Medicine* by Sir T.C. Allbutt and H.D. Rolleston in 1909. It illustrates the rather inconsistent attitude which British society has always shown towards drugs. Amid the horrifying stories of epidemic heroin use which seem to recur in the press periodically, mention is rarely made of the fact that Britain was the main importer of opium into China for much of the 19th century and fought two wars to protect the income derived from that source. Media protrayal of drugs almost always seems to imply that the use of drugs for pleasure is something relatively new, part of the youth culture of the second half of the 20th century, and that they necessarily represent a threat both to the health of the individual and to the well-being of society. Much of this seems to stem from the prohibition imposed on the recreational use of most psychoactive substances — it seems as though illegality almost inevitably equates with danger in the minds of many people.

In reality the greatest drug problems faced in British society today relate to the legitimate use of alcohol and tobacco. Together they contribute to at least 15 per cent of deaths in Britain each year (Tyler 1988). Cannabis is illegal but kills no one. Yet on 30 June 1989, 1,300 people were in prison for offences relating to cannabis (*Home Office Statistical Bulletin* 24/90).

In this chapter, the complicated relationship between drug use and crime will be explored and the implications for sentencing and treatment will be examined. The HIV pandemic has altered attitudes to the goals of drug treatment away from total abstinence, and the problems this presents to a criminal justice system which penalises the possession of drugs will be explored. Some drug users inevitably end up in prison and their care and treatment pose particular difficulties for the prison service.

Drug use and crime

In a society where the unauthorised possession of certain substances is against the criminal law, drug users inevitably come into contact with the criminal justice system on a frequent basis. The Inner London Probation Service Demonstration Unit (1990) divided drug and alcohol-related offences into three categories:

(a)   Drug or alcohol-*defined* offences are where the use or possession of a particular substance in itself constitutes a criminal offence. Possession of a controlled drug or driving while over the legal blood-alcohol limit are examples.

(b)   Drug or alcohol-*inspired* offences are committed in order to obtain a supply of the substance the offender wants. This group includes offences such as robbery or burglary to raise money for drugs as well as shoplifting bottles of sherry from the local off-licence.

(c)   Drug or alcohol-*induced* offences are committed while an individual is intoxicated by alcohol or drugs and while his or her perception of reality is affected to the extent that an offence takes place which would not otherwise have been committed. Violence resulting from alcohol or solvent use is an example of this type of offence. Drug-induced offending related to opioid use appears to be unusual. (The term 'opioids' is used in this chapter to refer to both naturally occurring opiates (such as heroin and morphine) and synthetically produced opioids including pethidine, dipipanone (Diconal) and methadone.)

Although alcohol and drugs may in these ways be a key factor in a wide variety of crime it is very difficult to gain a clear picture of the extent of crime related to substance use. Alcohol- or drug-defined crime can be measured easily and appears in the criminal statistics, but offences inspired or induced by drugs or alcohol are impossible to disentangle from similar offences committed without the influence of any substance. Such information would be difficult to collect accurately because in many situations it may be in the defendant's interests not to disclose the role of drugs or alcohol in the offence to the court. Examples of such disincentives may be fears about attracting police attention or a hard-line attitude by certain magistrates' courts to drug users.

Even where it is clear that an offender is also a drug user it would be wrong to assume that the individual's offending is necessarily and solely a result of drug use. Hammersley et al. (1989) interviewed Scottish prisoners and non-prisoners and divided them into those who used alcohol only, used cannabis and alcohol, used other drugs but not opioids, used opioids to a moderate extent and used opioids heavily. They obtained data on drug use frequency and other variables which revealed that while heavy opioid users committed crimes significantly more frequently than members of the other groups, the moderate opioid users in the sample did not. In fact polydrug use (using a number of different drugs, such as stimulants, barbiturates and tranquillisers) appeared to be more closely related to theft and delinquency than opioid use. They concluded that the need for opioids did not simply cause crime in this sample, but that crime and opioid use tend to influence each other.

While there is widespread acknowledgement that many drug users have been involved in criminal activity prior to the onset of drug use, the importance of drug use in precipitating criminal activity is given more emphasis by Parker et al. (1988). They examined the reasons for the increase in acquisitive crime in the Wirral between 1981 and 1985. This period was also marked by a massive increase in the use of heroin in this area. They found that the criminal careers of heroin users differed markedly from those of their non-heroin using peers. Of the heroin users who had been offending before their drug use commenced, the rate of conviction for acquisitive crime increased dramatically during the period 1981–85 compared to non-drug users who continued to offend. They also identifed a group who had passed through the period of adolescence (14–16 years) when the risk of conviction is greatest without attracting attention for offending. By their late teens or early twenties they appear in the statistics as recidivists with multiple convictions for acquisitive crime. The average age for the onset of heroin use in the Wirral at that time coincided with the point at which this group had started offending, indicating in the view of Parker et al. that heroin dependency had led this group into offending for the first time. They then interviewed a number of heroin users about their criminal activity and found that only 26 per cent reported an involvement in crime prior to their heroin use. Once they were involved in heroin use, 87 per cent reported that they had at some time financed their drug use illegally, and 64 per cent of the sample defined acquisitive crime as their primary method of financing the purchase of heroin.

Although the precise importance of drug use as a causative factor of crime (other than drug-defined crime) may be uncertain there are undoubtedly strong links, and this has led observers to conclude that responses to drug using criminals must deal both with drug use and crime. A simple law and order approach is inadequate.

Sentencing and treatment

Although the need to combine responses to drug use and to crime in the sentencing of drug using offenders may be evident, this has consistently posed difficulties for the criminal justice system. Until the Criminal Justice Act 1991 no specific sentencing provision for drug dependent offenders existed. Courts wishing to include treatment as part of a sentence had three options:

(a) to make a probation order with a condition of treatment by a named psychiatrist;
(b) to make a probation order with a condition of residence at a residential drug rehabilitation unit;
(c) to make a probation order with a condition that the probationer reside as directed by the probation officer.

The third option is similar in effect to the second but allows a little more flexibility if the treatment breaks down or if the needs of the offender change. Few probation orders with conditions of psychiatric treatment were made in respect of drug users because this option was limited to hospital-based drug dependence units (DDUs) by virtue of the psychiatric involvement required. Many DDUs refused to become involved because of doubts about the coercive nature of treatment in this situation. The same difficulties apply to probation orders with conditions of residence at drug rehabilitation centres, although some centres will accept residents subject to court orders particularly if the condition is the less specific 'to reside as directed by the probation officer'.

The Criminal Justice Act 1991 contains the provision, to be implemented in October 1992, that courts will be able to include a specific requirement in a probation order that an offender receives treatment for drug or alcohol dependence provided that three criteria are fulfilled:

(a)   that the offender is dependent on (or has a propensity to misuse) drugs or alcohol;
(b)   that the offender's dependency (or misuse) caused or contributed to the offence in respect of which the order is proposed to be made; and
(c)   that the offender's dependency is such as requires and may be susceptible to treatment.

This provision is more flexible than the previous condition of psychiatric treatment, since the treatment may be administered by a suitably qualified or experienced person: there is no expectation that such a person is necessarily a psychiatrist. This means that henceforth treatment as a requirement of a probation order could be undertaken by experienced drug workers in a range of different types of drug agency.

Inevitably this has reopened the debate about compulsory or coercive treatment. Although the offender's consent would be required before a probation order with a condition of treatment for drug dependence could be made, such consent is clearly given under a degree of duress, since withholding it may result in a more unpleasant outcome such as imprisonment. Many drug workers feel uneasy or unwilling about work with drug users under this degree of compulsion. The Advisory Council on the Misuse of Drugs (ACMD) in its report *Drug Misusers and the Criminal Justice System, Part 1* (1991) rejects the view that 'treatment for drug dependency should only be undertaken on a wholly voluntary basis and should, therefore, never form part of the sentence of a court'. They add, 'It has been pointed out to us that almost everyone who enters treatment for drug misuse does so under some degree of pressure, whether from family, employers or other sources: those who are impelled to enter treatment by a court are not in a fundamentally different position'. Though this may be true at the point of entry into treatment, the difference lies in the need to sustain the treatment over a period of time. While families or employees may be prepared to tolerate an individual moving in and out of treatment, or the individuals's circumstances may change so that a sustained effort becomes unnecessary, the treatment requirement of a probation order will remain in force for the duration of its existence. A drug user who is coerced into treatment by his mother's threat to throw him out of the family home if he does not seek help may find alternative accommodation and decide to return to drug use or may be able to convince his mother that he has made the effort but the time is not right. The compulsion to attend may disappear. The drug user subject to a probation order with a treatment requirement is still liable to be returned to court for breaching the terms of the order at any point during the currency of that requirement.

Little evidence exists as to the effectiveness or otherwise of treatment undertaken as part of a court order, possibly because such opportunities as have existed until now have not been widely used. In an unpublished study of referrals to the Lifeline drug project's two-week induction programme between 1980 and 1982, John Strang and Rowdy Yates found that drug users attending as a condition of bail had a much higher success rate (76 per cent) than those attending voluntarily (38 per cent). Success was measured by completion of the programme and referral on to some form of rehabilitation. This small study relates to an intensive two-week programme rather than a longer treatment plan with a lower level of intervention where sustaining motivation may be a problem. However, it does illustrate that the inevitable stress of a court appearance may be used constructively to enable drug users to consider their options.

Another small-scale study of drug users admitted as in-patients to the Bethlem Hospital was undertaken to examine the basis for an apparent prejudice on the part of drug professionals against admitting drug users with court appearances pending to drug withdrawal programmes. Brian Woollatt (1987) found that there was no statistical difference between those awaiting court appearances and those without a court appearance pending in terms of length of stay. He concluded that although no difference in outcome was evident, a forthcoming court appearance could be 'a powerful dynamic as clients engage with treatment agencies'.

In spite of the lack of evidence to suggest that treatment as part of a court order is likely to be detrimental to drug users, there is considerable apprehension about, and even resistance to, these provisions among workers in the drug field. Fears have been expressed about the prospect of drug users who would currently receive 'straight' probation orders being made subject to additional restrictions in relation to treatment. These are accompanied by concern about the likelihood of widespread breaches of treatment requirements which may involve drug agencies in playing a part in returning drug users to court. Accompanying this is often a doubt about the implications of formal involvement in a court order for the confidentiality of the drug user's relationship with the drug agency. Some drug workers also fear that the perceptions of the agency by drug users attending voluntarily may be affected if it appears to be working too closely with the criminal justice process. This last concern is probably linked to the doubt some workers inevitably feel about what may seem to be a change in their own role from 'helper' to 'supervisor of a court order'.

At the heart of all these concerns is the basic difficulty of reconciling the very different goals of the criminal justice system, which exists to investigate, prosecute and sentence offenders on behalf of society, and treatment, which is necessarily determined by the needs of the individual.

The Criminal Justice Act 1991 clarifies the basis upon which judges and magistrates should decide upon the appropriate sentence. Under the new provisions, to be implemented in October 1992, the seriousness of the offence is the determining factor in all cases, although the need to protect the public may also be taken into account. The goal of retributive 'just deserts' sentencing is the development of proportionality between culpability and sentence (Harvey and Pease 1987). This would be straightforward if a scale of penalties of escalating severity existed which could be imposed in direct relation to the seriousness of offences committed as measured by, for example, value of property stolen, quantity of drugs in possession, or levels of alcohol in the blood of a drunken driver. This purely mathematical relationship becomes more complicated where factors such as the emotional effects of an offence on a victim are taken into account, but it still appears relatively simple when penalties which can be made to increase in severity by numerical increments (fines, community service, imprisonment) are imposed. As Harvey and Pease show, guideline judgments can be used to provide a scale to determine the amount of a fine or length of a custodial sentence in relation to the severity of the offence.

Although the new sentencing structure appears to be based on retributive principles, the expansion of opportunities for treatment as part of a probation order would seem to owe more to the rehabilitative ideals of a bygone era. The other provisions relating to non-custodial or community-based sentencing in the Act are largely designed to increase the level of control and restriction, thus resolving what some saw as the ambiguity of the probation order which always encompassed both care and control (Celnick and McWilliams 1991). National standards for report writing and probation supervision are being introduced. Of course the probation order will remain a 'helping' sentence and may never fit neatly into the retributive scale, but the control elements are likely to become both more overt and more standardised.

The probation order with a condition of treatment for drug dependence should fit into the penal hierarchy at a level of severity above that of the probation order. This being the case, its use will be determined by the monetary value of the offence committed or the nature of the premises burgled, which will place the offender at a particular point on the scale of penalties. Only then will the need for treatment for a drug or alcohol problem be considered, at which point a referral will be made, and an assessment conducted concerning suitability for a probation order with a condition of treatment. Both the defendant and the drug agency would have to agree to such a sentence before it could be passed. It is hardly surprising that drug agencies, used to dealing with the needs of the individual drug user, show some scepticism and caution about their forthcoming involvement in the penal hierarchy.

On the other hand, proportional sentencing may result in fewer drug users going to prison, since many of the acquisitive offences committed to fund drug use may not be particularly serious in their own right. Until now an offender's past history has often played a major role in determining sentence, with individuals progressing through an informal tariff of non-custodial sentencing (for offences with a similar degree of severity) until imprisonment was used as a last resort. In future this progression through the tariff may be replaced by repeated sentences with a similar level of restriction for offences which do not increase in gravity.

A survey of magistrates in Inner London (Johns and Gossop 1990) revealed that most regarded psychiatric reports on drug users as useful, although more than half were critical of unclear wording, ignorance of the law and partiality towards the defendant in such reports. These magistrates may find the option of an expert assessment by a drug agency equally helpful in the future, and this likelihood creates a need for the adequate training of drug workers in providing appropriate reports for the court.

Johns and Gossop also discovered that a quarter of the magistrates in their sample did not regard a straightforward probation order as a valuable option for drug users, but nearly all were attracted by the idea of a probation order with a condition of treatment attached. At the time when that survey was performed the government Green Paper which provided the consultation stage of what ultimately became the Criminal Justice Act 1991 had recently been published. At that stage the notion of proportionality in non-custodial sentencing was still under discussion and this preference for dealing with drug users by means of a probation order with a condition of treament rather than with a 'straight' probation order seems to be based upon the magistrates' perceptions of the needs of drug using defendants, and of their own need to maintain control over the drug user's entry into treatment.

Such views are unlikely to change overnight and it will be essential for drug agencies and the probation service to work together to provide information to magistrates and judges about what treatment can be offered and under what circumstances referral is appropriate. At present many drug users are subject to probation orders with no additional requirements. According to the Advisory Council on the Misuse of Drugs (1991), the

Inner London Probation Service estimated that in 1989, 20 per cent of their caseload consisted of drug users, and the Norfolk Probation Service estimated that at least 15 per cent of those on whom social enquiry reports were prepared during a four-month period in 1990 were drug users. The ACMD recommends consideration of the need for additional training for probation officers to ensure that they have the skills and confidence to work with drug-misusing offenders. If such training were made available, it would reinforce the ability of probation officers to work with the majority of drug users on probation while, as the ACMD also suggests, 'conditions of treatment should be reserved for offenders convicted on relatively serious charges, when a custodial sentence would be the alternative outcome'.

Drug users may find the exacting requirements of a combined order difficult to adhere to, and the probation order with a condition of treatment may find a place in the penal hierarchy on a par with those more restrictive sentences where the offences are serious enough to merit such a response. The development of more formalised working arrangements and, where they are lacking, better understanding between drug agencies and the probation service is fundamental to the appropriate use and success of probation orders with treatment requirements. At present relationships vary from very good to more distant. Criteria for referral and acceptance, a 'gatekeeping' strategy, a code of confidentiality, an agreed procedure for dealing with non-compliance and a structure for the regular review of these arrangements must be properly established before the provisions are implemented, if treatment requirements are to be justly and properly managed from the outset.

If drug agencies receive more referrals from the criminal justice system in this way, they may well find they are dealing with a population which is different in profile to their usual client group. This may include, for example, more black people, who tend to be under-represented in their use of drug agencies but over-represented in the prison population.

Bild and Hayes (1990) point out that:

> Probation officers are in contact with people who experience their relationship with drugs as a positive, who are not seeking help and who would not present themselves to other agencies. Amongst this group will be a proportion who will become dependent and whose offending is likely to escalate. Of those who will be transitory, are some whose experimentation with drugs may include intravenous use or other unsafe practices: they all constitute a potential risk to themselves and others. They are in contact only because they have offended — and been caught!

While this may not appear to be the most auspicious time for intervention, 'Community based multi-agency programmes may accelerate the process by which drug users take "early retirement"' (Gilman and Pearson 1991). This may be of benefit both in terms of the needs of drug users and the communities in which they live. These communities, where high levels of social deprivation tend to be characteristic, have to bear the brunt of acquisitive crime committed to fund drug use and suffer the crippling effects of the fear of crime.

Harm reduction

The onset of the HIV pandemic has brought about a change of direction in drug treatment. While the situation is far from uniform, with different policies sometimes to be found in neighbouring health authorities, there has been a pronounced move away from abstinence as the only legitimate goal of drug treatment during the 1980s. Maintenance prescribing of pharmacologically pure drugs is nothing new; its place in the panoply of treatment options was recognised in the Rolleston report in 1926. There it was suggested that morphine or heroin prescription was a legitimate treatment in cases where withdrawal of drugs 'produced severe distress or even risk to life' or where 'experience showed that a certain minimum dose of the drug was necessary to enable the patients to lead useful and relatively normal lives, and that if deprived of this non-progressive dose they become incapable of work'.

The pattern changed in 1965 when an upsurge in the number of addicts notified to the Home Office was deemed to be due to excessive prescribing by some doctors. The second report of the Interdepartmental Committee on Drug Addiction made a number of recommendations designed to limit the availability of licit supplies of controlled drugs. This approach, combined with the rapid increase in the scale of heroin use among the young in the 1960s, led to a change in attitude in Drug Dependency Units (DDU) in the mid-1970s. The emphasis on abstinence became stronger and there was a shift away from offering injectable substitutes and towards the use of oral methadone with a treatment contract geared towards abstinence.

The latest epidemic of heroin use, which started in the early-1980s, has coincided with the spread of HIV, and the need to minimise that spread has resulted in a reassessment of priorities in the treatment of drug use. In 1987 the Advisory Council on the Misuse of Drugs in its report, *AIDS and Drug Misuse, Part 1*, suggested that this could be achieved by offering a wider range of services on terms that were likely to be acceptable to drug users and that this should include substitute prescribing and needle exchanges. This approach is known as 'harm reduction'.

In its report, *Drug Misusers and the Criminal Justice System, Part 1*, the ACMD goes on to recommend that work with drug misusing offenders should also be conducted in line with a philosophy of harm reduction. When applying the harm reduction philosophy to the criminal justice system it suggests that:

> The summit of the hierarchy of goals is not only to prevent the spread of HIV infection (although this will be relevant in many cases) but to extricate offenders from the revolving door of drug misuse, crime and custody.

There is some evidence to suggest that moving towards a harm reduction model and away from abstention as the only central ideal may reduce harm in a wider sense than simply in relation to AIDS. Bennett and Wright (1986) reported that although the small groups of heroin users they studied continued to use black market drugs in the year after they entered treatment, they reported doing so less frequently and in smaller doses while receiving prescribed heroin or reducing dosages of oral methadone. Fazey (1988) found that patients attending the Liverpool DDU continuously for a year said they were spending, on average, half as much per week on black market drugs as they had before they attended. Jarvis and Parker (1990) interviewed a group of London opioid users in 1987 who said they were less likely to commit offences while they were receiving treatment. Joy Mott (1991) concludes that:

> More generous prescribing of heroin and methadone during the course of medical treatment will not result in the elimination of the acquisitive offences committed by drug users. But [the evidence] does suggest that such treatment could reduce the extent to which many steal to raise funds to buy black market drugs. Prescribing heroin or other opioids is not the only treatment that might reduce illicit heroin use and curb the black market but it should not be completely rejected as an option during the course of treatment. . . . The evidence that the type of medical treatment offered to heroin users has implications for reducing and preventing crime cannot be ignored.

This suggests an approach to drug using offenders which recognises that, at the point at which they appear in court, abstinence may be an unrealistic goal. It is an approach based on a preparedness to countenance long-term prescribing of substitute drugs and above all an approach which is prepared to acknowledge that the drug user is likely to continue to use illicit drugs as well. It may even be necessary for agencies, while offering prescribed drugs, to provide information about the safer use of illicit drugs. While it appears that the abstinence model has been central to the work many probation officers have been involved in with drug users (Bild and Hayes 1990), many individuals working with the probation service have been informally and autonomously adopting degrees of harm reduction in relation both to drug use and other crime for many years. The fact that some probation officers committed to ideals of abstention and unwilling to consider continued drug use as an option are working alongside others who are prepared to incorporate harm reduction into their work with drug users, and that the client is unlikely to be given any choice about which officer supervises their probation order, creates inconsistencies. The lack of clear policy guidance may leave individual officers open to accusations of malpractice where problems arise and it becomes known that the officer was aware of a drug user's continued illicit drug use but has not acted on it.

In wider terms, policy and practice must be closely related, if a coherent strategy is to be adopted and injustice avoided. Where practice is so diverse this is clearly difficult. At least three probation services have now adopted harm-reduction policies and the ACMD (1991) recommends that: 'Agencies dealing with drug misusing offenders should adopt the principles of harm reduction so as to avoid setting unrealistic goals'.

Some workers in such agencies inevitably experience difficulty with this approach, since it poses ethical, moral and legal dilemmas in a situation where drug use is illegal and the past emphasis has been on abstention from use.

Northumbria Probation Service suggests that their staff may avoid apparent collusion with illicit drug use by setting clear ground rules for work with clients in writing if appropriate. Examples offered include:

(a)   The probation officer accepts that the client is using illicit drugs and is willing to work on the problems this produces in confidence.

(b)   However, any blatant evidence that the client is supplying drugs to others will lead to the police being notified.

(c)   Similarly, any concrete evidence of offending to buy drugs (i.e., evidence which could lead to successful prosecution, stolen credit cards etc.) will also lead to police involvement. (Gardiner and Talbot 1990.)

The guidelines emphasise the need for flexibility and offer the general principle that staff must '*act responsibly* and be able to demonstrate that they have done so to the satisfaction of management, and other parties, if called upon to do so'. While this is vague, the flexible approach required makes it difficult for more specific guidance to be given and staff are referred to their line managers for further advice.

The existence of such guidelines in Northumbria, Inner London and Merseyside probation services brings them more closely into line with other agencies working with drug users and is likely to facilitate the multi-agency approach which will be essential to the success of work with drug using offenders in the future.

Drug users in prison

Despite the growth and development of community based sentences, it is inevitable that many drug users will continue to be sent to prison. Some will have committed offences that are so serious that the sentencing court is unwilling to consider anything other than a custodial sentence. Others may have refused to consent to a community based sentence, or refused to cooperate once a community based sentence was passed. Many more will continue to experience prison before trial when they are remanded in custody.

A study quoted by ACMD (1987) found that a quarter of the 121 drug users in the sample had been in prison during the previous 12 months. A recent survey of the extent of drug dependence among the prison population confirms the fact that drug use and drug dependence is a significant issue in the prisons. Maden et al. (1991) conducted interviews with a randomly selected sample of 5 per cent of the male sentenced prison population and 25 per cent of the female sentenced prison population in 1988/9. They discovered that 11 per cent of the men they interviewed and 23 per cent of the women could be described as drug dependent during the six months prior to their imprisonment. Dependence was defined in this study as daily use, withdrawal symptoms on abstinence and an acknowledgement by the drug user of dependence. An extrapolation of the male sample suggested that between 3,400 and 4,500 of the sentenced male prison population were dependent on drugs before entering prison and may be at high risk of resuming drug use when they are released. Almost all of the drug dependent female prisoners had received some treatment in the past, and the majority said they would accept treatment if it were offered in prison. Half the men interviewed said they would accept treatment if it were offered in prison, and a further third said they intended to seek treatment after their release.

Apart from specialist facilities at Wormwood Scrubs Annexe and at Grendon Prison, both of which operate as therapeutic communities for male prisoners serving medium or long-term sentences, relatively little opportunity for the treatment of drug problems has been available to most prisoners until recently, and this situation is changing very gradually.

Where work with drug users has been developed it is often a result of the enthusiasm of one or two members of prison staff, either specialists such as probation officers or psychologists, or prison officers with a particular interest. While many of these initiatives are helpful to the individual prisoners concerned, they rarely seem to have been incorporated into the prison regime in such a way that they could be regarded as part of the 'core curriculum'. In many prisons activities such as drug groups, or pre-release courses which often feature inputs on drug use, are among the first casualties of staff shortages or other resource problems.

In 1987 the Prison Service offered guidance to prisons for the first time on the way drug users should be cared for at various stages in their prison sentences. Until then drugs had been regarded primarily as a security problem, and responsibility for the through-care of drug users had never been clearly defined. The guidelines allocated the tasks more clearly, with prison medical officers assuming initial responsibility for the assessment of any health problems, and the prison probation department undertaking subsequent responsibility for the prisoner's through-care including liaison with the field probation officer involved and with any community based drug agencies able to provide services to the prisoner during the sentence and after release.

Unfortunately this positive move was followed immediately by a new Prison Service circular instruction detailing ways in which prison security could be improved in relation to drugs. It included an emphasis on the need for vigilance when prisoners embrace their visitors and said that some prisoners could be instructed not to have physical contact with visitors or even made to have 'closed' visits if there was a suspicion that drugs might be passed in. These restrictions on visits, the prospect of extra searches, the likelihood of allocation to a secure rather than an open prison and the possibility of stigmatisation because of a perceived risk of HIV infection, all provided drug users in prison with additional disincentives to the disclosure of their drug problems to prison staff.

Although the need for security to stop drugs going into prison is clear, the timing of that circular instruction and the apparent lack of a common strategy between those with a security interest and those responsible for the through-care guidance was most unfortunate.

The 1987 through-care guidance was widely applauded, both inside and outside the prison service. The Prison Medical Directorate eventually decided that a more comprehensive approach was required and in 1989 convened a committee consisting of representatives from the Prison Service and the drug field to take the process forward. The result was a manual entitled *Caring for Drug Users: a Multi-disciplinary Resource for People Working with Prisoners*, which was published and distributed to all prisons in 1991. The manual confronts the difficulty of persuading drug users of the benefits of identifying themselves in prison and suggests that the availability of a detoxification programme may provide a benefit to drug users which might encourage them to disclose their drug use. This new approach, based on work undertaken at Holloway Prison by Dr Norman Hindson, is written in a more directive manner than is usual from the DPMS when addressing its doctors. After a brief preamble describing the benefits of a policy of detoxification, the general principle is asserted that: 'A detoxification programme will be offered, unless specifically contraindicated, where a prisoner presents with signs of addiction verified by the medical officer on examination (where necessary and practicable subsequently obtaining confirmation from the prisoner's previous medical adviser)'. A seven-day methadone detoxification programme for those withdrawing from opiates is mapped out, and suggestions for detoxifying users of other drugs are also made.

No evaluation is yet available of the impact of this approach on the treatment of drug using prisoners, though anecdotal information suggests that some doctors are not prepared to prescribe substitute drugs and will thus find it difficult to follow this instruction. Others appear to have adapted their practice and the debate for and against this method of treatment appears to have been occurring in prison hospitals.

The *Caring for Drug Users* manual was launched at a conference for staff representatives from the women's prisons in England and Wales. One year later a similar conference was held for staff representatives from all the young offender institutions. At the second conference the staff teams from the women's prisons reported on the encouraging progress they had made on implementing this approach over the previous year. The Prison Service's intention to ensure that the care of drug users in prison improves is further evidenced by the issuing of updated guidance on through-care (including an emphasis on confidentiality and acting only with the agreement of the drug user) and of a circular instruction (12/91) which accompanies the manual and revised guidelines. At the end of the guidelines is a checklist of factors to be considered in monitoring arrangements for the through-care of drug users which affords prisons, and those working with them, a means of evaluating progress.

The guidelines emphasise the role of community based drug agencies both in assessing and counselling prisoners and in providing help after release. It does appear that the number of drug agencies involved in prison work and the scale on which that work is taking place have increased quite dramatically over recent years. Some agencies now employ specialist prison workers and the only specialist agency, the Parole Release Scheme, which covers the South-East of England, has expanded rapidly. Whether the prisons' new-found enthusiasm for contact is the main factor in this increase in contact is difficult to tell. Although Prison Service policy is based upon community based agencies playing an integral role, the experience of some agencies which have tried to make and maintain working relationships with prisons suggests that it is still far from easy.

In general, individual prisons' contact with outside agencies of all sorts has developed in a rather *ad hoc* manner. Outside workers have usually gained access through a particular department, and information about which agencies are coming in, and via which department, is not usually coordinated within each prison. This means that three drug agencies could possibly be serving one prison through the probation department, the pre-release course and the hospital, each without being aware of the activities of the others. In some areas, outside organisations working with a particular prison in the drugs or HIV and AIDS fields have formed 'outsiders' groups which meet on a regular basis to discuss any common difficulties and to ensure that services are not being duplicated unnecessarily. If community based agencies are to play a role in the development of a strategy for caring for drug users then prisons themselves must do more to facilitate access and coordinate activity to ensure a comprehensive service. Perhaps one member of senior staff could be made responsible for liaison and negotiation with outside organisations.

At the beginning of any new contact it may also be helpful for outside agencies and prisons to negotiate written contracts in which the proposal for work to be undertaken is clearly set out, together with a process for its review if appropriate. Contracts could also contain agreements about issues such as confidentiality, facilities expected from the prison (room, escort etc.), the prison's expectations of outside workers (punctuality, regular attendance, for example) and arrangements for cancelling sessions so that external workers do not have to make wasted journeys and prisoners are not left waiting for workers who are unable to attend (Padel et al. 1992).

One difficulty faced by many community based drug agencies who would like to offer or extend existing services in prisons is funding. Prison work is expensive and time-consuming, since prisons are often situated at some distance from the urban centres where most agencies are found. Regional Health Authorities have been given funding to allocate to drug services for prison work, but the extent to which money has reached the relevant agencies and the criteria for its distribution seems to vary between regions. There is a need for the Department of Health and the Prison Service to clarify the basis on which funds are to be given to drug agencies (for example, whether they are to be paid for work undertaken with people held in prisons in the region, or with people from the region who may be imprisoned outside it) and to ensure consistent and long-term service provision.

The increased interest and awareness of the problems facing drug users in prison shown both by the Prison Service and by community based drug agencies has undoubtedly resulted in more opportunities for counselling, group work, through- and after-care than ever before. But many drug users, particularly those awaiting trial or serving short sentences, are still likely to fall through the net as long as insufficient resources are devoted to making the targets in the prison service's own checklist achievable. Staff training is of particular importance in enabling prison officers to look beyond drugs as a security problem and towards the positive work which can be done with drug users and in which they may be able to play a part.

Conclusion

As long as the possession of certain drugs remains illegal, an illicit market, funded in part by crime, will exist. Both drug-defined offences and crime committed to fund drug use will ensure that drug users continue to pass through the criminal justice system in large numbers. Until recently the expectations of the courts, probation services and prisons have been uniformly abstentionist, leaving drug users who were not willing simply to stop using drugs and allow themselves to be rehabilitated with few options.

The last five years have been characterised by a gradual change in emphasis as an awareness of the dangers of the HIV pandemic has prompted a reappraisal of the real risk posed by drug use (ACMD 1987). This in turn has resulted in a widespread move towards a harm reduction philosophy, first by drug agencies and then by others dealing with drug users. In terms of criminal justice this is inevitably a difficult process and, as it becomes more commonplace, tensions will inevitably manifest themselves in various areas.

If full advantage is to be taken of the opportunities presented by the new sentencing arrangements (including probation orders with conditions of treatment), by the adoption by some probation services of harm reduction policies and by the *Caring for Drug Users* initiative in prisons, the essential common ingredient is that sufficient time and resources need to be made available for the adequate training of staff and other personnel.

Simply introducing harm reduction policies, however small or large the change of emphasis, will only create difficulties if people who have responsibility for sentencing or supervising drug users or for their care within the prison system are not fully aware of the rationale behind the new approach. These potentially exciting changes will need considerable and long-term resources if they are to be translated from policy to practice in order to enable the criminal justice system to work more closely with drug treatment agencies for the benefit of drug users and society at large.

References

Advisory Council on the Misuse of Drugs (1987), *AIDS and Drug Misuse, Part 1* (London: HMSO).

Advisory Council on the Misuse of Drugs (1991), *Drug Misusers and the Criminal Justice System, Part 1. Community Resources and the Probation Service* (London: HMSO).

Bennett, T., and Wright, R. (1986), 'The Impact of Prescribing on the Crimes of Opioid Users', *British Journal of Addiction*, vol. 81, pp 265–73.

Bild, M., and Hayes, P. (1990), *The Problems Inherent in the Promotion of a Harm Reduction Strategy in an Agency Operating Within the Criminal Justice System* (Inner London Probation Service).

Celnick, A., and McWilliams, B. (1991), 'Helping, Treating and Doing Good', *Probation Journal* (December 1991).

Fazey, C.S.J. (1988), *Heroin, Crime and the Effect of Medical Treatment* (A report to the Home Office Research and Planning Unit).

Gardiner, J.D., and Talbot, J. (1990), *Northumbria Probation Service Dependency Manual* (Northumbria Probation Service).

Gilman, M., and Pearson, G. (1991), 'Lifestyles and Law Enforcement' in *Policing and Prescribing: The British System of Drug Control*, ed. D.K. Whynes and P.T. Bean (Basingstoke: Macmillan).

Hammersley R., et al. (1989), 'The Relationship between Crime and Opioid Use', *British Journal of Addiction*, vol. 84, pp. 1029–43.

Harvey, L., and Pease, K. (1987), 'Guideline Judgments and Proportionality in Sentencing' [1987] Crim LR 96.

Her Majesty's Prison Service (1991), *Caring for Drug Users: a Multidisciplinary Resource for People Working with Prisoners* (Home Office).

Inner London Probation Service (1990), *Drug and Alcohol Misuse: Summary of Demonstration Unit Interviews*.

Jarvis, G., and Parker, H. (1990), 'Can Medical Treatment Reduce Crime amongst Young Heroin Users', *Home Office Bulletin* 28.

Johns, A., and Gossop, M. (1990), 'Drug Use, Crime and the Attitudes of Magistrates', *Medicine, Science and Law*, vol. 30, No. 3.

Maden, A., et al. (1991), 'Drug Dependence in Prisoners', *British Medical Journal*, vol. 302, p. 880.

Mott, J. (1991), 'Crime and Heroin Use' in *Policy and Prescribing: The British System of Drug Control*, ed. D.K. Whynes and P.T. Bean (Basingstoke: Macmillan).

Padel, U., et al. (1992) *HIV Education in Prisons: a Resource Book* (Health Education Authority).

Parker, H., et al. (1988), *Living with Heroin* (Milton Keynes: Open University Press).

Strang, J., and Yates, R., *Non-voluntary Treatment of Drug Takers*. Unpublished.

Tyler, A. (1988), *Street Drugs*, 2nd ed. (London: Hodder and Stoughton).

Woollatt, B., *The In-patient Treatment of Drug Users when Court Cases are Pending*. Paper presented at the Third National Conference of the Association of Nurses in Substance Abuse 1987.

11

Perspectives on Race and Gender

Susan Edwards

Introduction

Much has been written on the subject of gender and criminal justice from women's experience of policing to their experience of sentencing. Research has focused, *inter alia*, on comparing the treatment of males and females in the criminal justice system and on wider jurisprudential questions examining the way in which statute, case law, legal method, as well as decisions in the legal process have been informed by sex role differences and expectations.

Additionally, much has been written about 'black' people's experience of criminal justice from policing to prison, but where gender and race interact, far less is widely known or appreciated about the particular experience of 'black' women at the hands of police either as suspects or offenders, before magistrates, in social inquiry reports, in medical or psychiatric reports, in court decisions to remand, in magisterial or judicial sentencing, or as victims. It is the politicisation of 'black' women together with the visibility of their unjust experience which provides the momentum for such a review. The conspicuous representation of 'black' women in prison disproportionate to their representation in the general population provides one of the several focal points for this chapter. The individual experiences of 'black' women, as wives and mothers of suspects, and their treatment by police, the treatment of 'black' women offenders — notably the treatment of immigrant women — and the treatment of domestic violence victims taken together raise certain fundamental questions about crime and more particularly about justice. This chapter draws together research on 'black' women's experience of criminal justice, as suspects and offenders and as victims and complainants.

First, the intention is to examine through empirical evidence and individual cases the experience of 'black' people, and 'black' women in particular, in the criminal justice system. Secondly, the intention is to scrutinise the explanatory debate which poses the question whether 'black' people and 'black' women are indeed more criminally inclined than non-blacks, through examining the part played by cultural disadvantage, institutionalised racism and individual racist attitudes held by those working in the criminal justice system in the production of disproportionately high arrest, charging, conviction and custodial sentence rates. This discussion also highlights rates of mental illness and raises the question of whether there exists a racism in psychiatric diagnosis as it pertains to the criminal offender, and focuses on racist assumptions as they affect the predilection to protect victims of racial harassment and of crime. Finally, I examine present policy designed to address institutionalised racism within recruitment of police and the legal professionals and discuss ways in which the criminal justice system, and notably the prison service, have tried to address the problem of racism in their midst.

These three aspects will be considered in the wider context of the evidence in the crime debate, and of race and crime within the broader penal policy perspective.

Experiencing criminal justice

Crime is, and always has been, predominantly a male activity. In 1989, for males the rate of known offending was 944 per 100,000 population, and 295 per 100,000 population for females. If official statistics are to be relied upon the crime problem is increasing year by year. The published figures (Home Office 1990a) show that the total number of notifiable offences reached 3,870,748 in 1989, compared to 3,715,767 in 1988, rising to an estimated 4.5 million in 1990 (Home Office 1992). All crimes before all courts, both indictable and summary offences, have risen. Of all offenders cautioned by the police and convicted by the courts, 83 per cent are males and 17 per cent females (a ratio of 5 males to every 1 female). The number of those cautioned and convicted of indictable offences has fallen, for males from 418,800 in 1979 to 399,300 in 1989, and for females from 90,400 to 76,200 in 1989. The reverse trend has been the case for summary offences (excluding motoring) which for both males and females has risen. For males, a total of 382,900 were cautioned and convicted in 1979 compared to 438,900 in 1989. For females, 63,000 were cautioned and convicted in 1979, compared to 135,500 in 1989. This summary increase for both male and female offenders has been in part a result of the Criminal Justice Act 1988 and the reclassification from either way to summary for certain offences, including theft of a motor vehicle (s. 37(1)), criminal damage (s. 38(1)), and common assault and battery (s. 39).

More than half of all crimes committed by males are committed by those under 21 years, to include 63 per cent of all burglaries, 58 per cent of all robberies, and 41 per cent of crimes of violence. For females the involvement of the under-21 age group is even more staggering, accounting for 52 per cent of all crimes of violence and over 60 per cent in crimes of burglary and robbery. However, it is the 17 years and under age group which is committing most crime. Thirty per cent of violent crime committed by females is committed by those under 17 years. Forty-five per cent of all female burglars are under 17 years, whilst 32 per cent of male burglars are under 17 years. Thirty-three per cent of all female robbers are under 17 years whilst 25 per cent of all male robbers are under 17 years.

Home Office guidelines for cautioning, whilst primarily drafted with the juvenile in mind, are being extended in certain cases to adult offenders, and following the Criminal Justice Act 1991, s. 68, persons aged 17 years are to be rated as young persons for certain purposes and as a consequence will be automatically included in cautioning programmes as a matter of policy. The programme of including young persons under 18 years of age in the juvenile courts (to be renamed youth courts) is part of government policy to reduce youth offending. It is difficult to discern what proportion of those offenders hitherto in the 17 to under-21 age group, both males and females, are indeed 17 years of age and therefore would be amenable to cautioning under the new guidelines. The application of cautioning programmes it is anticipated will vary from police force area to area, as experience has already shown. Variations in police cautioning practice regarding juvenile crime are already considerable (see chapter 9).

It is also to be noted that the Crown Prosecution Service is intending that cautioning should be used much more widely in all offences across all age groups as a means of dealing more speedily and economically with the crime problem.

Whilst the cautioning rate is lower for the adult offender in the 17 and under 21 years age group, it is precisely from this population of offenders that 17-year-old youths will be drawn. A dramatic rise then in 'youth' offenders and those automatically amenable to caution will be occasioned, indicated by the fact that according to the Home Office statistical officer, Gordon Barclay, the peak age of offending for all males has risen and for some categories has risen to 18 years. As Evans and Wilkinson's research (1990) highlights, the wide variations in cautioning rates between forces are in part a product of the lack of uniform criteria in deciding whether a case is cautionable or not, and local resources. But it is precisely this lack of uniformity which has facilitated the differential treatment of black people in respect of cautioning (discussed later).

Comparing male rates to female rates for cautioning, a higher proportion of females generally receive a caution. This generates cries of leniency toward females, but can be explained more accurately by the fact that a larger proportion of female offenders are first-time offenders and commit less serious offences than male counterparts. In 1989, the cautioning rate for female offenders was 44 per cent compared with 26 per cent for males for summary offenders, the cautioning rate for indictable offences for females was 11 per cent compared with 20 per cent for males.

In 1989 the average prison population was 48,610 of whom 1,767 (3.6 per cent) were females. The number of untried women defendants received into prison custody rose by 27 per cent between 1979 and 1989 from 2,431 to 3,085. Thirty per cent of untried and 47 per cent of convicted unsentenced women aged 21 and over remanded into custody were subsequently given non-custodial sentences compared with 23 per cent and 32 per cent respectively for men. This means that the majority of women remanded in custody subsequently receive a non-custodial penalty, whereas the majority of male remand prisoners go on to serve a prison sentence.

Moreover, a disturbing and inexplicably higher proportion of women than men currently sentenced to immediate imprisonment have no previous convictions. The Criminal Justice Act 1991, s. 29(1), emphasises sentencing for the offence charged and that offence alone:

An offence shall not be regarded as more serious for the purposes of any provision of this part by reason of any previous convictions of the offender or any failure of his to respond to previous sentences.

This might reflect the more humane face of a 'just deserts' penal policy, but there are well-founded fears that the interpretation of this section will disproportionately affect women first-time offenders and 'black' women first-time offenders especially, resulting in an even greater gender disparity than witnessed at the present time.

Race and crime: overcriminalised and overmedicalised?

From stop and search, to arrest, to the use of custody, the evidence is unequivocal: 'black' people are more likely to be arrested, charged, convicted, and to receive a custodial sentence than white people (Reiner 1989). Smith and Gray in the PSI study on *The Police and the People* (1983) found that 'black' people were more likely to be stopped than white people. The proportion for West Indians was 66 per cent, whilst it was 44 per cent for whites and 18 per cent for Asians. Willis (1983) also found that young 'black' males aged 16 to 24 years were stopped at roughly 10 times the average at two London police stations. Such evidence was found too by MacLean et al. in the *The Islington Crime Survey* (1987) (see chapter 1 above).

The arrest process reveals similar evidence of disparity. Stevens and Willis (1979) found that the arrest rate for Afro-Caribbeans 'was higher than for whites and Asians for every category of offence'. Home Office statistics show that of those arrested for an offence, about 18 per cent were 'black'-skinned although only 5 per cent of the London population are 'black' (*Home Office Statistical Bulletin* 5/89). The proportion of those arrested varies considerably depending on the offence. For burglary and assaults the proportion averaged about 20 per cent 'black', whilst for robbery and violent theft the proportion was around 50 per cent 'black'. For street robbery and snatches the proportion was over half, whilst for other offences of robbery it was around 40 per cent (*Home Office Statistical Bulletin* 6/89; Jefferson and Walker 1992).

A study of race and crime in the Metropolitan Police District found that 'blacks' were more likely than whites to be indicted for violence, sexual offences and robbery (Walker 1989). When cases reached the court, a higher proportion of cases brought against 'black' people resulted in a dismissal because of insufficient evidence than against white people (9 per cent compared with 6 per cent) and a higher proportion of 'black' defendants were acquitted of all indictable offences (15.3 per cent compared with 9.5 per cent).

Studies on the influence of race on sentencing have found that notwithstanding the fact that the London borough with the highest custody rate for Afro-Caribbeans also had the highest rate of ethnic minority population, when sentences of less than a month given for motoring offences were subtracted the result was a much higher custody rate for Afro-Caribbeans (Hudson 1989).

When cautioning rates are considered there is ample evidence to indicate that 'black' people are less likely to receive a caution for similar offences than white people (Landau 1981; Landau and Nathan 1983). A study by Hackney Council of 237 guilty pleas found that cautioning by the police was particularly underused against people from the 'black' or ethnic communities (Tipler 1986). Taken together such findings throw some light on how the provisions for cautioning in the Criminal Justice Act 1991 may have a disproportionate impact on 'black' youths. Evidence shows that 'blacks' are less likely to receive bail for similar offences than whites. And it remains to be seen how far recent government proposals to place more offenders on custodial remand, because of the rise in the so-called 'bail bandit' numbers, will have a keener impact on the 'black' community. Home Office research shows that 'black' people are twice as likely to be held in custody on remand.

At the end of the criminal justice process, 24 per cent of the female prison population are 'black' compared to 15.7 per cent of the male prison population; this figure rises for 1990 when 34 per cent of the female prison population are 'black' compared with 17 per cent of the male population (Home Office 1988; Home Office 1990b). It is to be noted that 4.4 per cent of the total population are 'black'. Male remand prisoners constitute one-fifth of the male prison population. Female remand prisoners constitute one-fourth of the female prison population. Of the untried unconvicted 'black' prison population 19 per cent of males are 'black' and 25 per cent of females 'black'. For males, 9 per cent of 'blacks', 8 per cent of Asians and 5 per cent of whites were remanded in custody. For females the position was similar: 4 per cent of 'blacks' and 2 per cent of whites. The Society of Black Lawyers' response to the Criminal Justice Act 1991 has been to conclude that 'black' people are eight times as likely to be imprisoned as white people (Herbert 1990).

Not only are 'black' people in prison, but they are also likely to be in prison for longer (cf. Browne 1990). The total population of sentenced female adults serving sentences over 18 months to life included 58 per cent of all whites sentenced, 83 per cent of all West Indian women sentenced, 95 per cent of all Indian women sentenced, 71 per cent of all Chinese sentenced and 77 per cent of all 'others' (including other ethnic groups and those refusing to specify race origin). The total population of sentenced male adults serving terms of four years and over, including life, consisted of 35 per cent of all whites sentenced, 44 per cent of all West Indians sentenced, 62 per cent of all Indians sentenced, 41 per cent of all Chinese/Arab mixed sentenced, and 44 per cent of all 'others' sentenced (Home Office 1990b).

'Black' men and women are also more likely to be medicalised. The medicalisation of 'black' people has been especially brought to the fore following the death in Broadmoor of Orville Blackwood, a 31-year-old Jamaican. He is the third young black patient to have died in similar circumstances. In 1991 a Channel 4 documentary highlighted the case of Randolp Ince who has been in hospitals since 1983 and in Broadmoor since 1987, who was allegedly given such high doses of drugs that he grew breasts and produced milk. Certainly the evidence suggests that 'black' men and women are over-represented amongst those members of the general population who find themselves diagnosed as suffering from some mental disorder. A recent study carried out by MIND found that Afro-Caribbean people are over-represented in section 136 referrals. In addition, a recent British study has shown that young African/Caribbean migrants are up to 25 times as likely as white people to be committed for detention under part III of the Mental Health Act 1983. Cope (1989) found that African/Caribbean people born in Britain were admitted at four times the white rate. A recent study conducted for NACRO (Browne 1990) examined the extent to which 'black' people are remanded for psychiatric reports when appearing in magistrates' courts, the nature and outcome of psychiatric remands, and the implications for the provision of services to 'black' people who have passed through the psychiatric remand process. Browne found that in a study of psychiatric remand, 36 (32 per cent) of the people given hospital orders without restrictions were known to be 'black'. Further evidence is provided by studies examining mental illness rates for 'black' people within the community. Cochrane (1977) found that the mental hospital admission rate for people born in England and Wales was 494 per 100,000 whilst the rate for the Caribbean-born community was 539. Further, Dean (1981) found that the number of first admissions for schizophrenia among 'black' people was three times the norm. Dr S.P. Sashidharan commented in the *Guardian*, 4 November 1989:

> The crisis in British psychiatry is not about large numbers of black people breaking down with any given psychiatric diagnosis but how such individuals are being inducted into the mental health services and being labelled as having serious mental illnesses.

On an individual basis the unsuccessful application in *R* v *Wolverhampton Coroner, ex parte McCurbin* [1990] 1 WLR 719 for judicial review following the death of Clinton McCurbin during an arrest and a head hold by the Wolverhampton police has further fuelled the criticism both of police and the criminal justice process for failure to afford equal protection under the law. In civil law, in claims for damages, the case of *Alexander* v *Home Office* [1988] 1 WLR 968 revealed the discrimination within the prison service: Alexander's application to work in the prison kitchen was turned down on several occasions and reports held on him at two prisons contained rude malicious imputations which were clearly racist.

The unsafe and unsatisfactory conviction of the Tottenham Three, and the recent trial of Alec Mason, a police officer, charged with stamping on the face of Harold Benn (*Guardian*, 2 April 1992) are all indicative of the individual experience of 'black' people up against the law.

Women, race and crime

When the question of women, race and crime is addressed, two major conceptual problems have blurred our vision. First, 'black' women's experience of and treatment by the criminal justice system has been subsumed in the experience of 'black' men. Second, 'black' women's experience has been homogenised with the experience of white women. As a result we have lost sight of the crucial interface between patriarchy and racism.

The involvement in the criminal justice system of 'black' women differs from community to community whether we are talking about Afro-Caribbean, Somali women, women from the Asian subcontinent, Indian women, Bangladeshi or Sikh women, or indeed Greek, Turkish or Arab women. The use of 'black' to describe the experience of all these groups can mislead, since non-white women share a particular treatment and experience of criminal justice which is distinct from white women, but there any attempt to generalise ends.

Asian women resent being defined along with 'black' women in an attempt to describe their oppression and experience. The complexities of tradition, custom, community, religion and patriarchal family structures all take on a different form and have a significantly different part to play in their experience of oppression. The eclipsing of 'black' women's experience by the experience of all women is not altogether surprising, as gender issues have struggled for recognition (e.g., Joseph 1982). More dangerously, however, women's experiences as victims more generally have been marginalised within crime and justice debates dominated by the issues of significance to the male left who have given priority to race above, and without, an appreciation of patriarchy.

Feminist criminologists have criticised the male left for the persistent gender blindness of their work (Heidensohn 1985; Edwards 1989; Morris and Gelsthorpe 1988). Some on the male left have replied to these criticisms (Young 1989), but mitigation is no defence to their grave omissions. A radical restructuring of political and criminological thought is urgently needed. Radical feminists have also been criticised by 'black' women writers and activists for marginalising the 'black' women's experience (Southall Black Sisters 1989; Mama 1989). Saadawi's criticism (1980) of Western feminists has highlighted their inappropriate commenting on 'black' women's issues and the need to experience racism as a 'black' woman as quintessential to writing about that experience. This approach has also contributed to white feminists deciding that they cannot be the spokeswomen for 'black' women's experience.

'Black' women offenders

Whilst I have already previously addressed some questions relating to the evidence of women's disproportionate involvement in crime, further evidence indicates that 'black' women are treated differently from white women in a number of ways. For example, 'black' women receive fewer cautions than white women (NACRO 1989). In their analyses of bail decisions, both NACRO and Women in Prison have indicated that a disproportionate number of 'black' women are remanded in custody. And finally, when it comes to considering imprisonment, 'black' women are disproportionately represented within the population and within the category of serving drug offenders. The percentage of women aged 21 and over sentenced to immediate custody for indictable offences rose from 3.8 per cent in 1979 to 6.8 per cent in 1989. The major increase in the length of prison sentences for drug offenders by the Crown Court probably accounts for much of this. Of 890 sentenced female offenders including adults and young offenders, 276 (31 per cent) are West Indian/Guyanese/African. Of this ethnic group 144 (52.2 per cent) are imprisoned for drug offences, 15 (5.4 per cent) for crimes of violence against the person, and 34 (12.3 per cent) for theft (Home Office 1990b). In addition, 'black' women find themselves imprisoned under immigration and nationality laws. Women may be detained at the ports of entry such as Heathrow and Gatwick. Figures for detention centres excluding Harmondsworth indicated that in 1983, 139 children under 17 and 813 women were held overnight (Women, Immigration and Nationality Group 1985).

'Black' women as associates of 'black' men

Much of the criminal justice response to 'black' women has been to regard 'black' men and women in the same light. First, the treatment of 'black' women is seen as inseparable from the treatment and perceptions of the 'black' community as a whole. Second, in the arena of 'black' women's victimisation, the protection of women is subordinated to a view of the community as a whole. Policing responses and policy approaches have been informed by paternalism or else a belief that self-determination in these communities, especially the Asian community, in respect of family matters is the way ahead. Allowing self-determination in certain issues and matters has led to a dangerous situation for victims of domestic violence who have been denied adequate protection from the police and the courts (Southall Black Sisters 1989).

Similarly in certain circumstances 'black' women are seen as accomplices. This view is discussed in some considerable depth in *R* v *Chrastny* [1991] 1 WLR 1381 and *R* v *Chrastny (No. 2)* [1991] 1 WLR 1385.

Women's treatment as relatives and the family of 'black' male suspects and offenders has led to unjust treatment. Floyd Jarret was arrested for suspected theft of a motor vehicle. Subsequently police officers searched his home after letting themselves in with his key. They pushed Mrs Jarret aside; she fell and died of a heart attack. Mrs Cherry Groce, the mother of Michael Groce, wanted for armed robbery, was shot and paralysed in consequence during a police raid at her home.

'On 30 September 1980 police went to the home of Mrs Clementine George in Sydenham, south London, demanding to see her son. When Mrs George, a Sunday school teacher, said he was not there, the police forced the door down and hit Mrs George, causing her "extensive bruising".' (*South London Press*, 6 April 1984, cited in *Policing against Black People* (Institute of Race Relations, 1985).)

'Black' women as victims

The treatment and experience of 'black' women as victims has much to do with the 'petty apartheid' in service delivery (Mama 1989, p. 23). Mama interviewed 54 Caribbean women, 40 Asian and six African women; in a report based on these data she criticises the Eurocentric feministic perspective. Southall Black Sisters (1989) highlight the dilemma posed: 'For black people the police in this country have always represented the most overtly repressive face of a racist State'. The majority of women had no confidence in police and contradictions were posed:

On the one hand, we are involved in campaigns against police brutality, deaths in police custody and immigration fishing raids. On the other, we are faced with daily beating, rape and sexual harassment.

Certainly police have tried to steer a way between respect for ethnic communities and family privacy and the need to protect victims from domestic violence. This fine balance has not been achieved and Asian and Afro-Caribbean women have felt that the interests of Asian and Afro-Caribbean men and family autonomy have been given priority over and above women's right to protection. This has led in some areas to a breakdown of relations between police and Asian and Afro-Caribbean women. The death of Vandana Patel in a domestic violence unit at Stoke Newington police station in 1991, where she was stabbed by her husband, highlights the dilemma. The meeting was arranged following the request of the local Asian women's refuge. The police for their part facilitated a multi-agency approach and self-determination of both parties by hosting the meeting. The consequences were disastrous. The police were blamed by some feminist groups who protested outside the station; other feminist groups also said they were confused, since on this occasion the police objective was to give priority to the interests and wishes of the woman concerned (Edwards, *Guardian*, 11 March 1991).

There are of course other examples where the police response has been negligent. Krishna Sharma in Southall had contacted police the night before she died, alleging beating from her husband. The police told her to go to a Citizens Advice Bureau which had been closed for eight years. Although she was found hanged and with bruises on her body a verdict of suicide was recorded in May 1984. Balwant Kaur was murdered at the Brent Asian women's refuge in 1985. Her husband planned to murder her and told accomplices of his plans. The accomplices informed the refuge, whose workers in turn told police. The refuge asked for a 24-hour patrol; the police attended the refuge but spoke to residents and later left. Later the husband broke into the refuge and Balwant was murdered.

Explanatory models of 'black' men's and 'black' women's involvement in crime

A pathological and social predisposition towards crime

How can 'black' women's involvement in crime and their experience as victims of crime be explained? Two major competing paradigms have presented a picture either of communities that are different from the white host indigenous population, where customs and mores differ and where a pathological tendency to crime, to violence in the home and to mental instability persists, or of communities where the disproportionate presence of black people in crime, victimisation and mental instability is clearly the product and function of a racist repressive and ideological State apparatus. Chiqwada (1991) is insistent when she lays the blame squarely on the shoulders of the police force. Gilroy (1987) argues that:

> ... to present 'black crime' as a primary cultural problem whether forged
> in the economic 'no man's land' between deprivation and restricted

opportunity, or secured in a spurious social biology, is a capitulation in the weight of racist logic.

More recently those disenchanted with the argument that all crime is an artefact of police activity and the activities of the criminal justice system, have returned realistically to examine both policing and cultural disadvantage in the form of social and economic provisions in areas where 'black' communities live. Jefferson (1991) grasps the nettle of reality and departs from this over-deterministic model of policing and high 'black' offending when he writes:

> But, when all is said and done, most commentators conclude that at least part of the explanation for higher black arrests has to be the result of higher offending behaviour. . . . For if blacks are disproportionately involved in known offending behaviour, they also have much higher rates of social disadvantage, being more likely to live in poorer housing in deprived areas, attend worse-off schools and, in the job market, to find manual (rather than non-manual) jobs or to be unemployed.

The belief that the home environment and especially 'black' parenting and 'black' mothering is to blame, persists. 'Black' parenting and family structure are at fault, coupled with loose sexual practices, unstable family ties and single parents. Such socio-pathological theorising has embraced the idea that high crime and victimisation rates are the response of family patterns and cultural deprivation. But even here with the most progressive of theorists the view is that the extent of crime within the 'black' community is real and of their own making. Solomos and Rackett (1991) noted that 'Lord Scarman partly explained the drift of black youngsters into crime and violence by reference to the weak family units of the West Indian communities'. Scarman rather felt it was the lack of a strong family unit which might lead to crime. Meanwhile, Conservative Party analysis of riots and 'black' involvement in crime (Solomos and Rackett 1991) paints the following profile:

> According to this model the cause of the riots lay not in the conflict between young people and the police but in the failure of families to control the actions of their children. Already in 1981 the government was looking at plans to involve parents in the consequences of offences committed by their children.

A similar picture is put forward by Gilroy (1987):

This unfortunate break-up of family association has seen the formation of substantial groups of blacks leaving home and banding together in numerous squats and communes, unemployed and completely disillusioned with society. Most of them have donned the mantle of Rastafarianism, or more precisely the criminal sub-cult of the dreadlock fraternity.

Analysis of offending rates amongst the 'black' community in 1992 will no doubt bring into the frame the issue of parental responsibility, a key predisposing factor to crime in Conservative criminological analysis. This question will appear of special significance in explaining crime in the 'black' community. The notion that 'black' people are intrinsically the problem will return with a vengeance as government thinking promotes its parental responsibility theory. It may not be then a question of refocusing on the individual, as Jefferson argues, but rescuing the black people and crime debate once again from individual over-determinism. The response of the government through the Criminal Justice Act 1991 has been to use the family as the means of controlling juvenile crime. The particular notion of parental responsibility applied here focuses on three aspects: requiring parents to take on a controlling and disciplining function and so making them responsible for their children's behaviour; requiring parents to take on financial responsibility for their children's fines; and finally making parents liable to pay a financial penalty (recognisance) should they fail to control their children. The emphasis on parental responsibility reflects a particular approach to crime prevention which embraces an accountability and disciplining function, which if parents fail results in criminal sanction.

In 1990 David Waddington (then Home Secretary), speaking on crime prevention when presenting the Criminal Justice Bill to the Commons, echoed a widely held government view that 'Crime begins at home'. Underpinning this view is a theoretical analysis which considers one of the primary causes of juvenile crime to be the lack of adequate care and control exercised by parents. David Waddington continues in this vein, 'Many offenders set off on the road to crime at an early age, often because their parents have not bothered to instil in them a sense of right and wrong and a respect for other people's property' (*Evening Standard*, 9 November 1990). John Patten's (then Minister of State at the Home Office) recent theorising on criminal behaviour goes a step further than merely placing the blame for delinquency on parents, by locating explanations in individual pathology rather than in social and economic factors or in deprivation: 'People sometimes freely choose to be bad, by quite deliberately harming other people or their property. There may be explanations, or mitigations, for it but badness is at the root.' (*Guardian*, 22 February 1990.)

Racism in private attitudes and public procedures

The second explanatory model illustrates the racism of the criminal justice system by identifying the high proportion of 'black' offending within individual racist attitudes, and the result of the exercise of discretion within institutionalised patterns and processes. The ideology of the police in respect of racist attitudes and stereotypes has been investigated severally from Smith and Gray (1983) to Graef (1989).

The Institute of Race Relations in their report, *Policing against Black People* (1985) wrote: '. . . the suspicion about the West Indian is that he is a criminal, a wild man. . . . the suspicion about the Asian is that he has sneaked in under the cover of night.' Superintendent Dick Holland of the West Yorkshire Police told the Police Federation in Oxford that the police 'must be prejudiced if they are to do their job properly'. In 1984 at the Police Federation conference, a police community relations officer referred publicly to 'our coloured brethren or nig-nogs'. In 1992 the Strathclyde Chief Constable cracked what he thought was a joke at his cricket club and was reprimanded by his police authority for racism (*Guardian*, 25 March 1992).

In the courtroom too there is a race blindness which results in racism through racial disadvantage and discriminatory treatment. In the case of *R v Thomas* (1989) 88 Cr App R 370, Mr Justice Otton was asked to exercise his power to stand by members of the jury. The application was made as four 'black' youths stood for trial before an all-white jury. Otton J's comments are particularly telling: 'At the end I must ask a simple question: is there a real risk that these four youths would not get a fair trial from an all-white jury? The answer is: There is no such risk.'

Within prison, too, research has shown (McDermott 1990; Genders and Player 1989) that 'black' people are systematically discriminated against and allocated the worst jobs — labouring and cleaning — whilst the better jobs are given to white prisoners. Indeed the case of *Alexander* v *Home Office* illustrates this well. In Wandsworth and Parkhurst prisons Alexander's several applications for work in the kitchens were refused. His initial assessment report at Wandsworth and induction report at Parkhurst contained these remarks:

He displays the usual traits associated with people of his ethnic background being arrogant, suspicious of staff, anti-authority, devious and possessing a very large chip on his shoulder which he will find very difficult to remove if he carries on the way he is doing.

He is an arrogant person who is suspicious of staff and totally anti-authority. He has been described as a violent man with a very large chip on his shoulder which he will have great difficulty in removing. He shows the anti-authoritarian arrogance that seems to be common in most coloured inmates. ([1988] 1 WLR 968 at p. 973.)

Throughout the criminal justice system institutionalised racism as well as individual racist attitudes lead to a differential treatment of 'black' people.

Conclusions

In the race, crime and gender arena three issues need to be urgently addressed. First, the racial discrimination in the criminal justice system needs to be challenged; second, the representation of those working as professionals throughout the system needs examining; and third, patterns of cultural disadvantage disproportionately experienced by 'black' people such as poverty, unemployment, housing and education need also to be addressed.

As part of a programme of resolving acknowledged discrimination the White Paper stated, 'There must be no discrimination because of a defendant's race, nationality, standing in the community or any other reason', but any structure to ensure that end has not been provided for in the Criminal Justice Act 1991. Section 95(1) provides that:

The Secretary of State shall in each year publish such information as he considers expedient for the purpose of:

(a)   enabling persons engaged in the administration of criminal justice to become aware of the financial implications of their decisions; or
(b)   facilitating the performance by such persons of their duty to avoid discriminating against any persons on the ground of race or sex or any other improper ground.

It is not clear whether the Judicial Studies Board and/or judges' and magistrates' training are to take into account race and sentencing.

The Criminal Justice Act includes a ban on racial discrimination by the police, the courts and prisons. How this will work remains to be seen. As in the Courts and Legal Services Act 1990, discrimination is covered by the statutory duty and by bringing the provision of legal services under the ambit of the Race Relations Act 1976.

In the committee stage of the Criminal Justice Bill considerable discussion was given over to the matter of targets and quotas of those working in the various professions (cf. *Parliamentary Debates (Hansard)*, *Lords*, 5th ser., vol. 529 (1991), col. 221).

The position *vis-à-vis* race and crime is deeply disturbing. There is overwhelming evidence that 'black' people get an overdose of 'just deserts' and are continually denied 'justice'.

There is a need for recruitment in all the criminal justice process agencies to reflect the needs and experiences of ethnic minorities and reduce institutionalised racism. The present position with regard to ethnic minorities in the police forces in England and Wales is striking: as of January 1990, there were some 1,306 officers from ethnic minority backgrounds. In the Metropolitan Police, for example, as of 28 May 1991, there were 515 officers from ethnic minorities, constituting 1.81 per cent of the force; this represented a small but steady increase over earlier years. By 13 January 1992, ethnic minorities constituted 1.95 per cent of the force, (0.57 per cent chief inspector, 0.66 per cent inspector, 0.82 per cent sergeant and 2.36 per cent of constable rank). Of 3,708 women, 125 were drawn from ethnic minorities, of whom 119 were uniformed officers and six detectives. The highest ranking female was of sergeant rank, of detectives all six were of constable rank. The retention rate is also improved. Improvement in recruitment of ethnic minorities into the profession will in due course impact on policing practice and public confidence.

The recruitment of ethnic minorities into the legal profession is also an ongoing problem of concern. Ethnic minorities are seriously under-represented in the professions of solicitors and barristers not to mention the judiciary, although recent efforts to recruit more 'black' magistrates are encouraging. An extimated 6 per cent of practising barristers are 'black'; there are no 'black' judges in the High Court, Court of Appeal or House of Lords, and only two out of 447 circuit judges are 'black' (cf. Bindman 1991, p. 1692).

There have been recent efforts to improve race relations policy in prisons (hitherto guided by Home Office circulars 28/91, 56/83, 25/84). The latest Home Office policy is stated in circular 13/1991:

> The prison department is committed absolutely to a policy of racial equality and to the elimination of discrimination in all aspects of the work of the Prison Service. It is opposed also to any display of racial prejudice, either by word or conduct, by any member of the Service in dealings with any other person.

This policy statement and the *Prison Service Race Relations Manual* cancelled all other circulars.

The emphasis is on ethnic minority recruitment and challenging racism in prison. Ethnic monitoring in prison includes many aspects of prison life including population, allocation of accommodation, work, education, training, and religious provision. Range setting is utilised as a means of achieving the correct ethnic mix rather than other mechanisms such as quotas.

However, the policy has a long way to go; range setting is problematic in that it varies from area to area, and fundamental issues need to be addressed conerning religious and cultural dietary 'laws'. Observance of these 'laws' is mandatory for those practising that religion, but they may still be regarded as cultural preferences by those in authority in the Prison Service: 'These preferences should be accommodated wherever possible' (*Race Relations Manual*, p. 67).

The term 'black' is confronted in the *Race Relations Manual* to prisons; as the manual makes clear, the generic use of the term 'black' to categorise non-whites may offend those from the Indian sub-continent. The position of Rastafarianism in the Prison Service's view of what does or does not constitute a religion is anomalous. As a consequence, responses to the needs of individual prisoners who practise Rastafarianism tend to vary in arbitrary ways as the individual's right to follow his or her convictions takes second place to the convenience of the prison establishment.

There is an ever increasing body of evidence indicating the extent of sexism and racism in the criminal justice system. Governmental efforts in respect of monitoring notwithstanding, discrimination persists and attempts to confront it continue to founder on the prevailing assumptions of the criminal justice process. The predominance of the theory of individual responsibility must be challenged if institutionalised bias is to be tackled in the rigorous and systematic way necessary to change the pervasive nature of racial and gender discrimination in our midst.

References

Bindman, G. (1991), 'Appointing judges without discrimination', 141 NLJ 1692.

Browne, D. (1990), *Black People, Mental Health and the Courts* (NACRO).

Chiqwada, R. (1991), 'The Policing of Black Women', in *Out of Order? Policing Black People*, ed. E. Cashmore and E. McLaughlin (London: Routledge).

Cope, R. (1989), 'The Compulsory Detention of Afro-Caribbeans under the Mental Health Act', *New Community*, April.

Cochrane, R. (1977), 'Mental Illness in Immigrants in England and Wales: an Analysis of Mental Hospital Admissions', *Social Psychiatry*, vol. 12, No. 1.

Crawford, A., Jones, T., Woodhouse, T. and Young, J. (1989), *The Second Islington Crime Survey* (Middlesex Polytechnic Centre for Criminology).

Dean, G. (1981), 'First Admissions of Native-born and Immigrant People to Psychiatric Hospitals in South-East England', *British Journal of Psychiatry*, vol. 139.

Edwards, S.S.M. (1989), *Policing 'Domestic' Violence* (London: Sage).

Evans, R., and Wilkinson, C. (1990), 'Variations in Police Cautioning Policy and Practice in England and Wales', *Howard Journal*, vol. 29, No. 3.

Genders, E. and Player, E. (1989), *Race Relations in Prisons* (Oxford: Clarendon Press).

Gilroy, P. (1987), 'The Myth of Black Criminality', in *Law, Order and the Authoritarian State*, ed. P. Scraton (Milton Keynes: Open University Press), pp. 107–20.

Graef, R. (1989), *Talking Blues* (London: Collins Harvill).

Heidensohn, F. (1985), *Women and Crime* (Basingstoke: Macmillan).

Herbert, P. (1990), *White Paper — Black Justice* (Society of Black Lawyers).

Home Office (1988) *Prison Statistics England and Wales 1988* (Cm 825) (London: HMSO).

Home Office (1990a), *Criminal Statistics England and Wales 1989* (Cm 1322) (London: HMSO).

Home Office (1990b), *Prison Statistics England and Wales 1989* (Cm 1221) (London: HMSO).

Home Office (1992), *Criminal Statistics England and Wales 1990* (Cm 1935) (London: HMSO).

Hudson, B. (1989), 'Discrimination and Disparity: the Influence of Race on Sentencing', *New Community*, vol. 16, no. 1, pp. 23–34.

Jefferson, T. (1991), 'Discrimination, Disadvantage and Police-work', in *Out of Order? Policing Black People*, ed. E. Cashmore and E. McLaughlin (London: Routledge), pp. 166–88.

Jefferson, T., and Walker, M. (1992), 'Ethnic Minorities in the Criminal Justice System' [1992] Crim LR 83.

Jones, T., MacLean, M. and Young, J. (1986), *The Islington Crime Survey: Crime Victimisation and Policing in Inner City London* (Aldershot: Gower).

Joseph, G. (1982) 'The Incompatible Menage a Trois, Marxism, Feminism and Racism' in Hartmann, H. and Sargeant, L., *The Unhappy Marriage of Marxism and Feminism* (London: Pluto).

Landau, S.F. (1981), 'Juveniles and the Police: Who is Charged Immediately and Who is Referred to the Juvenile Bureau?', *British Journal of Criminology*, vol. 21, pp. 27–46.

Landau, S.F., and Nathan, G. (1983), 'Selecting Delinquents for Cautioning in the London Metropolitan Area', *British Journal of Criminology*, vol. 23, pp. 128–49.

McDermott, K. (1990), 'We Have No Problem: the Experience of Race Relations in Prison', *New Community*, vol. 16, No. 2.

Mama, A. (1989), *The Hidden Struggle: Statutory and Voluntary Sector Responses to Violence against Black Women in the Home* (London: London Race and Housing Research Unit).

Morris, A. and Gelsthorpe, L. (1988) 'Feminism and Criminology in Britain', *British Journal of Criminology*, vol. 28, no. 2, pp. 93–110.

NACRO (1989), *NACRO Briefing, Women and Criminal Justice*.

Reiner, R. (1989), 'Race and Criminal Justice', *New Community*, vol. 16, No. 1 (October 1991), pp. 5–22.

Saadawi, N. El (1980), *The Hidden Face of Eve*, transl. S. Hetata (London: Zed Press).

Smith, D.J., and Gray, J. (1983), *Police and People in London*, vols 1–4 (London: Policy Studies Institute).

Solomos, J. and Rackett, T. (1991), 'Policing and Urban Unrest: in Cashmore and Mclaughlin, *Out of Order? Policing Black People* (London: Routledge).

Southall Black Sisters (1989), 'Two Struggles: Challenging Male Violence and the Police', in *The Boys in Blue: Women's Challenge to the Police*, ed. C. Dunhill (London: Virago), pp. 38–44.

Stevens, P. and Willis, C. (1979), *Race, Crime and Arrest* Home Office Research Study no. 58 (London: HMSO).

Tipler, J. (1986), *Is Justice Colour Blind?* (Social Services Research Note 6) (London: London Borough of Hackney, Directorate of Social Services, Research Development and Programming).

Walker, M.A. (1989) 'The Court Disposal and Remands of White, Afro-Caribbean and Asian Men' *British Journal of Criminology* vol. 29, no. 6, pp. 353–87.

Willis, C. (1983), 'The Use, Effectiveness and Impact of Police Stop and Search Powers', Research and Planning Unit, Paper no. 15 (London: HMSO).

Women, Immigration and Nationality Group (1985), *Worlds Apart, Women under Immigration and Nationality Law* (London: Pluto Press).

12

Sexual Offences

Lucia Zedner

Introduction

Sexual offences, sexual offenders and their victims occupy a higher profile on the criminal justice agenda than ever before. Greater public awareness of the incidence of rape, sexual assault and abuse of children, increased recognition of their long-term effects on victims, and a growing rate of reporting all combine to increase pressure on the criminal justice system to respond effectively to sexual offences. This chapter will focus on three key areas: the legal response to child sexual abuse; the scope of rape and the ending of the marital immunity; and finally, the treatment of sex offenders in prison. Each has excited the attention of academics, professionals and policy makers; each has been the subject of major government inquiries; and each is at the cutting edge of legal change. Despite the introduction or prospect of major reforms, all three areas remain the subject of grave concern.

Child sexual abuse

The response of the criminal justice system to sexual offences against children has attracted massive and continuing public disquiet in recent years. Every aspect of the legal response to child sexual abuse, from the problem of identification, through investigation and the decision to prosecute, to the trial itself, has come under intense scrutiny.

Problems in the way criminal justice agencies respond to sexual assault victims first attracted widespread public attention in a documentary on the Thames Valley Police which was broadcast in 1982. The programme revealed highly unsympathetic practices in the interviewing of rape victims and, in so doing, provoked a public outcry. It was clear that, at worst, existing police interview techniques inflicted further trauma tantamount to what has become known as 'secondary victimisation'. As a direct response, the Home Office issued a circular (25/1983) to the police drawing attention to public concern and insisting that sexual assault victims should be treated with tact and sensitivity. Amongst reforms proposed were that, wherever possible, female police officers should carry out questioning, medical examinations should be carried out quickly to allow the victim to wash and change, female doctors should be used if the victim so wished, and that repeat interviewing be avoided. Officers should be specially trained and victims given advice on medical treatment and the availability of support from organisations like Rape Crisis and Victim Support. Police forces across the country subsequently reviewed their practices, many introducing new procedures and facilities as a direct result. These included special suites in which to interview and conduct medical and forensic examinations of victims, and teams of women police officers trained to respond more sensitively (Temkin 1987, ch. 1). Welcome as these changes are, they cannot wholly eradicate the persisting view that 'nice girls do not get raped', nor the victim-blaming which such attitudes inevitably foster.

In all cases of sexual assault, unless there are clearly visible physical injuries, problems of proof are likely to be paramount. The victim's testimony is commonly essential to the success of the prosecution, whether it pertains to the absence of consent in rape or constitutes the sole evidence of the crime, as in many cases of child sexual abuse. With the aim of improving investigative techniques, to secure sound evidence, and to minimise the trauma for children interviewed repeatedly by police and social workers, a pioneer scheme was launched in 1984 by the Metropolitan Police in the London Borough of Bexley (Metropolitan Police and Bexley Social Services 1987). In establishing the practice of joint interviewing by police and social workers, the Bexley project provided a model of 'inter-agency cooperation' which was copied widely across the country. Doubts raised about the conduct and efficacy of the project did little to temper the speed and enthusiasm with which joint investigating was taken up (Kelly and Regan 1990; Byrne and Patrick 1990). Clearly it fulfilled an urgently felt need to find solutions to the problem of responding to child sexual abuse within the criminal justice system.

The difficulties entailed in inter-agency cooperation, in the management and investigation of child sexual abuse cases, re-emerged dramatically in the so-called 'Cleveland crisis' in 1987/8. The affair erupted when over 100 cases of sexual abuse were allegedly diagnosed during a five-month period in 1987 (compared with only two cases in the previous year). Children were diagnosed as having been abused on the basis of an extremely controversial test (reflex anal dilatation) and taken into local authority care in a series of dramatic 'dawn raids'. The absence of agreed diagnostic guidelines, insensitive implementation of place of safety orders, disagreements over instituting criminal proceedings, conflict between the medical, welfare, and criminal justice agencies involved, and the political involvement of local MPs supporting parental attempts to secure the return of their children combined in an explosive cocktail. The flood of national publicity which ensued generated considerable public disquiet. A committee of inquiry under Mrs Justice Butler-Sloss was swiftly set up, charged to find out what had gone wrong in Cleveland and to make recommendations to prevent its recurrence (Department of Health and Social Security 1988). The inquiry was damning in its condemnation of existing practice, of over-reliance on dubious diagnostic techniques, and of the lack of communication and understanding among the various agencies involved. Curiously, whilst the failure of the police to cooperate effectively with other agencies was a subject of particular criticism, greater disquiet about the competence of medical and welfare professionals gave the police an even more central role in the response to child sexual abuse.

Butler-Sloss's report made sweeping recommendations for the investigation and conduct of child sexual abuse cases, including effective cooperation between medical, welfare, police and voluntary agencies; the avoidance of repeated interviewing and examination for evidential purposes; and the establishment of 'special assessment teams' to make multi-disciplinary assessments of abuse cases. Proposals for inter-agency cooperation led quickly to the formal reappraisal of professional practices, for example, in the revision of DHSS guidelines, *Working Together* (1988).

The proliferation of preventative initiatives, helplines, and radical innovations in the workings of welfare and criminal justice agencies in the wake of Cleveland generated some initial confidence that the problem of child sexual abuse was now being tackled effectively. However, fresh controversy over alleged cases of 'satanic' or ritual abuse of children in Nottingham, Rochdale, Orkney and Kent led to renewed, ever more critical scrutiny of the system's response. By forcing the problem of child sexual abuse to the centre of public debate, the Cleveland crisis and the subsequent allegations of ritual abuse have prompted a wholesale reassessment of the criminal justice system's operation in this area. Yet heightened public anxiety and political sensitivity generated by these scandals has been less than conducive to measured, effective reform. Pressures for a more proactive role on behalf of police and prosecutors have clashed irreconcilably with equally insistent demands for the protection of the family from State interference (Frost 1990).

The growing centrality of criminal sanctions in Britain contrasts sharply with the non-punitive, non-legalistic approach to child sexual abuse pursued in many other European jurisdictions. In France, Sweden, Belgium, Holland and Germany, recourse to the police is rare, with long-term, voluntary family therapy pursued in place of punishment. In Britain, on the other hand, a number of factors combine to bring more cases into the criminal justice system every year. Although the desirability of prosecuting sexual offences against children where the offender is a member of the family remains a matter of heated debate amongst criminal justice professionals and academics, greater public awareness and concern has been an important pressure not only on the police but also on prosecutorial discretion. The 'public interest' element in the decision to prosecute is, therefore, ever more likely to weigh in favour of continuance.

A widespread decline of faith in the rehabilitative ideal has made diversion less and less acceptable. The re-emergence of a neoclassical approach to punishment demands that the offender receive his 'just deserts' for harm done, even if this entails further costs to his victim. Prosecution is lauded as a means of ensuring that blame is unequivocally, publicly attributed to the offender; that the child is relieved of any sense of guilt; and that 'the cycle of abuse' is thereby broken (Adler 1988). These forcible arguments in favour of instituting criminal proceedings must be countered, however, by persisting concern that 'without stringent safeguards prosecution may risk further victimising the abused child' (Morgan and Zedner 1992).

If criminal proceedings are increasingly accepted as appropriate in child sexual abuse cases, the difficulties of meeting the 'realistic prospect of conviction' test which is prerequisite to prosecution are only now being addressed. The great majority of offenders deny the abuse — in the Bexley experiment 86 per cent of suspects denied their guilt. Given that fewer than 50 per cent of children display any conclusive, physical evidence of abuse, the construction of a case relies heavily on the word of the child (Glaser and Spencer 1990). Their credibility as a witness, depending on such factors as age, maturity, intelligence, resilience, and their willingness and ability to testify, is therefore critical.

Until relatively recently, lack of confidence in children's reliability (recall, accuracy, ability to distinguish fact from fantasy, suggestibility, etc.) severely limited the value placed on their testimony in court (Naylor

1989). Recent psychological research has suggested, however, that children are able to give sound, truthful accounts no less reliable than testimony given by adults. A Home Office review of these research findings was highly influential in criticising the exclusion of children's evidence simply on grounds of age and in calling for the removal of the corroboration requirement. It stressed that 'the particular circumstances in which abuse is likely to occur means that other evidence will only rarely exist and will almost never meet current evidentiary standards' (Hedderman 1987). Following this and other pressures, the Criminal Justice Act 1988, s. 34, abolished the requirement that the unsworn evidence of a young child be corroborated and provided also that the unsworn evidence of one child be admitted to corroborate the evidence of another. It left untouched, however, the judge's discretion to decide the child's competence and retained the requirement of warning the jury of the dangers of convicting sexual offences on uncorroborated evidence by the complainant alone. Moreover, the distinction between sworn and unsworn evidence has not totally disappeared and so child witnesses are still liable to undergo fierce questioning to establish their appreciation of the responsibility to tell the truth (Wasik and Taylor 1991). The mixed messages sent out by this legislation were heavily criticised by John Spencer as the product of merely 'tinkering with little bits of the law relating to child witnesses without appreciating that there is a general problem to be considered' (Spencer 1988, p. 497).

Growing pressures to prosecute in child sexual abuse cases have furthered demands for recognition of the trauma caused to children called as witnesses. A number of innovations have been introduced and existing procedures modified in an attempt to minimise stress and thereby to improve the quality of evidence given. Considerable faith is placed in technological innovations designed to shield the child from direct confrontation with the defendant. Screens were first introduced in a trial involving sexual assault on five young children at the Old Bailey in 1987. Their use was taken up in many cases where it was felt that the child witness would have otherwise been too intimidated to give evidence and was endorsed when the case went to the Court of Appeal in 1989 (*R* v *X* (1989) 91 Cr App R 36). The grounds of the appeal, that 'it was an unfair and prejudicial act to erect the screen, the suggestion being that the jury might have been unduly influenced and unfairly prejudiced against the defendants', were rejected on the basis that the judge had a duty to see that the system operated fairly in respect of witnesses as well as defendants. Despite this affirmation of the use of screens, controversy continues to surround the adverse inferences which may be drawn in respect of the defendant. Screens proliferate in courts around the country, yet the question of whether or not their introduction inevitably sends messages to the jury about the need to protect the child witness from the baleful stare of the accused remains unanswered. What damage this symbolic message does to the fundamental principle that the defendant be presumed innocent until proved guilty may be difficult to calculate but this ought not to mean that it should be simply ignored.

Ultimately, the introduction of technology to allow the removal of the child from the court-room to give evidence by video link seems likely to replace the use of screens. Section 32 of the Criminal Justice Act 1988 permits a child witness in trials for sexual offences to give evidence by live television link from a separate room outside the court itself. Questions posed by counsel in court are heard by the child whose testimony is relayed to a monitor in the court-room. This statutory development affirms that there are times when the importance of receiving testimony from a witness, who would otherwise be too intimidated to give it, outweighs the possible prejudice to the defendant. Clearly this innovation may imply to the jury that children are at some indefinable risk from physical proximity with the accused such that they must be kept at a distance. As with screens, the inferences drawn by the jury are difficult to ascertain or to control. Yet again the potential damage done to the rights of the accused is apparently deemed less important than the imperative of protecting the witness.

As a means of reducing the trauma for child witnesses in sexual assault or abuse cases, the video link is only a partial solution. By no means all Crown Court centres are equipped with the necessary technology. As a result difficult decisions have to be made as to whether to transfer a case to a centre with such a link, thus risking the stress of further delays, or to have the case heard at a much earlier date, but without the link, in a local court (Temkin 1990, p. 410). The link does little to modify either the manner or tone in which cross-examination is conducted. The child may be spared physical proximity to the defendant or to an aggressive counsel, but questioning may be no less intimidating. The child has to cope instead with the additional strain of speaking on camera and responding to the demands of a disembodied voice. Ironically, where at its best, the child feels relatively comfortable with the technology and testifies easily, the emotional impact of his or her testimony on the jury may well be lost. Prosecuting counsel are likely, therefore, to be suspicious of the video link and its use may remain limited to those cases in which the child would otherwise be simply unable to testify. (Criticisms that use of the video link was frequently refused by judges in cases where the child was near to its 14th birthday have led to the raising of the age limit under the Criminal Justice Act 1991 from 14 to 17.)

In response to pressure for more far-reaching reforms, the Scottish Law Commission undertook a wide-ranging review of the entire question of vulnerable witnesses and specifically evidence by children (Scottish Law Commission 1990). In marked, and somewhat unfortunate contrast, a parallel committee (the Pigot committee) set up in England was charged to look only at the single issue of introducing videotapes as evidence in cases involving children (Home Office 1989). Unsurprisingly, this narrow focus was heavily criticised at the time for limiting the ability of the Pigot committee to consider the wider, interlocking problems requiring a solution of which the introduction of prerecorded evidence could be only a part.

Undaunted by the narrowness of its remit, the Pigot committee argued that children in cases involving sexual or violent assault should not be required to appear in court even if protected by screens or cross-examined by video link (Home Office 1989; McEwan 1990). Instead it recommended that the child's examination by both prosecuting and defence counsel should be conducted and videotaped as early as possible in advance, following a strict code of practice. These video recordings would then be made admissible at the trial rendering it unnecessary for the child to attend.

Following the Pigot committee, the Criminal Justice Act 1991 permits the prerecording of a first interview with the child to be admitted at the discretion of the judge as the child's evidence-in-chief. However, the government rejected Pigot's second recommendation that cross-examination should also be conducted and recorded in advance of the trial. Instead the child must be made available for cross-examination in person or by live video link on the day of the trial. This decision has been defended on a number of grounds. It is argued that the defence could not properly cross-examine a witness without full knowledge of the evidence to be called; that the likely need to cross-examine the child further in many trials would inflict worse trauma than being cross-examined just once on the day of the trial; that unacceptable delays would be caused if the child were not readily available; and that the very possibility that the child might have to be recalled undermined any argument that therapy could be begun in advance of the trial (Morgan and Zedner 1992, p. 136; Wasik and Taylor 1991, p. 129). Above all, the government pointed out that the showing of evidence-in-chief often precipitates a guilty plea, so avoiding the need to cross-examine the child at all. Any cross-examination carried out in advance would, therefore, have entailed unnecessary trauma for the child.

Whilst these justifications clearly have some weight, critics have argued that, by rejecting the second leg of the Pigot proposal and retaining live cross-examination on the day of the trial, the government has retained what is arguably the most harrowing aspect of the child witness's ordeal. As Temkin has argued: 'Child witnesses in sexual abuse trials are all too often put through the mill and doubly traumatised' (Temkin 1991, p. 315; John Spencer has also been a vociferous critic of this provision). There is little ground for thinking that the current legislation will do much to reduce this ordeal and demands for children to be removed altogether from the adversarial arena in trials for sexual offences will no doubt continue unabated.

The law on rape and the ending of the marital rape immunity

If concerns about child sexual abuse have focused on questions of policy and procedure, one of the most vexed subjects of judicial and legal scrutiny in doctrinal criminal law has been that of the law on rape within marriage. A series of cases has wrestled with the exemption to rape first laid down in the 18th century by jurist Sir Matthew Hale CJ in the *History of the Pleas of the Crown* (1736). Hale laid down that: 'the husband cannot be guilty of a rape committed by himself upon his lawful wife, for by their mutual matrimonial consent and contract the wife hath given up herself in this kind unto her husband, which she cannot retract'. This view has formed the basis of the common law ever since. Despite massive social, economic and cultural changes in respect of marriage, the immunity remained in force and largely unchallenged, until a number of cases (*R* v *Clarke* [1949] 2 All ER 448; *R* v *O'Brien* [1974] 3 All ER 663; *R* v *Steele* (1976) 65 Cr App R 22) sought to test its limits by establishing under what circumstances the marriage was deemed to be at an end and the wife's consent therefore revoked. In seeking to extend the number of exceptions to a husband's immunity from the charge of raping his wife, such cases progressively undermined the marital rape exemption. The Sexual Offences (Amendment) Act 1976 was commonly seen as an attempt to reaffirm the exemption since it was presumed that the use of the term 'unlawful' in defining rape was intended to denote non-consensual intercourse outside marriage only. This view prevailed even as recently as *R* v *J* (*Rape: Marital Exemption*) [1991] 1 All ER 759, in which Rougier J, at Middlesborough Crown Court, held that the 1976 Act clearly retained the exemption. Accordingly, further development of exceptions to it were, in his view, impossible without legislative intervention.

Objections to removal of the immunity were legion. Even in 1984, a majority of the Criminal Law Revision Committee concluded that sexual abuse within marriage was uncommon and that the law should, therefore, remain unchanged. Other objections included: the danger of encouraging wives to make malicious false allegations in order, for example, to obtain custody over children; the alleged tendency of wives to withdraw allegations in analogous cases of domestic violence; the damage done by criminal proceedings to any chance of reconciliation; and the difficulties of proof. Objections by such eminent academic lawyers as Glanville Williams no doubt proved a powerful inhibition to change. He argued that 'A charge of rape is too powerful (and even self-destructive) a weapon to be put into the wife's hands' and queried: 'Is it wise to arm her with such a powerful weapon as a charge of rape, when its use may greatly impair the happiness of both parties?' (Williams 1991, p. 206). He also doubted that the harm entailed in rape by the husband could be equivalent to that of the paradigmatic rape by an unknown assailant: '. . . it cannot be nearly so traumatic for the wife as stranger-rape' (ibid., loc. cit.).

In recent years, however, objections to the ending of the immunity have been challenged with increasing vigour. The fear of a flood of malicious allegations is countered by reference to those jurisdictions which recognise rape within marriage and also to the considerable personal costs faced by a rape complainant in pursuing criminal proceedings. The risk of withdrawn allegations should not, it has been argued, justify denying legal protection to those wives who are determined to follow through (Barton 1991, p. 74). The argument that hopes of reconciliation will be blighted is countered by graphic testimony by wives of the brutal, often long-term, abuse by spouses. The problems of proof are recognised, but evidentiary difficulties are legion in many areas of crime (not least rape by a cohabitant) and should not be a bar to criminalisation. Finally, the argument that 'the fearsome stigma of rape is too great a punishment for husbands' has been greatly undermined by growing evidence of the extent and severity of sexual abuse within marriage (Brooks 1989, p. 885). Whilst some cases will fall at the lower end of the scale, the view that rape within marriage is not 'real rape' seems less and less sustainable. In 1991, a study by Middlesex Polytechnic of 1,000 married women found that alleged rapes within marriage exceeded criminal rape by two to one. One in seven wives claimed to have been raped by their husbands, 50 per cent of violations were accompanied by violence or threats of violence, and 80 per cent had suffered more than one attack (Barton 1991, p. 73).

Seeking to test the limits of the law, the Crown Prosecution Service brought a series of cases resulting in *R* v *C (Rape: Marital Exemption)* [1991] 1 All ER 755, in which Simon Brown J, at Sheffield Crown Court, held firmly against the marital rape exemption. In *R* v *R*, the crux of the issue lay in the interpretation of the word 'unlawful' in the Sexual Offences (Amendment) Act 1976. The Court of Appeal [1991] 2 WLR 1065, and later

the House of Lords [1991] 3 WLR 767, took the view that 'no satisfactory
meaning at all could be ascribed to the word' and that it was mere
'surplusage'. In taking this view of the 1976 Act, it was possible simply to
sweep away Hale's dictum and declare the common law 'a fiction which
had become anachronistic and offensive'. The decision, did not, it was
argued, constitute the creation of a new law but merely the removal of an
outdated lie.

The propriety of such free judicial interpretation of a statute has not
passed without question. Whilst some have argued that the courts should
change rules which are clearly inappropriate and outdated, others insist
that criminal statutes affecting the liberty of the subject should be
construed strictly and any change left to Parliament. With a view to
instituting such legislative change, the Law Commission had been charged
to undertake a major review to consider the law of rape within marriage in
1990. As expected, although the conclusions of its final report *Rape within
Marriage* (1992) were in line with the decision of the House of Lords in *R
v R*, the Law Commission firmly favoured legislation over judicial
lawmaking. Whilst endorsing the ending of the marital rape immunity, it
stressed a number of procedural difficulties involved with such a reform.
The Law Commission's draft Bill proposed three clauses: ending the
marital rape immunity, extending anonymity to the husband, and making
the wife a compellable witness in a marital rape case. Whilst the extension
of anonymity to the husband is clearly necessary to protect the wife, the
third proposal has been criticised on the grounds that it will make many
women loath to call the police for fear of unleashing a process they cannot
control (Glasman 1991). Also, without some provision for financial
protection, many women will remain reluctant to bring a case for fear of
leaving themselves without home or money. Finally, if the law is not to be
undermined by unsympathetic judges, then guidance on sentencing is vital
to avoid cases such as that decided in October 1991, in which a judge
suspended a two-year sentence on a husband convicted of rape ((1991) 141
NLJ 1471). The claim that criminalising rape within marriage will 'devalue'
rape is only likely to be true if lenient sentences such as this are allowed to
pass unchallenged by the Attorney-General.

The treatment of sexual offenders

The extension of the law on rape and the increasing number of prosecutions
for child sexual abuse reflect a growing trend towards a more punitive
response to sexual offences. In the past decade there has been a
considerable growth in the numbers of sex offenders prosecuted. Sex

offenders are also increasingly liable to face incarceration on conviction. In 1979, 1,500 were sentenced to immediate custody, a decade later in 1989 the figure had risen to 2,400. On 30 June 1990, the prison system contained 3,166 offenders whose primary conviction was for a sexual offence. Of these, 2,006 were serving four years or more, including 170 sentenced for life. Figures for life sentences are independent of those sentenced for murder, arson etc. whose motive was sexual (HM Prison Service Directorate of Inmate Programmes 1991, p. 2).

The likelihood that numbers of sex offenders in the prison population will continue to grow is increased by recent changes in sentencing policy. The Court of Appeal's landmark guideline judgment on sentencing in rape cases, *R* v *Billam* [1986] 1 WLR 349, resulted in sharp increases in sentencing levels. In the year after *Billam*, 80 per cent of those convicted of rape received sentences of at least five years' imprisonment compared to only 30 per cent in 1984. In 1984, 10 rapists were sentenced to more than 10 years (including life imprisonment), in 1987 the figure had risen to 49, and in 1988 to 67 (Home Office 1990, p. 14). In *Attorney-General's Reference (No. 1 of 1989)* [1989] 1 WLR 1117, the Court of Appeal issued a guideline judgment on sentencing for incest and those cases where the offender was in a 'family relationship' with the victim too remote to constitute incest. It introduced a sliding scale of sentence lengths based on the age of the victim, the nature and occurrence of the offences and the degree of physical and psychological harm caused. In *Attorney-General's Reference (No. 7 of 1989)* (1990) 12 Cr App R (S) 1, a man convicted of the rape of his former cohabitee had his two-year sentence increased to four and a half years on appeal. Generally, custodial penalties for sexual crimes have been increased as part of a wider policy of 'being tough on violent crime'.

The population of sex offenders is likely to be increased further still by the Criminal Justice Act 1991. Section 2(2)(b) of the Act provides that an offender convicted of a sexual or violent offence may be sentenced to a longer term of imprisonment than that commensurate with the seriousness of their crime for such period 'as in the opinion of the court is necessary to protect the public from serious harm from the offender'. In thus legitimising longer sentences for the purposes of incapacitation or protection, the Act pays little apparent regard to the grave political, ethical and pragmatic doubts which have surrounded previous proposals for protective sentencing. Unhappily, the Act contains no procedural safeguards to ensure that these 'disproportionally' long sentences are given only where fully justified. Other than the most basic requirement that the court 'give reasons', there is, for example, no requirement for it to receive psychiatric reports in order to assess the likelihood of reoffending. Nor does the Act institute any of the mechanisms to monitor the continuing need for incapacitation recommended by the Floud committee (Floud and Young 1981). Still less does it give any guidance on the appropriate length of such protective sentences apart from requiring that they do not exceed the statutory maxima.

Officially, this new provision derives from the view that 'There are a small number of offenders who become progressively more dangerous and who are a real risk to public safety' (Home Office 1990, p. 14). Whilst this potential risk provides the justification for harsher sentences for sex offenders, it may be argued that provision for such sentences derives more from political expediency than demands for public protection. Although the government claims that 'Today, people are quite rightly much less tolerant of violence than they were and they expect violent crimes to be punished more severely' (Home Office 1990, p. 1), there is little evidence of burgeoning punitiveness on behalf of the public in relation to either sexual or violent offences. Rather, it could be argued that the move to reduce imprisonment for the mass of property offences relies, politically, on the introduction of tougher provisions for the most serious crimes. Criticisms have been made of the inconsistency entailed in promoting such a bifurcation in a sentencing policy supposedly premised on proportionality. Less attention has been paid to the likely impact on the prison population of longer sentences for those convicted of violent and sexual offences.

Given that the proportion of sexual offenders in prison is growing and seems set to rise further, it is no doubt timely to reflect on the stresses this trend entails for the management of penal regimes. The difficulties of managing sexual offenders in prison are well-documented. If their offences become known, they are often liable to verbal and physical abuse by fellow inmates. Accordingly, Prison Rule 43 provides for the segregation of prisoners on two grounds: when considered necessary by the prison authorities in order to maintain 'good order and discipline' or when requested by prisoners themselves 'for their own protection'. Currently, far more prisoners are segregated for their own protection than on the ground of keeping good order. This is not new: as the Chief Inspector of Prisons commented in his annual report for 1981:

It is generally accepted that most have committed offences which invoke the antipathy of other prisoners. Sex offenders, for example, have traditionally been the objects of inmate hostility, especially if they are accused or convicted of crimes against children.

Although segregation under Rule 43 is, therefore, a means of removing vulnerable prisoners such as sex offenders from the general prison population, it is far from an ideal or complete solution.

The conditions to which Rule 43 prisoners are removed vary considerably between establishments, but are generally acknowledged to be considerably worse than those in which the rest of the prison population is held. They enjoy fewer facilities and are frequently housed in inferior accommodation. Any improvement in their conditions is fraught with difficulty since it is liable to be seen as unwarranted favouritism. In 1986, for example, Douglas Hurd, then Home Secretary, insisted that Rule 43 conditions should not be improved at the expense of other inmates in the same establishment (*Guardian*, 3 April 1990). Whilst segregation provides for comparative safety, hostility by other prisoners is certainly not diminished. Food prepared by fellow inmates may be adulterated and it is common knowledge that tea is urinated in. Some prison officers, too, are known covertly to encourage or even actively participate in the victimisation of Rule 43 inmates. At worst, segregation 'gives other prisoners a perfect, almost legitimate target. The nonces become scapegoats, hidden away in a corner of the prison as a focus of inmate discontent' (Adam Sampson, Prison Reform Trust quoted in the *Guardian*, 3 April 1990).

Undoubtedly the most notorious assault on sexual offenders in recent years occurred during the Strangeways Prison riot in April 1990. Immediately the riot began, during a Sunday service in the prison chapel on 1 April 1990, a primary target of the inmates' fury was the isolation block, E wing. For much of the siege, persistent reports were given out that up to 20 Rule 43 inmates had been killed and others mutilated or forcibly injected with drugs. These horrific stories were deemed plausible just because the degree of animosity directed toward them was widely known. Although early reports proved to be exaggerated, inmates did assault, terrorise, and humiliate prisoners held on E wing. Five prisoners were subsequently tried for riot and for the murder of the one prisoner who died as a result of injuries sustained by being thrown repeatedly off the landing onto netting below. (They were acquitted of the murder charge.) Whilst the Strangeways riot was undoubtedly exceptionally violent, attacks on Rule 43 prisoners are by no means isolated incidents. In 1991, for example, the Home Office was obliged to pay £350 compensation to a convicted robber and burglar who was assaulted by fellow inmates who learned of his previous convictions for indecency with boys. The prison authorities were found to have been negligent in failing to keep his records secure.

Unsurprisingly, then, reliance on segregation as the primary means of responding to the discipline problems posed by sexual offenders in prison has been subject to increasing criticism. Experiments have been introduced where sex offenders remain on the normal wings at Grendon Underwood, Wormwood Scrubs, Littlehey, and Northallerton prisons. Such schemes rely not only on the authorities taking a very firm stance against any persecution, but above all on creating a regime which does not foster resentment, liable to be redirected at this most vulnerable group. The role of staff in defusing tension, the provision of opportunities for education, work and exercise to keep prisoners mentally and physically occupied, and the provision of humane living conditions must all be seen as necessary preconditions to integrating sex offenders into the wider prison population. Prisons which leave inmates brooding in their cells must inevitably foster trouble.

As a result of pressure by penal lobby organisations, most notably the Prison Reform Trust, and following evidence to its inquiry into Strange-ways, the Woolf report recommended that Rule 43 should henceforth apply only to those prisoners whose presence threatens the good order of the establishment and not to those removed 'in their own interests'. The government itself has come to recognise the injustice of using segregation to protect vulnerable prisoners. In its White Paper, *Custody, Care and Justice* (1991), it affirms that 'When a prisoner is victimised, the aim should be to restrict the victimiser and not the victim' (para. 5.23). A seeming contradiction in its thinking remains, however. Whilst accepting the recommendation made by the Woolf inquiry, the government fights shy of applying this amendment wholeheartedly. In the White Paper it anticipates a special exception in respect of sex offenders on the grounds that:

> It is not at present reasonable to leave these prisoners without special protection. . . . There will continue to be circumstances in which a vulnerable prisoner has to be segregated from other prisoners in his or her own interests. (Home Office 1991, paras 5.25 and 5.26.)

The intention may be that segregation should be used solely as an emergency device to provide immediate protection, to defuse tensions, and to allow for alternative arrangements to be made. The danger is that, unless severely delimited, it will allow for the continued use of Rule 43 on much the same grounds as at present. It is unfortunate that this caveat remains.

Rates of recidivism amongst sexual offenders are notoriously difficult to assess, varying from 0 to over 50 per cent in different studies (Prison Reform Trust 1990, p. 24). However, it is generally agreed both that there is a hard core of sexual offenders who have very high reconviction rates and that many more offences are committed than ever come to the attention of the criminal justice system. Those convicted of violent rapes and of paedophilia appear particularly prone to reoffending. Given the continuing, serious risk that such offenders pose to the public on release, the importance of developing prison regimes designed to treat, or at least to modify deviant behaviour, seems particularly acute. In the absence of such regimes, far from reducing the likelihood of reoffending, the damaging impact of incarceration reinforces those very feelings of inadequacy and of alienation which have been identified as causal factors in resort to sexual violence. More specifically, the vehement antipathy of fellow inmates may, as we have seen, result in threats and assaults on sexual offenders in prison. This may have several interrelated and unfortunate consequences. Those who suffer abuse may come to perceive themselves as victims, coincidentally blotting out the fact that they were once the perpetrators. As the Woolf inquiry into the Strangeways riots recognised:

> When Rule 43 prisoners are subject to assaults or worse, this makes them feel, with justification, that they are the victims. It focuses their attention on their own condition and away from what they have done to their victims. . . . Those offenders need to be assisted to avoid offending again. They must be required to confront their criminal conduct.

Many offenders do not recognise that their behaviour is wrong, and such feelings of victimisation can only further inhibit such recognition. Others seeking to avoid abuse may successfully conceal the nature of their offence. They may indeed be advised or assisted by the prison staff to invent 'alternative' offences in order to avert attack. Although widely condoned, such concealment is inimical to encouraging sexual offenders to face up to their crime. The Woolf inquiry, whilst recognising the reasons for such advice, nonetheless argued strenuously that 'to encourage prisoners, in effect, to lie about their offences in order to survive on normal location, is no solution to this problem' (Woolf report, para. 12.210). Above all, such a strategy renders the admission of the offender into any treatment programme almost impossible.

Until recently, treatment programmes for sex offenders have developed on an *ad hoc* basis in many prisons, relying heavily on local initiative and the enthusiasm of individual staff. As a consequence, the nature and quality of these programmes varies greatly, with little means of ensuring overall consistency, monitoring or evaluation. Penal reform organisations have lobbied government to recognise both the value of various treatment programmes for sex offenders and the dangers inherent in their *ad hoc* and largely uncoordinated development (Prison Reform Trust 1990). In March

1991, the Home Office finally launched a more coherent initiative. The Home Secretary announced that all sex offenders in custody were henceforth to be allocated to one of two programmes whilst serving their sentence. (The Home Secretary, Kenneth Baker, made this announcement at a conference, 'Working with the Sex Offender', organised by the Suzy Lamplugh Trust and the Criminal Bar Association, 7 June 1991.)

On conviction, sex offenders are to be sent to one of six assessment centres, at Albany, Dartmoor, Full Sutton, Maidstone, Wakefield and Wandsworth. In order to establish priority for treatment, psychological tests will be used to identify those likely to represent the greatest risk to the community on release, taking into account the inmate's previous convictions, evidence of inadequacy or addiction, sexual deviance etc. Thereafter, offenders will be allocated to one of two main treatment programmes at one of 20 prisons around the country. This approach of holding sex offenders in fewer prisons is intended to facilitate greater consistency of approach in the running of treatment programmes, to increase efficient use of resources and to provide a safe, supportive environment in which to conduct treatment. Well-intentioned as this may be, it clearly conflicts with the basic principle adopted by Woolf that prisoners should be held as close to their homes as possible. To confine this group of offenders to fewer prisons further from their homes runs counter to this recommendation and would seem to undermine the proposed setting up of mixed 'community prisons' (Home Office 1991, p. 52).

A 'core programme' will provide the basic means of treatment aimed at those offenders not deemed to be mentally ill and not, therefore, in need of psychiatric treatment. Based on cognitive behavioural programmes found to be successful in North America, it seeks to get offenders to face up to the consequences of their behaviour by making them aware of the impact of their crimes on the victim. A second 'extended programme' is intended for those deemed to represent the greatest risk on the grounds that they have 'other major deficits which contribute to their sexual offending, including inability to control anger . . . inability to express feelings and to communicate effectively, problems in managing stress, alcohol (and drug) abuse, and deviant sexual arousal' (HM Prison Service Directorate of Inmate Programmes 1991, p. 8). It is planned that both levels of treatment programme will be introduced progressively during 1992.

These new treatment programmes will be targeted at those serving sentences of four years or more. The justification given is that those serving longer sentences have generally committed the most serious offences and pose the greatest potential risk to the public. Given that most offenders convicted of child sexual abuse receive sentences of less than four years this assumption seems to be flawed. The prison service itself has recognised that those serving shorter sentences may also be dangerous and it is intended that those identified as 'high risk' will be offered places in treatment programmes if additional places are available. However, this targeting of longer-term offenders, together with the requirement that participation be voluntary, must surely limit participation considerably. What provision will be made for those not, for whatever reason, entering these programmes is as yet unclear.

More fundamentally, the official sponsorship of treatment programmes for sex offenders seems curious at a time when the role of the prison as an agent of rehabilitation, or indeed any idea of treating or reforming offenders, is out of vogue. The decline of the rehabilitative ideal from its heyday in the 1960s is partly attributable to a growing body of research casting grave doubts over the ability of penal institutions to tackle the root causes of offending behaviour. Treatment programmes for sexual offenders have been far from immune from such criticism. The Prison Reform Trust, in a recent review of the subject concluded: 'There is, as yet, little or no evidence to indicate that such provision has a significant effect on reconviction rates' (Prison Reform Trust 1990, p. 13). Others view some sexual offenders as quite simply untreatable. Note, for example, the view of Henry Field, consultant psychiatrist working for the Home Office that: 'Some offenders are untreatable and that is the end of the matter. There is no solution for people who have a deviant personality' (quoted in *The Times*, 21 July 1989). Even those who endorse treatment programmes fear that if poorly planned or executed, such intervention may actually increase the risk of reoffending.

In fairness, the Home Office has made no claim that the new programmes will effect any miracle 'cure'. Even where attitudes and behaviour appear to be successfully modified during the course of the programme, any such changes may not be permanent. The desire to meet the expectations of therapists provides an immediate incentive to manifest apparent improvement without fully eradicating the risk of future reversion to deviant sexual acts. Moreover, the artificial, largely single-sex, environment of the prison provides few natural analogies to the temptations to be faced in the outside world. In view of this obvious difficulty, the core treatment programme contains elements which aim 'to help an offender to recognise situations that create a potential for relapse and to identify ways of controlling deviant behaviour or avoiding high risk situations' (HM Prison Service Directorate of Inmate Programmes 1991, p. 8). How far such strategies can indeed enable offenders to resist temptation outside the controlled world of the prison remains to be seen. In the case of those sentenced for sexual offences against children within the family, instigating family-based therapy within prison is particularly problematic. The difficulties of bringing the family together, guilt about the very presence of the offender in prison, and a consequent blurring of the attribution of blame combine to hinder effective treatment.

Growing recognition that prison is far from unproblematic as a means of responding to many sexual offenders and that, at worst, it may reinforce offending behaviour has led to the development of community-based treatment programmes. In 1989, 21 of the 56 probation areas in England and Wales were running treatment programmes for those convicted of child sexual abuse. Interdisciplinary ventures and hospital-based schemes are also increasing. These trends have been tentatively recognised by the courts. In a 'wholly exceptional' case, *Attorney-General's Reference (No. 4 of 1989)* [1990] 1 WLR 41, a father convicted of incest with his daughter and originally given 18 months' imprisonment, was on appeal given a three-year probation order with conditions. Material factors included the interests of the victim (his daughter), the early admissions of the offender, his previous good conduct and character and the unlikelihood of any recurrence. Lord Lane stressed intensive work being done by social workers and probation services in an attempt to rehabilitate and to reunite the family. Given the major problems which beset the success of prison-based treatment, it may be that treatment in the community, such as that provided privately by the Gracewell Clinic since 1988, offers a model for future development (Wyre 1990).

Conclusion

Where once sexual offenders were pictured as unknown strangers striking in lonely alleys at night, revelations of the extent of sexual violence within the home have forced a wholesale reassessment of the problem. Heightened public sensitivity to the vulnerability of victims has supported calls for greater intervention: 'It is increasingly accepted that the criminal law should not stop at the door of the family home' (Morgan and Zedner 1992, p. 115). Yet criminal proceedings and penal sanctions are far from being an unproblematic 'solution' to sexual offences against women and children. Insensitive intervention by the criminal justice system risks inflicting yet further harm on the victim. Whilst punishing sexual offenders may serve the purposes of public condemnation, retribution and temporary incapacitation, custodial sentences do little to reduce offending behaviour and may do much to exacerbate it. Treatment programmes offer some hope of reform, but unless adequately resourced and carefully executed they have little chance of effecting lasting change. Whether, indeed, it is reasonable or realistic to look to the criminal justice system to tackle the underlying problems that lead to sexual offending must remain open to doubt.

References

Adler, Z. (1988), 'Prosecuting Child Sexual Abuse: A Challenge to the Status Quo', in *Victims of Crime: A New Deal?*, ed. M. Maguire and J. Pointing (Milton Keynes: Open University Press).

Brooks, R. (1989) 'Marital Consent in Rape' [1989] Crim LR 877.

Davies, G. (1991), 'Children on Trial? Psychology, Video technology and the Law', *The Howard Journal of Criminal Justice*, vol. 30, no. 3, pp. 177–91.

Byrne, K., and Patrick, N. (1990), 'Bexley Bounces Back', *Social Work Today*, 24 May 1990.

Department of Health and Social Security (1988), *Report of the Inquiry into Child Abuse in Cleveland 1987*, (London: HMSO).

Department of Health and Social Security, and Welsh Office (1988), *Working Together: A Guide to the Arrangements for Inter-agency Cooperation for the Protection of Children from Abuse* (London: HMSO).

Floud, J., and Young, W. (1981), *Dangerousness and Criminal Justice* (Cambridge Studies in Criminology, vol. 47) (London: Heinemann).

Frost, N. (1990), 'Official Intervention and Child Protection: the Relationship between State and Family', in *Taking Child Abuse Seriously*, by the Violence against Children Study Group (London: Unwin Hyman).

Glaser, D., and Spencer, J.R. (1990), 'Sentencing, Children's Evidence and Children's Trauma' [1990] Crim LR 371.

Glasman, C. (1991), 'Women Judge the Courts', 141 NLJ 395.

Grubin, D. and Gunn, J. (1991) *The Imprisoned Rapist and Rape* (London: HMSO).

Hedderman, C. (1987), *Children's Evidence: The Need for Corroboration*, Home Office RPU paper, no. 41 (London: HMSO).

HM Chief Inspector of Prisons (1987), *A Review of the Segregation of Prisoners under Rule 43* (London: Home Office).

HM Prison Service Directorate of Inmate Programmes (1991), *Treatment Programmes for Sex Offenders in Custody: A Strategy* (London: Home Office).

Home Office (1989), *Report of the Advisory Group on Video Evidence* (London: HMSO).

Home Office (1990), *Crime, Justice and Protecting the Public: the Government's Proposals for Legislation* (Cm 965) (London: HMSO).

Home Office (1991), *Custody, Care and Justice: the Way ahead for the Prison Service in England and Wales* (Cm 1647) (London: HMSO).

Jefferson, M. (1991), 'Marital Exemption in Rape' *Journal of Criminal Law*, vol. 55, part 3, pp. 357–60.

Kelly, L., and Regan, L. (1990), 'Flawed Protection', *Social Work Today*, 19 April 1990.

Law Commission (1992), *Rape within Marriage*, (Law Com. No. 205) (London: HMSO).

Lloyd, C. and Walmsley, R. (1989), *Changes in Rape Offences and Sentencing* (London: HMSO).

McEwan, J. (1990), 'In the Box or on the Box: the Pigot Report and Child Witnesses' [1990] Crim LR 363.

Metropolitan Police and Bexley Social Services (1987), *Child Sexual Abuse: Joint Investigative Programme, Final Report* (London: HMSO).

Morgan, J., and Zedner, L. (1992), *Child Victims: Crime, Impact, and Criminal Justice* (Oxford: Oxford University Press).

Naylor, B. (1989), 'Dealing with Child Sexual Assault: Recent Developments', *British Journal of Criminology*, vol. 29, pp. 395–407.

Prison Reform Trust (1990), *Sex Offenders in Prison* (London: Prison Reform Trust).

New Law Journal editorial (1991), 'Rape after the House of Lords' (1991) 141 NLJ 1471.

Scottish Law Commission (1990), *Report on the Evidence of Children and Other Potentially Vulnerable Witnesses* (Scottish Law Commission Study No. 125).

Smith, L.J.F. (1989), *Concerns about Rape* Home Office RPU Research Study, no. 106 (London: HMSO).

Spencer, J. (1988), 'Children's Evidence: How not to Reform the Law', *New Law Journal*, 15 July 1988, pp. 497–99.

Spencer, J. and Flin, R. (1990) *The Evidence of Children: The Law and the Psychology* (London: Blackstone Press).

Spencer, J. Nicholson, G., Flin, R. and Bull, R. (1990) *Children's Evidence in Legal Proceedings: An International Perspective* (Cambridge: Cambridge University Press).

Temkin, J. (1987), *Rape and the Legal Process* (London: Sweet & Maxwell).

Temkin, J. (1990), 'Child Sexual Abuse 2', 140 NLJ 410.

Temkin, J. (1991), 'Doing Justice to Children', 141 NLJ 315.

Wasik, M., and Taylor, R.D. (1991), *Blackstone's Guide to the Criminal Justice Act 1991*, (London: Blackstone Press).

Wells, C. (1985), 'Law Reform, Rape and Ideology' *Journal of Law and Society*, vol. 12, no. 1, pp. 63–75.

Williams, G. (1991), 'The Problem of Domestic Rape', 141 NLJ 205.
Woolf, Lord Justice (1991), *Prison Disturbances April 1990: Report of an Inquiry* (Cm 1456) (London: HMSO).
Wyre, R. (1990), 'Treatment at Gracewell', in *Report of an Interdisciplinary Conference. Working with the Sex Offender. Issues for Policy and Training: Prevention and Treatment* (London).

13

Mental Health Problems

Adrian Grounds

Mental health issues in the criminal justice system have attracted increased
attention during recent years. Mentally disordered offenders have been the
subject of policy initiatives encouraging diversion (Home Office 1990a),
and services for them are currently the subject of a major government
review (Department of Health and Home Office 1991a; 1991b; 1992a;
1992b). Issues of mental health have also featured in two broader areas of
concern in the criminal justice system, namely prisons and miscarriages of
justice. The Woolf report on prison disturbances included the mentally
disordered amongst those who should be diverted from prison (Home
Office 1991a), and criticisms of available medical services are regularly
expressed by the Chief Inspector of Prisons (Home Office, 1990b; 1991).
An efficiency scrutiny of the Prison Medical Service was carried out in 1990
and may have a far-reaching impact in due course on the way in which
medical care in prisons is provided (Home Office 1990c). In the miscarriages of justice which have shaken the English criminal justice system,
medical and psychological evidence has played a role in the cases which
have come to prominent public attention, and this has been based on a
developing body of research on the psychological and psychiatric basis of
unreliable confessions (Gudjonsson 1992).

This chapter will review some contemporary issues concerning provision
for mentally disordered offenders, particularly the policy of diversion to
health and social services, and its prospects for successful implementation

in the context of the current reforms of the National Health Service (Department of Health 1989).

In August 1990 the Home Office and Department of Health jointly issued a circular on provision for mentally disordered offenders (Home Office Circular 66/90) (Home Office 1990a). The accompanying letter from the NHS Management Executive commenced with the explicit statement:

> Government policy is that, wherever possible, mentally disordered people should receive care and treatment from the health and social service authorities rather than be cared for within the criminal justice system. (EL(90)168, para. 1).

The circular urged that powers enabling the diversion of mentally disordered offenders away from the criminal justice system should be used to their fullest possible extent.

Diversion policy, as it has become loosely termed, embraces three ideas. First, the term is used in a relatively narrow sense to refer to avoiding prison custody; secondly, it is more broadly understood as diversion from criminal proceedings and criminal justice agencies; and thirdly it is used to denote transfer to health and social services. Diversion can be therefore variously understood as a specific prison issue, an issue of criminal justice policy, and as an issue of health and social services provision. Each of these will be considered, but first a brief outline of the available avenues for diversion will be given.

Current provision

There are many routes for diverting mentally disordered people into psychiatric care before and during the process of criminal proceedings. First, the police, who may be the initial agency to deal with a mentally disordered suspect, may attempt to arrange a medical assessment in the police station or a direct admission to hospital. If the police suspect mental disorder in someone behaving in a disturbed manner in a public place, they can take the person to a place of safety, which may include a hospital, for assessment (s. 136 of the Mental Health Act 1983). The police are often a front line agency, and may in effect act as a community psychiatric resource. Contact with the mentally ill is not uncommon in police practice and the majority of such contacts do not involve the patient as a suspect of crime but as a subject of concern or assistance, particularly in inner city areas. Ever since the 19th century the law has included provisions for police constables to remove mentally disordered people from public places to hospital without medical consultation.

Mental health may be a matter taken into account by the Crown Prosecution Service in deciding whether a prosecution is in the public interest, and both bail information schemes and public interest case assessment schemes can be helpful in bringing a history of psychiatric disorder to the attention of the CPS. If the person is proceeded against and appears in court there are powers to remand the person to hospital for assessment or for treatment as an alternative to remand in prison custody (ss. 35 and 36 of the Mental Health Act 1983). At or before the trial stage there are the possibilities of being found unfit to plead or acquitted on the grounds of insanity, and a new, flexible range of disposals in these cases has now become available (Criminal Procedure (Insanity and Unfitness to Plead) Act 1991). At the sentencing stage two specific medical disposals are available for the mentally disordered: first, a hospital order (s. 37 of the Mental Health Act 1983), with or without a restriction order; and secondly a probation order with a condition of psychiatric treatment, which may be suitable for those who will cooperate with treatment and supervision, particularly on an out-patient basis. Sentenced prisoners who require psychiatric hospital treatment during sentence can be transferred under s. 47 of the Mental Health Act 1983. The law thus provides numerous avenues for moving the mentally disordered into psychiatric care. However, these legal powers are primarily to achieve admission to hospital, and the structure of mental health legislation does not reflect the move that is taking place in the locus of psychiatric provision away from the hospital and into the community. The framework of powers to detain in hospital has remained broadly the same for three decades against a background of a shrinking hospital estate in local psychiatric services.

The range of NHS provision to which mentally disordered offenders may be diverted is not as full or comprehensive as is required. The special hospitals, which give treatment in conditions of maximum security for detained patients, provide about 1,800 beds nationally (Broadmoor, Rampton and Ashworth Hospitals). The task of reforming excessively custodial and non-therapeutic regimes in the long-established special hospitals continues to be a major one. Following a critical report on services in Broadmoor Hospital in 1988 (National Health Service Health Advisory Service and Social Services Inspectorate 1988), a new health authority (the Special Hospitals Service Authority) was established in 1989 by the Department of Health to manage the special hospitals. It is too early to assess how effective the new authority will be in achieving a reformed culture at ward level in the hospitals. Doubts about this prospect have already been expressed (Bynoe 1992), and the report of the Inquiry into Complaints about Ashworth Hospital (Department of Health 1992a) provides further evidence of the huge task the Authority is facing.

Provision within regional health authorities of hospital units with a medium level of security was recommended in the interim report of the Butler committee (Home Office and Department of Health and Social Security 1974), with an initial target of 1,000 beds (2 per 100,000 population) being set by the Glancy committee (Department of Health and Social Security 1974). This target has not been met and the number of beds in Regional Secure Units on 31 January 1991 was 597 (Department of Health and Home Office 1991b). Psychiatric hospitals and units in district health authorities are largely open units and the availability of local locked wards providing intensive nursing and medical care is inconsistent and in some regions minimal. Community-based forensic psychiatry services are also poorly developed.

The pattern of NHS hospital provision therefore results in a number of problems. Whilst in many respects hospital provision is better for mentally ill people who commit grave offences than for those who commit minor offences, the small number of beds in regional secure units results in strict gate-keeping with restrictive admission criteria, and most units only accept individuals who are judged likely to improve and be discharged within two years. There is no long-term medium-security hospital provision. Provision of medium security is inadequate: at their current level, existing units cannot meet the security needs of minor offenders, they cannot provide long-term care, and they represent a bottleneck for special hospital patients requiring transfer as a first step towards eventual discharge to the community.

Forensic psychiatry services are generally organised on a regional basis with one or more consultants in each region working from their regional secure unit. The units tend to take patients whose behaviour has posed a significant risk to others, and many have been convicted of offences of serious violence. The units are not able to provide a service of emergency admission for acutely mentally ill people who require short-term containment. It has become clear now that another gap in provision has opened up for people who do not require the level of security of the regional secure unit but nonetheless are not easily manageable in their local open psychiatric wards. Many of these patients are petty offenders. Some require short periods of containment, others are more chronically ill and disabled. Amongst this group tend to be found the minor, recidivist mentally disordered offenders who trouble the police, magistrates' courts and remand prisons. Generally their psychiatric care will be the responsibility of local, district mental health and social services.

Two studies which have attempted to measure the size of the residual group of mentally disordered people who require specialist facilities have reached similar conclusions. Wykes et al. (1982) investigated the needs of long-term mentally ill patients based in the community in Camberwell and estimated that the proportion of those requiring special supervision or security because they were a danger to themselves or a serious nuisance or a danger to others, was 13 per 100,000 population. Guderman and Shore (1984), examining the same problem in Massachusetts, also estimated a projected need for specialist facilities totalling 15 beds per 100,000 population for the residual group of patients who could not be catered for in community facilities. These findings suggest that, in planning services for the mentally ill, it should be recognised that there may be in the order of 15 per 100,000 population who will require secure, supportive long-term care in specialised facilities. A major contemporary challenge for social and psychiatric services is how this can be done in the context of inadequate current levels of provision and continuing, severe public-expenditure constraints.

One frequently rehearsed argument is that psychiatric hospital closure programmes should stop. However, as Bowden (forthcoming) cogently argues, the problem posed by chronically mentally ill offenders in the community does not result from the closure of traditional mental hospitals. It was the liberalisation and opening of large mental hospitals a generation ago which led to the translocation of chronic psychotic people into the community. The process could not be reversed without a return to wholesale incarceration, which would be clinically and ethically unacceptable. Other ways forward have to be found.

Administratively, local general psychiatry services need to develop closer working relationships with their local criminal justice agencies. Currently in Britain, psychiatric services at local level may have close liaison and joint planning arrangements with social service departments, general practitioners, other medical specialties and community agencies in the voluntary sector or statutory sector such as local housing departments. In contrast, mental health services are unlikely to have similar arrangements with their local courts, police and probation services, with whom mechanisms of referral and contact tend to be more indirect and formal.

Remand prisoners

The Mental Health Act 1983 powers noted above, which enable courts to remand mentally disordered defendants to hospital as an alternative to prison, came into operation in October 1984, and were introduced because, in the words of the Ministerial statement:

> . . . the mentally ill should be treated in hospital, wherever possible, and [the government] did not wish the courts to have to send sick people to prison. (*Hansard*, Written Answer, 23 October 1984.)

However, the numbers of remands to hospital under the Mental Health Act 1983 since that time have remained low. Currently the number of cases remanded to hospital by the courts for assessment or treatment is approximately 300 annually. The number remanded in custody for medical reports is about 20 times greater. As a means of shifting medical remands from prison to hospital, the new powers have not worked.

The process and outcome of remands in custody of mentally disordered defendants was examined in a recently completed study at HMPs Brixton, Holloway and Risley (Dell et al. 1991). The study involved a follow-up of 952 mentally disordered men and women from the time of reception in custody to final court disposal. The core samples consisted of newly received prisoners thought by prison doctors to have psychotic illness or known to have histories of psychosis; prisoners recognised as mentally handicapped; prisoners referred to outside psychiatrists; and those on whom psychiatric reports were requested. These cases represented remand prisoners whose referral to prison doctors caused, or showed need to cause, psychiatric intervention in the remand process. About half the sample consisted of people with psychotic illnesses.

Only a small proportion of the individuals studied had been charged with grave offences of violence. Most offences were relatively minor: thefts and public nuisance offences (criminal damage, threatening behaviour, possession of an offensive weapon, vagrancy) predominated, particularly in the London prisons. In Brixton, for example, men in the main research sample were four times more likely than the general population of Brixton receptions to have been charged with a public order, vagrancy or criminal damage offence, and they were half as likely to have been charged with offences involving personal violence. People with a diagnosis of psychosis were particularly likely to have been charged with criminal damage and other 'public order' types of offences. In the London samples (Brixton and Holloway), 40 per cent and 43 per cent respectively of those on whom information was available had been living in unsettled lodgings, hostels or on the streets prior to reception, i.e., they had no proper home. In the Risley samples the figures were 32 per cent and 15 per cent for the men and women respectively.

The research indicated that remands in custody of the mentally disordered were not carried out primarily because of the nature of their offences, but because of their need for social and psychiatric help, and the remand prisons were being used for the purpose of psychiatric assessment in these cases. Very few of those who did not achieve medical disposals returned to prison to serve custodial sentences. Remands in custody of the mentally disordered were an inefficient, ineffective and inhumane way of securing psychiatric assessment and treatment. Referrals to outside doctors lengthened the time spent on custodial remand and people who were judged sufficiently ill to require detention in hospital remained in prison for longer than those not accepted for hospital. The results pointed to a need for comprehensive availability of diversion schemes, a range of alternative social as well as hospital provision, and a greater urgency in dealing with the mentally ill who do appear in the remand prison population. It is also questionable whether remands in custody for the primary purpose of psychiatric assessment constitute a justifiable use of the prison system and whether the powers of courts to remand to prison for the purpose of obtaining a psychiatric report are justifiable in the light of the policy statement in the Home Office Circular 66/90, quoted above.

The problem of the mentally disordered in remand prisons needs to be considered at three levels of analysis. First there is a problem of resources. There is some unmet need for local security, and a small number of mentally disordered remand prisoners are not achieving hospital disposals because of its absence. There is also a requirement for social as well as hospital provision. Our picture of alternatives to custody should not consist only of hospital beds. In many cases it is housing that is required, and psychiatric assessments could be done in the community.

The second level of analysis has to look at the system at a whole. We are dealing not only with a resource problem, but a system problem. There has to be recognition of the incentives that make the system work the way it does and that bring the mentally disordered into the remand prisons. Remanding in custody rather than to hospital for assessment is easier for courts, cheaper for health authorities, helpful to NHS staff, and provides prison doctors with the psychiatric assessment work in which they take a traditional pride. These financial, legal and professional incentives need to be reversed if diversion policies are to succeed. In particular, the powers of the courts to remand in custody for medical reports should be restricted or repealed, as has been recently recommended in the joint departmental review (Department of Health and Home Office 1991c).

However, even if the issues of resources and system incentives are dealt with, there remains a third level of underlying difficulty, which is a matter of social expectations and policy. It appears that the courts consider psychiatric assessment and help to be needed for a considerably wider range of offenders than are regarded by psychiatric services as needing psychiatric care. There is a discrepancy between what criminal justice agencies expect of psychiatric services, in terms of assessment, treatment and social control, and what the services define as their role.

Court diversion schemes

One of the most important initiatives to reduce custodial remands of the mentally disordered has been the development of court-based psychiatric assessment schemes. Two recent studies have considered the extent and effectiveness of these schemes. Joseph (1992) has provided a detailed evaluation of the 'duty psychiatrist' scheme he established at Bow Street and Marlborough Street magistrates' courts, and his results indicate that a substantial number of remands in prison custody were probably avoided through the operation of the scheme. Of the 201 referrals seen between February 1989 and September 1990, the mean time from arrest to assessment was six days, and for the 65 defendants who were admitted to hospital, the mean time from arrest to admission was 10 days. This contrasted with a mean of 50 days between arrest and hospital admission for a comparable sample of men remanded in custody to HMP Brixton during the study period. Joseph estimated that the scheme did result in extra costs to NHS psychiatric services, primarily through extra hospital bed usage, but this was offset by greater financial savings to the prison service through reduced time on remand. By extrapolation, he suggested that the nationwide provision of similar schemes might result in a reduction in the total number of custodial remands by 5,000 annually, which is equivalent to over three-quarters of all medical custodial remands. Savings to the prison service might amount to about £7.5 million annually, and increased costs to the health service about £5 million annually.

Although criminal justice agencies may regard the need for such schemes as compelling, their place on the agenda of purchasing health authorities and providers of psychiatric services is less prominent. A recently published survey commissioned by the Department of Health and carried out by Blumenthal and Wessely (1992) indicated that only 25 per cent of purchasing health authorities had established a policy for diversion of mentally disordered offenders, and 50 per cent of purchasers had no current or future purchasing plans relating to diversion. Over half the provider services had no plans for regular attendance at magistrates' courts. On the basis of their national survey the authors identified 48 psychiatric assessment schemes already in operation and a further 34 under development in December 1991. In conclusion, the authors noted:

> Overall, we found considerable activity in both the criminal justice system and the health service in response to Home Office Circular 66/90, and considerable goodwill, with the occasional exception. However the response remains fragmented, and occasionally fragile. (Blumenthal and Wessely 1992, p. 26.)

Sentenced prisoners

A major study of mental disorder and psychiatric treatment needs in the sentenced prison population was published by the Home Office in 1990 (Gunn et al. 1990). The research, based on psychiatric interviews with a 5 per cent representative sample of sentenced prisoners, estimated prevalence rates of 1.9 per cent for psychotic disorders, and 19.6 per cent for alcohol or drug dependence (pre-offence). In the assessment of psychiatric treatment needs it was estimated that 3 per cent (i.e., approximately 1,100) of the sentenced population required treatment in NHS psychiatric hospital beds. The in-patient treatment needs were distributed across all levels of security, but the greatest proportional shortfall in bed provision was at medium-secure level, and the need for long-term medium-security hospital provision was emphasised.

Prison health services

Two major reviews of medical services relating to mentally disordered offenders have taken place in the last three years: a rapid 'efficiency scrutiny' of the prison medical service (Home Office 1990c), and a longer overall review by the Department of Health and the Home Office (the Reed committee) (Department of Health and Home Office 1991a).

Efficiency scrutiny

The efficiency scrutiny of the prison medical service was carried out in a brief period and recommended that the prison medical service should be reorganised and should no longer be primarily a provider but instead a purchaser buying in contracted medical services from outside the prison. The scrutiny team recommended a target date of 1 April 1992 for completing initial contract negotiations. (The report was published in July 1990.) The response of the prison medical service to the scrutiny team report was officially to welcome it but then to argue against rapid implementation. A joint Home Office and Department of Health working party established to examine the scrutiny recommendations emphasised in relation to the mentally disordered that contracting in a psychiatric service required a 'step-by-step approach' (Directorate of Prison Medical Services 1991, para. 3.20). At the present time it is planned that a small number of pilot schemes focusing on psychiatric services for remand prisoners should be in place by the end of 1992, and they should be evaluated before progressing further.

Smith (1992) has argued that the scrutiny recommendations do not go far enough and the purchasing of prison health services should also be carried out by the NHS. He points out that the skills and expertise of need evaluation and purchasing are better developed in health authorities than in the prison service:

> ... purchasing authorities should be able to purchase for prisoners at the same time as purchasing for the rest of the community and so get a broader range of services at better prices. (Smith 1992, p. 135.)

The Reed committee

In November 1990 the Department of Health announced that a joint Department of Health and Home Office review of provision for mentally disordered offenders and others requiring similar services would be established.

In 1991 a first set of reports, covering hospital, prison and community services was issued, and a second group of reports, including recommendations on staffing and finance, was issued for consultation in 1992. (Department of Health and Home Office 1992a, 1992b). A Ministerial response is expected in the autumn.

The reports begin with the principle that mentally disordered people requiring care and treatment should receive it from health and personal social services rather than in the criminal justice system. It is acknowledged that practice falls short of what is desirable. In planning services, ideal criteria are that care should be provided:

(a)   as far as possible in the community rather than in the institutional settings;

(b)   under conditions of no greater security than is justified by the degree of danger that individuals present to themselves or others;

(c)   in such a way as to maximise rehabilitation and the chances of sustaining an independent life;

(d)   as near as possible to patients' own homes or families if they have them.

Broadly the reports emphasise the need to develop diversion schemes in each district, better local collaborative arrangements between criminal justice agencies and health and social services, and core psychiatric teams to provide assessment and care. There is recognition of a need for more medium-security provision (which should increase from the current level of approximately 600 to at least 1,500 beds). The need for specialist bail hostels is also endorsed.

The report most eagerly awaited was that concerning finance (Department of Health and Home Office 1992a). The finance advisory group recommended that district health authorities should be responsible for purchasing a comprehensive range of provision for mentally disordered offenders, that regional health authorities should set performance indicators and hold districts to account for purchasing the full range of services, and regions themselves should operate in a framework of objectives set out by the NHS Management Executive. The purchasing of services by district health authorities should include special hospital care, which at present is provided at no cost to district health authorities because special hospitals receive central government funding. This constitutes a financial disincentive to resuming local care. At the time of writing it is unclear what level of new resources and political commitment will follow the final reports of the review.

The reports begin to highlight structural difficulties which are difficult to overcome. Strategic planning is hindered by the fact that the agencies which have to deal with mentally disordered offenders are numerous and do not share coterminous boundaries. Secondly, the development of services for mentally disordered offenders has to take place in the context of the reforms of the National Health Service (Department of Health 1989) which introduced separation of purchasers and providers of health services and gave greater autonomy to purchasing district health authorities. However, in this field it is criminal justice agencies that most want good services for mentally disordered offenders, and they generally do not have the power to purchase the services, nor are there widespread formal arrangements enabling criminal justice agencies to influence health purchasing decisions. There is therefore a strong case for having health representatives in the area criminal justice liaison committees to be established following the Woolf report.

On closer analysis the reports have a number of specific weaknesses, most crucially in the funding recommendations. The finance advisory group recommends targeted funding to increase medium-security provision, and specific grants to social services and voluntary agencies, but there are no similar recommendations for targeted funding to develop district-based NHS services (Department of Health and Home Office 1992a). The current financial constraints on district health authorities make this a difficult time for the development of marginal services, and the likelihood of service developments in the absence of earmarked funding is low. In addition, the reports envisage a key role for regional health authorities in the coordination and planning of services, including the appointment of regional forensic advisers, for example. This may be unrealistic. No account appears to have been taken of the likelihood of future changes in the role of regional health authorities as the NHS reforms gather pace and it becomes commonplace for provider NHS units to be self-governing trusts which are not directly answerable to regional health authorities, but to the NHS Management Executive and its outposts. The future role of regional health authorities is uncertain and may contract so that they become primarily regulators of the market, with purchasing and planning functions becoming more fully delegated to districts (Ham 1992). Despite the Ministerial support which lay behind the initial establishment of the joint Department of Health and Home Office review, the outcome of its recommendations is not yet known. It is encouraging that the objective of more effective service provision for mentally disordered offenders is included as a health target in the Government White Paper, *The Health of the Nation* (Department of Health 1992b), but resource expectations are not high.

Diversion policy

This chapter ends by returning to the theme with which it began. Whilst the broad policy of diversion is widely agreed, it also requires some critical scrutiny. There is no doubt that the policy has merits from pragmatic, economic and humanitarian points of view. But at the same time it has to be recognised that diversion effectively removes a category of offender from the operation of the criminal justice system, and as a corollary removes a category of victims from the operation of criminal justice too. There are few mechanisms for ensuring that the discretion to exercise diversion is operated fairly and that requirements of justice are met. Similar cases may be given wholly different outcomes depending on the availability and efficiency of local services. Diversion of mentally disordered offenders may be seen as part of a wider process of seeking to respond to offending in ways which do not involve entry into the criminal justice system. The need to respond to offending does not disappear; it is just displaced on to clinical and social work practitioners who have to manage it by informal means.

References

Blumenthal, S., and Wessely, S. (1992), *The Extent of Local Arrangements for the Diversion of the Mentally Abnormal Offender from Custody* (London: Institute of Psychiatry and Kings College Hospital Medical School).

Bowden, P. (forthcoming, due 1993), 'Future Provision for Mentally Disordered Offenders: a Personal View', In *The Mentally Disordered Offender in an Era of Community Care*, ed. A.T. Grounds and W. Watson (Cambridge: Cambridge University Press).

Dell, S. et al. (1991), *Mentally Disordered Remanded Prisoners: Report to the Home Office* (Cambridge: Institute of Criminology).

Department of Health (1989), *Working for Patients* (Cm 555) (London: HMSO).

Department of Health (1992a), *Report of the Inquiry into Complaints about Ashworth Hospital* (Cm 2028) (London: HMSO).

Department of Health (1992b), *The Health of the Nation* (Cm 1986) (London: HMSO).

Department of Health and Home Office (1991a), *Review of Health and Social Services for Mentally Disordered Offenders and Others Requiring Similar Services: the Reports of the Service Advisory Groups; an Overview with Glossary* (London: Department of Health; Home Office).

Department of Health and Home Office (1991b), *Review of Health and Social Services for Mentally Disordered Offenders and Others Requiring Similar Services: Report of the Hospital Advisory Group* (London: Department of Health; Home Office).

Department of Health and Home Office (1991c), *Review of Health and Social Services for Mentally Disordered Offenders and Others Requiring Similar Services: Report of the Prison Advisory Group* (London: Department of Health; Home Office).

Department of Health and Home Office (1992a), *Review of Health and Social Services for Mentally Disordered Offenders and Others Requiring Similar Services: Report of the Finance Advisory Group* (London: Department of Health; Home Office).

Department of Health and Home Office (1992b), *Review of Health and Social Services for Mentally Disordered Offenders and Others Requiring Similar Services: Report of the Staffing and Training Advisory Group* (London: Department of Health; Home Office).

Department of Health and Social Security (1974), *Revised Report of the Working Party on Security in NHS Psychiatric Hospitals* (London: Department of Health and Social Security).

Directorate of Prison Medical Services (1991), *Contracting for Prison Health Services: a Consultation Paper* (London: Home Office).

Gudeman, J.E., and Shore, M.F. (1984), 'Beyond De-institutionalisation: a New Class of Facilities for the Mentally Ill', *New England Journal of Medicine*, vol. 311, pp. 832–6.

Gudjonsson, G. (1992), *The Psychology of Interrogations, Confessions and Testimony* (Chichester: John Wiley).

Gunn, J., et al. (1990), *Mentally Disordered Prisoners* (London: Home Office).

Ham, C. (1992), 'What Future for the Regions?', *British Medical Journal*, vol. 305, pp. 130–1.

Home Office (1990a), *Provision for Mentally Disordered Offenders* (Home Office Circular 66/90) (London: Home Office).

Home Office (1990b), *HM Prison Brixton: Report by HM Chief Inspector of Prisons* (London: Home Office).

Home Office (1990c), *Report on an Efficiency Scrutiny of the Prison Medical Service* (London: Home Office).

Home Office (1991), *Report of Her Majesty's Chief Inspector of Prisons, January 1990–March 1991* (London: HMSO).

Home Office and Department of Health and Social Security (1974), *Interim Report of the Committee on Mentally Abnormal Offenders* (Cmnd 5698) (London: HMSO).

Joseph, P. (1992), *Psychiatric Assessment at the Magistrates' Court* (London: Home Office and Department of Health).

National Health Service Hospital Advisory Service and Social Services Inspectorate (1988), *Report on Services at Broadmoor Hospital* (London: Department of Health).

Smith, R. (1992), 'Prison Medicine: beginning again', *British Medical Journal* vol. 304, pp. 134–5.

Woolf, Lord Justice (1991), *Prison Disturbances April 1990: Report of an Inquiry* (Cm 1456) London: HMSO).

Wykes, T., et al. (1982), 'Needs and the Deployment of Services', in *Long Term Community Care: Experience in a London Borough*, ed. J. K. Wing (Cambridge: Cambridge University Press).